ARE WE ALONE IN THE COSMOS?

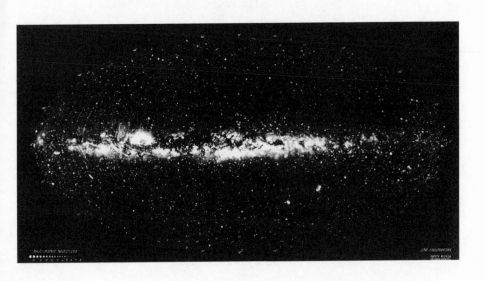

THE GUIDE TO
THE SEARCH FOR
EXTRATERRESTRIAL INTELLIGENCE

ARE WE ALONE IN THE COSMOS?

THE GUIDE TO THE SEARCH FOR EXTRATERRESTRIAL INTELLIGENCE

Edited by
Ben Bova and Byron Preiss

Science Editor
William R. Alschuler

Contributing Editor
Howard Zimmerman

ibooks
new york
www.ibooksinc.com

DISTRIBUTED BY SIMON & SCHUSTER, INC
BOOK-OF-THE-MONTH CLUB
NEW YORK

Opening each chapter is the footprint of Apollo 11 astronaut Neil A. Armstrong in the
lunar dust, taken on July 20, 1969. *(Photo Courtesy NASA)*

Half-title page: The whole celestial sphere, as seen from Earth,
in galactic coordinates. The Milky Way (center) shows the plane of our
galaxy. The tail of the constellation Scorpius and the teapot of Sagittarius
are just above and below the galactic center. The small, slanting "dash"
below the Milky Way at left is M 31, the Andromeda Galaxy—
the most distant object visible to the naked eye.
(Sky map: Lund Observatory, Courtesy the American Museum of Natural History.)

William Alschuler dedicates this book to his daughter, Elise B. Alschuler
Ad Astra per Aspera!
(To the stars, no matter the difficulty!)

CONTENTS

PREFACE

The technology to actively search for extraterrestrial intelligence was invented in the late 20th century. But the reasons for the search are as old as humankind itself. As a species, we want to know, need to know, if we are alone in the universe or are part of a larger community of intelligent beings.

Humans are self-reflective animals. We question our acts, our motives, our lives, and our reasons for being alive. As far as we can determine, even though the Earth is teeming with life forms we are the only species on the planet that spends time examining this internal landscape. We find companionship with many different species, from dogs to reptiles to birds and insects. But we cannot find introspective souls anywhere among them. Hence, our search for life outside of our world is focused on discovering signs of intelligence, not merely signs of the existence of life elsewhere.

We are seeking out kindred spirits; we are looking for intellectual companionship among the stars. Most professionals involved in space science agree that the discovery of extraterrestrial life will be the single most important discovery ever made by humankind. But the holy grail is the confirmation of the existence of intelligent creatures. This alone can tell us that we are not unique.

I write this at a propitious moment for the ongoing search. It was recently announced that the discovery of another solar system, 44 light years away and containing at least three planets, has been confirmed by two independent sources. Until the announcement, each of the twenty or so prior extrasolar planetary discoveries has been of a single world orbiting a star. Now we know that a solar family consisting of multiple planets like our own is not unique, and many scientists believe it will ultimately be proven to be common.

We still have not found any planets the size of Earth orbiting other stars, but this is not a matter for concern. It merely reflects the limitations of our current technology. The observational hardware and software will improve, and smaller, Earthlike planets will surely be discovered. If we find artificial, intelligent signals originating from one of them, it will be the dawn of a new age.

Such a discovery will bring about a revolution in our thinking and understanding, which will be reflected in our art, our science, our philosophy and religion—those aspects of human culture that we feel represent the best of our species. Confirmation that we are not alone will dramatically increase the knowledge of our place in the cosmos, and it will alter the nature of our interior landscapes forever.

Howard Zimmerman
Contributing Editor

ARE WE ALONE IN THE COSMOS?

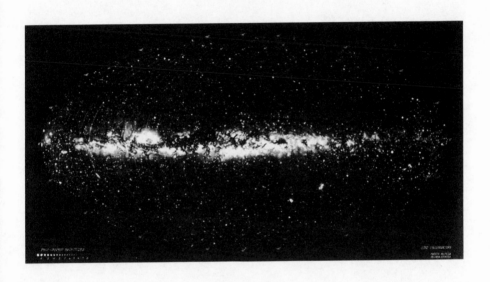

THE SEARCH FOR ALIEN CONTACT IN THE NEW MILLENNIUM

INTRODUCTION

ARE WE ALONE?

by

DONALD GOLDSMITH

Throughout human history, the question Are we alone in the cosmos? has neither lost its appeal nor provided an answer. As a result, SETI (the search for extraterrestrial intelligence) remains, as its critics have scoffed, a science without a subject matter. This condition exposes SETI to attack on two fronts. Many scientists refuse to pay serious attention to SETI because its endeavors lack substance, while UFO enthusiasts insist not only that the subject exists—in the form of extraterrestrial visitors to our planet—but also that nay-saying scientists must belong to a conspiracy in which governmental authorities conceal this Earth-shaking news from an otherwise quaking public.

A decade ago, one might have predicted that these two forces would squeeze SETI out of existence, unable either to secure the funding that accompanies and signifies scientific acceptance or to maintain its proper distance from pseudoscientific groups seeking to establish contact with extraterrestrials here on Earth. Part of this prognosis seemed to come true in 1993, when the United States Congress passed a law forbidding further government spending on SETI. In addition, throughout the 1990s progressively larger segments of the population, responding to increased reports of abduction by alien visitors, tended to accept the conclusion that extraterrestrial civilizations continually interact with our society. Nevertheless, the dawn of the new millennium finds the search for extraterrestrial intelligence flourishing as an ongoing scientific discipline, still in its infancy but poised to reach new levels of activity and understanding during the first decades of the 21st century.

What evidence supports the bold statement of the previous sentence, the seemingly paradoxical result that the search for extraterrestrial intelligence is doing fine without finding anything? Let us make a brief tour through the fields of SETI, and judge for ourselves whether this positive conclusion receives verification.

PROGRESS IN SOLVING THE DRAKE EQUATION: THE DISCOVERY OF EXTRASOLAR PLANETS

By far the most exciting news in the search for other intelligent life forms consists of the recent and ongoing discoveries of planets in orbit around stars similar to the Sun. Though only a few years have passed since the first extrasolar planet was confirmed, the observations implying their existence have been carefully rechecked and reanalyzed, allowing astronomers to reject alternative hypotheses and to reach the firm conclusion that at least a few percent of all sunlike stars have planets.

On the one hand, these discoveries confirm what all astronomers had long suspected: Since our Sun provides us with a fully representative star, and since the Sun formed along with its planets some 4.6 billion years ago, we may reasonably expect that many, if not most, stars likewise formed along with their own planetary systems, billions of years ago. On the other hand, until late 1995, proof of this reasonable hypothesis was lacking, because the detection of planets orbiting other stars lay beyond astronomers' capabilities. We certainly cannot hope to see these extrasolar planets, whose weak reflected light disappears in the enormously greater glow from their parent stars. The 20 or so actual detections all rely on extremely detailed observations of the light from the star itself. Spread out into its spectrum, this starlight shows tiny changes in its frequencies and wavelengths (that is, in its exact colors). These changes repeat in a cyclical manner, and presumably arise from the Doppler effect, which reveals changes in the speed with which a light-emitting object is moving toward or away from an observer. Astronomers conclude that an object is orbiting the star, tugging it with its modest gravitational force as it does so. The time interval over which the cycle of changing colors repeats itself should correspond to the orbital period, and the amounts by which the colors change indicates the mass of the object that tugs at the star.

All the new planetary discoveries have revealed objects with masses that range from about one-half to nearly ten times Jupiter's mass. To astronomers, these masses imply the discovery of giant planets similar to Jupiter, the Sun's largest planet, and exclude the possibility that the

Doppler-effect method has found miniature stars. Only objects that have at least 80 times Jupiter's mass can undergo the nuclear-fusion processes that define a star; lower-mass objects deserve the name of planets, though they may not have formed in exactly the same way as the sun's planets. A conservative minority of astronomers, however, believe that the newly discovered extrasolar planets may prove to be "brown dwarfs," objects that formed in the same way that astronomers think stars do (by the gravitationally induced contraction of a single mass of gas, rather than by the steady agglomeration of cometlike objects called planetesimals). Since brown dwarfs may have the same masses as truly giant planets (5 to 50 times Jupiter's mass), part of the argument of planets versus brown dwarfs may be seen as a semantic one.

About half of the extrasolar planets orbit their stars at startlingly small distances, only about 5 percent of the distance from the Sun to the Earth. Astronomers generally agree that giant planets cannot form at these distances from their stars; instead, any planets orbiting so close to their stars must have formed at much greater distances, comparable to the distance of Jupiter from the Sun, and then moved inward, perhaps from tidal effects arising from the disk of planet-forming material as it slowly evaporated. These close-in planets offer poor prospects for life, but they do signal the actual existence of extrasolar planets.

The remaining newfound planets present a more comforting picture to those who search for life. Like the close-in planets, these objects have masses comparable to Jupiter's, hardly a surprising result once we recognize that the Doppler-shift method most easily reveals the planets with the largest masses (and also those with the smallest distances from their stars, a fact that may bias us in assessing the numbers of the close-in planets). The half-dozen or so planets discovered with "ordinary" separations from their stars orbit at distances comparable to those between the Sun and Mars.

In April 1999, the world's leading planet hunters announced their discovery of the first system of planets orbiting another star. To the giant planet already discovered around the Sunlike star Upsilon Andromedae, some 45 light years from our solar system, they added two more, which likewise have masses comparable to Jupiter's. Unlike the first planet discovered in this system, which orbits its star every 4.6 days at a distance only 1/20 of the distance between the Earth and the Sun, the two newfound planets have average distances from their star of 0.8 and 2.5 times the Earth-Sun distance, so they orbit with periods of 8 months and 4 years, respectively, and would occupy the orbits of Venus and the largest asteroids if they were magically transported into the solar system.

To scientists interested in SETI, the discovery of these extrasolar planets, and especially of the three-planet system around Upsilon Andromedae, connotes significant progress. Until a few years ago, we could assign an accurate value to only one term in the Drake Equation, the calculation that summarizes our knowledge and ignorance about the prevalence of extraterrestrial civilizations (see the essays by Frank Drake and David Brin, Chapter 3). Now we can attach a reasonably good value to a second term, the fraction of stars that have planets, setting a lower boundary of a few percent, and rounding off to a value between 0.05 and 0.5. This may seem vague—until we realize that the previous lower bound lay below 0.000000001.

THE REMAINING TERMS IN THE DRAKE EQUATION

What can we say about the remaining five terms in the Drake Equation? (See The Drake Equation: A Reappraisal.)

They are:

- The fraction of all planets that have conditions suitable for life
- The fraction of those planets on which life actually develops
- The fraction on which life evolves what we call intelligence
- The fraction of those intelligent populations that develop into civilizations capable of interstellar communication
- The average lifetime of these civilizations

Relatively little progress has been made in assigning numbers to these terms of the equation, though the new planet discoveries already imply that at least a modest fraction, say 10 or 20 percent, of all planets lies within the "habitable zones" of their stars.

On the question, *How many of the planets suitable for life actually produce the living article?* the exciting, though still controversial, news burst on the world in August 1996, with the announcement that ALH 84001, a meteorite from Mars found in the Antarctic ice cap, carries signs of ancient life on the red planet. ALH 84001's Martian origin can be verified by the exact correspondence of the abundances of its chemical elements (including those in trapped air bubbles) to those measured on Mars by the Viking spacecraft, and its age, measured by the decay of radioactive minerals. These factors single out this meteorite as the only truly ancient rock (more than 4 billion years old) among the dozen or so identified Martian meteorites. A number of independent lines of reasoning strongly suggested that this rock carries evidence of ancient life, but during the two and a half years since the initial announcement, much of this evidence has been vigorously disputed, not over its factual basis but over its interpretation.

The current status of the evidence can be summarized as highly intriguing but not at all proven. All the scientists agree that it would be amazing if the first ancient rock from Mars showed convincing proof for life. The few rocks found on Earth with ages close to 4 billion years show no evidence of life whatsoever, even though single-celled life had quite likely come to flourish by the time that the rocks formed. What we need, and may soon have, are missions to Mars that actively explore the surface, looking for likely rocks to bring home, possibly even drilling into the Martian permafrost to see whether life might exist on Mars even now, protected by the soil against the harsh environment. Three automated spacecraft, one Japanese and two from NASA, are now sailing toward Mars, destined to arrive as the year 2000 begins. Two of these explorers will enter orbits around the planet, obtaining detailed observations of its surface from altitudes of a few hundred miles, while the third, NASA's Mars Polar Lander, will make humanity's first contact with the ground close to one of Mars's polar caps.

Using a giant parachute to brake its descent through the thin atmosphere, the Polar Lander will land about 500 miles from the south pole of Mars. Five minutes before this landing, the spacecraft will release two sturdy probes to fall onto the surface. Each probe will excavate a small crater, punch through the crater bottom for another few feet, then drill into the Martian soil and use laser beams to heat some of the dirt and grit that it digs up. This heating will vaporize the lighter compounds in the soil, which the instruments on each probe can measure to determine how much water and carbon dioxide has been trapped within the soil below Mars's surface. The Polar Lander itself will use a robotic arm to scoop some Martian soil from just below the surface, which it will bake in an oven, again releasing compounds that have been trapped in the surface material. A microphone on board the lander will allow us to hear, for the first time in human history, the high-pitched hum of the winds on Mars.

Further decades should allow us to send similar automated explorers to Europa, Jupiter's satellite with a possible worldwide ocean beneath its icy crust. We will also explore Titan, Saturn's large moon, the only solar-system satellite with a thick atmosphere (and one made mostly of nitrogen, like Earth's), where pools of liquid ethane may offer potential sites for the origin and development of life; the Cassini-Huygens mission to the Saturnian system, scheduled to arrive in the year 2004, includes a probe that will descend through Titan's opaque atmosphere and make initial measurements of the surface conditions.

These and subsequent attempts to determine the prevalence of life will help us to determine the values of the third and fourth terms in the Drake Equation. Eventually, we may know not only the first four terms but all of them, including the fraction of planets with life that produce a civilization, and the lifetime of an average civilization once it attains the ability to communicate over interstellar distances. Each of these terms comes heavily freighted with implications about the origin and persistence of life and intelligence. If we could only find, and then establish communication with, another civilization, we might quickly learn all the answers by tapping that civilization's experience and insight. In other words, a successful SETI effort offers rewards not only of finding friends in the cosmos, but also of resolving the Drake Equation and its cosmic meaning.

THE CURRENT STATUS OF SETI SEARCHES: HOW SHOULD WE SEARCH?

What progress has now been made, and can soon be made, in SETI searches? In order to answer this question, we must also set a standard by asking ourselves, *What is the proper procedure for a SETI search?* In answering this question, we have no course but to make the best guesses available to science; the best answer will appear only after the search has become successful.

As described in the essay by Michael J. Klein, twenty years ago astronomers achieved a broad consensus that the most efficient way to search for civilizations roughly similar to our own consists of a serious, long-term effort to find their radio and television broadcasts, either those beamed outward in deliberate hopes of attracting attention or those on which we manage to "eavesdrop" with sufficient sensitivity and fine-tuning. SETI scientists can add to this approach with other techniques described in this and other essays, but radio searches appear to be, as they have seemed for decades, the single most effective means of finding another civilization. Let us look at the leading ongoing attempts to find our cosmic neighbors by the radio waves they may emit.

PROJECT PHOENIX AND THE ONE-HECTARE TELESCOPE

The SETI project with the highest visibility and funding has transmogrified itself, changing from what was once a NASA effort to find other civilizations into a private attempt to do so. After Congress commanded NASA to cut off all funding for SETI in 1993, the scientists most directly involved in what had been the U.S. government's project successfully reconstituted themselves as the SETI Institute. Supported by private donations, the SETI Institute has taken its equipment throughout the world, in effect buying time on large radio telescopes in the United States and Australia. The Institute's appropriately named Project Phoenix has thus continued to make radio searches for other civilizations.

Like previous efforts, these searches have found numerous non-natural signals, all of which have turned out to be human-made sources of radio interference. While continuing its present efforts, the SETI Institute has also created a plan to build a much larger collecting area for radio waves than any now available, in an observatory largely devoted to SETI. In January 1999, the SETI Institute and the Radio Astronomy Laboratory of the University of California at Berkeley announced that they will collaborate in constructing an array of radio dishes that collectively will cover an area of one hectare, equal to that of a square one hundred meters on a side. This array, called the One Hectare Telescope or "1HT," should achieve the observational effect of a single giant antenna from 500 or more individual small dishes, essentially the ubiquitous antennas a few meters in diameter that receive television signals from satellites in stationary orbit above the Earth. By combining the signals received by all these dishes, we can derive a radio view of the cosmos that has the same angular resolution as one obtainable with a single dish whose diameter equals the span of the antenna array.

The 1HT's total collecting area will equal about one-seventh of the surface area of the world's largest radio antenna, the 300-meter dish near Arecibo, Puerto Rico. Because only a tiny fraction of the Arecibo telescope's observing time has been or will be devoted to SETI, the 1HT will represent a significant improvement in astronomers' ability to search for weak radio signals. Furthermore, the 1HT will provide SETI astronomers with an advantage unavailable at the Arecibo dish, called "multi-beaming." By interweaving the signals from its individual dishes in sophisticated ways, the array can make high-resolution observations along hundreds of directions on the sky simultaneously. These lines of sight lie within the relatively wide-angle field of view seen by each of the antennas. Combining the signals from all the dishes allows the array to examine a host of much smaller regions within that field, each of which might contain a potential source of signals from an extraterrestrial civilization, or an object of astronomical interest. All of the funding for the 1HT is to come from private sources; the SETI Institute now faces the task of raising several million dollars to pay for it. The University of California will furnish the site for the project, probably near the existing Hat Creek Observatory in northern California, and will oversee the operation of the array.

The One Hectare Telescope will represent by far the largest system dedicated to SETI. Its heart will be not the field of antennas that gather radio photons, but rather the hardware and software that processes the signals from all the separate antennas. Aware that they face a formidable challenge in processing the flood of data anticipated from the 1HT, the SETI astronomers engaged in the project foresee that development at the signal-processing "back end" will never cease; instead, progressively better means of searching the data for signs of another civilization should emerge from increased skill and experience.

Project Phoenix and the One Hectare Telescope do not, of course, represent the only attempt to use radio techniques to search for other civilizations. Among the most noteworthy ongoing efforts, we should salute the team in Massachusetts led by Paul Horowitz, which has completely rebuilt and reconstituted an old radio telescope and its receivers, turning it into a dedicated instrument for SETI. For more than a decade, this relatively modest antenna has been devoted to a full-time search for extraterrestrial radio signals. Although it has surveyed the sky many times, Horowitz's search, like all others, has covered only a modest portion of the total spectrum of possibilities.

Why is this so? In all radio searches for other civilizations, one of the greatest challenges lies in the mind-boggling number of potential frequencies that might carry a non-natural signal, evidence that would reveal another civilization's existence. After examining all the different frequencies that might be used for communication, and all the frequencies of photons that the universe emits naturally (which will interfere with, or even hide completely, any artificial photon pulses), most SETI scientists have concluded that the band of radio frequencies most likely to contain interstellar transmissions lies approximately between 1,000 and 10,000 megahertz. This conclusion, which Michael J. Klein explores in his essay, still leaves a huge number of frequencies to search—assuming that it is correct. From our knowledge of how radio waves pass through interstellar space, we may have to search frequency channels as narrow as 0.1 hertz each, with the result that the most promising radio band contains 100 billion separate frequency channels! A large portion of any SETI radio search must therefore be devoted to searching through an enormous number of channels. Thanks to improvements in computer software and computer speeds, this task now seems doable.

PROJECT SERENDIP AND THE SETI@HOME PROGRAM

Hoping to bring success closer, scientists at the University of California in Berkeley have created a program that employs personal computers to make SETI searches. For a good many years, SETI scientists have deployed a program called Project SERENDIP, which consists of a means of storing on tape some of the signals received by radio telescopes such as the giant dish at Arecibo. The SERENDIP scientists make no attempt to direct where the telescope looks; instead, they "piggyback" on other astronomers' efforts, recording data in whatever direction the telescope happens to be pointed. Over a number of years, this rather randomly oriented approach comes close to duplicating the effects of a carefully planned sky survey.

But the SERENDIP project generates an immense amount of data— too much to be easily analyzed quickly with even the most modern computers. Building on the philosophy behind SERENDIP, some of its scientists decided to farm out the data-analysis task, not to a single large computer but to thousands or millions of small computers, which have become quite powerful in comparison to earlier versions. The two SERENDIP scientists most directly involved in this effort, Daniel Werthimer and David Anderson, call their program for searching through the accumulated mass of data "SETI@home." If you go to the Internet (at the address http://setiathome.ssl.berkeley.edu), you can

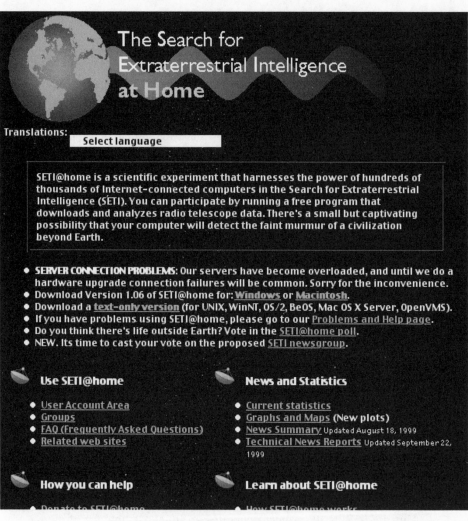

Figure 1. The SETI@HOME home page tells you what the search is all about and how to join the over one million people currently signed up to receive the software for their computers.

download the software that will allow your computer to examine small chunks of the data recorded in radio searches of the sky, searching for possible non-natural signals. The program runs whenever the computer's screen saver does—that is, whenever the computer is not in actual use. (See Figure 1.)

DO SETI SEARCHES LIMIT THEMSELVES TOO SEVERELY BY RELYING ON RADIO?

SETI searches by radio have passed from infancy into adolescence, with relatively bright prospects for improvement, even though no one can accurately predict when ultimate success will occur. Before we consign all our eggs to the radio basket, however, we ought to ask whether an overzealous concentration on these radio searches might cause us to reject one or more likely successes by using other techniques. Radio searches have gained favor from the relatively low cost and immensely high speed of electromagnetic radiation, which promotes communication by radio waves within our own society and (so we conclude) elsewhere in the cosmos. To the extent that other civilizations resemble our own, this logic appears impeccable, so long as we are attempting to eavesdrop on another civilization's internal communication. But if we ask, How could a civilization best signal its existence across interstellar distances?, we may well find that laser beams offer advantages superior to those of radio.

Laser beams consist of photons, which form all types of electromagnetic radiation, including gamma rays, X rays, ultraviolet, visible light, infrared, microwaves, and radio. Most lasers operate in the visible-light domain of the electromagnetic spectrum, producing beams of radiation that consist of a nearly pure color (that is, of one particular wavelength and frequency of light). Such beams can be "collimated"—kept from spreading out as they travel through space—with great efficiency. In theory, a maser beam, the microwave analogue of a laser beam, could experience similar collimation, but in practice, we can achieve this result far more easily with lasers—and so could another civilization. Even though laser beams cost more than masers or radio beacons to run (because visible-light photons each have much larger energies than microwave or radio photons, and someone must pay for this energy), they don't cost much in the broad scheme of things, and they can be recognized across distances of many light years. The SETI Institute and the Planetary Society are now investigating the feasibility of making improved searches for laser broadcasts, which advanced civilizations might already be using either for their own interstellar communication or for signaling their existence to those developing civilizations whose technological abilities now allow them to detect these laser beams.

The possibility of finding other civilizations by detecting laser light leads to the broader question of how we can determine the best means of finding other civilizations. Earthbound astronomers, who have become expert in using the different parts of the spectrum of electromagnetic radiation to study the universe, judge that somewhere in this spectrum lies the most obvious, and therefore the likeliest, means of communication between technologically-adept civilizations. Are the astronomers, however, missing what hindsight will reveal as still better possibilities? What about, for example, using tachyons (particles that travel faster than light), for interstellar communication? Einstein's theory of relativity allows the existence of tachyons, particles that always travel more rapidly than light, whose name derives from the Greek word for swift. These particles exist, so far as we know now, only in physicists' imagination; no experiment has suggested their actual existence.

Tachyons have many remarkable properties (on paper). When we seek to accelerate particles that move more slowly than light, we must add energy to do so, but for tachyons the situation reverses, and we must add energy in order to slow them down! To slow them down "all the way" to the speed of light demands an infinite amount of energy, the same amount required to accelerate an "ordinary" particle to this speed. Without going further into the amazing properties of tachyons, we may note one key aspect of their hypothetical existence that diminishes their usefulness for interstellar communication. Our present understanding suggests no way for tachyons to interact with ordinary matter such as ourselves. This leaves open the untestable possibility that tachyons continually pass by the Earth and everything else we call matter, profoundly unaffected and incapable of demonstrating even their existence. Until we can demonstrate that tachyons do exist and can find a way to interact with them, we may have to leave the tachyon civilizations (should they exist!) to themselves, and count ourselves among the tachyon-challenged.

WHO WILL SPEAK FOR EARTH?

No one said that SETI would easily yield a positive result. To be successful, the search for other civilizations must solve the problem of discovering, by luck or insight, information about those civilizations sufficient to allow us to establish a means of communication. We have considered radio and other forms of electromagnetic radiation, as well as hypothetical tachyons, in our brief analysis. These may prove more than enough—or not even a useful beginning. Confronted with this difficulty, some might be tempted simply to wait for the arrival of extra-terrestrial visitors to Earth, an event much bruited in the tabloids but utterly lacking in the verification that would be trivially available over worldwide networks. (For those who believe that repeated visits to Earth have been concealed by our leaders, let me propose the equally likely hypothesis that everyone save yourself is an alien, pretending to act "normally" in order to observe you more accurately.) A more optimistic view adopts the following approach: To find the closest galactic neighbors with whom we might communicate, first assume that these civilizations have reached at least our level of technological ability. Civilizations less developed than ourselves, either through choice or because their evolution has not brought them technology, will remain undetected for the time being. This suggests using our best means to listen for, and to broadcast if we choose, signals sent between civilizations, or perhaps only the signals that a civilization leaks into space accidentally, as we leak part of our radar, television, and radio transmissions into space.

At first glance this advice to follow our own technological development in choosing a SETI strategy may appear just as Earth-centered as any fantasy of "E.T.'s" landing to check us out. In one sense, this is so: The advice presupposes that the evolution of life forms in the universe leads through something like our technological stage—that is, through a world whose communications are dominated by photon-borne messages. We have no way to be sure that this is so, but we may note that the hypothesis above is one of Earth-averageness, not Earth-centeredness. The concept of searching for civilizations with roughly our own technology presupposes that our history as a society has been at least roughly encompassed by a sizable fraction of all other civilizations. Most of these have presumably progressed to some stage far more advanced than anything we can imagine, and might use some superior means of communication (sometimes whimsically called zeta waves by SETI scientists) of which we are absolutely ignorant. However, if we simply sit on our assets waiting for the day that we discover zeta waves, our prospects for interstellar communication are highly limited in the near term. Furthermore, if the typical technological development pattern passed through radio on the way to zeta waves, then any civilization that now has zeta waves can, if it chooses, contact those less advanced civilizations who still know only radio. As Carl Sagan noted, they will "wheel the old radio telescopes out of the museums" if they seek to speak to their underdeveloped neighbors.

Of course, we can't be sure of anything that a far more technologically advanced civilization might have on its mind—such as, for example, whether the whole notion of contacting "backward civilizations" might be a total bore, or an intrusion on cosmic evolution, or a project to be left for high school science projects and occasional masters' theses on anthropology. Some scientists have speculated that if highly advanced civilizations have come to exist in the Milky Way, at least some of them will want to lord it over the entire galaxy. Hence the fact that we remain free from extraterrestrial dominance (or so most of us believe) shows that civilizations must be extremely rare—otherwise at least one of them would have succeeded in colonizing the galaxy, and with it our planet, which they may call Quork 484. In my opinion, these speculations suffer from a scientifically rationalized form of Earth-centeredness. I believe that it is logically impossible to draw a conclusion that rests on how a civilization sufficiently advanced to colonize a galaxy would behave, since any such conclusion imposes our cultural attitudes on a highly different (to put it mildly) situation.

This may or may not be high-class reasoning. I do feel safe in asserting that civilizations more like ourselves in technological development are more likely to establish contact with us than those less like ourselves. This might imply that we should expect to make contact first with a civilization not greatly in advance of our own, rather than stumbling upon a veritable Athens of the Milky Way. Unfortunately, we have no way of knowing the relative numbers of Earthlike and far more advanced civilizations. Lacking the relative abundances of these two vague categories, my assertion, although eminently reasonable, has no chance of being proven correct until we do establish contact.

All our exploration of the solar system, difficult and time-consuming by human standards, highlights the fact that it's a long way to the stars. Alpha Centauri is 50,000 times farther from us than Jupiter, so the Voyager spacecraft, which took about two years to reach Jupiter and its moons, would require 100,000 years to travel to Alpha Centauri. It is these immense interstellar distances that make UFO reports so highly unlikely to be evidence of interstellar spacecraft! I discount all UFO reports as evidence of extraterrestrial visitors on the grounds of our knowledge of (1) the difficulty of interstellar travel; (2) how unusual a suggestive UFO sighting is, and the difficulty that humans have in recording unusual events correctly; and (3) most of all, the lack of anything other than personal accounts rather than hard evidence.

Most UFO reports appear to refer to natural phenomena, and the ones that don't are the least reliable. (Those interested in the subject of UFOs should consult a marvelous book by Philip Klass, *UFOs Explained.*) On a still more basic level, my desire (shared by many, I believe) is for contact with another civilization. Alleged extraterrestrial spacecraft that merely fly over or even kidnap an occasional human for inspection without leaving any information are not making contact in my book—not when the television networks would be glad to give them a special program, possibly even without commercials. Hence I find UFO reports unconvincing twice over, one because they don't appear to represent extraterrestrial spacecraft, and also because if they were visitors from other worlds, their occupants apparently have little to do but observe us without broadcasting their presence to a waiting world. Being far more advanced than we, these visitors can surely avoid detection; the odd fact would then be that they are glimpsed at all. The popular movies and television programs that feature UFOs speak to the human desire to believe that unseen powers watch over us, guiding us for good or evil purposes. This leaves the tremendous unanswered questions, Why bother? and Why not simply wipe humanity off the planet if we provoke disdain or are perceived as a free lunch?

The first UFO report that I will take seriously is the report that we have detected an extraterrestrial signal. This is so because I know that to send a ten-minute television program to Alpha Centauri, to arrive with a signal strength that our technology could capture, would cost a few thousand dollars. To send this program not four light-years but a thousand light-years, again with an intensity level accessible to a civilization like ours, would cost a few hundred thousand dollars. And this is a conservative estimate—it might even cover modest salaries for the stars of the program. The cost of this broadcast falls so far below the cost of any expedition, and its transmission proceeds so much more rapidly, that it should appeal to any civilization that does not have unlimited resources.

Which brings me to a key point that deserves serious attention: Who will speak for Earth? Until contact is established, SETI efforts must concentrate on detection, not broadcasting. Detection promises results now; broadcasting represents casting bread on the waters for an unknown waiting period. If you think that communication will never occur if all civilizations share this attitude, remember that we continuously broadcast radio signals as we leak radio, television, and radar photons into space.

I believe that sooner or later SETI searches will find a clearly artificial signal. When that happens, it will already be too late to have a reasoned discussion about the reply that we might return. The paranoid side of the human psyche suggests that one country might detect a signal but attempt to keep it secret, presumably from its own population as well as the rest of the world. If we put to one side the operational value of keeping such a secret, as well as the enjoyable speculation that this plan has been in operation for years (in which case much of our leaders' behavior becomes more easily explicable), I claim that no such secret could be kept for long. The president's closest advisors cannot resist spilling their beans about far smaller matters. If this is so, we return to the question of what we as a planet might plan now to do when we receive a definitive signal.

Through one of society's many ironies, advice from scientists seems destined to be ignored if the scientists wait to offer advice until clear proof of a signal appears. The matter will then appear too important to consult an expert. On the other hand, if the scientific community were to engage in debate today over the appropriate reply to an extraterrestrial message, they will most likely be laughed at. But when the moment arrives, the existence of a model message prepared by the world's scientists could provide the focus for worldwide discussions and would remind us that it is a planet, not a political subset of its population, that has established contact with another civilization.

I have proposed that the International Astronomical Union and the International Astronomical Federation create a committee to encourage the process of formulating a reply to an artificial extraterrestrial signal. This committee would raise interest within the community of scientists and scholars, who in turn might succeed in awakening interest among the general public. If not, the proposed message or messages would nonetheless make a key step toward producing a consensus, prior to the detection of a signal, as to what Earth's reply should contain. I am not so optimistic as to believe that general agreement would arise among scientists, let alone in the public at large. On the other hand, I am optimistic that to awaken debate over the contents of our reply—even at the price of derisory mention among those who find all of SETI a worthless endeavor—would prove beneficial. We may not establish contact in our lifetimes, and discussion of our reply may therefore prove highly premature. Nevertheless, it can't hurt to be ready.

What should Earth say to the cosmos? Since my goal is to produce consensus, I won't make any specific suggestions, but I can note the

precursor of a reply message and our present abilities in sending information. In 1974, to celebrate the upgrading of the surface of the
Arecibo radio antenna, scientists used it in the reverse sense to broadcast an interstellar message in the direction of the globular star cluster
M13 in the constellation Hercules, 25,000 light-years from Earth. The
message was broadcast at a frequency of 2.38 Ghz—outside the "water
hole" band of frequencies, from 1.42 to 1.65 Ghz, that Michael Klein
discusses in his essay—and contained 1,679 bits of information. Each
bit consisted of a single item, in this case whether the transmitter was
or was not broadcasting at a particular moment. Even repeated a few
times over, the message took only few minutes to send.

In the year 26988 or so, if anyone in the star cluster M13 happens
to have a powerful receiver tuned to 2.38 Ghz and attached to an
antenna pointed in our direction, our message might be detected and
recorded as a suggestive, nonrandom set of on-off pulses. If those
detecting the signal notice, that 1,679 is the product of two prime
numbers (23 and 73), they may hit on the idea of arranging the "bits"
into a rectangular grid, 23 columns by 73 rows, or 23 rows by 73
columns, and using two different colors, one for the "on" bits and
another for the "off" bits. If they do so, one of the two choices will
produce a meaningless blur, but the other will shout (so we think) with
the cry of "intelligent beings over here!" The recipients of our message
will see a crude representation of a human figure, a map of the solar
system, symbols representing the most important elements in our kind
of life, and the structure of the DNA molecule, which governs the
process of replication in every organism on Earth. They can mull the
message over and might decide to reply, in which case we can expect
to hear from them, presumably at the same frequency at which we
sent the message, in about the year 51988.

The Arecibo radio message raises some important issues. For me,
the most important are these: Should scientists celebrating an
improved antenna be the ones who decide whether, when, and what to
broadcast to other civilizations? If not, then who? It may be noted that
the Arecibo message was a one-shot affair, and was directed to a star
cluster sufficiently distant that we can hardly expect any consequences on a human time scale. (Of course, with just this philosophy
we have come close to ruining our planet on a human time scale.) The
chief moral that I draw from the Arecibo message is that the issue of
who should compose a message from Earth deserves more attention
than it has received until now. Beyond that, another issue emerges: Do

we really want to send such a low-budget picture into space? Our technology is now entirely capable (and already was in 1974) of sending a message that would contain not a thousand or so bits of information but a hundred million or so, without taking any more time to broadcast than the few minutes consumed by the Arecibo message. A hundred million bits can be used to convey the contents of several thousand printed pages, or a few thousand detailed pictures. This seems to me to represent a capability sufficient to sidestep much of the potential argument over message content, since it offers the opportunity to include a host of diverse, even possibly conflicting, information and opinions.

On the other hand, maybe we shouldn't try to paint ourselves in living color. Lewis Thomas suggested that we might try broadcasting nothing but Bach, on the theory that we should start by bragging; perhaps it's worth a try. Ernst Fasan has proposed a basic principle of truthfulness-that is, anything might reasonably be included so long as it is true. The difficulty with this principle is that we humans (could it be true of other civilizations' members?) are notoriously slow to agree on what is true.

I propose another principle, the democratic principle: Anything is acceptable in a reply message so long as it has been openly discussed and, in some vaguely defined sense, agreed upon. This is a principle for ourselves, not for the recipient of our messages. They may have strange forms of political organization (just what those are is one of the prime pieces of information we might hope to learn), but it is we ourselves who must speak for Earth.

The astrophysicist Philip Morrison has called SETI "the archaeology of the future," comparing the search for another civilization's signal to the excavation of the remains of a bygone civilization on Earth. In both cases we are looking into the past-on Earth because the information has been long buried; in space because it has taken many years to reach us. The difference is that archaeology examines the past of Earth, but SETI attempts to examine its future, by discovering what paths other civilizations, many with longer histories than ours, have traveled in past times. It appears likely that insight into our future can be plucked from the airwaves-once we know how and where to look. Once a signal has been detected, the way that we think about our planet will change. Those who care about the future might do well to plan now for the time that the signal arrives-a watershed in the history of Earth that will change us from a silent to a communicating planet.

CHAPTER 1

LIFE IN THE UNIVERSE

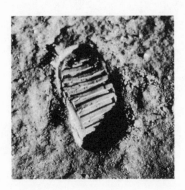

Is there intelligent life on Earth? Before we begin to seek extraterrestrial intelligence we must arrive at some understanding of just what we mean by intelligence. Might there be intelligent nonhuman life on Earth?

Ben Bova introduces the idea of the search for good suns and their good planets, by introducing the concept of a star's habitable zone. The late Isaac Asimov's essay on the question of intelligence in general is as valid now as when he wrote it for the prior edition of this book. It produces a soundly workable definition of just what we should look for when we turn our probing senses toward the heavens. Diana Reiss reports on an "alien" intelligence that lives here on Earth: the dolphins. Hal Clement gives a detailed prescription for what kind of worlds might harbor intelligent life.

The one fact that overwhelms all others is that we have only a single example of intelligent life on which to base all our conjectures: ourselves. While Copernicus removed the Earth from the center of the Universe and Darwin showed that humans are not separate from the other life forms on our planet, when it comes to intelligent life we are alone on the center of the stage.

So far.

SURVEYING THE COSMOS

By

BEN BOVA

L ook out at the sky on a moonless night. Not from the streets of a brightly lit, dusty, and polluted city, but from an open field far out in the countryside. Or from the chill dark of the desert, the kind of barren emptiness where astronomy began long millennia ago. Or, best of all, from the deck of a ship in the middle of the ocean.

There you can see the sky in all its splendor. Stars fill the darkness wherever you look, and the glowing sweep of the Milky Way arches overhead like a river of faintly shimmering light.

You will be able to see more than two thousand stars on such a night with your unaided eyes. Which of them might be the home of an intelligent civilization? Which ones should we direct our attention to as we search for the first contact with extraterrestrial intelligence?

In 1609 Galileo became the first astronomer to turn a telescope toward the stars. He found that there were far more than the few thousand we can see with the naked eye. Stars that were invisible to the unaided eye showed up even in his little thirty-power telescope. The Milky Way itself was revealed as a vast assemblage of stars, so many stars so distant from us that their light blends together to form the band of brightness that we see.

As astronomers built larger and larger telescopes they found more and more stars. Giant stars. Dwarf stars. Some stars were blue, some red, some yellow like our own Sun. Some pulsated as if they were breathing in and out.

OUR GALAXY AND OTHERS

By the middle of the twentieth century astronomers had learned that the Milky Way is actually a vast, pinwheel-shaped *galaxy* that contains more than 100 billion (10^{11}) stars and enough loose gas and dust to create billions more. And there are billions of other galaxies, far beyond our own, many of them much larger than our Milky Way.[1]

The distances to the stars in our galaxy are immense, mind-boggling. Even light, the fastest thing in the Universe, takes years to travel between the stars. Light moves at 186,000 miles per second (300,000 kilometers per second). It takes light eight minutes to go from the Sun to Earth, a distance that averages roughly 93 million miles. Light from the Sun reaches Pluto, the farthest known planet of our solar system, in five hours and thirty minutes.

To reach the nearest star, Alpha Centauri, light from the Sun must travel 4.3 *years*. If you drew a map in which the Earth-to-Sun distance was shrunk to one inch, the distance between the Sun and Alpha Centauri would be 4.3 miles. And that is the closest star to our solar system.

Astronomers use the *light-year* as a yardstick to measure distances in space. The distance that light travels in one year is close to 6 trillion miles (nearly 10 trillion kilometers).[2]

The Milky Way Galaxy is a vast double spiral of stars about 100,000 light-years across and 12,000 light-years thick at its core. Our solar system lies off to one side of the Milky Way, roughly 30,000 light-years from its center, where the Galaxy is about 2,000 light-years thick. The Sun travels around the galactic center in an orbit that takes 250 million years to complete.

With a hundred billion stars in our galaxy alone, which are the most likely to harbor intelligent life? What regions of the sky should we be searching to find signals from alien civilizations? Or are we alone in the Galaxy, perhaps alone in the Universe? Could it be that

---

1. *Beware of Hollywood's use of the word* galaxy. *In most motion pictures the word is mistakenly used to mean a solar system, a system consisting of a star and its planets. The proper astronomical definition of the word* galaxy *is a system of billions of stars, such as our own Milky Way or the great spiral in Andromeda.*

2. *Astronomers also use a slightly larger unit, the* parsec, *in measuring distances. One parsec equals 3.26 light-years. Think of the light-year as the astronomers' "foot" and the parsec as their "yard."*

intelligence, or even life itself, is a fluke, a statistical accident that is so unlikely it has occurred only once?

What do the stars tell us?

STELLAR LIFE CYCLES

The first and most impressive fact is that there are so *many* stars. It is difficult to believe that around all those billions of billions we are the only living creatures, the only intelligence.

Stars come in many sizes and colors. Some appear to be single stars, such as our Sun. Others are double. Sirius, the brightest star in our sky is a double star. There are triple star systems (Alpha Centauri is a triple), and even more complex systems of multiple stars.

A star's color is a clue to its surface temperature. Astronomers have set up a classification system that ranks color and temperature. (See Table 1.) The system originally was strictly alphabetical, with A representing the hottest stars, and so forth. Over the years, though, it was found that B stars are actually hotter than A, so some classifications were dropped and others added until the current lineup evolved: O, B, A, F, G, K, M. Astronomers have no trouble remembering the order. They simply recall the mnemonic, "Oh, Be A Fine Girl, Kiss Me!" Obviously all this happened before the women's movement hit astronomy.

Astronomers have learned much about the life cycles of stars. Yes, stars have life cycles much as human beings do. Stars are born, go through a certain lifespan, then weaken and die. Some of them die in violent explosions. For most stars the life span is measured in billions of years. Our Sun, for example, is probably a bit less than 5 billion years old and has at least another 5 billion years of steady, dependable life ahead of it before it becomes unstable and ultimately collapses and fades out.

How can astronomers learn the life histories of stars that take billions of years to play out? We only see the stars in an instant of time; even several centuries of observation is little more than a snapshot. The very multiplicity of the stars comes to the astronomers' aid. By taking snapshots of thousands, millions, billions of stars, the astronomers can put them together into a sort of family album that, coupled with computer models of stellar evolution, shows young stars, old stars, middle-aged stars—stars in every stage of their eons-long life cycles.

STAR BIRTH, STAR DEATH

Astronomical cameras have captured new stars in the midst of birth. *Protostars*, dark clumps of interstellar gas and dust, have been photographed in the process of formation. A few years later the telescopes were turned to the same protostars and they were no longer dark! They had begun to shine. New stars had been born.

Stars begin as cold, dark clouds of gas and interstellar dust. Such clouds condense until their central regions become so hot and compressed that hydrogen in the core is forced to begin fusion reactions, creating helium and the energy that we ultimately see as starlight.

A star remains stable as long as it is fusing hydrogen into helium at its core. For most stars this stable middle age spans billions of years. However, the rate at which hydrogen is consumed depends on the mass of the stars. Hot blue giants such as Rigel and Spica are burning up their core hydrogen so fast that they will have stable life spans of only a few hundred million years, at best, instead of the billions of years that less massive, cooler stars have.

Stars also die. When they have used up the energy sources within them they collapse and go dim. Some of them explode so violently as they collapse that they can outshine an entire galaxy—briefly. Such *supernova* explosions are rare: Perhaps one occurs in our galaxy every 500 years, on average. In 1987 a supernova blasted out in the Large Megellanic Cloud, a companion to the Milky Way, the closest supernova observed since 1604.

When a star dies its fate is determined by its original mass. The Sun will not explode, according to astrophysical theory. Some 5 billion years from now the Sun will have exhausted its core hydrogen and will begin to swell and turn into a red giant star. Its bloated outer envelope may engulf the Earth itself. Even if it does not, in its red giant phase our friendly Sun will glow so fiercely that life on Earth will become impossible.

Ultimately the Sun will collapse, going from a red giant to a white dwarf. It will shrink to about the size of the Earth, a hundreth of its present diameter. The matter inside the Sun will become so compressed that a spoonful of it would weigh thousands of tons. Then slowly, over countless eons of time, the Sun will cool down and go dark, a burned-out stellar cinder.

Many white dwarfs have been seen. The star Sirius is accompanied by a white dwarf, a star with a mass similar to the Sun's but a size of only a few thousand miles across. Since Sirius is known as the Dog Star, its tiny companion has been dubbed the Pup.

More massive stars undergo more spectacular death throes. A supernova explosion releases as much energy in twenty-four hours as the Sun does in a billion years! Most of the star's material is ejected into space, and any planets that might have been orbiting the star are undoubtedly demolished utterly. Yet death can lead to new life: The material ejected by the earliest supernovas enriched the interstellar medium with heavy elements that eventually became the building blocks for new stars.

Nor does a supernova explosion entirely destroy the star. For a star with an original mass of more than about twice the Sun's, the core collapses into matter so dense that a spoonful would weigh billions of tons. The atomic particles are squeezed so hard that they coalesce to form neutrons. The star shrinks to a mere few miles in diameter and is composed entirely of neutrons (with, perhaps, a surface skin of pure iron).

Neutron stars have been observed despite their diminutive size, thanks to the fact that many of them are *pulsars*, which emit powerful beams of radio energy in regularly timed bursts. The first pulsar, discovered in 1967, put out such precise pulses of radio waves that at first astronomers thought they might have discovered signals from an extraterrestrial civilization. The radio pulses, each ten to twenty milliseconds long, came every 1.33730113 seconds. Their timing was more accurate than the finest quartz watches.

Further study, however, showed that the pulsars are natural phenomena, not signals from an alien life form. The key piece of evidence proving that pulsars are neutron stars came from the Crab Nebula, the visible and expanding remains of a supernova that was observed by Chinese and Japanese astronomers in A.D. 1054. In 1969 astronomers found a pulsar at the heart of the Crab Nebula's wildly distorted cloud of gas. Not only does it emit bursts of radio energy, it even winks on and off visibly, as shown on a synchronized TV detector.

Stars of more than about 8 times the Sun's mass undergo an even stranger fate when they reach the end of their life cycles.

When the core of such a massive star collapses in a supernova explosion, more than 3 solar masses remain and not even the formation of neutrons can stabilize it. Most of the star's matter is ejected into space in the supernova explosion, but the core of the star shrinks under the immense force of gravity even beyond the tiny size of a neutron star. The core keeps on collapsing and disappears into a *black hole*. The gravitational force is so titanic that the star's core is pulled down into a dimensionless point.

Not even light waves can escape the incredible gravitational force. The star disappears from our Universe. As the old saw says, the star "digs a hole, jumps in, and then pulls the hole in after it."

Astronomers have detected pinpoints in the sky that are sources of fierce X-ray emanations. They deduce that these locations are sites of black holes, where some of the gases surrounding the exploded stars are being sucked into insatiable gravitational wells, generating X rays as the stars fall into oblivion.

PLANETS OF OTHER STARS

The one form of life that we know of exists on the surface of a planet. Therefore we should seek out other planets as possible abodes of extra-terrestrial intelligence.

Spacecraft have investigated all the planets of our solar system except tiny, distant Pluto. Although the chances that some form of life may exist on Mars cannot be absolutely ruled out, and we simply do not yet know enough about the outer planets and their moons to deter-mine if life exists there, it seems clear that no *intelligent* life exists on the other worlds of our solar system.

For extraterrestrial intelligence we must look to the stars.

The stars are so far away that any planets they may harbor are too dim for ground-based telescopes to detect. Astronomers on Alpha Centauri (if any exist there) could not see the Earth, nor even detect giant Jupiter, with the same kind of telescopes we have on Earth.

However, the InfraRed Astronomy Satellite (IRAS), launched in 1981, detected clouds of dust around several stars, including bright Vega. Astronomers conclude that such dust clouds are either the raw materials for building planets or the leftovers after the process of planet-building is completed. Interplanetary space in our own solar system is strewn with dust; we see some of it in the *zodiacal light*, a band of faint luminosity along the line of the Sun's path through the sky created by the reflection of sunlight off the dust particles. (You need a dark night, far from the city, to see it.)

But in an amazing turn of events, we have detected, through infer-ence, the existence of extrasolar planets via *ground-based* observations. In October of 1995, Michael Mayor and Didier Queloz of the Geneva Observatory in Switzerland reported finding an extrasolar planet orbiting the star 51 Pegasi in the constellation of Pegasus. Their discovery was not based on a sight observation, but rather inference from an observed variation in the light from the star in question. Spectrum features of 51 Pegasi were seen to periodically shift from the red toward the blue end of the spectrum and back. The only logical and rational explanation for this cycle is the presence of a planet orbiting the star.

A more recent ground-based survey of 107 Sun-like stars by a team at San Francisco State University and U.C. Berkeley, led by Geoffrey Marcy and R. Paul Butler, turned up six more planets based on such Doppler shifts. That seemed to open the floodgates, as there are now more than 20 extrasolar planets that have been identified (see Table 1 in Chapter 3) through this method. The results are both unexpected and exotic, as several planets seem to be two to ten times the mass of Jupiter, and some orbit their stars at extraordinarily close distances while other apparently possess quite eccentric orbits. Aside from the Doppler shift, one other piece of evidence may indicate the presence of extrasolar planets.

The Sun spins on its axis very slowly, roughly once a month. Many stars spin hundreds of times faster. Astrophysicists have calculated that, although the Sun may have spun quite rapidly at first, its rotation was probably slowed by the processes that created the planets and the drag of the primordial solar wind. Fast-spinning stars, perhaps, either have no planets or are too young for planetary systems to have formed around them and slowed their spin. (See Chapter 3.)

There is an enormous number of slow-spinning stars in the Milky Way. As Table 2 shows, G-type stars such as our Sun tend to spin quite slowly. Has their spin rate been slowed by planetary systems that we cannot yet see?

THE CONDITIONS FOR LIFE

Even if *all* the stars of the Milky Way were accompanied by planets, that does not mean that every planet would harbor life—or intelligence.

It took nearly 5 billion years for intelligence to arise on Earth. During all that time the Sun has remained steady in its output of energy, and the Earth has remained in a stable orbit around the Sun.

If the Sun's energy output had fluctuated significantly—if it had grown suddenly much brighter or dimmer, or exploded even mildly—life on Earth would have been wiped out. Our life depends on having liquid water available. Only a few-percent change in the Sun's energy output could freeze the oceans or boil them away.

And the Earth's orbit is very nearly circular. This means there is comparatively little change in global temperature during the course of a year. If our orbit took Earth as far from the Sun as Mars is, and in as close as Venus, our water would alternately freeze and boil. The chances for life would be slim.

The Sun has remained stable for 5 billion years and has at least another 5 billion years of placid stability ahead of it. Not all stars are so well behaved. Table 2 shows that the hottest stars are stable for only a relatively short time, perhaps too short for life to arise, certainly too short to expect intelligence to evolve—assuming Earth-like rates of evolution.

The very bright giant stars such as Rigel are not stable long enough for life to flower. Not until we consider the cooler main-sequence F and G class stars do we find stable life spans long enough for life to develop. (Remember, we are using the only example of life and intelligence that we know of—ourselves—as our yardstick here.)

Curiously, it is exactly these cooler main sequence yellow, orange, and red stars that show the slow spin rates that may be associated with planetary systems. So on two counts we can reject the hot young giant stars as likely abodes for intelligent life.

ROOM ENOUGH FOR LIFE

Life needs an abode that is "thermally habitable."

The temperature of a planet must be right for life to exist on it. Earth is thermally habitable for life based on liquid water. Jupiter may be also, deep beneath its outer cloud deck, where heat upwelling from the Jovian core may have created a vast planetwide ocean of water. Jupiter's moon Europa appears to be covered with water ice; there is some reason to suspect that liquid water may exist beneath the frozen surface.

The farther planets of our solar system are apparently too cold for liquid water. They may be suitable for life based on ammonia or methane, however.

A star will heat up objects within a certain space around it, depending on the star's surface temperature. There is a zone around each star, then, that can be called thermally habitable for a given form of life.

For our own solar system, the thermally habitable zone for liquid-water life extends from somewhere between the orbits of Venus and Earth barely out to the orbit of Mars. Another thermally habitable zone for possible ammonia-based life includes Jupiter and Saturn, as well as their moons, and possibly Uranus and Neptune as well.

Table 1   STAR CLASSES

Class	Surface Temperature	Color	Examples
O	above 45,000°F	blue-violet	rare
B	45,000–20,000	blue	Rigel, Spica
A	20,000–13,500	blue to white	Sirius, Vega
F	13,500–11,000	white to yellow	Canopus, Procyon
G	11,000–9,000	yellow	Sun, Capella, Alpha Centauri A
K	9,000–7,000	orange	Arcturus, Aldebaran, Alpha Centauri B
M	less than 7,000	red	Betelgeuse, Antares, Alpha Centauri C

Table 2   LIFE SPANS AND SPIN RATES OF STARS

Star Class	Stable Life Span	Typical Spin Rate
B	8 to 400 million years	60 to 90 miles per sec.
A	400 million to 4 billion years	30 to 60 miles per sec.
F	4 to 10 billion years	30 to 60 miles per sec.
G	10 to 30 billion years	0 to 30 miles per sec.
K	30 to 70 billion years	0 to 30 miles per sec.

To be a good prospect for having a life-bearing planet, a star should have as large a thermally habitable zone (or zones) as possible. (See Chapter 1.) The larger the zone the better the chances of one or more planetary orbits being in it. Also, the planet's orbit should remain within the zone all the time; it is difficult to imagine life evolving on a planet that is thermally habitable only part of its year. Planets associated with multiple star systems may have complex orbits that swing them in and out of one or more thermally habitable zones.

The stars with the largest thermally habitable zones are obviously the hot, young giants. But these stars are short-lived. They do not remain stable long enough to allow life to develop. The dinosaurs never saw Rigel or Spica; they were not shining yet. Such bright blue giants will be long gone before any planets near them have had the time to evolve life.

The stars with the longest stable lifetimes are the cool, dim red dwarfs. They burn their hydrogen fuel so slowly that they can remain stable for tens of billions of years. But they are so cool that their thermally habitable zones must be small, and the chances of having a planet orbiting inside such a zone seem slim.

It is no surprise, then, that we live on a planet that orbits a yellow star. Such stars are warm enough to have a respectably sized thermally habitable zone, and long-lived enough to allow life—even intelligence—to evolve.

There are billions of such stars in the Milky Way Galaxy. Of the forty stars closest to us, there is one F type, three G types, and twenty-nine K and M stars. This count includes only the brightest members of double and multiple star groups. Four of these stars are suspected of having unseen dark companions. Each of them might have Earth-type planets orbiting within thermally habitable zones, bearing life and even intelligence civilizations.

THE GEOGRAPHY OF THE MILKY WAY

As a starting rule of thumb, lacking evidence except for the example of ourselves, we can say that we should not expect to find intelligence on planets circling stars that are less than roughly 5 billion years old.

We know that the young giant stars do not meet this criterion. The cool K- and M-class dwarf stars have much longer life *expectancies* than the Sun. But are they actually older than the Sun? We know that some are not; some of them are just becoming stable after their formation out of protostar globules. Moreover, the thermally habitable zones of K and M dwarfs must be perilously slim.

Looking further afield, let us consider the "geography" of the Milky Way Galaxy in our quest to determine where extraterrestrial intelligence may be found.

The Milky Way is a spiral galaxy very much like the beautiful spiral in Andromeda, M31.[3] The most distant object visible to the naked eye, M31 is about two million light-years away.

---

3. *M31 is the thirty-first item of 107 objects listed in the 1784 catalogue of Charles Messier, a French astronomer who especially sought to discover new comets. His catalogue was originally intended as a guide to fellow comet-seekers, identifying fuzzy objects that are not comets and not worth bothering with. Or so he thought. Thirty-four of the "Messier objects" are galaxies, the rest are star clusters or interstellar clouds within the Milky Way.*

The core of our own Milky Way Galaxy (which lies in the direction of the constellation Sagittarius) must be thick with stars, as the core of M31 and other spiral galaxies are. But we never see the core optically because it is hidden behind thick clouds of interstellar dust. Radio and infrared observations have been able to penetrate the dust to some extent. These observations, plus the studies of the cores of other spiral galaxies, show that the region is so rich with stars that they are probably no more than a single light-year apart, at most.

Such studies of the Milky Way's core also indicate that something very energetic is blazing away at the heart of our galaxy. Possibly a giant black hole is gnawing away at the Milky Way's core, gobbling whole stars while discharging radio, infrared, and high-energy radiation.

Most of the stars at the cores of spiral galaxies are much older than the stars in their arms. Red giant stars are common in the core regions, and astrophysical theory shows that stars become red giants only after they have used up most of their original hydrogen and left their long life of stability behind them. There are few hot young blue giants in galactic cores; these are found almost exclusively in the spiral arms.

Because the core regions of spiral galaxies seem to be populated predominantly by different types of stars than the spiral arms, astronomers refer to the two different stellar constituencies as Population I and Population II. This can cause some confusion.

Population I stars are the kind found in the spiral arms. Our Sun is a Population I star. These are youngish stars; their brightest members are blue giants such as Rigel. Population I stars contain a relatively high proportion of elements heavier than hydrogen and helium, although "relatively high" never amounts to more than a few percent. Yet astronomers refer to the Population I stars as "metal rich." ("Metal," in this usage, means any element heavier than helium.)

Population II stars are those found in the core regions of a galaxy. They are old. Their brightest members are red giants, stars that have gone through many billions of years of stability and have now become bloated and swollen. Population II stars are mostly "metal poor."

The heavy-element content of a star is an important clue to its history. Why are the stars in the Milky Way's core metal-poor while the stars in the spiral arms are metal-rich? Because the elements heavier than helium have been created inside the stars. Consider the following:

The Milky Way must have been quite different 10 or 15 billion years ago—a span of time two to three times longer than the Sun's age. It is almost misleading to use the name Milky Way that far back in time, because there were no stars to make it shine.

Our galaxy presumably began as an immense dark cloud of gas, at least 100,000 light-years across. The gas was almost entirely hydrogen, the lightest and simplest of all the elements, probably with a smattering of the second-lightest element, helium.

CREATION OF THE CHEMICAL ELEMENTS

The first stars to form, then, had no significant amounts of elements heavier than helium. All the heavier elements, up to iron, were "cooked" inside the stars. During the long eons of a stable star's life, its fusion processes transmute hydrogen into helium. When the core hydrogen supply becomes depleted the star begins "burning" helium to create carbon, oxygen, and neon. These elements eventually are themselves used as fuel for further fusion processes that create still-heavier elements.

Once helium-burning begins at a star's core its outer envelope begins to swell. The star grows into a red giant.

When the star has reached the point where its fusion processes are creating atoms of iron, it has also reached the end of its tether. When iron undergoes fusion the process *absorbs* energy rather than releasing it. The star is suddenly bankrupt. It collapses, either into a white dwarf (as the Sun eventually will) or into the explosive fury of a supernova, as discussed above. In the star-shattering cataclysm of a supernova, the elements heavier than iron are created.

The earliest stars in the Milky Way began with nothing more than hydrogen and helium. They created the heavier elements and spewed them into interstellar space when they exploded. These atoms served as the building blocks for the next generation of stars. The explosions that marked the deaths of the earliest stars enriched the interstellar medium with clouds of heavy elements. It was from those clouds that new stars were created.

Judging by the heavy-element content of the stars, most astrophysicists estimate that the Sun must be at least a third-generation star, a grandchild of the original stars of the Milky Way. The elements inside the Sun were created in the cores (and supernova explosions) of ancient stars. The atoms that make up the solar system were once thousands of light-years away, deep inside other stars. The atoms of our own bodies were created in those distant stars. We are truly stardust.

Those earliest stars, however, *could not produce life.* They began

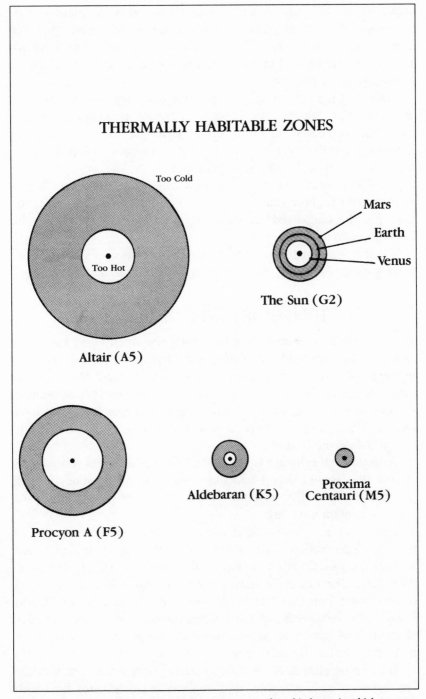

Figure 1. The shaded region around each star represents the orbital area in which temperatures are moderate enough that life may be possible. The orbits are all drawn to the same scale. (*Diagram supplied by Ben Bova. Art by Elizabeth Wen.*)

with nothing but hydrogen and helium. If there were any planets orbiting around them, those planets could be made of nothing but hydrogen and helium. Nothing else existed! There was no carbon, no oxygen— none of the elements that are needed to create the complex chemical phenomenon we call life.

Second-generation stars? It is possible that they would have most of the heavier elements, including the nitrogen, potassium, iron, and such that are needed for life to exist. Planets of such stars might be able to support life, even our own kind of water-based life, if those elements were present in sufficient quantities.

If life has arisen on planets circling second-generation stars there is no reason to suppose that it could not eventually attain intelligence. Certainly the long-lived red dwarf stars provide plenty of time for intelligence to develop.

Granting that intelligence could arise on the planets of second-generation stars, could such races develop high civilizations and technology?

THE IMPORTANCE OF METALS

This depends on the abundance of natural resources. Fossil fuels such as coal and oil should be available, since these are the result of biodegrading plant and animal matter. What about metals? (And here we mean metals in the usual definition of the word, not the astrophysicist's.) Our technology here on Earth is built on copper, iron, nickel, tin, etc. Our history rings with the sounds of the Bronze Age, the Iron Age, the Steel Age, the Uranium Age.

Astronomical evidence is hazy here. Theory shows that second-generation stars should have a lesser abundance of metals than we third-generation types. But certainly there should be *some* metals on second-generation worlds.

How much metal is enough? There is no way for us to tell. Planets of second-generation stars might have iron mountains and gold nuggets lying on the open ground. Or they might have very little available metal. The planet Jupiter in our own solar system might easily contain more iron than the Earth does, but it would be mixed with 317.4 Earth masses of hydrogen, helium, methane, ammonia, and other elements, and buried at the bottom of an ocean that is thousands of miles deep. Not easily accessible.

If there are planets of second-generation stars where heavy metals are abundant and available, those planets could be sites for highly advanced civilizations. But what if intelligence arises on a world where heavy metals are not available?

First recognize that while intelligence per se does not depend on the existence of metals, *life* does. There is an atom of iron at the heart of every hemoglobin molecule in your bloodstream. Good health depends on trace amounts of iron, zinc, and other metals.

The human race rose to intelligence before the discovery of metalworking. Humans used bone, rock, clay, and wood for their earliest technology. Yet history shows that once metals became available our race took giant strides forward. Metals allowed our ancestors to build effective plows. And swords. And chariots. And radio telescopes. Today our skyscrapers and computers and engines and spacecraft are made largely of metals. Metals are strong, tough, and cheap.

Could an intelligent race build spacecraft and computers without metals? Could they build radio telescopes with which to receive our signals or send their own?

Today we humans use Space Age materials such as plastics and composites. But the machinery that produces them is made of stainless steel, copper, brass, and other metals. Cavemen, or even ancient Greeks, could not have produced boron-filament composites or polystyrene plastics. They did not have the metals with which to produce them.

Would a metal-poor second-generation intelligent race be stymied in its attempts at technology? Who can say? *Our* technology certainly depends on metals, and that is the only example we have to consider—so far.

Another important point: The entire world of electricity and magnetism would never have been discovered without copper and iron. It is difficult to see how the entire chain of study and application of the electromagnetic force—from Volta through Faraday, Maxwell, Hertz, and Marconi to radio telescopes and television and superconducting magnets—could have taken place on a metal-poor planet. And where would our technology be without electricity? Back in the mid-nineteenth century, at best.

It just might be possible for an intelligent race on a metal-poor world to build a complex technology out of nonmetals. However, tribes on Earth that never had easy access to metals never developed a complex technology. Coincidence, or cause and effect?

If our own history is any guide, it is the heavy metals that lead to high technology. They also form a natural gateway into the world of electromagnetism and the whole concept of "invisible" forces that act over a distance, such as gravity. We can trace a direct line from humankind's use of heavy metals to electromagnetics, nuclear power, space exploration, and the search for extraterrestrial intelligence.

Indeed, as we scan the stars with out radio telescopes, we are implicitly seeking intelligent races that have developed a technological civilization, a civilization that can build radio telescopes, a civilization that uses metals.

If there are second-generation worlds rich enough in metals to give rise to technological civilizations, then their races must be much older and presumably wiser than we are. Second-generation races that do not have metals may be gamboling innocently through some local variation of Eden. They will not have radio telescopes to either receive or transmit intelligent signals.

First-generation stars, if any still exist, will have no life at all.

Add to this the fact that the core of the Milky Way is being bathed with lethal amounts of hard radiation from the black hole (or whatever it is) that is blazing away there, and we must come to the conclusion that the place to search for intelligent signals is in our own neighborhood, here among the spiral arms of the Galaxy.

Gone is the old science-fiction dream of an immense galactic empire, presided over by the older and wiser races that exist at the heart of the Galaxy. Perhaps there was one there once, a second-generation race that had enough metal available to expand outward. Perhaps, as suggested by writer/editor Stanley Schmidt, the cataclysm that is destroying the core of the Milky Way is the result of an industrial accident, some bit of interstellar technology that went awry. If so, the accident certainly wiped out the home worlds of the race that caused it.

Our search for intelligent life should begin, then, in our own region of the Milky Way's spiral arms. We should eliminate stars that are too young to have developed intelligence, and not spend too much effort on those that are too dim to have a wide thermally habitable zone.

That leaves stars close in physical makeup to our Sun: yellow or orange, late F-, G-, and K-type stars that are still living out their long eons of stability before they begin to swell into red giants.

That simplifies our search. It eliminates literally billions of stars.

And still leaves a few billion to examine.

TERRESTRIAL INTELLIGENCE

by

ISAAC ASIMOV

Intelligence on Earth is not really rare. Octopi are quite intelligent if compared to other invertebrates; crows are quite intelligent if compared to other birds; primates are quite intelligent if compared to other mammals.

However, there is only one type of organism in existence that is sufficiently intelligent to have developed a complex technology, and there we are speaking of ourselves and our immediate ancestors, the various hominids.

It worked this way. The earliest australopithecines, about five million years ago, were no taller than chimpanzees, slighter in build, and with a brain no larger. The australopithecines had, however, developed a backward bend in the lumbar region of the spine that made it possible for them to walk erect easily and in preference to any other form of locomotion. That distinguished them from all four-legged animals. Bears and chimpanzees might walk on their hind legs temporarily, for instance, but not continually and not by preference.

Erect posture freed hominid forelimbs for holding and manipulating. By bringing objects to close examination by sense organs, and by manipulating those objects, hominids flooded their brains with information. Any chance mutation that increased the size or complexity of the brain and enabled it to process the information more efficiently had survival value and was selected for. The brain, therefore, evolved explosively, and human beings now have far larger brains than any ape.

What counts is not only a large brain but a comparatively small body. Elephants and whales have brains that are larger than human brains, but the bodies of those creatures are so massive that the brain/body ratio is small. The human brain makes up 2 percent of the mass of the human body. Those of elephants and whales make up far less than 2 percent.

Some of the smaller monkeys (marmosets, for instance) have brain/body ratios actually larger than human beings, but the brain, in absolute size, is much smaller than ours.

Only dolphins have brains as large and complex as those of human beings (or somewhat more so, actually) and bodies as small. They might be of human intelligence, but they live in the sea so that their bodies are streamlined and they lack any appendages that are in any way equivalent to human hands.

The large-brained elephant does have an appendage, its trunk, that might almost be compared to a hand, but actually, two such appendages, not one, are needed for the development of technology-based intelligence. One appendage is needed for holding and one for manipulating. In the case of 90 percent of human beings, the left hand is preferentially used for holding and the right for manipulating. (It is reversed in the other 10 percent.)

The result is that *Homo habilis*, the first organism sufficiently human to be included in the genus "Homo," once it evolved nearly 2 million years ago, was capable of shaping stone into tools. Other animals might use tools, and some might even be able to modify natural objects to make them more fit for use, but only members of genus *Homo* have ever been able to deliberately modify something as ordinarily intractable as stone. It is with the development of stone tools that hominids first differentiated themselves from all other forms of life.

Then, about 500,000 years ago, probably earlier, *Homo erectus* learned to make use of fire. No non hominid has ever, under any circumstances, learned to do anything with fire but flee from it. This matter of fire is an even sharper differentiation than stone tools. All technology depends on fire; depends, that is, on the use of sources of energy other than that in living muscle, sources that are dependable, portable, and human-made in any amount. Thus, wind and running water are examples of inanimate energy that can be used by any organism, but they are not dependable or portable and must be taken only as they are found by any organism without a technology. (Fire is not possible in water, which means that dolphins, however intelligent, cannot develop a technology.)

Now, then, how do we define intelligence? I see no point in trying to define what it *is*. Not only would that be too complicated a task, but it is unnecessary. Far better to define what it *does*.

For our purposes, a species is intelligent if it can develop a complex technology.

One usefulness of this definition is that it makes it unnecessary to delve into psychology and philosophy. One doesn't have to be concerned with inner being and inner thoughts. One merely looks at what is being accomplished.

Another usefulness of the definition is that we don't have to bother with intelligence on the individual, or even the minor group level. Undoubtedly, some human individuals are more intelligent than others, but which are more intelligent and to what degree depends upon the precise definition you care to give to individual intelligence and the manner in which you decide to measure it. There is enough uncertainty and controversy over both definition and measurement to give us a feeling of relief at not having to deal with it.

The fact is that an individual human being, or even a small group, left to itself cannot develop a technology, except very slowly as the group expands. (There are romantic stories, such as *Robinson Crusoe*, which seem to demonstrate the reverse, but Crusoe started with a shipload of equipment and the memories of a technology.)

Let us restrict intelligence, then, to nothing smaller in scale than the *species*, and to *the development of a technology* as the measure of intelligence for our purposes.

But what do we mean by a technology? Spiders build webs. Ants, bees, and termites build complicated dwelling places and develop complicated societies with specialized activities. Some social insects do things that look very much like agriculture, herding, enslavement, and so on. Beavers build dams and significantly change the environment in their own favor.

On the other hand, Paleolithic humanity had only the sketchiest kind of technology, nothing that we would consider an *advanced* technology. (And what is an *advanced* technology, by the way? What we have naturally seems advanced to ourselves, but another species with a far more advanced technology, or even we ourselves a thousand years from now, might consider our present technology primitive, and therefore useless as an indication of intelligence.)

But please note that I didn't define intelligence as the *possession* of a technology, but the *development* of a technology. In estimating whether a species is intelligent or not, it is insufficient to look at it and judge it at a specific time.

In every species of organism we know, other than the human being and its immediate ancestors, significant alterations in behavior take place only as a result of evolutionary change, which is very, very slow. A spider, building a web today, does so exactly as members of its species, or closely allied species, would have done a million years ago, or will do a million years from now.

Undoubtedly, web-building evolved and grew more efficient with time, but only at the general rate of biological evolution. The same is true for the most complicated of termite societies, for dam-building among beavers, and so on.

Even creatures as intelligent as gorillas, elephants, or dolphins live now, we suspect, as they have always lived, and will always live as long as they do not evolve. (Some monkeys have been reported to learn new varieties of behavior, which shows they have the beginnings of intelligence.)

Only human beings, *without* significant biological evolutionary change, can alter their behavior radically as a result of *cultural* evolution, through the accumulation of information, and the deliberate conception of "improvement."

Cro-Magnon man, twenty-five thousand years ago, had a brain as good as ours and was as intelligent as we. The measure of that intelligence is not the technology that the Cro-Magnons had or that we have, but the *change* in technology that has taken place in those twenty-five thousand years without any significant change in the quality of the brain. The change is slow at first, but it is cumulative and eventually becomes rapid; but even slow change is indicative of intelligence.

Zero change with time, whatever the appearance of technology, is what we might refer to as "instinct" rather than intelligence.

But if intelligence is to be found only in our own species and its immediate ancestors among all the tens of millions of species that have inhabited our world in the last 3.5 billion years, is it possible that human beings can now put their intelligence to work to *create* an intelligent species?

We have built computers and sometimes these are considered "thinking machines" and people talk of the possibility of "artificial intelligence."

To begin with, what is a computer?

A computer is a device capable of doing things that, throughout history, we have associated with intelligence, and not with the instinct of animals or the mechanical behavior of machines.

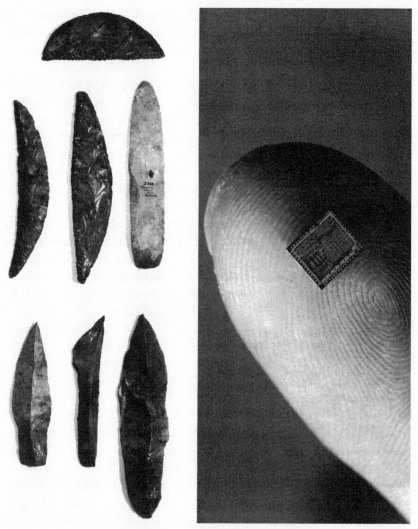

Figure 1. Chipped tools from the Paleolithic, and a modern computer chip. The continued development of a technology is the hallmark of intelligence. *(Courtesy American Museum of Natural History and Delco Electronics.)*

For instance, we associate the solution of mathematical problems with human intelligence. No other living organism can do it, and, until the 1940s, calculating devices have been simple indeed and have clearly and obviously worked only by something we might call "artificial instinct" rather than "artificial intelligence."

Modern computers, however, solve problems that are truly complex, and do so with such speed that human beings cannot compete with them at all. The temptation is to think of machines that can do *mental* labors that are far beyond us as certainly intelligent and even superintelligent.

And yet such computers show no true intelligence. A modern computer, however advanced, does nothing it is not directed to do. It is working with electrical impulses that do not get tired, do not make mistakes, and are transmitted at the speed of light. It is engineering that gives the *illusion* of intelligence. The human brain does get tired, does make mistakes, and works much more slowly, but that is the penalty of not being too-simply "wired," of not being driven by instinct.

A typical modern computer, set to working, will do what it does forever without change. Even if it is so designed as to improve its responses by considering past events, that improvement is sharply limited. No computer or group of computers existing now or in the foreseeable future can start from scratch and develop a technology, so they are not intelligent by the definition I have presented.

But computers do change, if not as a result of their own inner capacities, then because human beings are forever building new ones of improved design. Will we ever be the agents for the evolution of computers that *are* examples of true "artificial intelligence"?

I doubt it. One must first understand the true complexity of the human brain as it has evolved over 3.5 billion years. The human brain consists of 10 billion neurons and 90 billion auxiliary cells. No computer, either now or in the foreseeable future, is going to contain 100 billion switching units.

And even if a computer were to contain so many units, the neurons of the brain are interconnected with extraordinary complexity, each being connected to dozens or thousands of others in a manner that passes our understanding. Computers don't have even the beginnings of such complexity.

And even if we learn to duplicate the complexity, too, then the fact remains that the units in computers are switches that move from on to off and back to on, and nothing more. The neurons of the brain, on the other hand, are enormously complex structures of macromolecules of various types whose functions we do not entirely understand.

True artificial *intelligence* is not something we can easily attain, or may even want to. It is much easier to produce more human beings (indeed, a major problem of humanity today is that we produce too

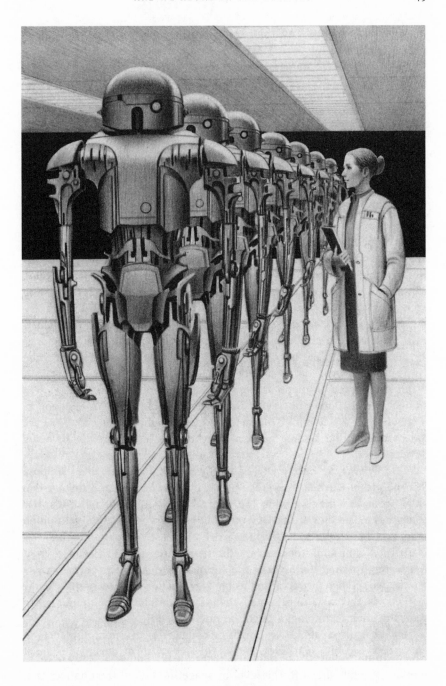

Figure 2. Intelligent, mobile robots play a big role in science fiction, such as these positronically designed characters from an early Asimov robot story. *(Art: Ralph McQuarrie.)*

many human beings and that there is a perilous oversupply) than to produce and multiply enormously complex computers.

Better to develop computers that are better and better at *artificial instinct*, leaving the intelligence to ourselves. Computers are tools and can become magnificent tools, and why should we want more than that?

It is in the highest degree unlikely, of course, that Earth is the only world in the Universe that has developed life. It seems quite possible than any world with the physical and chemical characteristics of Earth may develop life, and there may conceivably be millions of such Earth-like planets in each of billions of galaxies.

Even if this is so, we don't know where any of these life-bearing planets exist, and have no reasonable system (other than hit-and-miss searching) for finding them. (That has been called feeling about in a large dark room for a small black cat that might not be there in the first place.)

But then, even if there are life-bearing planets and, in one way or another, we encounter one, what are the chances of intelligent life upon it? If we cling to our definition of intelligence, we might ask instead: What are the chances of our finding upon it a technology in the process of being developed?

The only way we have a chance of guessing at an answer is to suppose that the planet Earth is an average planet in every respect and that we can judge from its one case what the general situation might be. Thus, our planet has existed for a total of 4,600 million years and it is only 2 million years ago that *Homo habilis* appeared and began to develop a technology at the level of making stone tools. What's more, it is only 200 years ago that reached the level of the steam engine. And it is only 20 years ago that we reached the Moon and technology reached the level of spaceflight.

If this is the kind of situation that is representative of the Universe generally, then technologies might be rare indeed.

I once calculated that there might be as many as 640 million planets in our galaxy capable of bearing life. Even if all of them developed life, it might well be that on only 280,000 of such planets would we find any species capable of developing a technology; that on only 28 of them would we find an industrialized world; and that only 2 or 3 would have advanced to the level of spaceflight. And the chances that any of them would have advanced to the point where interstellar flight was practical would be virtually zero.

But that supposes that all life-bearing worlds are as old as Earth and no more. The Universe, however, was already 10 billion years when Earth was formed. It might, by then, have formed many millions of life-bearing worlds and, even at the most pessimistic, many dozens of technologies capable of space flight even before Earth was anything more than part of the swirling cloud of dust and gas that eventually formed our solar system. In that case, there must surely have been time for alien intelligences to have explored the Galaxy thoroughly.

Enrico Fermi, faced with that possibility, asked, "Then where is everybody?"

The fact that in Earth's history no aliens have reached us (as far as we know, and never mind the UFO-maniacs) would indicate that other advanced technologies like our own are indeed excessively rare. Another possibility is that whether or not they are excessively rare the problem of interstellar flight defeats them all. Still another possibility is that we have indeed been discovered but that the discoverers refrain from interfering with us, knowing that technological societies are rare indeed and any that might develop must be protected and cared for.

But suppose *we* are the ones who go out and explore and come across life-bearing planets, with or without technologies? (Using my definition of intelligence, we don't have to worry about having to decide whether some alien species is intelligent or not, and fearing that its intelligence might be so different from our own in kind as to be unrecognizable. We are looking for *technology* and that, being a material system, should be simpler to recognize than something as inchoate and as hard to pin down as abstract intelligence.)

If technologies are rare or nonexistent, can we feel all the safer in exploring the Universe? After all, what can nontechnological life do against our sophisticated weapons? Well, ask yourself, how technologically advanced is the AIDS virus?

Any life-bearing planet might have its dangers. Possibly the least dangerous are those that carry advanced technologies. Species that possess such technologies might well be fascinated by us and be much more anxious to learn about us than to do us harm. And we, of course, could learn from them.

First contact between two advanced technological civilizations might well result in a fusion of knowledge that might benefit each one extremely.

But what if we encounter a technology as far beyond ours as ours is beyond that of a chimpanzee? Does that mean the superior aliens would instantly wipe us out as despicable vermin? Is that how reasonable human beings feel toward chimpanzees? We have reached the stage where we are anxious to protect and preserve chimpanzees. We study them and try to teach them to communicate by gesture and are delighted with every small success. Why may not those more advanced than ourselves be at least as humane?

Will the very ability of the superior beings to care for us and condescend to us prove unbearable to us? After all, a chimpanzee probably isn't bright enough to appreciate how much brighter a human being is. We, however, are quite likely to be bright enough to realize our own inferiority, and that realization might destroy us.

Still, there is a difference between a more advanced technology, and a more advanced intelligence. A more advanced technology, however far beyond us, can be learned—just as Archimedes, if he were brought into our world as a young man, could easily learn our advanced mathematics.

And yet, what are the chances of encountering a more advanced intelligence? How intelligent can an intelligent species become?

We can easily imagine a larger brain, a more complex brain, a more efficient brain, one more capable of making leaps of creation, of grasping conclusions, of foreseeing consequences—of doing anything that we associate with high intelligence.

Yet as a brain grows larger and more complex, might it not also become more unstable, more capable of sudden and disastrous breakdowns? For all we know, the complexity of the brain and the intensity of intelligence may reach a point where the possibilities of breakdown match the benefits of creation, and after that further advance is impractical.

And—conceivably—we may ourselves be near that point at this time, so that the chances of meeting any species more intelligent is small indeed.

Maybe.

THE DOLPHIN:
A NONTERRESTRIAL
INTELLIGENCE

BY

DIANA REISS

Historically it has been a tacit assumption that humans demonstrate a unique intelligence evidenced by our capacity for symbolic language, tool-use, self-awareness, self-reflection, and consciousness, that sets us apart from other species. Parenthetical to this assumption is the question whether intelligence in humans and other animals differs in kind or only in degree. This assumption regarding the unique quality of human intelligence is not only heard in discussions regarding our relationship to the rest of the biological world, but is also now being heard in speculations about the probability of extraterrestrial intelligence.

Theoretical discussions about extraterrestrial life have included a wide range of assumptions about intelligence. Some scientists argue that the rise of intelligence may be a convergent process, a widespread phenomenon throughout the universe. Others argue that "true" intelligence might only evolve in a handed humanoid species capable of developing language, tool use and technology. If we ever find extraterrestrial life, bioastronomers may face the same problems that currently challenge biologists and psychologists who study communication and other cognitive abilities of other species on this planet. Common problems include how we decode the communication systems of non-human species and how we recognize and characterize intelligence in those life forms.

In searching for evidence of intelligent behavior in other species on this planet we often fall into the search by looking for intelligence as we know it, measuring intelligence by how closely the behavior of other animals approximates our own. Other species have to deal with different social and environmental demands and types of information in their daily lives. Aside from using their own forms of species-specific behaviors and signaling, they may also employ strategies and behavior patterns that are quite alien to us. This raises two important and interrelated questions concerning our ability to discern intelligence in other species:

1) How well can we recognize intelligent behavior in non-human, and in particular, a nonprimate species?
2) If individuals of a species behave "intelligently" but in unfamiliar ways would we recognize it and interpret it as intelligent?

Studies in comparative and experimental psychology with other species have demonstrated our ability to compare and assess the cognitive abilities of diverse species and ask precise questions about their perceptual and problem-solving abilities. For example, we can easily recognize goal-directed behavior in the relatively intelligent marine invertebrate, the octopus, as it performs a familiar activity of opening a closed jar to obtain a food item. But intelligent behavior in other species might go unnoticed if the behavior is unfamiliar to us. Our perceptions about the behavior and intelligence of other species, like our perceptions of other aspects of our world, are implicitly shaped by what we know and what we expect to find. This is a serious difficulty that confronts us in our investigations of comparative intelligence.

THE DOLPHIN

The dolphin is a superb model for challenging our abilities to understand communication and intelligence in a nonhuman, nonprimate and "nonterrestrial" species. It provides a unique opportunity to gain insights into evolutionary strategies at work in the adaptation of these large-brained mammals from a terrestrial to completely marine environment. Since ancient times people have been fascinated by the highly social dolphin (Fig.1). During the past forty years speculation about the intellectual and communicative abilities of the gregarious bottlenose dolphin (*Tursiops truncatus*) has captured the interest and imagination of both the scientific community and the general public. A long history of anecdotal reports and recent scientific studies of the cognitive achievements of dolphins leave little doubt that they are highly intelligent mammals and scientists have tried to capture the rich cognitive life of dolphins through systematic observational studies and experimental investigations conducted in oceanaria and in the field.

Dolphins and whales, members of the order of mammals called Cetacea, made a return to an aquatic existence in the early Eocene period nearly 60 million years ago, just after the dinosaurs became extinct. The fossil record and skeletal features indicate the dolphin's ancestors were terrestrial mammals which evolved from Condylarthra, a family of archaic ungulates. (Cows, deer and goats are modern ungulates.) Most of the typical mammalian appendages and characteristics, such as earflaps, tail, legs and hair (e.g., erectile hairs) that can normally be used to convey information between terrestrial mammals were lost in the radical streamlining of the dolphin's body in its adaptation from a land-based to a totally marine existence. The skulls of archaic whales document a progressive migration of the nostrils from the rostral (front) region of the head, to the current position of and merger into the blowhole on the top of the head which facilitates breathing at the water's surface.

The dolphin brain has evolved differently from that of primates and many other mammals and shows specialized features not found in the brains of terrestrial mammals. Anatomical studies of the dolphin brain have revealed that it is large relative to body weight and that dolphins, like humans and the higher primates, show a high degree of encephalization, the relative enlargement of the cerebral cortex. Furthermore, the cortex of the cetacean brain is thin compared with other mammalian brains of similar size while dolphins actually exceed humans and other mammals in the degree of convolution of the cerebral cortex. Convolution of cortical folds is a means of packing more surface area of the brain in a given volume. Although the importance of these differences in the dolphin brain is not well understood, the concept of an Encephalization Quotient (EQ), which is a measure of relative brain-body size ratio, can offer insight into the level of cognitive development in cetaceans. For example, primates have the highest EQ among terrestrial species with values up to 7.0 for humans and 2.4 for chimpanzees. However, a number of odontocete species (toothed cetaceans) possess EQ values that range higher than chimpanzees and other great apes. Therefore, the EQ data suggest a level of intelligence or cognitive processing in some cetaceans that is closer to the human range than are our nearest primate relatives.

Despite the vastly different evolutionary histories between dolphins and primates, they share to some degree the common feature of brain laterality. Neuroanatomical studies and behavioral observations of dolphins have indicated a high degree of hemispheric independence as well as hemispheric asymmetry. This means that the different hemispheres of the brain are involved in different processes. For example, certain populations of dolphins "strand feed," a foraging strategy in which dolphins actually chase fish onto muddy river banks and then slide up onto the mud to capture their stranded prey. During strand feeding dolphins have shown a right-eye viewing preference. Also, studies of sleep in dolphins have revealed unihemispheric sleep: each hemisphere of the brain sleeps at different times. The discovery that dolphins sleep differently than most terrestrial mammals is not surprising since they are voluntary breathers and thus have to control their breathing and maintain a level of consciousness at all times.

The dolphin brain is also well adapted for hearing and vision in water. Due to the density of water, sound travels about four and a half times faster in the ocean than in air, and their auditory cortex is well adapted for perceiving and interpreting acoustic information at requisite speeds. Dolphin vision is also well adapted for a marine existence; the dolphin has a specialized lens in its eye and a double-slit pupil, which facilitates both underwater and in-air vision as well as the ability to see through the water-air interface.

Although the size and complexity of the dolphin's brain suggests the potential for a high degree of intelligence, we have to rely on their behavior, not brain structure, when we attempt to characterize their intelligence. Elucidating the cognitive abilities of any organism requires an understanding of the social and environmental context in which it resides. Observations of dolphins in the field and oceanaria indicate that they live in highly complex social groups often referred to as 'societies'. They reside in large groups, often numbering in the hundreds, which are composed of much smaller sub-groups of age and gender-related individuals. These sub-groups include nursery groups composed of mothers and their young, juvenile male and female groups, and adult male or female groups. The social structure found in dolphin societies is called a fission-fusion type social structure. It is found in chimpanzee societies as well, in which individuals spend much time maintaining, reaffirming, and forming new relationships and coalitions with other members of their social group. Their behavior is marked by a high degree of interdependence and cooperation evidenced in their foraging, mating and survival strategies. For example, dolphin females have been observed to engage in shared watching and guarding of their young within nursery groups. While foraging for food, it has been observed that certain individuals will actively participate, while others stay on the periphery of the group. The latter are usually mothers attending their young or another female "aunting" or babysitting while the mother is feeding.

Dolphins, like other animals, use a variety of signals in different modalities to exchange information and to modify messages. These different types of signals include acoustic and visual signals (e.g. body postures, swimming formations, and behaviors such as pectoral fin rubbing, tail slapping, etc.), tactile signals, and perhaps gustatory (taste) signals. However, since the 1960s, there has been a particular fascination with the subject of dolphin vocal communication. This may be due to several factors. In the 1960s there were reports in the scientific and popular press by John Lilly, a neurophysiologist, suggesting that the large-brained and highly social dolphins might possess a complex languagelike communication system. While Lilly's reports of brain complexity were accurate, his later work suggesting that dolphins had their own complex language and could be taught to imitate human speech sounds was more speculative than scientific. However, the possibility of complex communication in another large-brained mammal sparked the imagination of many. Another factor contributing to the sustained interest in dolphin vocal communication was the fact that dolphins have a very large and complex auditory cortex capable of high level sound processing. Lastly, acoustic communication would be an optimal means of communication in an aquatic environment when long distance signaling is required or when murky water prohibits visual signaling.

What do we really understand about vocal communication in dolphins? Dolphins use a wide and varied repertoire of complex vocalizations and show turn-taking behavior in their acoustic exchanges. Their vocalizations have been characterized into three broad classes of signals. They use broadband "clicks" called sonar or echolocation for navigation and perception. When echolocating, dolphins emit click sequences of sonic and ultrasonic frequencies that bounce off objects and features in their environment. The returning echoes provide the dolphins with "acoustic images" of environmental features. The non-handed dolphin has not developed a technology like ours that is reflected in scientific and industrial achievements. However, through the evolutionary process the animal itself has undergone important changes leading to the emergence of a sensory system with functional equivalence to one of our most notable technological achievements: sonar. A second class of signals includes wide-band sounds such as squawks, yelps, pops, etc, that dolphins use in a variety of different social interactions including mating, chasing, and agonistic bouts. And the third class of signals is variable-pitch narrow-band whistles, often emitted in complex sequences and exchanged between individuals in turn-taking patterns.

There have been a number of conflicting reports about the nature of dolphin whistle repertoires. Several studies have indicated that each dolphin uses its own "signature whistle," an individually distinctive one, that accounts for 70-95% of its whistle repertoire. Some scientists have speculated that this whistle could function like an individual's "name" informing others of its identity. These calls have been primarily recorded in contexts of separation or when animals are temporarily isolated from members of their social group. Other studies conducted at our laboratory, have provided different but equally compelling evidence that dolphins use a much larger whistle repertoire than just "signature whistles." By recording different social groups of dolphins residing in different oceanaria we discovered that they use a large and varied whistle repertoire and many whistle types are shared by individuals within and across social groups. Interestingly, all dolphins we recorded produced the *same* predominant whistle, not a different "signature whistle." In contrast to reports of predominant signature whistles, our studies indicated that dolphins share the *same* predominant "contact call," but produce it individually in different ways. In other words, each dolphin has its own way of producing or "articulating" the same whistle which might facilitate individual recognition as well as communication. Rather than a different whistle identifying each individual, it is how each individual produces the same call that serves to identify them. Individual recognition through the use of a shared contact call has been reported in many other terrestrial mammals, and finding a shared contact call in dolphins is not surprising since they evolved from terrestrial mammals.

At our laboratory we have also investigated whether young dolphins learn their whistle repertoires. Vocal learning, the ability to acquire, produce and use new sounds, is rare in the biological world. It has previously been reported only in humans and birds; humans learn language and birds learn songs. Notably, humans and birds show parallels in their stages of vocal acquisition that include a stage of vocal play called babbling. We found that young dolphins also learn their whistle repertoires and show similar stages during vocal acquisition to those in humans and birds. Finding parallel stages in vocal learning in three species from different phyla is striking and suggests a convergence of strategies in these vocal learners. Additionally, dolphins do not appear to show critical or sensitive periods for vocal learning. Dolphins, like humans, show vocal plasticity through adulthood, providing compelling evidence for what is probably an "open" communication system.

Research investigating other cognitive abilities of the dolphin has suggested that, like primates, they show advanced capabilities for classifying, remembering, and discovering relationships among events. Bottlenose dolphins have demonstrated proficiency in comprehending artificial gestural 'languages' generated by experimenters. The results of these studies have demonstrated that dolphins can process semantic and rule-governed sequences of gestures. They even showed great proficiency in interpreting these gestures when they were extremely degraded while being shown on TV monitors. Recently two studies demonstrated the dolphins' ability to match what they perceive by echolocation with what they perceive visually. Their ability to do this task provides evidence that the dolphins get "acoustic images" of objects through the use of echolocation and demonstrates the integration of these two senses (sight and hearing).

As mentioned above, cetaceans are the only mammals other than humans that clearly demonstrate vocal learning. Dolphins show a strong proclivity for vocal mimicry of their own species-specific whistles and other sounds. At our laboratory we investigated the dolphin's communicative and cognitive abilities through experimental studies. In one study, we presented dolphins with an underwater keyboard. Their use of specific keys, each displaying a different visual form, resulted in specific whistles (synthetic sounds) being broadcast into their pool, and specific objects (toys) or interactions were offered. Without explicit training the dolphins spontaneously imitated the model sounds and extended their own productions of whistle facsimiles to their interactions with the "paired" or associated toy or activity. They demonstrated contextually appropriate use of their versions of the model whistles they had acquired on their own. Furthermore, the dolphins produced apparent *combination whistles* composed of two of the discreet computer-generated whistles and used these novel productions in appropriate behavioral contexts thus suggesting the possibility that dolphins may purposefully combine elements within their own whistle repertoires. These results do not provide evidence that dolphins use specific signals in referential ways, as analogs of "words," but demonstrate that they readily acquire strong associations between sounds and environmental stimuli on their own.

Dolphins have shown certain behavior patterns that compel us to examine their level of self-awareness and their understanding of the contingencies of their own behavior. For example, care-giving behavior has been reported in dolphins and in other toothed whales. Individuals have been seen "standing by" or physically supporting injured animals from below with their bodies, not eating until the injured animal recovered or died. Notably, throughout history there have been numerous reports of dolphins supporting and saving drowning sailors and swimmers. How do we interpret this behavior? Do these animals really know what they are doing or is this supportive behavior merely an instinctive or adaptive response to the stimulus of an injured creature? Perhaps the answer to this question lies in the degree of plasticity of their response to new and changing situations. For example, Ken Norris, an eminent marine biologist, reported the following scenario. An adult pilot whale *(Globicephala macrorhynchus)*, fatally wounded by a whaling boat, was drifting toward the whaling vessel. Two other pilot whales approached the individual and, rising on either side of the dead animal, pushed it down and away from the boat, vanishing below with the dead whale. This behavior departs from a stereotypic response of holding up an injured individual, and the behavior was appropriate for this context. There have also been numerous reports in which individuals of one species of cetacea have protected individuals of other species of cetacea. Individuals have been seen biting harpoon lines trailing from injured individuals. The specificity, appropriateness, and plasticity of their behavior strongly suggests that the individuals comprehend something about the contingencies of the situation and their own behavior. Whether such observed sequences should be considered acts of altruism or simply cases of care-giving behavior is unclear, but the behavior is a familiar pattern we recognize and hold up as a hallmark of civilized behavior and intelligence in our own species.

Another striking example of this level of consciousness in dolphins comes from observations of dolphin play. Dolphins residing in oceanaria show a high degree of inventive play with other animals and objects. In our laboratory we frequently observe dolphins engaging in long periods of toy play and object manipulation using various parts of their bodies; these nonhanded mammals are quite skilled at manipulat-

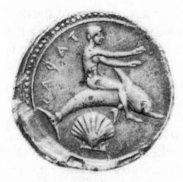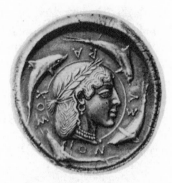

Figure 1. Greek coins, circa 480 B.C.E., are an example of humanity's long and close association with the dolphins.

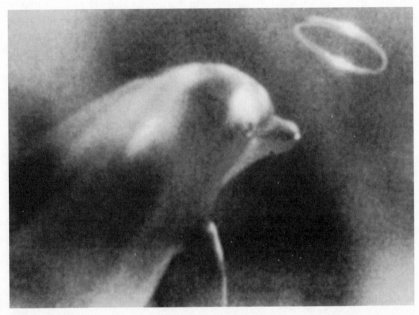

Figure 2. The "halo" is a ring of air that this dolphin has snorted out of its blowhole. The dolphin plays with its creation as the ring rises to the surface. *(Photo: Copyright Diana Reiss.)*

ing objects in their environment. However, we also observed the dolphins creating their own objects of play, bubble rings, rings formed of air which they expel from their blowhole. The dolphins assume a horizontal position near the bottom of the pool and then jerking their heads upward, produce what appears as a silver ring of air, similar in form to a smoke ring blown from the mouth of a smoker (Fig. 2). The dolphins orient to the rings they produce, following and playing with them in various ways as they rise to the water surface. Sometimes they bite the rings, smack them with their tails, or put their rostrums through the center of the rings as they would with a solid toy ring. We marveled as we watched dolphins blow one ring, then a second ring at a faster velocity, which merged with the first ring and formed a larger hoop-sized ring, which the dolphins then swam through. We observed one instance in which one dolphin was producing bubble rings and an observing dolphin swam to the tank floor, picked up a piece of fish and put it into a rising ring of air. As the ring rose, the piece of fish spun wildly in the turbulence of the rising torus, as the dolphins closely watched and followed it to the surface. This behavior was repeated several times. This activity struck me as a familiar pattern of exploratory behavior and a planned activity in which the animals understood something about the contingencies of their actions.

Finally, there have been a number of recent attempts to determine whether bottlenose dolphins show behavioral evidence of mirror self-recognition; a capacity only demonstrated in humans and ape species. Although past dolphin studies have yielded provocative results, none have brought forth evidence of a conclusive nature. At our laboratory we have recently embarked on a rigorous study, the preliminary results of which provide strong behavioral evidence that bottlenose dolphins are capable of recognizing themselves in a mirror.

In summary, dolphins show many of the cognitive abilities and behavioral patterns hailed as hallmarks of intelligence in humans and other large-brained primates. Finding such similarities in the cognitive abilities across species suggests a convergence in survival strategies that may emerge from sufficiently complex brains.

BREAKING THE LONG LONELINESS

An anthropologist Loren Eiseley wrote an essay called "The Long Loneliness" in which he suggested that we isolate ourselves from the rest of the biological world by how we view intelligence and that intelligence cannot be conceived of in just human terms. Scientists must find the delicate balance between anthropomorphism, falsely assigning human traits to other animals, and anthropocentrism, human-based assumptions about intelligence and behavior. But how do we achieve this fine balance as we interpret the behavior of other species? Scientists apply Lloyd Morgan's law of parsimony which states, "In no case may we interpret an action as the outcome of the exercise of a higher mental faculty if it can be interpreted as the exercise of one that stands lower on the psychological scale." The law of parsimony continues to be a foundation for scientific investigation and guides our interpretation of data. It is clear that parsimony is critical for any scientific investigation, but it can also be problematic if over applied. For example, *all behavior*, including human behavior, was described by traditional behaviorists as mindless responses to external environmental stimuli. Contemporary cognitive psychologists reject this view and instead attempt to understand the various kinds of cognitive processes that underlie our behavior.

The tacit assumption that humans demonstrate a unique type of intelligence as evidenced by our capacity for symbolic language, tool-use, self-awareness, self-reflection and consciousness still prevails but growing evidence from behavioral and cognitive research with other species challenges the basis of the assumption that our intelligence is different in kind. The pyramidal model of evolution with humans at the top has been replaced with the view of evolution as a spreading structure with diverse life forms. There are both convergent and divergent processes at work and a variety of strategies operating throughout the biological world that enable different species to survive and flourish in their respective environments. Hopefully, we will become more skilled at discerning a wider spectrum of intelligence. Ultimately, our interpretation of the behavior of other species and our understanding of different types of intelligence will depend on what we are looking for, how we are looking, what we expect to find and whether we choose to break the long loneliness or maintain it.

ALTERNATIVE LIFE DESIGNS

By

HAL CLEMENT

Scientific opinions, supposedly based on evidence rather than dogma, are tentative by nature. There is no way yet to say with confidence where in the Universe, except on the one planet where we have already found it, there may be life. We can only draw inferences on the matter, as early scientists inferred the shape of the Earth and later ones the existence and nature of the electron.

We may hope that our ideas about life distribution will some day, like our Earth-shape theory, get solid support from further evidence; but so far this is only a hope, dimmed by the fact that any reasoning about extraterrestrial life demands data from the haziest fringes of our knowledge about chemistry and astronomy. I will try in what follows to show where the haziness lies.

The speculation falls into two major parts. We must try to decide what life itself requires for existence, which is fortunately not quite the same as deciding what life is; and we must then settle what environments the Universe offers that may reasonably be expected to provide such needs, and where these may be found. Essentially, we will be discussing chemistry and astronomy.

A warning: Scientists are expected to be objective—that is, to keep their wishes out of their opinions. I am not sure how closely I approach this ideal. I like to suppose that life is extremely common in the Universe, just as at least one television evangelist prefers to believe, for, he says, biblical reasons, that it can exist nowhere but on Earth. You will have to decide for yourself how far my wish has influenced my thinking in sections containing the words, or even the thought, "It seems likely to me that . . ."

Read this essay critically, therefore, and if you are moved afterward to go out and study biology, chemistry, physics, astronomy, or several of them, my feelings will certainly not be hurt.

First, then, life's needs.

All things we regard as living assimilate material from their sur- roundings and incorporate selected parts of it into their own architec- ture; they respond in various ways to changes in their environments; they reproduce their kind with more or less accuracy and repair injury to their structures. Some nonliving things, such as fires and crystals growing in solution, show certain of these abilities, but I can think of nothing not alive that has them all.

I do not see how all this can be done without a very complex chem- ical and mechanical structure. I am leaving the supernatural out of consideration, as science must; this is not because we can disprove it— we cannot—but because we can't work with it. Anyone with a normal imagination can produce an endless number of supernatural explana- tions for anything, and there is no objective way of choosing among them. Hence, for this essay's reasoning, life involves complex chem- istry.

It also involves *solution* chemistry, material in the liquid state. The gas state does not permit definite mechanical structure; if its molecules were close enough to each other for the forces between them to pro- duce a fixed pattern, the substance wouldn't be a gas. A solid, at the other extreme, is too organized; it does not allow atoms and molecules to move around freely enough for the things that have to happen in a living creature. An organism may have solid structural parts, like our bones and teeth, and *handle* gas as we do when we breathe, but its essential chemistry goes on in solution.

Therefore, we need liquid. An easily available liquid.

I don't say it has to be water, though we know water will work. Nei- ther do I suggest that any liquid whatever, such as mercury or lava, would be appropriate. Mercury is quite a rare element on Earth; there is reason to believe that it is comparably rare elsewhere in the Universe, and a planet with enough of this substance to form oceans and lakes, and be available in quantity for life forms, seems pretty unlikely. Melted rock has to be at what we would consider very high tempera- tures, which implies that much of the complex molecular structure that seems necessary for life could not hold together.

Four materials seem most likely to me, a priori, to be reasonable life solvents. Five others might be added to the list without too much strain on a science-fiction-oriented imagination.

The first four are all hydrogen compounds, which makes them common on theoretical grounds, and three of these are known to be plentiful on various planets we have studied. The fourth is less defensible, perhaps. Hydrogen is observed to be the most common element in the Universe; it appears that about 921 out of every 1,000 atoms that exist are of this simple substance (and plain hydrogen is one of the five others mentioned above).

The elements that combine with hydrogen in my first four suggested liquids are also common; they are the four "hydrogen bonding" atoms of the second period of the chemical table—carbon, nitrogen, oxygen, and fluorine. The liquids are, then, methane, ammonia, water, and hydrogen fluoride.

Liquids? Methane, ammonia, and hydrogen fluoride are all gases under what we consider ordinary conditions. I am claiming, however, that life need not be confined even to such close-to-ordinary conditions as our own ocean-bottom thermal jets, where water, too, would be gas if it weren't for the pressure. All four of these substances are solid if the temperature is low enough, liquid if the temperature is not too high and the pressure is high enough, and gaseous regardless of pressure if the temperature is high enough. Figure 1 gives the approximate ranges. Its vertical scale, temperature, is in Kelvins, used in science because it has no negative—zero Kelvins means there is no heat energy; you can't get less. The bottom section of each column is the temperature range at which the substance is solid; water melts to liquid at 273 Kelvins, for example.

Hydrogen fluoride is the least likely of the four to form oceans and be the common liquid even on a planet with the right temperature and pressure conditions. The trouble is that such worlds are likely to have silicate rock crusts, which are rich in oxygen (there is more oxygen in the top few feet of the solid Earth than in all the air overhead); and hydrogen fluoride will react with such material to form water and silicon tetrafluoride, a gas under what we consider ordinary conditions. The latter, whether gaseous or liquid, can be expected to undergo further reactions that will eventually tie most of the fluorine up in insoluble minerals, just where we find it on Earth.

Water we know about. It forms the basis of Earth's oceans and Earthly life fluids; we know it works as a biological solvent. It has been suggested that it is the only liquid which can, on the basis of some of its really unique properties.

One of the most striking of these is that it expands when it freezes, so that ice floats on liquid water—a rare trait indeed. This prevents oceans and large lakes from freezing all the way to the bottom in winter, thus protecting the life in them from freezing too. I grant the weight of this argument; but on the other hand, the expansion makes things much harder for a water-based life form that actually does get frozen. Its cells tend to be punctured or burst by the growing ice crystals. Try letting an apple or a potato freeze in your ice cube compartment, if nothing of the sort has ever happened around you by accident, and see what the item is like after it thaws out. The expansion argument seems to me to work both ways; other solvents might actually be *better* than water.

The best substitute is probably ammonia, which is a remarkably waterlike compound in spite of its odor. I am not referring to the cleaning liquid sold in grocery stores, which is ordinarily about 2 percent ammonia in water, but the real NH_3, which, as Figure 1 indicates, is a gas under normal pressure until we cool it down quite a bit (or a gas at normal temperature unless we squeeze it pretty hard). At low enough temperature and/or high enough pressure, ammonia looks like water, pours and flows like water, and dissolves pretty much the same things in the same way, though not always to the same extent, as water. While details differ, pretty much the same sort of chemistry can go on in ammonia solution as in water solution, as a great deal of laboratory work has shown.

Water and ammonia have molecules whose electrical charges are not smoothly distributed, so they have surface regions distinguishable by positive or negative polarity. This has a profound effect on their ability to dissolve other materials, as well as on their melting and boiling points (hydrogen fluoride is also polar; see how these three compare with all the others on the temperature graph, Figure 1).

Methane, the third of the "most probable" liquids, is not polar. This does not mean that it won't dissolve anything, only that it prefers other nonpolar substances to things like salt. Salts are vital to life as we know it—but so are the highly nonpolar substances we call fats and oils, which our very polar water does not dissolve very well. Living things get around these problems. Nothing is *completely* insoluble in any given liquid, and there are molecules called *detergents* that are chainlike in shape and have one end that is polar and soluble in polar liquids, while the other end is nonpolar and soluble in nonpolar liquids.

Methane's lack of polarity is responsible for it being liquid at much lower temperatures than water, or hydrogen fluoride. The five other substances mentioned as possible solvents are, as Figure 1 shows, even more extreme in this respect; and like methane, their dissolving powers would favor nonpolar chemicals.

There are chemicals other than the solvent liquids that go into life architecture, of course. They are, here on Earth, mostly compounds of elements already mentioned: carbon, whose atom can fasten to as many as four others at once and hence be involved in extremely complex structures; the hydrogen-bonders nitrogen and oxygen; and hydrogen itself. One not mentioned before but playing a critical part is phosphorus; nearly as ubiquitous, but not as clearly necessary, is sulfur, though sulfur may play the role of oxygen in some cases.

Very tiny amounts of other elements such as cobalt, zinc, molybdenum, copper, and, in at least one type of creature, vanadium, also play active parts in life chemistry. I consider it most unlikely, however, that these were used by the original, simplest organisms that started the biology game on our planet; it seems much more probable to me that life learned to use them later, as children learn to use casually found objects as tools, with natural selection preserving the more effective chemical tricks. I could be wrong, since these elements were present from Earth's beginning; indeed, they are present in the interstellar gas and dust from which the Earth and solar system presumably condensed. If they were *essential* from the beginning, however, life is a much less probable phenomenon than I like to believe, since their concentration is quite low.

The *essential* original life compounds were presumably ones that were simple enough to have formed with fairly high probability during random molecular collisions in solution and then tended to polymerize. That is, they combined with each other to form much more complicated chains of molecules, such as cellulose, which uses only carbon, hydrogen, and oxygen; proteins, requiring the same three plus nitrogen (some of these *now* contain sulfur and iodine as well); and DNA, which also requires phosphorus. Exactly what went on is still being worked out; we don't know.

All these structures depend heavily on the four-bond capacity of carbon to attain their complexity. It has been suggested that other atoms with the same capacity might be used by some exotic life form. The most obvious candidate is silicon, and more recently the silicone group (not the same thing; it has two oxygen atoms as well as a silicon one) has also been suggested. There are three principal, though certainly not conclusive, objections to these ideas. First, the Earth's crust is about one quarter silicon by weight, and much less than 1 percent carbon; it would seem that if silicon could have been used, it would have been. Second, the four-bond capacity is not the only property of either atom; silicon is noticeably larger than carbon. One familiar result of this size difference is that carbon dioxide is a gas under Earthly conditions, while silicon dioxide (quartz, amethyst, chalcedony, etc.) is not only hard enough to be used for jewelry but is highly insoluble in both polar and nonpolar liquids (remember the importance of the liquid state). Third, silicon does not form *hydrogen bonds*, intermediate-strength chemical links firm enough to keep a human being from collapsing into a puddle of warm jelly but weak enough to permit muscles to flex without preliminary treatment by a blowtorch. Only the second-period atoms carbon, nitrogen, oxygen, and fluorine are small enough to do this.

Figure 2 shows "skeletons" of molecules that meet both the above qualifications and are found as structural members in much of Earthly life. The arms, numbered for convenience on the purine skeleton, indicate points where other atoms or groups of atoms may join them to make more complex units; for example, starting with the purine and adding oxygen atoms to arms 2 and 6, a hydrogen to arm 8, and methyl groups (methane molecules with one hydrogen removed so they also have an "arm") to 1, 3, and 7 gives us caffeine. Adding a hydrogen to the oxygen on 6 and taking the methyl away from 1 turns the caffeine into theobromine, if you prefer chocolate to coffee. Starting back with the skeleton and putting hydrogens at 2, 7, and 8 and an amino group (ammonia with a hydrogen removed) at 6 gives adenine, one of the key bricks in the DNA molecule and also in ATP (adenosine triphosphate, the "battery" involved in the energy reactions of, as far as I am aware, all known life forms on this planet).

We certainly do not know whether these skeletons and the other common ones I haven't listed are the only possible structural items for living beings. It seems most unlikely to me that they are. Earth creatures use only about twenty of the hundreds of possible fairly simple amino acids, and only a few of the possible simple sugars. I am inclined to attribute this to historical accident; groups containing these particular items were the first to acquire the self-replicating ability.

I have not yet written a *Robinson Crusoe* type of space epic, but if I ever do, my marooned hero's chief problem will be finding living tissue, either plant or animal, that he can digest and assimilate. Even on

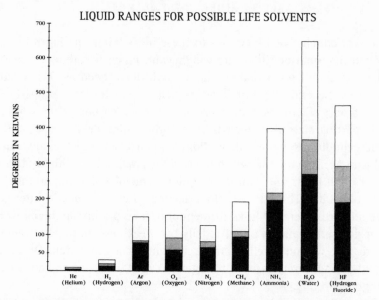

Figure 1. The black portion of each bar indicates the temperature range in which each substance is a solid. The shaded portion shows the range at which each substance is a liquid at normal pressure; the clear portion shows the range at which each substance is a liquid at elevated pressure. (*Diagram supplied by Hal Clement. Art by Elizabeth Wen.*)

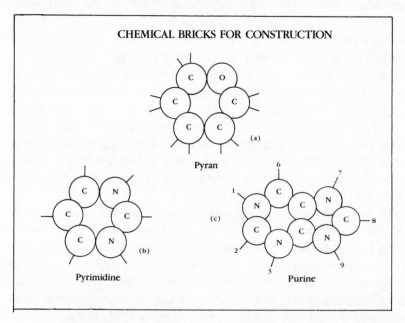

Figure 2. The building of life. (a) Pyrans combine with hydrogen and hydroxide to form simple sugars. (b) Pyrimidines and (c) Purines combine with various atoms to form molecules important for life. Numbered bonds are referred to in the text. (*Diagram supplied by Hal Clement. Art by Elizabeth Wen.*)

Earth there are lots of kinds we can't handle: Though cotton (cellulose) is a polymer of a simple sugar, and botulism toxin a protein, neither can be processed properly by human digestive enzymes (I didn't use snake venom as an example because Crusoe could digest that with no trouble). I think a Crusoe's chances of finding a native meal would be pretty small on any other planet, even if its temperature were in the right range to provide liquid water and a comfortable oxygen concentration.

Temperature raises one more question. The various liquids suggested earlier imply, if indeed they all will work, a very large possible temperature range for life, from two or three Kelvins up to six hundred or so. The obvious problem with very high temperatures is that complex structures such as proteins and polysaccharides (starch, cellulose) break up or at least change their structure when heated too strongly—watch the white part (protein) of an egg as it cooks. This is not an insuperable difficulty; some structures are more stable than others, and in fact Earth has life forms carrying on comfortably at temperatures well above the normal boiling point of water, around the suboceanic thermal jets.

Recent discoveries confirm that life can exist (and may have originated) in conditions which, while well within the limits proposed here, we would consider extremely hot and with a "nonstandard" chemistry. The first of these examples, mentioned above, is the life found at mid-ocean vents. Movies, measurements and samples brought back by deep submersibles show that albino crabs and starfish, and tube worms, along with bacteria and archaea, flourish at the edges of these vents. The streams of water emerging from these vents are rich in minerals dissolved from the accompanying lava, but poor in carbon, and there is essentially no visible light (some infrared radiation is present but is thought not to contribute to metabolism). The archaea, one-celled microbes without nuclei, and some of the bacteria live in zones where the temperature is 110° C (230° F) and the water would boil except for the extreme pressure. An example is *sulfolobus*, which metabolizes sulfur and hydrogen. Since on early Earth oxygen was almost entirely bound up in the solid minerals, the atmosphere was rich in ammonia and methane and the surface was much hotter than it is now, it has been suggested that the sulfur-eating archaea may be representative of the earliest forms of terrestrial life.

A range of bacteria and archaea of similar sorts are also found in surface volcanic vents, fumaroles and hot springs, and in the latter their colorful colonies are sometimes mistaken for mineral deposits. And then there is the news that deep drilling to depths of more than one and a half miles has recovered bacteria that metabolize formate, lactate, iron and manganese dioxide. One such creature, *bacillus infernus*, may represent a deeply buried population of microbes that add up to more living mass than all other living things combined. All of these thermophiles enlarge the range of life conditions beyond "the usual" and should inform our search for life elsewhere. In fact, NASA is supporting research on such "extremophiles" for exactly that reason.

There is a complex little creature which puts even the extremophiles to shame in its apparent ability to survive a huge range of conditions. The phylum of tardigrades ("water bears") holds more than 750 species, all around a half millimeter in length, with barrel-shaped bodies, four pairs of stubby legs tipped with claws, and a neckless head with external pincers. They are found in many different wet environments. What is amazing is that they have been known to survive a hundred years in dry hibernation, twenty hours at temperatures one twentieth of a degree above absolute zero, and twenty months at 140 degrees above absolute zero (minus 209° F). They have also survived 240° F, pressures of 1000 atmospheres, and hard vacuum. They can survive exposure to hydrogen sulfide, carbon dioxide, ultraviolet and even X-ray doses 500,000 times the fatal human dose. These creatures could be sent across the universe with almost no life support, yet you can find them in moss in your local park or wetland. It is an open question why they evolved such extraordinary survival abilities.

With low temperatures, another difficulty arises. The rate of a chemical reaction, be it involved in digestion of a meal or in contraction of a muscle, depends in a complicated way on temperature; broadly speaking, the colder the slower. Essentially, a reaction takes place because things tend to fall downhill; that is, to yield to forces. There are forces that tend to fasten carbon atoms to oxygen atoms, forming carbon dioxide; yielding to them is a "fall," and the collision at the end of the fall shows up as heat energy from, say, burning charcoal. However, charcoal does not start burning unassisted; the carbon atoms (and, indeed, the oxygen atoms in their molecules) are stuck to each other and have to be forced apart before the reaction can start; you have to light the grill. The supplied kick is called *activation energy*; the bigger the activation energy of a particular reaction, the more it is slowed down by cooling.

It looks, therefore, as though the chemicals in a liquid nitrogen ocean might never get around to reacting at all in living style. There is a possible answer here, too, however, though not as definite a one as at the hot end of the scale.

Even at our own body temperatures, most of our personal reactions would be going very slowly by themselves. It should take hours to use up a lungful of oxygen, weeks to digest a hamburger. The reason it does not is the phenomenon called catalysis.

A catalyst is a substance that reacts easily (low activation energy) with, in our example, the carbon or the oxygen to produce something else; the something else, still with very low activation energy, then reacts with the oxygen or carbon to form carbon dioxide and the original catalyst. They help reactions by, in effect, tunneling through the activation energy wall. Living creatures use catalysts, usually complex compounds we call *enzymes*. You use your lungful of oxygen in seconds, digest your hamburger in an hour or two, because you have the appropriate enzymes.

I don't know what enzymes exist that would help out at liquid nitrogen temperatures; I'm not sure there really are or can be any. If there are, I can't be sure that the resulting life speeds would be anywhere near our own, so that creatures with the behavior patterns of Earthly animals would be possible.

To summarize the chemical situation, I consider it likely that ammonia as well as water can act as a reasonable life solvent, and possible though perhaps rather less likely that such non-polar materials as methane and nitrogen might do so. The structural chemistry of life will probably depend largely on compounds of the second row of the periodic table—carbon, nitrogen, and oxygen—and the ever-present hydrogen.

I can't make up my mind how likely it is that phosphorus could be replaced in the DNA ladder or whatever equivalent alien life might use for self-replication. With the size, the charge arrangement, and the availability of the atom all relevant, it is just possible that phosphorus rather than the traditional carbon might prove to be the really essential element for life.

Likely, or fairly likely, temperatures seem to extend from perhaps fifty Kelvins (liquid nitrogen with dissolved impurities; liquid hydrogen and helium strain even my optimism) up to around six hundred or a bit more (near the critical temperature of water, the top of the bar in Figure 1, above which water *must* be gaseous).

The remaining questions are astronomical: Are there many environments providing these chemicals in this temperature range in the universe? Where do we find them? Or, accepting practical restrictions on present science, where would we expect to find them?

The answer to the first question seems to be affirmative. At the moment, astronomers generally feel that planets probably exist near most if not all suns. This has not always been the belief; in my undergraduate days, the accepted theory of planet formation assumed a near collision of stars, a most unlikely event implying that there could be only one or two planetary systems in our entire Milky Way. It is possible that new evidence will force opinion to swing back, of course—science is not a religion—but the present arguments seem much stronger to me than the collision ones ever did (but remember, I *wanted* even in those days to believe in lots of planets). It is therefore reasonable to suppose at the moment that there are billions or hundreds of billions of planets in our Milky Way and hundreds of millions of times as many in the Universe. The questions that remain are how many of these provide environments in which life could exist, and would life come into existence wherever conditions are suitable?

The preceding paragraph's reasoning assumes that planets are associated only with stars. This may not be true. It is easy to imagine cosmic dust accumulating to form small, low-mass objects, just as it is believed to have accumulated to form the larger, more massive ones we call stars, and a Milky Way swarming with sunless planets is quite conceivable, but I am not sure how well actual calculations of the behavior of cosmic clouds shrinking under their own gravity would support the picture. It is hard to see, moreover, how such planets could get warm enough even for liquid nitrogen life unless they somehow accumulated, during formation, rather surprising amounts of uranium, thorium, potassium-40, or other radioactive materials. These elements were not, we believe, present in the earliest clouds of material in space, but were "cooked" in the cores of aging suns and distributed by the "stellar wind" ejected from what astronomers call red giants and by the explosion of supernovas. The earliest stars and planets to form would have contained little but hydrogen and helium, and planets in very old objects such as globular star clusters may be only lifeless gas giants.

The temperature that sunless planets would reach from starlight and other distant radiation sources would be three or four Kelvins at their surfaces. I could, and have, gotten around this in science-fiction stories, but in this more serious discussion we'll leave sunless planets out of consideration.

STELLAR TEMPERATURE & BRIGHTNESS

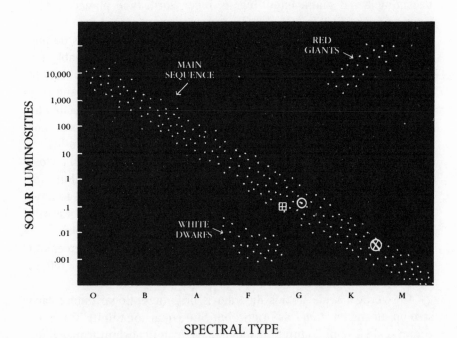

SPECTRAL TYPE

Figure 3. A schematic representation of the relationship between temperature and brightness for stars. Our Sun is represented by a dot in a circle. The F star indicated in the text is shown as a boxed plus mark, and the red dwarf is shown as an X in a circle. (*Diagram supplied by Hal Clement. Art by Elizabeth Wen.*)

Stars or suns—the words are synonymous in astronomy—do warm their planets, however; the questions are merely how big and how hot is the star, and how far from it is the planet?

A star is a nuclear reactor whose output depends on its mass; the more material it has, the denser and hotter it is at the center, and the faster its nuclear fusion reaction gulps hydrogen. Our own Sun has, we believe, been shining for about 4.5 billion years, and can go on for another 5 or 6 billion before the fuel is so thoroughly used up that major changes will occur in its structure (we think it will expand, becoming a red giant, engulfing its inner Earth-type planets before running out of fusible material altogether).

A star twice as massive would have sixteen times the sun's output, and last only about an eighth as long. A sun like Rigel, probably ten times Sol's mass and tens of thousands of times as bright, is unlikely to remain stable for more than ten million years. If it had planets, and they were far enough out and had time enough to cool to the solid state and form oceans, life might come into existence; but it would not have time to evolve very far before the star would roast or swallow the worlds.

In the other direction, a red dwarf like Proxima Centauri—the closest known star outside our planetary system—could simmer along for half a trillion years or so with little change, and if it happened to have a planet close enough for something to be liquid (not necessarily water), there would plenty of time for life to originate and evolve.

Classification of nearby stars has shown that about 90 percent fit on the *main sequence*, which is the line running from upper left to lower right in Figure 3.

The vertical scale in this diagram is brightness (logarithmic; each step up means ten *times* as bright; our Sun equals one unit). The horizontal scale is temperature; the letters have historical significance only, but are still used by astronomers to describe stars. B stars are very hot, M are relatively cool (compared to our Sun, which is a G).

The main sequence, we believe, contains stars in what might be called adulthood, burning their hydrogen at the rate set mainly by their masses. The ones in the upper right, the red giants, are nearly out of hydrogen and are having their senile fling, wasting what they have left at hundreds or thousands of times the Sun's rate. The bottom center ones are white dwarfs, the cooling corpses, still pretty hot by our standards, but out of fuel and no longer kept inflated by nuclear reactions. On the main sequence, mass goes up with brightness as mentioned; off it, the connection is much less reliable.

It seems likely, from the foregoing, that we should hope most reasonably to find the environments mentioned earlier, and hence life, on planets: first, of main-sequence stars from a little left of and above the Sun—hotter and more massive, but still capable of a couple of billion years on the main sequence to give evolution a chance—and on downward to the right; and second, of stars that formed relatively recently from gas and dust that have cycled at least once through earlier suns and contain respectable numbers of heavy atoms. This would leave out globular star clusters, believed to be very ancient; possibly much of the central part of the Milky Way; and the so-called elliptical galaxies. It still leaves in the disc or spiral arm regions of spiral galaxies and many, many billions of stars. My personal opinion is that life, since I believe firmly that it results from the operation of natural laws, *will* come into existence fairly quickly wherever conditions are suitable.

What evidence we have, and there is a good deal, indicates that the number of stars in the Milky Way increases in the low-right direction on the temperature-brightness diagram; that is, there are relatively few of the hot, bright, upper-left members, and enormous numbers of the cooler, dim red dwarfs. There is no lack of stage settings—and, I would be willing to bet, no lack of life.

The hot end for reasonable search planning might be somewhere in the F region, say a star three times as bright as ours, at about the plus mark in Figure 3. It would be 40 percent more massive than the Sun, so should have roughly half or a little less of Sol's nine- or ten-billion-year main-sequence lifetime. This should be ample for evolution. An Earth-like planet would have a temperature of six hundred Kelvins if it was about as far from this star as Earth is from our Sun—what astronomers call an *astronomical unit*. However, for water to be a liquid at six hundred Kelvins, tremendous pressure is needed, and an atmosphere heavy enough to furnish this pressure would also have a strong greenhouse effect (this should not need explaining, these days). The closest habitable planet to our F star would therefore be more like two astronomical units out—perhaps farther; exact greenhouse effects are dependent on detailed atmospheric composition and extremely tedious to calculate—and would have a year of about twenty-eight of our months. The range of possible life, if this essay's arguments are essentially correct, would extend out to Pluto's average distance or thereabouts, where the liquid would be nitrogen and the year a couple of our centuries. This is lots of room. Toward the faint-star extreme (not *at* it; see Figure 3 again, right-hand "X" mark) would be a red dwarf of about 1 percent of our Sun's brightness and a quarter of its mass. A planet would have to be within about a tenth of an astronomical unit to receive the same heat flow as we do; such a world would have a year about three weeks long.

A complicating factor in this world's climate would be the likelihood that it would be in tidal lock with its sun, as our moon is with the Earth—that is, one hemisphere would be in perpetual daylight, the other in endless night. With a dense enough atmosphere, heat might still be carried around to the night side fast enough to keep all the gas and liquid from turning solid; the world would now have a really fascinating environment range. Working out the details of such planets is part of the fun of writing careful science fiction. I do not eliminate such a planet as a possible base for life.

By the time we are three astronomical units from our red dwarf, though—about twice as far as Mars is from our own Sun—we are down to the liquid-nitrogen temperature zone. There can easily be planets within such a distance, of course; the system in which we live has four, or five if you count our moon, no farther out than Mars. Any of these *might* have acquired enough material during formation to have a decent atmosphere and a liquid phase. Apparently only two of ours did, and Venus then lost its liquid; but this shows why deciding *how many* life-bearing planets there may actually be is still largely guesswork. I believe the number to be very large indeed; but we need more research on just what occurs on the large scale as planetary systems form, and on the small atomic and molecular one as life comes into being.

I feel quite sure that both sets of phenomena can eventually be explained by the operation of natural laws; but some of you younger folks will have to do a lot of the work. I won't last long enough, probably, to learn the answer, even though discovery is the greatest entertainment I can imagine and like most people I intend to keep enjoying myself as long as I possibly can. Good luck to *you*.

CHAPTER 2

Seti Through The Ages

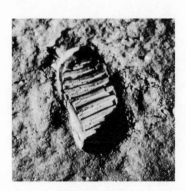

The idea of extraterrestrial intelligence has a long and curious history, dating back at least as far as human experience has been recorded in writing.

Thomas R. McDonough shows how humans have sought to make contact with "others," and—perhaps more important—how our efforts have been the reflection of the times and the societies in which they were made. In short, the search for other intelligences has often been a mirror of our own human yearnings and limitations.

The ancient Peruvians who drew the mysterious figures across the desert plain of Nazca, for example, may have intended those drawings as meditation aids rather than attempts to contact extraterrestrials. It is our generation that looks at the Nazca figures in the context of SETI. More soberingly, if we cannot tell with any assurance why the Peruvians drew those figures, what can we expect to understand of the workings of totally alien minds, if and when we contact them?

One of the earliest and best portrayals of a totally alien mind was written by the late Stanley G. Weinbaum in his memorable tale, "A Martian Odyssey." First published in 1934, this intriguing science-fiction story was immediately hailed as a classic, which it remains to this day. The Mars that Weinbaum describes does not really exist; we know that, thanks to the advance of the space sciences. But the Martian character Tweel will stick in your memory even after SETI succeeds and we find real extraterrestrials.

E.T.: PHONE ARISTOTLE!

By

THOMAS R. MCDONOUGH

T*he sky above the bleak Middle Eastern landscape was shattered by the saucer-shaped vehicle that slowly settled down onto the desert. Zeke, the only human witness, shrieked with terror at the bright flames of its rocket thrusters that dazzled the eye even at midday, while its roar deafened his ears. He threw himself down on the ground in fear.*

After the bluish-green saucer had landed, a door slid open, and one by one four space-suited humanoids stepped out onto the ground, placing brass boots carefully onto the sand, staring at the barren land through their faceplates. Emblems of animals were etched onto the sides of their bright red suits.

A loudspeaker on the craft boomed out in the strange tones of the unearthly language. The spacemen unloaded four small helicopters and unfolded their blades. One of them entered a chopper and turned it on. Its roar echoed throughout the valley.

Another alien spotted Zeke and turned on his psychrotronic transmitter-translator. The sounds of the words echoed inside poor Zeke's brain: "On your feet, dude. We have a job for you!"

Science fiction, right? Actually, believe it or not, it's the Bible, freely translated into modern English. It's from the book of Ezekiel, one of the strangest stories in the Old Testament, a story that sounds like a scriptural close encounter of the third kind. It's one of many curious stories that have been passed down from ancient times. Intriguing stories like these make even hard-core skeptics like myself wonder whether perhaps, some time in the distant past, we may have been visited by another civilization.

Since it seems reasonable that there may be other civilizations in the Universe, and since there is no law of physics that prevents interstellar travel, it is logical to ask the question: have we ever been visited in the past? For this chapter, I'll put aside the phenomenon of unidentified flying objects (UFOs) to examine the intriguing question of whether there might be some *historical* record of past visitations. And I'll show the connection between early attitudes about extraterrestrial intelligence and modern efforts to search for it.

Let's look at some of the evidence, from bizarre stories of ancient history up to the interstellar messages that our civilization is sending out in the twentieth century.

OTHER ANCIENT-ASTRONAUT CANDIDATES

Looking beyond the Bible, we find many intriguing stories and pictures. On the cliffs of the Sahara Desert are found paintings known as the Tassili frescos. As old as 6,000 B.C., these figures look unearthly, but there is good evidence that these are pictures of natives wearing ritual costumes (see Fig. 1).

Some ancient Mayan carved figures may look a bit like an astronaut about to blast off in an Apollo space capsule, but they clearly portray masked Mayans dressed for rituals. The problem is that masks with exaggerated features of symbolic significance are common among tribal people all over the world, and there is no reason to assume that they necessarily are representations of extraterrestrial beings.

Then there is the case of the Nazca drawings on the low coastal desert of Peru. An extinct civilization drew huge pictures of birds and other creatures on the desert, pictures not evident to the pedestrian, but which are quite visible from the air and, to a limited extent, from the surrounding hills.

They have even been suggested to be landing fields for alien vehicles, though it's not clear why a civilization advanced enough to engage in interstellar travel would need a landing field in the desert. More likely, the Nazcas believed that the gods were up there in the sky. After all, they could see the Sun God rise in the morning, and the Moon God come out at night, and hear the Thunder Gods when they were angry during a storm, flashing their weapons in the sky. It is reasonable that the Nazcas might want to send messages by making big drawings in the sand that the gods above could see easily, such as: "Send more rain, and while you're at it, drop a few stiff lighting bolts down on our enemies over there." Some of the same motifs, probably part of important rituals, are found on Nazca pottery (see Fig. 2).

The ancients studied the sky because their lives depended on it. During the year, the constellations rose and fell, telling them when to plant and when to harvest. They knew that the five bright planets (Mercury, Venus, Mars, Jupiter, and Saturn) were special because they wandered slowly among the thousands of "fixed" stars, although until the telescope arrived, they couldn't know that these were also worlds like ours. Occasionally, a star would appear mysteriously, and this was cause for great worry, because it meant that something was dramatically disrupting the slow, predictable backdrop of the gods. It was taken as an omen that something major was about to happen, or perhaps it was signaling something that had just occurred: the death of a king, war, famine. Today, we know these apparitions were actually supernovas (exploding stars) and comets (huge chunks of dirty ice flying between the planets).

What I look for in claims of ancient extraterrestrial visitations is some evidence from the old accounts that ancient people knew something that they could not have known using the science of their time. For example, one of the most fundamental of all numbers in science is the speed of light. It's something that cannot be measured except by telescopic observations of Jupiter's moons or with some moderately advanced technology. So if I came across some ancient record stating that the speed of light was so many cubits per heartbeat, and if that number were roughly equivalent to 300,000 kilometers per second, I would be extremely impressed. Yet I know of no such revelation.

Still, intriguing tales abound in history. Carl Sagan, in the book he wrote with the Soviet astrophysicist I. S. Shklovskii, *Intelligent Life in the Universe*, disclosed a remarkable tale from the ancient Persian Gulf suggesting contact between humans and extraterrestrials. He quoted an ancient Babylonian account:

"In the first year there made its appearance from a part of the Persian Gulf which bordered upon Babylonia, an animal endowed with reason, who was called Oannes. [According to the account of Apollodorus] the whole body of the animal was like that of a fish; it had under a fish's head another head and also feet below, similar to those of a man, except joined to the fish's tail. His voice too and language was articulate and human. . . . This Being, in the day-time used to converse with men but took no food at that season; and he gave them an insight into letters and sciences and every kind of art. He taught them to construct houses, to found temples, to compile laws, and explained to them the principles of geometrical knowledge."

But every human society invents myths of its origins, usually a mixture of history and fantasy. Tempting though it is to interpret these as extraterrestrial visitations, we have to look for hard evidence. If we ever find a laser buried, undisturbed, underneath a Babylonian temple, we'll know either that the ancients were really visited by aliens, or someone has planted a hoax. Up to now, no one has found any artifact that has been studied by independent laboratories that couldn't have been built right here on Earth.

A fascinating modern case sometimes interpreted as extraterrestrial contact is that of the African tribe called the Dogon. Living in Mali, the Dogon people have an oral tradition filled with several interesting bits of astronomical lore, information that would seem to have been unavailable to them until recently. As reported in Robert K. G. Temple's book *The Sirius Mystery*, the Dogon claim to have been visited by beings from the star Sirius, and they say that that star has a companion that moves around it every fifty years. The amazing fact is that Sirius has a companion invisible to the naked eye that indeed orbits around it every fifty years, and this companion—a white dwarf—was not discovered until the ninteenth century. Furthermore, the Dogon describe that companion as being the smallest and heaviest object in the sky, and while that is not absolutely true, it is correct that a white dwarf star is vastly denser than an ordinary star.

Fascinating and impressive, but science writer Ian Ridpath, writing in the journal *Skeptical Inquirer*, finds all kinds of flaws in the argument. He points out that the primary star Sirius has such a short lifetime that life could not have survived there for very long, and probably could never have arisen there. Furthermore, before it became a white dwarf, the companion was presumably a red giant star and perhaps a nova (a star which blew off its outer layers). Both stages would destroy any nearby planets. It is a hostile environment, nothing like the one around the mild-mannered, stable star we are fortunate enough to have in our own system. And he finds that the Dogon believe that Sirius had *two* companions, not one. Astronomers find only one companion.

According to Ridpath, it turns out that the Dogon really say that the companion's orbit is one hundred years, not fifty, and they celebrate the renewal of the world every sixty years, not fifty. And the natives do not actually claim that they were visited from Sirius. They only make vague statements about Sirius that, with a lot of optimism, can be interpreted as implying that they have been influenced by visitors from Sirius.

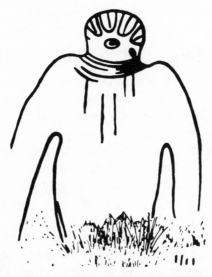

Figure 1. Taken from a rock fresco at the Tassili site in the Sahara, this image has been mistaken for an alien in a space suit by Erich von Daniken and others. It is almost certainly an illustration of a local inhabitant in ritual garb.

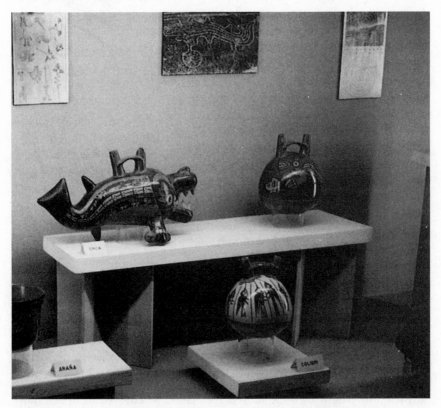

Figure 2. The curious lines inscribed on the Plain of Nazca (center photo above) are also found as a motif in local pottery (the ceramic fish). It must have had a significance to the local inhabitants, probably of a religious nature. (*Photo William R. Alschuler.*)

DUELING PHILOSOPHERS

Whether or not our ancestors were visited by aliens, the possibility that other worlds could exist was one that many of them pondered. The ancients, in those days before the telescope, had only a few paths open to them for their speculation about the Universe: They could extrapolate from the example of the Earth and suppose that there could be other Earths. They could use philosophy and conclude, as Aristotle did, that this must be the only world. Or they could rely on faith, and conclude that because the Bible said nothing about other worlds, that there could not be other worlds.

The concept of worlds other than the Earth existing and even being populated is one that has emerged from diverse philosophies and religions from ancient times to the present. Often rejected in the end, it has come to dominate our thinking. In 400 B.C., the Greek philosopher Metrodorus of Chios wrote, "It is unnatural in a large field to have only one shaft of wheat and in the infinite Universe only one living world."

Aristotle's reasoning to the contrary dominated Western civilization for two thousand years. Astronomers and philosophers have had to fight a battle against the rigidity of his reasoning. Just as thinkers had to fight for centuries to overcome the idea that the Earth was the center of the Universe—because to think otherwise diminished the standing of human beings—they also had to fight to support the idea that there could be other worlds in the Universe. This too diminished man's standing. It meant that our planet might not be the noblest in the Universe.

Some scientists paid dearly for their opposing beliefs. Galileo was forced to recant by the Church, his books were banned, and he died under house arrest. One heretical Italian went so far in his thinking as to earn the ultimate penalty. Giordano Bruno, a contemporary of Galileo, was a philosopher who questioned many of the beliefs of the Church in the sixteenth century. He was convinced that there was an infinite number of worlds in the Universe, which contradicted the Aristotelian ideas that the Church had embraced. This was only one of Bruno's many heresies, and in the end the Church paid him the ultimate compliment for his intellectual daring by burning him at the stake in the year 1600.

The invention of the telescope in 1608 opened up the Universe. Now the blind could see. It would allow the planets to be revealed as worlds like ours, and new planets were eventually found: Uranus, Neptune, Pluto. Might there be more? The telescope allowed us to see that the Milky Way was made up of multitudes of stars. It eventually enabled us to see that some of the faint fuzzy objects visible to the naked eye at night were actually made of stars, too—groups we now call galaxies. And it showed that the Milky Way was but one out of many galaxies.

With each major step in astronomy, we have learned that the Universe is larger than we had thought it. And we have learned that there is nothing obviously unique here. The Sun is an ordinary star, just like billions of others in our galaxy. The chemicals out of which humans are made are widely distributed, not rare, in the Universe. And there is now real evidence that planets are a normal part of the evolution of many stars. All of this suggests today that life may be common in the Universe.

The great seventeenth-century astronomer Kepler believed that there were inhabited worlds in the sky. Kepler, the man who proved that planets move in elliptical orbits about the Sun, even "deduced" the existence of intelligent beings on our moon. He noted a large circular feature that Galileo had observed, which we now know is just a crater. But Kepler asserted that it was created by a civilization of beings who "make their homes in numerous caves hewn out of that circular embankment." In this error, Kepler pioneered the type of reasoning that has led to numerous claims in later times that indistinct objects barely visible through telescopes, vaguely resembling human artifacts, on our moon and Mars, proved the existence of intelligent life there—arguments that continue to this day.

In the seventeenth century, the great French philosopher and mathematician René Descartes was able to write, "It seems to me that the mystery of the incarnation and all the other advantages which God bestowed on man do not preclude the possibility that he might have granted infinitely many others, very great, to an infinity of other creatures." But there were many who opposed Descartes's views. One such opponent, Dutch philosopher Gerhard DeVries, wrote, "There are indeed many and weighty authors who would stand in the battle line for the lunar inhabitants. Nevertheless, victory is certainly ours for they are not easily armed by fate or reason."

Alexander Pope's "Essay on Man" summed up the attitude of the eighteenth century's most daring thinkers:

> He, who through vast immensity can pierce
> See worlds on worlds compose one universe,

Observe how system into system runs,
What other planets circle other suns,
What varied Being peoples every star,
May tell why Heaven has made us as we are.

PHONING E.T.

All these ideas prepared civilization so well for the idea of life on other worlds that many people in 1835 were taken in when the *New York Sun* ran a series of newspapers articles about the famous British astronomer Sir John Herschel, who was observing the sky from a new telescope in South Africa. The paper claimed that the scientist had seen creatures on the Moon, and included drawings of critters who looked just like apes. They had "short and glossy copper-colored hair and had wings composed of thin membranes . . . They are doubtless innocent and happy creatures, not withstanding some of their amusements would but ill comport with our terrestrial notions of decorum." The poor astronomer had no idea that reporter Richard Locke was inventing completely phony stories about Herschel's legitimate observations. The Moon Hoax suckered in half of New York City and, amazingly, many people continued to believe in it even after the reporter confessed his crime.

In the 1820s, the German mathematician Karl Friedrich Gauss had suggested that we could announce our existence to the Universe for the benefit of other civilizations that might be out there. He wanted to plant trees in a large area in Siberia in the shape of a right triangle to demonstrate Pythagoras's theorem. This would prove to them that we were at least smart enough to pass high school geometry! As modern SETI researcher Frank Drake likes to say, the result of this proposal was an echo of so many research proposals today: "Not Funded."

The greatest boon to ninteenth-century public interest in SETI was American astronomer Percival Lowell, whose startling "detection" of Martians had long-lasting effects on astronomy and science fiction. It all started in 1877 when he learned that an Italian astronomer, Giovanni Schiaparelli, had reported seeing *canali* on Mars. Schiaparelli just meant *channels*—not necessarily artificial features—but Lowell thought he meant *canals*, which required a civilization to build them.

Sure enough, when Lowell looked through his telescope at Mars, he thought he could see canals. Thus began the century-long hunt for the canals of Mars and the civilization that built them, a search that was to end only when spacecraft flew by the planet and photographed the surface. The problem is that Mars is covered with dark splotches that change from month to month with the Martian seasons. And the difficulty is that when you look through the soupy atmosphere of the Earth at distant Mars, the eye connects these blotches with straight lines. (Photos don't capture this effect very well.) Thus Mars sometimes appears to be crisscrossed by these faint straight lines, and Lowell and other astronomers inspired by him made elaborate maps of these "canals."

To Lowell, these features meant that a civilization must have built the canals to bring water from the Martian ice caps (since confirmed to be real, made of water and carbon dioxide). He supposed that the civilization would use the canals to support crops in warmer regions, and that these crops were the splotches that varied seasonally. It was a magnificent theory, although one that not every astronomer of the time agreed with. But his books about the Martian civilizations were enormously popular, leading to the public fascination with Mars, and inspiring H. G. Wells' novel, *The War of the Worlds*, and countless imitations.

Many other astronomers were cautious about Martians. Sir Robert Ball was such a one. In 1893, he wrote:

"That there may be types of life of some kind or other on Mars is, I should think, very likely . . . Speculations have also been made as to the possibility of there being intelligent inhabitants on this planet, and I do not see how anyone can deny the possibility, at all events, of such a notion . . .

"We have also heard surmises as to the possibility of the communication of interplanetary signals between the Earth and Mars, but the suggestion is a preposterous one. Seeing that a canal 60 miles wide and 1,000 miles long is an object only to be discerned on exceptional occasions and under most favorable circumstances, what possibility would there be that, even if there were inhabitants on Mars who desired to signal this Earth, they could ever succeed in doing so?"

French astronomer Camille Flammarion had speculated in 1892 that, in the distant future, civilization might find a way of communicating across interplanetary space. But he said it would require some completely new invention. What he didn't realize was that the invention of which he spoke wouldn't take centuries to arrive—it was right there on Earth at that very moment. The fantastic new technology was radio.

Sir Robert Ball not only rejected optical communication, he also pooh-poohed the idea of interplanetary radio communication. He said that one would need a transmitter "sixteen million times as efficient" as radio's "most honored champions" predicted. It would have blown Sir Robert's mind to learn that we now communicate over billions of miles to our spacecraft at the edge of the solar system. Unfortunately, he was born too early to have heard of Arthur C. Clarke's First Law: "When a distinguished but elderly scientist states that something is possible, he is almost certainly right. Whenever he states that something is impossible, he is very probably wrong."

Radio actually turns out to be an excellent method for SETI (according to current thinking), and radio pioneers Nikola Tesla and Guglielmo Marconi were quick to listen for Martian radio signals. Tesla was the brilliant and eccentric Yugoslavian inventor who fought with Marconi over credit for the invention of radio. Tesla has become something of a cult figure today, complete with a rock band named after him half a century after his death. He was confident that life existed on other planets, especially Mars.

In 1901, Tesla recorded that he had detected strange signals on his most powerful receiver at Colorado Springs. He concluded that the regular pattern of these rhythmic signals must be produced by intelligent life on other worlds, attempting to communicate with Earth, and he proposed that Venus or Mars were the most probable sources. History later repeated itself in 1967, when scientists in England detected rhythmic radio sounds. Those signals in fact were from space, and the scientists at first thought that they too had detected another civilization. But we now know that the 1967 sounds were from pulsars, spinning neutron stars (supernova remnants), not other civilizations.

In 1902, the distinguished British physicist Lord Kelvin visited the United States and announced that he agreed with Tesla that Mars was signaling Earth. The Englishman said that New York was the "most marvelously lighted city in the world," and that it could be the only place on the Earth visible to the Martians. He said further that "Mars is signaling . . . to New York."

By the Roaring Twenties, radio was booming commercially. Marconi also thought he had detected signals from Mars. In 1924, during a close approach of Mars, the U.S. military conducted a search for radio signals from Mars, even assigning a code expert to decode the Martian signals. One civilian observer detected radio signals recorded on a moving strip of film and concluded that they represented a human face. (Not the last time that people would claim to have detected human faces on Mars.) It was actually terrestrial radio interference, probably produced by the growing number of human radio stations, some of whose signals bounced all the way around the planet, reflected by the ionosphere.

The strange radio signals that Tesla and Marconi detected from time to time could have come from a number of sources. Civilization had learned to use powerful electrical machinery, which often produced radio noise as a by-product, especially when sparks were created. Automobile ignitions or the running of an elevator motor could have generated such regular, artificial noises. It is also likely that some of the early investigators were fooled by natural signals called whistlers, produced by distant lightning, that sound artificial.

This concern with Martians came to a peak in 1938, when Orson Welles broadcast what was to become the most famous radio show in history. He did an updated version of H. G. Wells's *War of the Worlds*, and he did it in an unprecedented docudrama style, as if it were an ordinary broadcast interrupted by news bulletins from reporters in the field. To an audience of millions, the radio announced invasion and destruction by the evil Martians as they rampaged across the American countryside, viciously slaying all humans they encountered. Thousands of listeners panicked, and for a few hours SETI was transformed for some of these people to a search over their shoulder for Martians coming down the street.

MARTIANS MEET THE SPACE AGE

Throughout much of the last century, astronomers have been so embarrassed by the exaggerated claims of the detection of other civilizations that they became gun-shy about the idea of life on other worlds. In the first half of the twentieth century, the idea of extraterrestrial life fell into disrepute in the eyes of scientists, while it flourished in the genre of science fiction. It wasn't until Sputnik was launched in 1957 that ideas in the science-fictional trash heap, such as space travel and alien beings, began to return to respectability.

That started a long uphill battle for serious SETI undertaken by scientists such as Giuseppe Cocconi, Philip Morrison, Frank Drake, and Carl Sagan. They marshaled arguments from what we now knew about the origin of life on Earth and what astronomy revealed about conditions elsewhere in the Universe. Gradually, they convinced much of the scientific community that the idea of life on other worlds was respectable.

Ironically, there has now been a counterrevolution in the form of a handful of scientists who think that we are, after all, alone in the Universe. Scientists, of whom the most outspoken is Frank Tipler, have produced an array of arguments that conditions on Earth are truly unique and that life simply could not arise elsewhere in the Universe. So, strangely, a few scientists have returned to the days of Aristotle, when philosophers sitting at their desks could conclude that an entire vast Universe, about which we still know so little, is empty of extraterrestrial life.

To most scientists this is an absurd conclusion. A Universe empty of anyone but us is conceivable, but it's too early to jump to such a conclusion. After all, we have barely begun to search the skies with a handful of telescopes, at a few frequencies, in a limited number of programs, looking for evidence of other possible civilizations. And so many of the modern discoveries of the twentieth century seem to point in the direction of life elsewhere: the ease of producing organic molecules under conditions like those on primitive Earth; dust rings around nearby stars similar to those that led to the formation of the planets; the detection of probable planets around other stars; and the discovery of vast clouds of chemicals in interstellar space—the same chemicals out of which we are made, such as water, carbon monoxide, alcohol, and many others.

While Lowell left a bad taste about E.T.s in the mouths of scientists, we still owe him a debt of gratitude. Not only did he stimulate public interest in astronomy, but he even indirectly inspired one of the most remarkable space projects of the twentieth century, the Viking missions to Mars. The question of whether there was *life* on Mars lingered long after astronomers relegated to embarrassed silence the speculations of a civilization there. This fascination with the red planet led to a continuing series of space probes, something that probably would have been even more astounding to Lowell than actual Martians.

The first successful one was Mariner 4, which flew by Mars in 1965. It revealed a bleak, cratered landscape showing no signs of canals, one that seemed to have no potential for life of any kind, much less an advanced civilization. The surface looked like our moon. Later spacecraft changed our attitudes once more. They showed that there were huge canyons apparently cut by water on Mars. So it turns out that Schiaparelli was right after all. There are channels on Mars. But not canals.

The fascination with Mars continued, supported by the fact that it was the nicest place in the solar system for life as we know it (apart from Earth). Thus NASA sent two Viking spacecraft to land on Mars. The experiments on board tried to detect chemical reactions due to life, but gave ambiguous results. The concensus is that they did not detect life at the two barren points examined.

Recently the U. S. has sent a series of probes to Mars. The Mars Surveyor/Orbiter imaged the surface in great detail. The images confirm the hints from older probes that there are locations that were once flooded by water. They also reveal multilayer stratigraphy in canyon walls that look sedimentary and also water-cut (see Fig. 3). The so-called "Face on Mars" was shown to be a small cluster of hills and plateaus, and the nearby "pyramids" also naturally fractured hills, rather than an alien project to signal Earthlings as asserted by a former NASA technician. Both the U. S. and Soviet space programs have ambitious plans to send more advanced spacecraft there, culminating most likely in a human visit.

And not only have interplanetary spacecraft left Earth, but the first *interstellar* spacecraft have been launched. In 1972, Pioneers 10 and 11 were launched toward Jupiter and Saturn on trajectories that would eventually shoot them out of the solar system. In 1983, Pioneer 10 became the first human hardware ever to cross the orbits of Pluto and Neptune and leave the Sun forever.

Meanwhile, two Voyager spacecraft were launched in the footsteps of the Pioneers. These were bigger, more advanced probes also designed to fly by Jupiter and Saturn, with Voyager 2 destined to add Uranus and Neptune to its list of worlds explored. Like the Pioneers, they will eventually escape the Sun's gravity completely, and wander endlessly through the Galaxy.

Taking advantage of this, NASA put messages on all four spacecraft, designed to be understandable by an alien civilization. The Pioneers each have a plaque of a man and woman, together with a little astronomical information. The Voyagers bear a more sophisticated message, a kind of videodisk with pictures, human speech, and music. It would take them thousands of centuries to travel to the nearest star if they were aimed at it (which they're not). But one day, perhaps billions of years from now, some creature may find a drifting, pitted spacecraft, and know that two-legged creatures built it.

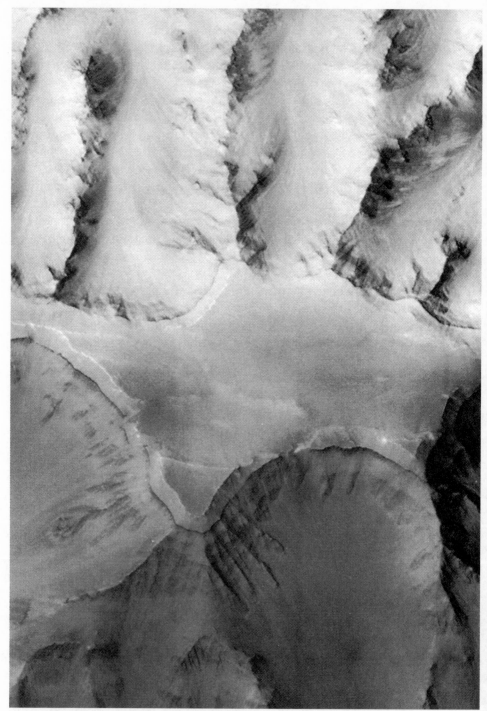

Figure 3. This image, shot by Mars Orbiter, is an aerial view of a portion of Valles Marineris, the Grand Canyon of Mars. It clearly shows sedimentary layers revealed in the canyon walls. The simplest explanation for the layers is that they were deposited by water in an earlier era, and of the canyon itself that it was cut by flowing water at a later time. *(Photograph: Courtesy Jet Propulsion Laboratory/NASA.)*

THE FUTURE

So where do we stand now? We are fortunate to live in the first period in the history of this planet when we may be able to answer the questions that theologians, philosophers, and scientists have fruitlessly argued for thousands of years. With our observatories and spacecraft we at last have the capability of detecting some kinds of life if it is out there.

There is presently no convincing evidence that Earth has been visited at any time in the past—at least, no evidence compelling to the majority of scientists. There's always the possibility that some paleontologist may find an interstellar lunch box mingled with the bones of a long-dead dinosaur. Or perhaps deep in the archives of the British Museum there may be some ancient cuneiform tablet bearing the equation $E = mc^2$, just waiting to be deciphered by a patient scholar.

While there are intriguing mysteries—and one can never completely rule out the possibility that aliens may have interfered with human history—most cases put forth in sensationalistic books like *Chariots of the Gods?* turn out to have been produced by our ancestors (or by the author), not alien visitors. It is the *lack* of imagination in the authors of such books that creates most of the mystery: they are not as smart as our ancestors.

But the next few years may see the answer to the ancient debate of the Greeks. We may finally know whether we live in a Universe as one shaft of wheat in an otherwise empty desert, or whether, as many scientists suspect, we are in a vast field covered with life as far as the telescope can see.

"A MARTIAN ODYSSEY"

By

STANLEY G. WEINBAUM

Jarvis stretched himself as luxuriously as he could in the cramped general quarters of the *Ares*.

"Air you can breathe!" he exulted. "It feels as thick as soup after the thin stuff out there!" He nodded at the Martian landscape stretching flat and desolate in the light of the nearer moon, beyond the glass of the port.

The other three stared at him sympathetically—Putz, the engineer, Leroy, the biologist, and Harrison, the astronomer and captain of the expedition. Dick Jarvis was chemist of the famous crew, the *Ares* expedition, first human beings to set foot on the mysterious neighbor of the earth, the planet Mars. This, of course, was in the old days, less than twenty years after the mad American Doheny perfected the atomic blast at the cost of his life, and only a decade after the equally mad Cardoza rode on it to the Moon. They were true pioneers, these four of the *Ares*. Except for a half-dozen moon expeditions and the ill-fated de Lancey flight aimed at the seductive orb of Venus, they were the first men to feel other gravity than earth's, and certainly the first successful crew to leave the Earth-Moon system. And they deserved that success when one considers the difficulties and discomforts—the months spent in acclimatization chambers back on earth, learning to breath the air as tenuous as that of Mars, the challenging of the void in the tiny rocket driven by the cranky reaction motors of the twenty-first century, and mostly the facing of an absolutely unknown world.

Jarvis stretched and fingered the raw and peeling tip of his frostbitten nose. He sighed again contentedly.

"Well," exploded Harrison abruptly, "are we going to hear what happened? You set out all shipshape in an auxiliary rocket, we don't get a peep for ten days, and finally Putz here picks you out of a lunatic ant-heap with a freak ostrich as your pal! Spill it, man!"

"Speel?" queried Leroy perplexedly. "Speel what?"

"He means *'spiel'*," explained Putz soberly. "It iss to tell."

Jarvis met Harrison's amused glance without the shadow of a smile. "That's right, Karl," he said in grave agreement with Putz. *"Ich spiel es!"* He grunted comfortably and began.

"According to orders," he said, "I watched Karl here take off toward the North, and then I got into my flying sweat-box and headed South. You'll remember, Cap—we had orders not to land, but just scout about for points of interest. I set the two cameras clicking and buzzed along, riding pretty high—about two thousand feet—for a couple of reasons. First, it gave the cameras a greater field, and second, the under-jets travel so far in this half-vacuum they call air here that they stir up dust if you move low."

"We know all that from Putz," grunted Harrison. "I wish you'd saved the films, though. They'd have paid the cost of this junket; remember how the public mobbed the first Moon pictures?"

"The films are safe," retorted Jarvis. "Well," he resumed, "as I said, I buzzed along at a pretty good clip; just as we figured, the wings haven't much lift in this air at less than a hundred miles per hour, and even then I had to use the under-jets.

"So, with the speed and the altitude and the blurring caused by the under-jets, the seeing wasn't any too good. I could see enough, though, to distinguish that what I sailed over was just more of this grey plain that we'd been examining the whole week since our landing—same blobby growths and the same eternal carpet of crawling little plant-animals, or biopods, as Leroy calls them. So I sailed along, calling back my position every hour as instructed, and not knowing whether you heard me."

"I did!" snapped Harrison.

"A hundred and fifty miles south," continued Jarvis imperturbably, "the surface changed to a sort of low plateau, nothing but desert and orange-tinted sand. I figured that we were right in our guess, then, and this grey plain we dropped on was really the Mare Cimmerium which would make my orange desert the region called Xanthus. If I were right, I ought to hit another grey plain, the Mare Chronium, in another couple of hundred miles, and then another orange desert, Thyle I or II. And so I did."

"Putz verified our position a week and a half ago!" grumbled the captain. "Let's get to the point."

"Coming!" remarked Jarvis. "Twenty miles into Thyle—believe it or not—I crossed a canal!"

"Putz photographed a hundred! Let's hear something new!"

"And did he also see a city?"

"Twenty of 'em, if you call those heaps of mud cities!"

"Well," observed Jarvis, "from here on I'll be telling a few things Putz didn't see!" He rubbed his tingling nose, and continued, "I knew that I had sixteen hours of daylight at this season, so eight hours—eight hundred miles—from here, I decided to turn back. I was still over Thyle, whether I or II I'm not sure, not more than twenty-five miles into it. And right there, Putz's pet motor quit!"

"Quit? How?" Putz was solicitous.

"The atomic blast got weak. I started losing altitude right away, and suddenly there I was with a thump right in the middle of Thyle! Smashed my nose on the window, too!" He rubbed the injured member ruefully.

"Did you maybe try vashing der combustion chamber mit acid sulphuric?" inquired Putz. "Sometimes der lead giffs a secondary radiation—"

"Naw!" said Jarvis disgustedly. "I wouldn't try that, of course—not more than ten times! Besides, the bump flattened the landing gear and busted off the under-jets. Suppose I got the thing working—what then? Ten miles with the blast coming right out of the bottom and I'd have melted the floor from under me!" He rubbed his nose again. "Lucky for me a pound only weighs seven ounces here, or I'd have been mashed flat!"

"I could have fixed!" ejaculated the engineer. "I bet it vas not serious."

"Probably not," agreed Jarvis sarcastically. "Only it wouldn't fly. Nothing serious, but I had my choice of waiting to be picked up or trying to walk back—eight hundred miles, and perhaps twenty days before we had to leave! Forty miles a day! Well," he concluded, "I chose to walk. Just as much chance of being picked up, and it kept me busy."

"We'd have found you," said Harrison.

"No doubt. Anyway, I rigged up a harness from some seat straps, and put the water tank on my back, took a cartridge belt and revolver, and some iron rations, and started out."

"Water tank!" exclaimed the little biologist, Leroy. "She weigh one-quarter ton!"

"Wasn't full. Weighed about two hundred and fifty pounds earth-weight, which is eighty-five here. Then, besides, my own personal two hundred and ten pounds is only seventy on Mars, so, tank and all, I grossed a hundred and fifty-five, or fifty-five pounds less than my everyday earth-weight. I figured on that when I undertook the forty-mile daily stroll. Oh—of course I took a thermo-skin sleeping bag for these wintry Martian nights.

"Off I went, bouncing along pretty quickly. Eight hours of daylight meant twenty miles or more. It got tiresome, of course—plugging along over a soft sand desert with nothing to see, not even Leroy's crawling biopods. But an hour or so brought me to the canal—just a dry ditch about four hundred feet wide, and straight as a railroad on its own company map.

"There'd been water in it sometime, though. The ditch was covered with what looked like a nice green lawn. Only, as I approached, the lawn moved out of my way!"

"Eh?" said Leroy.

"Yeah, it was a relative of your biopods. I caught one—a little grasslike blade about as long as my finger, with two thin, stemmy legs."

"He is where?" Leroy was eager.

"He is let go! I had to move, so I plowed along with the walking grass opening in front and closing behind. And then I was out on the orange desert of Thyle again.

"I plugged steadily along, cussing the sand that made going so tiresome, and, incidentally, cussing that cranky motor of yours, Karl. It was just before twilight that I reached the edge of Thyle, and looked down over the grey Mare Chronium. And I knew there was seventy-five miles of *that* to be walked over, and then a couple of hundred miles of that Xanthus desert, and about as much more Mare Cimmerium. Was I pleased? I started cussing you fellows for not picking me up!"

"We were trying, you sap!" said Harrison.

"That didn't help. Well, I figured I might as well use what was left of daylight in getting down the cliff that bounded Thyle. I found an easy place, and down I went. Mare Chronium was just the same sort of place as this—crazy leafless plants and a bunch of crawlers; I gave it a glance and hauled out my sleeping bag. Up to that time, you know, I hadn't seen anything worth worrying about on this half-dead world—nothing dangerous, that is."

"Did you?" queried Harrison.

"*Did I!* You'll hear about it when I come to it. Well, I was just about to turn in when suddenly I heard the wildest sort of shenanigans!"

"Vot iss shenanigans?" inquired Putz.

"He says, 'Je ne sais quoi,'" explained Leroy. "It is to say, 'I don't know what.'"

"That's right," agreed Jarvis. "I didn't know what, so I sneaked over to find out. There was a racket like a flock of crows eating a bunch of canaries—whistles, cackles, caws, trills, and what have you. I rounded a clump of stumps, and there was Tweel!"

"Tweel?" said Harrison, and "Tveel?" said Leroy and Putz.

"That freak ostrich," explained the narrator. "At least, Tweel is as near as I can pronounce it without sputtering. He called it something like 'Trrrweerrlll.'"

"What was he doing?" asked the captain.

"He was being eaten! And squealing, of course, as anyone would."

"Eaten! By what?"

"I found out later. All I could see then was a bunch of black ropy arms tangled around what looked like, as Putz described it to you, an ostrich. I wasn't going to interfere, naturally; if both creatures were dangerous, I'd have one less to worry about.

"But the birdlike thing was putting up a good battle, dealing vicious blows with an eighteen-inch beak, between screeches. And besides, I caught a glimpse or two of what was on the end of those arms!" Jarvis shuddered. "But the clincher was when I noticed a little black bag or case hung about the neck of the bird-thing! It was intelligent! That or tame, I assumed. Anyway, it clinched my decision. I pulled out my automatic and fired into what I could see of its antagonist.

"There was a flurry of tentacles and a spurt of black corruption, and then the thing, with a disgusting sucking noise, pulled itself and its arms into a hole in the ground. The other let out a series of clacks, staggered around on legs about as thick as golf sticks, and turned suddenly to face me. I held my weapon ready, and the two of us stared at each other.

"The Martian wasn't a bird, really. It wasn't even birdlike, except just at first glance. It had a beak all right, and a few feathery appendages, but the beak wasn't really a beak. It was somewhat flexible; I could see the tip bend slowly from side to side; it was almost like a cross between a beak and a trunk. It had four-toed feet, and four-fingered things—hands, you'd have to call them, and a little roundish body, and a long neck ending in a tiny head—and that beak. It stood an inch or so taller than I, and—well, Putz saw it!"

The engineer nodded. "*Ja!* I saw!"

Jarvis continued. "So—we stared at each other. Finally the creature went into a series of clackings and twitterings and held out its hands toward me, empty. I took that as a gesture of friendship."

"Perhaps," suggested Harrison, "it looked at that nose of yours and thought you were its brother!"

"Huh! You can be funny without talking! Anyway, I put up my gun and said 'Aw, don't mention it,' or something of the sort, and the thing came over and we were pals.

"By that time, the sun was pretty low and I knew that I'd better build a fire or get into my thermo-skin. I decided on the fire. I picked a spot at the base of the Thyle cliff, where the rock could reflect a little heat on my back. I started breaking off chunks of this desiccated Martian vegetation, and my companion caught the idea and brought in an armful. I reached for a match, but the Martian fished into his pouch and brought out something that looked like a glowing coal; one touch of it, and the fire was blazing—and you all know what a job we have starting a fire in this atmosphere!

"And that bag of his!" continued the narrator. "That was a manufactured article, my friends; press an end and she popped open—press the middle and she sealed so perfectly you couldn't see the line. Better than zippers.

"Well, we stared at the fire a while and I decided to attempt some sort of communication with the Martian. I pointed at myself and said 'Dick'; he caught the drift immediately, stretched a bony claw at me and repeated 'Tick.' Then I pointed at him, and he gave that whistle I called Tweel; I can't imitate his accent. Things were going smoothly; to emphasize the names, I repeated 'Dick,' and then, pointing at him, 'Tweel.'

"There we stuck! He gave some clacks that sounded negative, and said something like 'P-p-p-root.' And that was just the beginning; I was always, 'Tick,' but as for him—part of the time he was 'Tweel,' and part of the time he was 'P-p-p-proot,' and part of the time he was sixteen other noises!

"We just couldn't connect. I tried 'rock,' and I tried 'star,' and 'tree,' and 'fire,' and Lord knows what else, and try as I would, I couldn't get a single word! Nothing was the same for two successive minutes, and if that's a language, I'm an alchemist! Finally I gave it up and called him Tweel, and that seemed to do.

"But Tweel hung on to some of my words. He remembered a couple of them, which I suppose is a great achievement if you're used to a language you have to make up as you go along. But I couldn't get the hang of his talk; either I missed some subtle point or we just didn't *think* alike—and I rather believe the latter view.

"I've other reasons for believing that. After a while I gave up the language business, and tried mathematics. I scratched two plus two equals four on the ground, and demonstrated it with pebbles. Again Tweel caught the idea, and informed me that three plus three equals six. Once more we seemed to be getting somewhere.

"So, knowing that Tweel had at least a grammar school education, I drew a circle for the sun, pointing first at it, and then at the last glow of the sun. Then I sketched in Mercury, and Venus, and Mother Earth, and Mars, and finally, pointing to Mars, I swept my hand around in a sort of inclusive gesture to indicate that Mars was our current environment. I was working up to putting over the idea that my home was on the earth.

"Tweel understood my diagram all right. He poked his beak at it, and with a great deal of trilling and clucking, he added Deimos and Phobos to Mars, and then sketched in the Earth's Moon!

"Do you see what that proves? It proves that Tweel's race uses telescopes—that they're civilized!"

"Does not!" snapped Harrison. "The Moon is visible from here as a fifth magnitude star. They could see its revolution with the naked eye."

"The Moon, yes!" said Jarvis. "You've missed my point. Mercury isn't visible! And Tweel knew of Mercury because he placed the Moon at the *third* planet, not the second. If he didn't know Mercury, he'd put the Earth second, and Mars third, instead of fourth! See?"

"Humph!" said Harrison.

"Anyway," proceeded Jarvis, "I went on with my lesson. Things were going smoothly, and it looked as if I could put the idea over. I pointed at the Earth on my diagram, and then at myself, and then, to clinch it, I pointed to myself and then to the Earth itself shining bright green almost at the zenith.

"Tweel set up such an excited clacking that I was certain he understood. He jumped up and down, and suddenly he pointed at himself and then at the sky, and then at himself and at the sky again. He pointed at his middle and then at Arcturus, at his head and then at

Spica, at his feet and then at half a dozen stars, while I just gaped at him. Then, all of a sudden, he gave a tremendous leap. Man, what a hop! He shot straight up into the starlight, seventy-five feet if an inch! I saw him silhouetted against the sky, saw him turn and come down at me head first, and land smack on his beak like a javelin! There he stuck square in the center of my sun-circle in the sand—a bull's eye!"

"Nuts!" observed the captain. "Plain nuts!"

"That's what I thought, too! I just stared at him open-mouthed while he pulled his head out of the sand and stood up. Then I figured he'd missed my point, and I went through the whole blamed rigamarole again, and it ended the same way, with Tweel on his nose in the middle of my picture!"

"Maybe it's a religious rite," suggested Harrison.

"Maybe," said Jarvis dubiously. "Well, there we were. We could exchange ideas up to a certain point, and then—blooey! Something in us was different, unrelated; I don't doubt that Tweel thought me just as screwy as I thought him. Our minds simply looked at the world from different viewpoints, and perhaps his viewpoint is as true as ours. But—we couldn't get together, that's all. Yet, in spite of all difficulties, I *liked* Tweel, and I have a queer certainty that he liked me."

"Nuts!" repeated the captain. "Just daffy!"

"Yeah? Wait and see. A couple of times I've thought that perhaps we—" He paused, and then resumed his narrative. "Anyway, I finally gave it up, and got into my thermo-skin to sleep. The fire hadn't kept me any too warm, but that damned sleeping bag did. Got stuffy five minutes after I closed myself in. I opened it a little and bingo! Some eighty-below-zero air hit my nose, and that's when I got this pleasant little frostbite to add to the bump I acquired during the crash of my rocket.

"I don't know what Tweel made of my sleeping. He sat around, but when I woke up, he was gone. I'd just crawled out of my bag, though, when I heard some twittering, and there he came, sailing down from that three-story Thyle cliff to alight on his beak beside me. I pointed to myself and toward the north, and he pointed at himself and toward the south, but when I loaded up and started away, he came along.

"Man, how he traveled! A hundred and fifty feet at a jump, sailing through the air stretched out like a spear, and landing on his beak. He seemed surprised at my plodding, but after a few moments he fell in beside me, only every few minutes he'd go into one of his leaps, and stick his nose into the sand a block ahead of me. Then he'd come shooting back at me; it made me nervous at first to see that beak of his coming at me like a spear, but he always ended in the sand at my side.

"So the two of us plugged along across the Mare Chronium. Same sort of place as this—same crazy plants and same little green biopods growing in the sand, or crawling out of your way. We talked—not that we understood each other, you know, but just for company. I sang songs, and I suspect Tweel did too; at least, some of his trillings and twitterings had a subtle sort of rhythm.

"Then, for variety, Tweel would display his smattering of English words. He'd point to an outcropping and say 'rock,' and point to a pebble and say it again; or he'd touch my arm and say 'Tick,' and then repeat it. He seemed terrifically amused that the same word meant the same thing twice in succession, or that the same word could apply to two different objects. It set me wondering if perhaps his language wasn't like the primitive speech of some earth people—you know, Captain, like the Negritoes, for instance, who haven't any generic words. No word for food or water or man—words for good food and bad food, or rainwater and seawater, or strong man and weak man—but no names for general classes. They're too primitive to understand that rain water and sea water are just different aspects of the same thing. But that wasn't the case with Tweel; it was just that we were somehow mysteriously different—our minds were alien to each other. And yet—we *liked* each other!"

"Looney, that's all," remarked Harrison. "That's why you two were so fond of each other."

"Well, I like *you!*" countered Jarvis wickedly. "Anyway," he resumed, "don't get the idea that there was anything screwy about Tweel. In fact, I'm not so sure but that he couldn't teach our highly praised human intelligence a trick or two. Oh, he wasn't an intellectual superman, I guess; but don't overlook the point that he managed to understand a little of my mental workings, and I never even got a glimmering of his."

"Because he didn't have any!" suggested the captain, while Putz and Leroy blinked attentively.

"You can judge of that when I'm through," said Jarvis. "Well, we plugged along across the Mare Chronium all that day, and all the next. Mare Chronium—Sea of Time! Say, I was willing to agree with Schiaparelli's name by the end of that march! Just that grey, endless plain of weird plants, and never a sign of any other life. It was so monotonous that I was even glad to see the desert of Xanthus toward the evening of the second day.

"I was fair worn out, but Tweel seemed as fresh as ever, for all I never saw him drink or eat. I think he could have crossed the Mare Chronium in a couple of hours with those block-long nose dives of his, but he stuck along with me. I offered him some water once or twice; he took the cup from me and sucked the liquid into his beak, and then carefully squirted it all back into the cup and gravely returned it.

"Just as we sighted Xanthus, or the cliffs that bounded it, one of those nasty sand clouds blew along, not as bad as the one we had here, but mean to travel against. I pulled the transparent flap of my thermoskin bag across my face and managed pretty well, and I noticed that Tweel used some feathery appendages growing like a mustache at the base of his beak to cover his nostrils, and some similar fuzz to shield his eyes."

"He is a desert creature!" ejaculated the little biologist, Leroy.

"Huh? Why?"

"He drink no water—he is adapt' for sandstorm—"

"Proves nothing! There's not enough water to waste anywhere on this desiccated pill called Mars. We'd call all of it desert on Earth, you know." He paused. "Anyway, after the sand storm blew over, a little wind kept blowing in our faces, not strong enough to stir the sand. But suddenly things came drifting along from the Xanthus cliffs—small, transparent spheres, for all the world like glass tennis balls! But light— they were almost light enough to float even in this thin air—empty, too; at least, I cracked open a couple and nothing came out but a bad smell. I asked Tweel about them, but all he said was 'No, no, no,' which I took to mean that he knew nothing about them. So they went bouncing by like tumbleweeds, or like soap bubbles, and we plugged on toward Xanthus. Tweel pointed at one of the crystal balls once and said 'rock,' but I was too tired to argue with him. Later I discovered what he meant.

"We came to the bottom of the Xanthus cliffs finally, when there wasn't much daylight left. I decided to sleep on the plateau if possible; anything dangerous, I reasoned, would be more likely to prowl through the vegetation of the Mare Chronium than the sand of Xanthus. Not that I'd seen a single sign of menace, except the rope-armed black thing that had trapped Tweel, and apparently that didn't prowl at all, but lured its victims within reach. It couldn't lure me while I slept, especially as Tweel didn't seem to sleep at all, but simply sat patiently around all night. I wondered how the creature had managed to trap Tweel, but there wasn't any way of asking him. I found that out too, later; it's devilish!

"However, we were ambling around the base of the Xanthus barrier looking for an easy spot to climb. At least, I was. Tweel could have leaped it easily, for the cliffs were lower than Thyle–perhaps sixty feet. I found a place and started up, swearing at the water tank strapped to my back–it didn't bother me except when climbing–and suddenly I heard a sound that I thought I recognized!

"You know how deceptive sounds are in this thin air. A shot sounds like the pop of a cork. But this sound was the drone of a rocket, and sure enough, there went our second auxiliary about ten miles to westward, between me and the sunset!"

"Vas me!" said Putz. "I hunt for you."

"Yeah; I knew that, but what good did it do me? I hung on to the cliff and yelled and waved with one hand. Tweel saw it too, and set up a trilling and twittering, leaping to the top of the barrier and then high into the air. And while I watched, the machine droned on into the shadows to the south.

"I scrambled to the top of the cliff. Tweel was still pointing and trilling excitedly, shooting up toward the sky and coming down head-on to stick upside down on his beak in the sand. I pointed toward the south and at myself, and he said, 'Yes–Yes–Yes'; but somehow I gathered that he thought the flying thing was a relative of mine, probably a parent. Perhaps I did his intellect an injustice; I think now that I did.

"I was bitterly disappointed by the failure to attract attention. I pulled out my thermo-skin bag and crawled into it, as the night chill was already apparent. Tweel stuck his beak into the sand and drew up his legs and arms and looked for all the world like one of those leafless shrubs out there. I think he stayed that way all night."

"Protective mimicry!" ejaculated Leroy. "See? He is desert creature!"

"In the morning," resumed Jarvis, "we started off again. We hadn't gone a hundred yards into Xanthus when I saw something queer! This is one thing Putz didn't photograph, I'll wager!

"There was a line of little pyramids–tiny ones, not more than six inches high, stretching across Xanthus as far as I could see! Little buildings made of pygmy bricks, they were, hollow inside and truncated, or at least broken at the top and empty. I pointed at them and said 'What?' to Tweel, but he gave some negative twitters to indicate, I suppose, that he didn't know. So off we went, following the row of pyramids because they ran north, and I was going north.

"Man, we trailed that line for hours! After a while, I noticed another queer thing: they were getting larger. Same number of bricks in each one, but the bricks were larger.

"By noon they were shoulder high. I looked into a couple—all just the same, broken at the top and empty. I examined a brick or two as well; they were silica, and old as creation itself!"

"How you know?" asked Leroy.

"They were weathered—edges rounded. Silica doesn't weather easily even on Earth, and in this climate—!"

"How old you think?"

"Fifty thousand—a hundred thousand years. How can I tell? The little ones we saw in the morning were older—perhaps ten times as old. Crumbling. How old would that make *them?* Half a million years? Who knows?" Jarvis paused a moment. "Well," he resumed, "we followed the line. Tweel pointed at them and said 'rock' once or twice, but he'd done that many times before. Besides, he was more or less right about these.

"I tried questioning him. I pointed at a pyramid and asked 'People?' and indicated the two of us. He set up a negative sort of clucking and said, 'No, no, no. No one-one-two. No two-two-four,' meanwhile rubbing his stomach. I just stared at him and he went through the business again. 'No one-one-two. No two-two-four.' I just gaped at him."

"That proves it!" exclaimed Harrison. "Nuts!"

"You think so?" queried Jarvis sardonically. "Well, I figured it out different! 'No one-one-two!' You don't get it, of course, do you?"

"Nope—nor do you!"

"I think I do! Tweel was using the few English words he knew to put over a very complex idea. What, let me ask, does mathematics make you think of?"

"Why—of astronomy. Or—or logic!"

"That's it! 'No one-one-two!' Tweel was telling me that the builders of the pyramids weren't people—or that they weren't intelligent, that they weren't reasoning creatures! Get it?"

"Huh! I'll be damned!"

"You probably will."

"Why," put in Leroy, "he rub his belly?"

"Why? Because, my dear biologist, that's where his brains are! Not in his tiny head—in his middle!"

"*C'est* impossible!"

"Not on Mars, it isn't! This flora and fauna aren't earthly; your biopods prove that!" Jarvis grinned and took up his narrative. "Anyway, we plugged along across Xanthus and in about the middle of the afternoon, something else queer happened. The pyramids ended."

"Ended!"

"Yeah; the queer part was that the last one—and now they were ten-footers—was capped! See? Whatever built it was still inside; we'd trailed 'em from their half-million-year-old origin to the present.

"Tweel and I noticed it about the same time. I yanked out my automatic (I had a clip of Boland explosive bullets in it) and Tweel, quick as a sleight-of-hand trick, snapped a queer little glass revolver out of his bag. It was much like our weapons, except that the grip was larger to accommodate his four-taloned hand. And we held our weapons ready while we sneaked up along the lines of empty pyramids.

"Tweel saw the movement first. The top tiers of bricks were heaving, shaking, and suddenly slid down the sides with a thin crash. And then—something—something was coming out!

"A long, silvery-grey arm appeared, dragging after it an armored body. Armored, I mean, with scales, silver-grey and dull-shining. The arm heaved the body out of the hole; the beast crashed to the sand.

"It was a nondescript creature—body like a big grey cask, arm and a sort of mouth-hole at one end; stiff, pointed tail at the other—and that's all. No other limbs, no eyes, ears, nose—nothing! The thing dragged itself a few yards, inserted its pointed tail in the sand, pushed itself upright, and just sat.

"Tweel and I watched it for ten minutes before it moved. Then, with a creaking and rustling like—oh, like crumpling stiff paper—its arm moved to the mouth-hole and out came a brick! The arm placed the brick carefully on the ground, and the thing was still again.

"Another ten minutes—another brick. Just one of Nature's bricklayers. I was about to slip away and move on when Tweel pointed at the thing and said 'rock!' I went 'huh?' and he said it again. Then, to the accompaniment of some of his trilling, he said, 'No—no—,' and gave two or three whistling breaths.

"Well, I got his meaning, for a wonder! I said, 'No breath?' and demonstrated the word. Tweel was ecstatic; he said, 'Yes, yes, yes! No, no, no breet!' Then he gave a leap and sailed out to land on his nose about one pace from the monster!

"I was startled, you can imagine! The arm was going up for a brick, and I expected to see Tweel caught and mangled, but—nothing happened! Tweel pounded on the creature, and the arm took the brick and placed it neatly beside the first. Tweel rapped on its body again, and said 'rock,' and I got up nerve enough to take a look myself.

"Tweel was right again. The creature *was* rock, and it didn't breathe!"

"How you know?" snapped Leroy, his black eyes blazing interest.

"Because I'm a chemist. The beast was made of silica! There must have been pure silicon in the sand, and it lived on that. Get it? We, and Tweel, and those plants out there, and even the biopods are *carbon* life; this thing lived by a different set of chemical reactions. It was silicon life!"

"La vie silicieuse!" shouted Leroy. "I have suspect, and now it is proof! I must go see! *Il faut que je—*"

"All right! All right!" said Jarvis. "You can go see. Anyhow, there the thing was, alive and yet not alive, moving every ten minutes, and then only to remove a brick. Those bricks were its waste matter. See, Frenchy? We're carbon, and our waste is carbon dioxide, and this thing is silicon, and *its* waste is silicon dioxide—silica. But silica is a solid, hence the bricks. And it builds itself in, and when it is covered, it moves over to a fresh place to start over. No wonder it creaked! A living creature half a million years old!"

"How you know how old?" Leroy was frantic.

"We trailed its pyramids from the beginning, didn't we? If this weren't the original pyramid builder, the series would have ended somewhere before we found him, wouldn't it?—ended and started over with the small ones. That's simple enough, isn't it?

"But he reproduces, or tries to. Before the third brick came out, there was a little rustle and out popped a whole stream of those little crystal balls. They're his spores, or eggs, or seeds—call 'em what you want. They went bouncing by across Xanthus just as they'd bounced by us back in the Mare Chronium. I've a hunch how they work, too—this is for your information, Leroy. I think the crystal shell of silica is no more than a protective covering, like an eggshell, and that the active principle is the smell inside. It's some sort of gas that attacks silicon, and if the shell is broken near a supply of that element, some reaction starts that ultimately develops into a beast like that one."

"You should try!" exclaimed the little Frenchman. "We must break one to see!"

"Yeah? Well, I did. I smashed a couple against the sand. Would you like to come back in about ten thousand years to see if I planted some pyramid monsters? You'd most likely be able to tell by that time!" Jarvis paused and drew a deep breath. "Lord! That queer creature! Do you picture it? Blind, deaf, nerveless, brainless—just a mechanism, and yet—immortal! Bound to go on making bricks, building pyramids, as long as silicon and oxygen exist, and even afterwards it'll just stop. It won't be dead. If the accidents of a million years bring it its food again, there it'll be, ready to run again, while brains and civilizations are part of the past. A queer beast—yet I met a stranger one!"

"If you did, it must have been in your dreams!" growled Harrison.

"You're right!" said Jarvis soberly. "In a way, you're right. The dream-beast! That's the best name for it—and it's the most fiendish, terrifying creation one could imagine! More dangerous than a lion, more insidious than a snake!"

"Tell me!" begged Leroy. "I must go see!"

"Not *this* devil!" He paused again. "Well," he resumed, "Tweel and I left the pyramid creature and plowed along through Xanthus. I was tired and a little disheartened by Putz's failure to pick me up, and Tweel's trilling got on my nerves, as did his flying nosedives. So I just strode along without a word, hour after hour across that monotonous desert.

"Toward mid-afternoon we came in sight of a low dark line on the horizon. I knew what it was. It was a canal; I'd crossed it in the rocket and it meant that we were just one-third of the way across Xanthus. Pleasant thought, wasn't it? And still, I was keeping up to schedule.

"We approached the canal slowly; I remembered that this one was bordered by a wide fringe of vegetation and that Mudheap City was on it.

"I was tired, as I said. I kept thinking of a good hot meal, and then from that I jumped to reflections of how nice and home-like even Borneo would seem after this crazy planet, and from that, to thoughts of little old New York, and then to thinking about a girl I know there—Fancy Long. Know her?"

"Vision entertainer," said Harrison. "I've tuned her in. Nice blonde—dances and sings on the *Yerba Mate* hour."

"That's her," said Jarvis ungrammatically. "I know her pretty well—just friends, get me?—though she came down to see us off in the *Ares*. Well, I was thinking about her, feeling pretty lonesome, and all the time we were approaching that line of rubbery plants.

"And then—I said, 'What 'n Hell!' and stared. And there she was—Fancy Long, standing plain as day under one of those crack-brained trees, and smiling and waving just the way I remembered her when we left!"

"Now you're nuts, too!" observed the captain.

"Boy, I almost agreed with you! I stared and pinched myself and closed my eyes and then stared again—and every time, there was Fancy

Long smiling and waving! Tweel saw something, too; he was trilling and clucking away, but I scarcely heard him. I was bounding toward her over the sand, too amazed even to ask myself questions.

"I wasn't twenty feet from her when Tweel caught me with one of his flying leaps. He grabbed my arm, yelling, 'No—no—no!' in his squeaky voice. I tried to shake him off—he was as light as if he were built of bamboo—but he dug his claws in and yelled. And finally some sort of sanity returned to me and I stopped less than ten feet from her. There she stood, looking as solid as Putz's head!"

"Vot?" said the engineer.

"She smiled and waved, and waved and smiled, and I stood there dumb as Leroy, while Tweel squeaked and chattered. I *knew* it couldn't be real, yet—there she was!

"Finally I said, 'Fancy! Fancy Long!' She just kept on smiling and waving, but looking as real as if I hadn't left her thirty-seven million miles away.

"Tweel had his glass pistol out, pointing it at her. I grabbed his arm, but he tried to push me away. He pointed at her and said, 'No breet! No breet!' and I understood that he meant that the Fancy Long thing wasn't alive. Man, my head was whirling!

"Still, it gave me the jitters to see him pointing his weapon at her. I don't know why I stood there watching him take careful aim, but I did. Then he squeezed the handle of his weapon; there was a little puff of steam, and Fancy Long was gone! And in her place was one of those writhing, black, rope-armed horrors like the one I'd saved Tweel from!

"The dream-beast! I stood there dizzy, watching it die while Tweel trilled and whistled. Finally he touched my arm, pointed at the twisting thing, and said, 'You one-one-two, he one-one-two.' After he'd repeated it eight or ten times, I got it. Do any of you?"

"*Oui!*" shrilled Leroy. "*Moi—je le comprends!* He mean you think of something, the beast he know, and see it! *Un chien*—a hungry dog, he would see the big bone with meat! Or smell it—not?"

"Right!" said Jarvis. "The dream-beast uses its victim's longings and desires to trap its prey. The bird at nesting season would see its mate, the fox, prowling for its own prey, would see a helpless rabbit!"

"How he do?" queried Leroy.

"How do I know? How does a snake back on earth charm a bird into its very jaws? And aren't there deep-sea fish that lure their victims into their mouths? Lord!" Jarvis shuddered. "Do you see how insidious the monster is? We're warned now—but henceforth we can't trust even our eyes. You might see me—I might see one of you—and back of it may be nothing but another of those black horrors!"

"How'd your friend know?" asked the captain abruptly.

"Tweel? I wonder! Perhaps he was thinking of something that couldn't possibly have interested me, and when I started to run, he realized that I saw something different and was warned. Or perhaps the dream-beast can only project a single vision, and Tweel saw what I saw—or nothing. I couldn't ask him. But it's just another proof that his intelligence is equal to ours or greater."

"He's daffy, I tell you!" said Harrison. "What makes you think his intellect ranks with the human?"

"Plenty of things! First, the pyramid-beast. He hadn't seen one before; he said as much. Yet he recognized it as a dead-alive automaton of silicon."

"He could have heard of it," objected Harrison. "He lives around here, you know."

"Well how about the language? I couldn't pick up a single idea of his and he learned six or seven words of mine. And do you realize what complex ideas he put over with no more than those six or seven words? The pyramid-monster—the dream-beast! In a single phrase he told me that one was a harmless automaton and the other a deadly hypnotist. What about that?"

"Huh!" said the captain.

"*Huh* if you wish! Could you have done it knowing only six words of English? Could you go even further, as Tweel did, and tell me that another creature was of a sort of intelligence so different from ours that understanding was impossible—even more impossible than that between Tweel and me?"

"Eh? What was that?"

"Later. The point I'm making is that Tweel and his race are worthy of our friendship. Somewhere on Mars—and you'll find I'm right—is a civilization and culture equal to ours, and maybe more than equal. And communication is possible between them and us; Tweel proves that. It may take years of patient trial, for their minds are alien, but less alien than the next minds we encountered—if they *are* minds."

"The next ones? What next ones?"

"The people of the mud cities along the canals." Jarvis frowned, then resumed his narrative. "I thought the dream-beast and the silicon-monster were the strangest beings conceivable, but I was wrong. These creatures are still more alien, less understandable than either and far less comprehensible than Tweel, with whom friendship is possible, and even, by patience and concentration, the exchange of ideas.

"Well," he continued, "we left the dream-beast dying, dragging itself back into its hole, and we moved toward the canal. There was a carpet of that queer walking-grass scampering out of our way, and when we reached the bank, there was a yellow trickle of water flowing. The mound city I'd noticed from the rocket was a mile or so to the right and I was curious enough to want to take a look at it.

"It had seemed deserted from my previous glimpse of it, and if any creatures were lurking in it—well, Tweel and I were both armed. And by the way, that crystal weapon of Tweel's was an interesting device; I took a look at it after the dream-beast episode. It fired a little glass splinter, poisoned, I suppose, and I guess it held at least a hundred of 'em to a load. The propellent was steam—just plain steam!"

"Shteam!" echoed Putz. "From vot come, shteam?"

"From water, of course! You could see the water through the transparent handle and about a gill of another liquid, thick and yellowish. When Tweel squeezed the handle—there was no trigger—a drop of water and a drop of the yellow stuff squirted into the firing chamber, and the water vaporized—pop!—like that. It's not so difficult; I think we could develop the same principle. Concentrated sulphuric acid will heat water almost to boiling, and so will quicklime, and there's potassium and sodium—

"Of course, his weapon hadn't the range of mine, but it wasn't so bad in this thin air, and it *did* hold as many shots as a cowboy's gun in a Western movie. It was effective, too, at least against Martian life; I tried it out, aiming at one of the crazy plants, and darned if the plant didn't wither up and fall apart! That's why I think the glass splinters were poisoned.

"Anyway, we trudged along toward the mud-heap city and I began to wonder whether the city builders dug the canals. I pointed to the city and then at the canal, and Tweel said 'No—no—no!' and gestured toward the south. I took it to mean that some other race had created the canal system, perhaps Tweel's people. I don't know; maybe there's still another intelligent race on the planet, or a dozen others. Mars is a queer little world.

"A hundred yards from the city we crossed a sort of road—just a hard-packed mud trail, and then, all of a sudden, along came one of the mound builders!

"Man, talk about fantastic beings! It looked rather like a barrel trotting along on four legs with four other arms or tentacles. It had no head, just body and members and a row of eyes completely around it. The top end of the barrel-body was a diaphragm stretched as tight as a drum head, and that was all. It was pushing a little coppery cart and tore right past us like the proverbial bat out of Hell. It didn't even notice us, although I thought the eyes on my side shifted a little as it passed.

"A moment later another came along, pushing another empty cart. Same thing—it just scooted past us. Well, I wasn't going to be ignored by a bunch of barrels playing train, so when the third one approached, I planted myself in the way—ready to jump, of course, if the thing didn't stop.

"But it did. It stopped and set up a sort of drumming from the diaphragm on top. And I held out both hands and said, 'We are friends!' And what do you suppose the thing did?"

"Said, 'Pleased to meet you,' I'll bet!" suggested Harrison.

"I couldn't have been more surprised if it had! It drummed on its diaphragm, and then suddenly boomed out, 'We are v-r-r-riends!' and gave its pushcart a vicious poke at me! I jumped aside, and away it went while I stared dumbly after it.

"A minute later another one came hurrying along. This one didn't pause, but simply drummed out, 'We are v-r-r-riends!' and scurried by. How did it learn the phrase? Were all of the creatures in some sort of communication with each other? Were they all parts of some central organism? I don't know, though I think Tweel does.

"Anyway, the creatures went sailing past us, every one greeting us with the same statement. It got to be funny; I never thought to find so many friends on this God-forsaken ball! Finally I made a puzzled gesture to Tweel; I guess he understood, for he said, 'One-one-two—yes!—two-two-four—no!' Get it?"

"Sure," said Harrison. "It's a Martian nursery rhyme."

"Yeah! Well, I was getting used to Tweel's symbolism, and I figured it out this way. 'One-one-two—yes!' The creatures were intelligent. 'Two-two-four—no!' Their intelligence was not of our order, but something different and beyond the logic of two and two is four. Maybe I missed his meaning. Perhaps he meant that their minds were of low degree, able to figure out the simple things—'One-one-two—yes!'—but not more difficult things—'Two-two-four—no!' But I think from what we saw later that he meant the other.

"After a few moments, the creatures came rushing back—first one, then another. Their pushcarts were full of stones, sand, chunks of rubbery plants, and such rubbish as that. They droned out their friendly greeting, which didn't really sound so friendly, and dashed on. The third one I assumed to be my first acquaintance and I decided to have another chat with him. I stepped into his path again and waited.

"Up he came, booming out his "We are v-r-r-riends' and stopped. I looked at him; four or five of his eyes looked at me. He tried his pass-word again and gave a shove on his cart, but I stood firm. And then the—the dashed creature reached out one of his arms, and two finger-like nippers tweaked my nose!"

"Haw!" roared Harrison. "Maybe the things have a sense of beauty!"

"Laugh!" grumbled Jarvis. "I'd already had a nasty bump and a mean frostbite on that nose. Anyway, I yelled 'Ouch!' and jumped aside and the creature dashed away; but from then on, their greeting was 'We are v-r-r-riends! Ouch!' Queer beasts!

"Tweel and I followed the road squarely up to the nearest mound. The creatures were coming and going, paying us not the slightest attention, fetching their loads of rubbish. The road simply dived into an opening, and slanted down like an old mine, and in and out darted the barrel-people, greeting us with their eternal phrase.

"I looked in; there was a light somewhere below, and I was curious to see it. It didn't look like a flame or torch, you understand, but more like a civilized light, and I thought that I might get some clue as to the creatures' development. So in I went and Tweel tagged along, not with-out a few trills and twitters, however.

"The light was curious; it sputtered and flared like an old arc light, but came from a single black rod set in the wall of the corridor. It was electric, beyond doubt. The creatures were fairly civilized, apparently.

"Then I saw another light shining on something that glittered and I went on to look at that, but it was only a heap of shiny sand. I turned toward the entrance to leave, and the Devil take me if it wasn't gone!

"I suppose the corridor had curved, or I'd stepped into a side pas-sage. Anyway, I walked back in that direction I thought we'd come, and all I saw was more dimlit corridor. The place was a labyrinth! There was nothing but twisting passages running every way, lit by occasional lights, and now and then a creature running by, sometimes with a pushcart, sometimes without.

"Well, I wasn't much worried at first. Tweel and I had only come a few steps from the entrance. But every move we made after that seemed to get us in deeper. Finally I tried following one of the creatures with an empty cart, thinking that he'd be going out for his rubbish, but he ran around aimlessly, into one passage and out another. When he started dashing around a pillar like one of these Japanese waltzing mice, I gave up, dumped my water tank on the floor, and sat down.

"Tweel was as lost as I. I pointed up and he said 'No—no—no!' in a sort of helpless trill. And we couldn't get any help from the natives. They paid no attention at all, except to assure us they were friends—ouch!

"Lord! I don't know how many hours or days we wandered around there! I slept twice from sheer exhaustion; Tweel never seemed to need sleep. We tried following only the upward corridors, but they'd run uphill a ways and then curve downwards. The temperature in that damned anthill was constant; you couldn't tell night from day and after my first sleep I didn't know whether I'd slept one hour or thirteen, so I couldn't tell from my watch whether it was midnight or noon.

"We saw plenty of strange things. There were machines running in some of the corridors, but they didn't seem to be doing anything—just wheels turning. And several times I saw two barrel-beasts with a little one growing between them, joined to both."

"Parthenogenesis!" exulted Leroy. "Parthenogenesis by budding like *les tulipes!*"

"If you say so, Frenchy," agreed Jarvis. "The things never noticed us at all, except, as I say, to greet us with 'We are v-r-r-riends! Ouch!' They seemed to have no home-life of any sort, but just scurried around with their pushcarts, bringing in rubbish. And finally I discovered what they did with it.

"We'd had a little luck with a corridor, one that slanted upwards for a great distance. I was feeling that we ought to be close to the surface when suddenly the passage debouched into a domed chamber, the only one we'd seen. And man!—I felt like dancing when I saw what looked like daylight through a crevice in the roof.

"There was a—a sort of machine in the chamber, just an enormous wheel that turned slowly, and one of the creatures was in the act of dumping his rubbish below it. The wheel ground it with a crunch—sand, stones, plants, all into powder that sifted away somewhere. While we watched, others filed in, repeating the process, and that seemed to be all. No rhyme nor reason to the whole thing—but that's characteristic of this crazy planet. And there was another fact that's almost too bizarre to believe.

"One of the creatures, having dumped his load, pushed his cart aside with a crash and calmly shoved himself under the wheel! I watched him being crushed, too stupefied to make a sound, and a moment later, another followed him! They were perfectly methodical about it, too; one of the cartless creatures took the abandoned pushcart.

"Tweel didn't seem surprised; I pointed out the next suicide to him, and he just gave the most human-like shrug imaginable, as much as to say, 'What can I do about it?' He must have known more or less about these creatures.

"Then I saw something else. There was something beyond the wheel, something shining on a sort of low pedestal. I walked over; there was a little crystal about the size of an egg, fluorescing to beat Tophet. The light from it stung my hands and face, almost like a static discharge, and then I noticed another funny thing. Remember that wart I had on my left thumb? Look!" Jarvis extended his hand. "It dried up and fell off—just like that! And my abused nose—say, the pain went out of it like magic! The thing had the property of hard ex-rays or gamma radiations, only more so; it destroyed diseased tissue and left healthy tissue unharmed!

"I was thinking what a present *that'd* be to take back to Mother Earth when a lot of racket interrupted. We dashed back to the other side of the wheel in time to see one of the pushcarts ground up. Some suicide had been careless, it seems.

"Then suddenly the creatures were booming and drumming all around us and their noise was decidedly menacing. A crowd of them advanced toward us; we backed out of what I thought was the passage we'd entered by, and they came rumbling after us, some pushing carts and some not. Crazy brutes! There was a whole chorus of 'We are v-r-r-riends! Ouch!' I didn't like the 'ouch'; it was rather suggestive.

"Tweel had his glass gun out and I dumped my water tank for greater freedom and got mine. We backed up the corridor with the barrel-beasts following—about twenty of them. Queer thing—the ones coming in with loaded carts moved past us inches away without a sign.

"Tweel must have noticed that. Suddenly, he snatched out that glowing coal cigar-lighter of his and touched a cartload of plant limbs. Puff! The whole load was burning—and the crazy beast pushing it went right along without a change of pace! It created some disturbance among our 'v-r-r-riends,' however—and then I noticed the smoke eddying and swirling past us, and sure enough, there was the entrance!

"I grabbed Tweel and out we dashed and after us our twenty pursuers. The daylight felt like Heaven, though I saw at first glance that the sun was all but set, and that was bad, since I couldn't live outside my thermo-skin bag in a Martian night—at least, without a fire.

"And things got worse in a hurry. They cornered us in an angle between two mounds, and there we stood. I hadn't fired nor had Tweel; there wasn't any use in irritating the brutes. They stopped a little distance away and began their booming about friendship and ouches.

"Then things got still worse! A barrel-brute came out with a push-cart and they all grabbed into it and came out with handfuls of foot-long copper darts—sharp-looking ones—and all of a sudden one sailed past my ear—zing! And it was shoot or die then.

"We were doing pretty well for a while. We picked off the ones next to the pushcart and managed to keep the darts at a minimum, but suddenly there was a thunderous booming of 'v-r-r-riends' and 'ouches,' and a whole army of 'em came out of their hole.

"Man! We were through and I knew it! Then I realized that Tweel wasn't. He could have leaped the mound behind us as easily as not. He was staying for me!

"Say, I could have cried if there'd been time! I'd liked Tweel from the first, but whether I'd have had gratitude to do what he was doing—suppose I *had* saved him from the first dream-beast—he'd done as much for me, hadn't he? I grabbed his arm, and said 'Tweel,' and pointed up, and he understood. He said, 'No—no—no, Tick!' and popped away with his glass pistol.

"What could I do? I'd be a goner anyway when the sun set, but I couldn't explain that to him. I said, 'Thanks, Tweel. You're a man!' and felt that I wasn't paying him a compliment at all. A man! There are mighty few men who'd do that.

"So I went 'bang' with my gun and Tweel went 'puff' with his, and the barrels were throwing darts and getting ready to rush us, and booming about being friends. I had given up hope. Then suddenly an angel dropped right down from Heaven in the shape of Putz, with his under-jets blasting the barrels into very small pieces!

"Wow! I let out a yell and dashed for the rocket; Putz opened the door and in I went, laughing and crying and shouting! It was a moment or so before I remembered Tweel; I looked around in time to see him rising in one of his nosedives over the mound and away.

"I had a devil of a job arguing Putz into following! By the time we got the rocket aloft, darkness was down; you know how it comes here—

like turning off a light. We sailed out over the desert and put down once or twice. I yelled 'Tweel!' and yelled it a hundred times, I guess. We couldn't find him; he could travel like the wind and all I got—or else I imagined it—was a faint trilling and twittering drifting out of the south. He'd gone, and damn it! I wish—I wish he hadn't!"

The four men of the *Ares* were silent—even the sardonic Harrison. At last little Leroy broke the stillness.

"I should like to see," he murmured.

"Yeah," said Harrison. "And the wart-cure. Too bad you missed that; it might be the cancer cure they've been hunting for a century and a half."

"Oh, that!" muttered Jarvis gloomily. "That's what started the fight!" He drew a glistening object from his pocket.

"Here it is."

CHAPTER 3

Searching The Cosmic Haystack For ETI

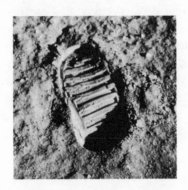

When you flip a coin there is a fifty-fifty chance that it will turn up heads. What are the chances of finding extraterrestrial intelligence if we search the sky diligently?

No one can say. We simply do not know enough about the universe to be able to tell. Our ignorance is as wide as the starry galaxies, as deep as the void of space.

We do not even know for certain that stars other than our Sun harbor Earth-like planets where life might take root. Astronomer David Latham, a leader in the hunt for other solar systems and the sub-stars called brown dwarfs, presents the evidence for the existence of planets orbiting other stars. The new results lead to the conclusion that many stars should host planetary systems, since a high percentage of the initial stellar targets has yielded evidence of planets. Where observations are lacking, scientists can sometimes use mathematics and statistics to help explore a new area. Frank Drake, one of the fathers of SETI, discusses the equation he devised for the purpose of assessing the chances of finding an extraterrestrial civilization.

Your humble editor wishes to make an un-humble declaration here. The first suggestion that organic molecules might exist in space was made by me, in 1962. Since my prediction was published in a science-

fiction magazine, hardly anyone paid attention to it. But it was a serious prediction made in a nonfiction article about what would one day come to be called SETI.

The following year saw the actual discovery of hydroxyl molecules (OH) in interstellar space, soon followed by discoveries of complex organic molecules. If the chemicals of life exist among the stars, is it likely that they came together only once to form intelligent creatures?

Yet there is the possibility that no ETI exists. After all, no one has contacted us yet. David Brin, physicist and award-winning science-fiction author, examines the implications of this interstellar silence.

Although radio telescope searches have failed to turn up any intelligent signals from extraterrestrials so far, they have found the chemical constituents of life among the stars. Radio signatures of organic chemicals in interstellar clouds have encouraged the belief that life may be an inherent feature of the Universe and not a fluke occurrence on our one little lonely world.

LOOKING FOR
EXTRASOLAR PLANETS

by

DAVID LATHAM

Humans have walked on the Moon. The Apollo astronauts were even able to do a little exploring in their few short excursions onto the lunar surface, scooting from this crater to that rock aboard their electric rover. But, the Apollo missions were not much more than expensive and well-planned camping trips. Long-term self-sustained survival on the lunar surface may be within the reach of our technology now, but establishing a lunar colony still eludes our willingness to foot the bill. Nevertheless, the Apollo missions had a profound impact on our collective image of what it takes for a planet to be habitable. Seen from deep space the Earth is mostly blue and white: blue from the liquid water in the oceans and white from the clouds of water vapor in the atmosphere. It is easy to imagine that we could be comfortable on other worlds like this one. All we have to do is find them. To the generation that grew up watching Captain Kirk and the *Enterprise* jump from one habitable planet to the next, it all seems so natural.

In reality we do not yet know of any other planet just like the Earth. The closest thing is Mars, right here on our doorstep in our own solar system. But, Mars is so much more distant than the Moon that nobody talks about colonizing Mars without first establishing a permanent lunar base. Beyond that, Mars is ridiculously close compared to the nearest stars, which are more than a million times farther away. Finding extrasolar planets like the Earth will not be easy, but it will be trivial compared to visiting them.

Over the past few years, astronomers have made dramatic progress in the search for extrasolar planets. Ten years ago there was only one confirmed extrasolar planet candidate, the unseen companion that my team found orbiting the solar-type star HD 114762. Most astronomers found that candidate a bit hard to swallow, because it was several times more massive than Jupiter, the largest planet in our own solar system, yet the orbital period of 84 days placed the companion in an orbit similar to Mercury's, close to the parent star, in the hot inner regions where the theorists said the temperatures would be too high for a giant planet to form. All the gas and volatile material would have been swept away from the inner regions leaving behind only high melting-point minerals and rocks. Such material might be suitable for building planets like the earth, but it would fall far short, by a factor of 100 or more, from providing enough raw material to build giant planets like Jupiter.

As long as there was only one candidate for a giant planet in a short-period orbit, there was a convenient way out. The small amplitude for the periodic variation in HD 114762's velocity along the line of sight might not be due to the gravitational pull of an orbiting planet. Instead it might be due to a normal low-mass stellar companion, with the plane of the orbit oriented almost exactly face-on to the line of sight. In this case the observed velocity variations would be small due to projection effects, not to the mass of the companion being so small that it would have to be a planet.

All the doubts about the feasibility of there being giant planets in tight orbits evaporated with the discovery of a planet in a low-amplitude orbit with a period of four days around the solar-type star 51 Pegasi. For any reasonable orientation of that orbit, the mass implied for the companion was similar to that of Jupiter. This discovery proved to be a watershed. Within months the floodgates had opened, with a rush of discoveries of additional giant planets orbiting other solar-type stars.

Finally there was progress in a quest that began 5 centuries ago with the Copernican Revolution and the realization that the Sun is a star and the stars are suns. If the Sun was orbited by a retinue of planets, why couldn't many other stars have their own solar systems? Surely some of those extrasolar planets would support life, and perhaps other thinking beings. In the last 100 years or so the realization has dawned that for there to be life like ours, liquid water must exist at the planet's surface and thus only a certain zone around a star is likely to allow water-based life (see the chapter by Ben Bova). However, our new search techniques, as powerful as they are, do not allow us to choose to find such planets. We have to take what our searches find easiest: massive planets in small orbits.

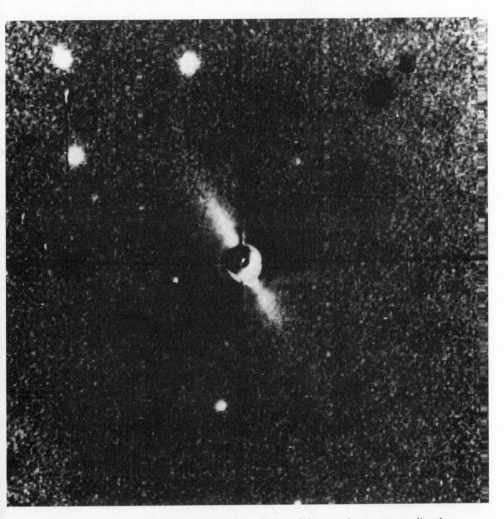

Figure 1. This computer-processed image shows the faint disk, seen edge-on, surrounding the star Beta Pictoris. The star's image was cancelled out to allow the faint disk to be seen. The black cross is a computer artifact. *(Photo: Courtesy NASA.)*

PLANETS VS. BROWN DWARFS

Stars are thought to form by the gravitational collapse of clouds of interstellar gas and dust. We know that stars have formed throughout the history of the Milky Way Galaxy, because we see clusters of stars with ages that date from all different times in the lifetime of the Galaxy. The oldest clusters are the globulars, magnificent congeries of vast numbers of stars that must have formed roughly 15 billion years ago, even before the Galaxy itself had finished collapsing into its present configuration, a highly flattened disk. It is in the disk that star formation has continued throughout the history of the Galaxy, and where we now find the youngest stars. We see evidence for this in the open clusters, which cover a wide range of ages, judging from the way their massive stars have evolved. Messier 67, for example, has an age of 4 billion years, roughly the same as the Sun, while the Hyades are close to half a billion years old, and the Pleiades are five times younger than that.

Even younger are the regions of recent star formation in Orion and Taurus, where we see stars that are still in the final stages of gravitational collapse, heading towards the main sequence, where they will settle down and start fusing hydrogen in their cores a few million years from now. Yet, most of these very young stars are already accompanied by stellar companions.

It appears to be the natural outcome of star formation that most stars come in binaries. Among the solar-type stars in the neighborhood of the Sun, surveys show that it is more likely for a star to have a stellar companion than not. Many of these stellar secondaries are too dim or too close to their primary stars for astronomers to detect them directly. Instead their presence is inferred from the orbital motion that they induce in the primary star by their gravitational pull.

The first binary orbits were derived more than 150 years ago, based on visual measurements of the slow changes of stellar positions on the plane of the sky. The stars' positions traced out elliptical orbits and, applying Kepler's laws of orbital motions, allowed an estimate to be made of their masses. Typical periods amounted to decades, because these periods were typical of stars near enough and widely enough separated to be visible, and also allowed most of an orbit to be observed before the observer died of old age!

Then, almost 100 years ago, with the application of spectroscopy to the measurement of Doppler shifts for stars, it became possible to determine stellar motions in the third dimension, along the line of sight. The Doppler technique proved to be much better suited for discovering short-period orbits, because the speed of the motion increases when the separation of the two stars in a binary is smaller, allowing detection of orbits too small to resolve visually.

In principle the techniques used for the detection of unseen planetary companions are the same as for stellar secondaries in binaries. The main difference is that planets are much less massive than stars, so the amount of motion induced in the parent star is correspondingly smaller. One can also detect somewhat larger objects which are not-quite stars.

When the mass of a proto-star is smaller than about 7% or 8% of that of the Sun, it can't reach the central pressures and temperatures needed to fuse hydrogen in its core, and it is doomed to cool slowly and to fade into obscurity. Substellar objects larger than planets that form the same way that stars form, by the gravitational collapse of interstellar clouds, are usually called brown dwarfs.

In contrast, planets are thought to form by a very different mechanism, by the accumulation of gas and dust in a flat circumstellar disk. This scenario implies that planets must have much smaller masses than their parent stars, because the circumstellar disks are made of the debris left over from the formation of the star, and there is less material to work with.

Circumstellar disks turn out to be a common phenomenon among the youngest stars, as evidenced by the frequent occurence of infrared luminosities beyond that of more mature stars of the same class observed for young proto-stars in star-formation regions (see Fig. 1). The cold dust in the circumstellar disk absorbs radiation from the central proto-star in the visible. This raises the temperature of the dust enough for it to glow faintly at long wavelengths, where the star itself is dim because it is compact and has much less emitting surface than the dust disk. By the time young stars reach an age of 10 million years, they are rarely observed to have infrared excesses anymore, which means that their disks have dissipated. It is tempting to speculate that the disk material has been used up in the process of planet building, although there is little direct evidence of this process in action.

The smallest mass that a brown dwarf can have is not well determined from the theory of star formation, nor is the largest mass that a planet can have well constrained by the theory of accretion of objects in a circumstellar disk. It may be that the two different mechanisms produce masses that overlap, so that two objects could have the same mass, yet one might be called a brown dwarf and the other a planet. Alternatively, there might be a gap in the mass between the two mechanisms, leading to a "brown dwarf desert" as has been advocated by some astronomers. Presumably this ambiguity will get resolved after astronomers have discovered enough objects in the transition region between planets and brown dwarfs so that the general characteristics of the two populations can be deduced (see Fig. 2). Astronomers often quote the masses for planets and brown dwarfs in terms of the mass of Jupiter, which happens to be, rather conveniently, a thousand times smaller than the mass of the sun. There is at present no consensus on the mass corresponding to the transition region between planets and brown dwarfs, but my guess is that this transition occurs somewhere around 10 to 30 Jupiter masses (1/100th to 3/100ths the mass of the Sun).

ASTROMETRY

Astrometry is the branch of astronomy dedicated to the measurement of stellar positions and their change with time (here the term stellar position really means the precise direction that a star appears in the sky, specified by two angles). Astrometrists have something of a reputation for adopting a painstaking approach to their work, which is seen as tedious by many, and no wonder, because changes to stellar positions are for the most part extremely small and slow, and thus are difficult to measure and generally require years of observing for reliable and definitive results.

One of the time-honored applications of astrometry has been the study of binary stars and the derivation of binary orbits, as mentioned above. This tradition dates back to the pioneering work of William Herschel who discovered (to his surprise) that some of the double stars he was observing followed slow curved paths around each other. Herschel had assumed that his doubles must be the result of accidental alignments between two unrelated stars, the fainter ones likely being farther away. The first orbital solution for a binary star was published in 1828, for the system Xi Ursae Majoris, where the two visible stars take 60 years to complete one revolution. (Each of the visible stars in Xi UMa is itself a close binary, one with a period of two years and the other with a period of four days, but that is another story.)

For many binaries the separation between the two stars is too small to be resolved with the telescope being used, and/or the secondary is so

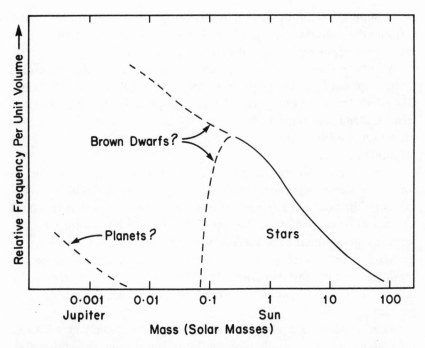

Figure 2. The relative populations per cubic light year of stars, planets, and brown dwarfs. Solid lines are based on observation, while dashed lines represent extrapolations. The brown dwarf population might be numerous (rising curve) or rare (falling curve). *(Diagram supplied by Bruce Campbell.)*

faint that it is lost in the glare of the primary. All is not lost in such cases. Astrometrists can still learn a lot about the orbit, even when they can only measure the motion of a single stellar image. Astrometric searches for planetary companions are in fact an extreme example of the case where the secondary is unseen, with the additional difficulty that the mass of the planetary companion is much smaller than a star, and the motion that it induces in its parent star is correspondingly much smaller.

Astrometrists realized long ago that they might detect evidence for extrasolar planets if they could achieve the demanding level of astrometric precision required, and planet searches were mounted at several observatories during the 1930s to the 1960s. The instrument of choice was a long focal-length refractor using photographic plates. Small planets in short-period orbits, like Earth or Venus, were well beyond the detection limits for these telescopes. The best hope was to look for giant planets in wide-swinging orbits, similar to Jupiter. There would be no hope of overnight success in this game. Nevertheless, a few brave astrometrists bought into the game, despite the knowledge that success might require the dedication of their entire careers.

A famous example of an astrometrist whose search for extrasolar planets spanned his entire professional career is Peter van de Kamp. One of his favorite targets with the 61-cm Sproul Refractor at Swarthmore College was Barnard's star, a very nearby M dwarf that is too faint to be visible to the naked eye because it has such a low intrinsic brightness.

The apparent faintness of Barnard's star was actually an advantage for van de Kamp, because he could take longer exposures without overexposing the image of Barnard's star itself. This meant that there would be enough images of faint background stars on his photographs to serve as good references for his measurements of the positions of Barnard's star. With photographic astrometry it is hard to work on the brightest nearby stars because of the lack of enough reference-star images on the photographs with which to form a background "grid" of positions.

Another advantage of Barnard's star was its relatively small mass, only about one quarter that of the Sun. This meant that the reflex motions induced by a Jupiter-sized planet orbiting Barnard's star would be four times larger than for a star like the Sun.

Van de Kamp obtained more than 20,000 exposures of Barnard's star over a span of almost 40 years. In a preliminary report on his work in 1963 he announced the detection of an astrometric wobble in the position of Barnard's star corresponding to a Jupiter-sized object orbiting the star with a period of 24 years. Then, 12 years later, towards the end of his career, he found it necessary to revise this conclusion and to add a second planet with a period of 12 years. Apparently the wobble had not followed the pattern expected for just a single planetary companion over the intervening years, and the deviations could be accommodated only by introducing a second planet into the model.

Other astrometrists have tried to confirm the astrometric wobble reported for Barnard's star by van de Kamp, but without success. A close inspection of van de Kamp's results reveals that the wobbles he reported are very close to the limit of what he could hope to detect under ideal conditions. It appears that the planetary signatures that he saw in his data were not due to planets after all, but to subtle systematic trends left over in his reduced positions (nobody knows exactly what the trends came from). It was a noble effort, but one doomed to failure by the limitations of the available technology.

Van de Kamp was not alone in his failure. In my opinion there is not yet a single convincing published example of an extrasolar planet detection based on astrometry. But, astrometry from space holds great promise for the future, and I expect space astrometry missions to have an enormous impact on our understanding of extrasolar planets.

RADIAL VELOCITIES AND DOPPLER SHIFTS

The application of photography to stellar spectroscopy was pioneered more than 100 years ago. That new technology made it possible for astronomers to start mass-producing accurate stellar radial velocities (the component of the star's motion along the line of sight) by measuring the Doppler shifts on stellar spectrograms. Many stars proved to have velocity variations that could be nicely explained as the result of orbital motion. Such stars are called spectroscopic binaries.

The study of spectroscopic binaries has a long and rich history. For example, the Eighth Catalogue of Orbital Elements of Spectroscopic Binary Systems, published in 1989, has 1469 entries, including an orbital solution for the fainter component of the famous visual binary Xi UMa that was mentioned earlier. That orbit was based on 47 spectrograms obtained with the Mills spectrographs at the Lick Observatory over the period 1902 to 1929, and was first published in 1931 by Louis Berman. The remarkable thing about the orbit is not the short 4-day period, but rather the small velocity amplitude of 5 km/s, which implies that the mass of the unseen companion could be as small as 35 Jupiter masses, if the orbit happens to be viewed edge-on. As far as I am aware, this is the first published example of a spectroscopic orbit where the minimum mass of the companion is well below the substellar limit and therefore might be a brown dwarf.

Orbital solutions for spectroscopic binaries have an unfortunate ambiguity: They can not specify the inclination of the plane of the orbit to the line of sight, and thus they can only give a minimum mass for the companion. If the orbit happens to be viewed at some inclination other than edge-on, then the actual mass of the companion must be larger than the minimum value.

There is a second ambiguity that applies to both spectroscopic and astrometric binaries for the case where the companion is too faint to be detected, which obviously includes planetary companions. The problem is that the mass of the primary star can not be determined from the orbit alone, yet the mass of the companion depends on the mass of the primary. Thus the mass of the primary star must be estimated from other information, such as its spectral type, and subtracted from the total mass estimated from the orbit, before the (minimum) mass of the companion can be calculated.

In 1980 a Canadian team led by Gordon Walker and Bruce Campbell undertook a pioneering effort to search for giant planets orbiting nearby stars. For 12 years they monitored the velocities of 21 bright stars with the spectrograph of the Canada-France-Hawaii 3.6-m telescope on Maun Kea. To achieve long-term stability in their velocity system, they developed an innovative technique for calibrating the wavelengths of their stellar spectra with a hydrogen-fluoride gas absorption cell. When they began their program the Canadian team fully expected to discover several giant planets. At the end of the project they concluded that not one of their solar-type targets showed any reflex motion that could be attributed to a substellar companion, at least for orbital periods shorter than 15 years and companion masses larger than 1 to 3 Jupiter masses.

The Canadians had sufficient velocity precision to detect any of the low-mass radial-velocity planet candidates reported over the past few years, but apparently by bad luck none of their chosen targets are orbited by such companions. Nevertheless, this effort was successful in demonstrating that the velocities of solar-type dwarf stars could be monitored to detect reflex orbital motions as small as the 12 m/s induced in the solar spectrum by Jupiter over its 12-year period.

THE DISCOVERY OF EXTRASOLAR PLANETS

The first discovery of a Jupiter-sized planet orbiting another solar-type star, 51 Pegasi, came in 1995 from the Swiss team of Michel Mayor and Didier Queloz. They had recognized that substellar companions were proving to be rare, and had set out to survey a larger sample of 142 solar-type stars with the new Elodie spectrometer on the 1.93-m reflector at the Haute Provence Observatory in France. The orbit has a period of only 4 days, and therfore could be confirmed almost immediately by a team led by Geoff Marcy and Paul Butler using the Hamilton spectrograph at the Lick Observatory. The Lick team had been monitoring 107 solar-type stars for 8 years and were poised to make their own discoveries. With the 51 Peg success to inspire them, they were soon able to announce in quick succession five more planet candidates: 70 Virginis, 47 Ursae Majoris, 55 Cancri, tau Bootis, and upsilon Andromedae.

Two of the new Lick planets, companions to tau Boo and upsilon Andromedae, shared with 51 Peg the completely unexpected characteristic of an extremely short period of 3 or 4 days, corresponding to orbits 20 times smaller than that of the earth. Initial concerns that such planets could not survive the high temperatures so close to their parent stars were soon allayed. The gravity of the planets would be plenty strong enough to retain their outer layers despite the intense heat.

Then the burning question became, how do you make giant planets in such tight orbits? Although formation of the planets in situ by gravitational collapse could not be ruled out, a preferred explanation soon emerged. These planets were probably formed at a much larger distance from their parent star, in a region where the temperatures were cool enough for ices to freeze out, with the accretion of a planetary core followed by the gravitational accumulation of vast quantities of gas onto the core to build up the total mass. Then the planet must have migrated inwards due to drag in the still-dense circumstellar disk. The trick was to stop this migration before the planet spiraled all the way into the parent star, and to park the planet in an orbit with a period of about 4 days as observed. The parking process is not yet properly understood.

For orbits so close to the parent star, the tidal forces raised on the planet would be enormous. This would quickly synchronize the axial rotation of the planet with the orbital period, just like the Earth has done to the Moon, so that the same side of the planet would always face the parent star. It would also circularize the orbit, effectively erasing any chance of deducing something about the formation of the planet from the characteristics of the orbit that we observe now.

The first two planet candidates with eccentric orbits, HD 114762 and 70 Vir, seemed to be at odds with the traditional view that planets form by accretion of objects in a flat circumstellar disk. All the gas and dust and planetesimals in the disk should be in nearly circular orbits, and sticking a lot of this material together to make a giant planet should lead naturally to a circular orbit. It was proposed that one way to explain the eccentric orbits observed for HD 114762 and 70 Vir would be to suppose that the companions were brown dwarfs despite their minimum masses of 9 and 7 Jupiter masses, respectively. Then their eccentric orbits would be the natural result of the infall associated with their formation by gravitational collapse. However, this does not appear to be the right explanation. As additional planets have been

TABLE 1

MASSES AND ORBITAL DATA OF EXTRASOLAR PLANETS						
STAR NAME	DIST(LY)	SP TYP	MIN MASS	ORB SIZE	ECCENT	PERIOD
	(OF STAR)	(STAR)	(x JUP)	(AU)	(0=CIRC)	(days)
DETECTED USING HIGH RESOLUTION OPTICAL SPECTROSCOPY						
HD 187123	156	G5	0.52	0.04	0	3.1
TAU BOOTIS	50	F7V	3.64	0.04	0	3.3
HD 75289	94	G0V	0.42	0.05	0	3.5
51 PEGASI	50	G2-3V	0.44	0.05	0.01	4.2
UPSILON ANDROMEDAE(b)	54	F8V	0.69	0.06	0.04	4.6
UPSILON ANDROMEDAE(c)	SAME	SAME	2	0.74	0.23	241.3
UPSILON ANDROMEDAE(d)	SAME	SAME	4.1	2.2	0.36	1280.6
HD 217107	120	G8IV	1.3	0.07	0.14	7.1
RHO 1 55 CANCRI (b)	45	G8V	0.85	0.12	0.03	14.7
RHO 1 55 CANCRI (c)	SAME	SAME	3.2	6-7	?	7000?
GLIESE 86	35	?BINARY	3.6	0.11	0.04	15.8
HD 195019	65	G3IV-V	3.4	0.14	0.03	18.3
RHO CORONA BOREALIS	55	G0V	1.1	0.23	0	39.6
HD 168443	108	G5	5	0.28	0.54	58
GLIESE 876	15	M4V	1.9	0.21	0.37	60.9
HD 114762*	94	F9V	9.7	0.39	0.33	84
70 VIRGINIS	59	G4V	7.4	0.43	0.4	116.7
HD 210277	68	G0	1.36	1.15	0.45	437
16 CYGNUS B	85	G2.5V	1.74	1.7	0.65	802.8
47 URSA MAJORIS	46	G0V	2.42	2.1	0.03	1093
14 HERCULIS	60	K0V	3	2.5	0.35	2000
LALANDE 21185 (c)	8.2	M2	0.9	2.5	0	1900
LALANDE 21185 (b)	SAME	SAME	1.6	10	0	10,000?
IOTA HOROLOGII	?	G0V	2	0.93	0.16	312
DETECTED ON AN OPTICAL TV IMAGE						
TMR 1 (MAY BE A BROWN DWARF)			600-1000	1500 (MIN.)	?	?
PLANETS ORBITING PULSARS, DETECTED BY RADIO EMISSION						
PSR1257+12	1600	PULSAR	2 @M (EARTH) 1@M(MOON)			
PSR1620-26	20,000	PULSAR/WHITE DWARF		1 PLANET		
PSR 0329+54		PULSAR	1@ 2M (EARTH)			16.9
KEY: SP TYP=THE STAR'S SPECTRAL TYPE (THE SUN IS A G2V ON THIS SCALE); MIN MASS=MINI-MUM PLANET MASS IN JUPITERS (ACTUAL MASS IS UNCERTAIN BECAUSE ORBIT TILT IS UNKNOWN); ORB SIZ=HALF THE MAIN ORBIT AXIS, IN EARTH ORBIT RADII (AU); ECCEN=ORBIT ECCENTRICITY WHERE 0=CIRCULAR AND .6 IS VERY ELONGATED); PERIOD=ORBITAL PERIOD IN DAYS.						

Table 1. This table gives data for extrasolar planets and their parent stars as of 8/18/99. The entries are arranged by orbit size for the first planet found in each system (the periods follow the same order). The prevalance of hi-mass planets in small orbits is due to observational selection; they are easiest to detect. What is surprising is the number of cases of very elongated orbits. In our system comets follow such orbits, not planets. (*Source: Data from websites by Marcy et. al. and Willman.*)
*Discovered 1989, confirmed 1996.

discovered, many of their orbits have proven to be rather eccentric (see Table 1).

The observation that many of the "radial-velocity" planets have eccentric orbits has led to the idea that something besides drag may be involved in moving the planets from the cold regions further out where they were formed into the inner regions closer to their parent stars where we observe them. This alternative mechanism could be gravitational encounters between planets. In this scenario several planets at more or less the same distance from the parent star would be formed initially. Sooner or later there would be close encounters between planets, and one might be perturbed into an elongated orbit taking it into the inner regions of the system, while the other would be bounced into a more distant orbit, often getting ejected completely from the system. This mechansim explains nicely the two main characteristics for extrasolar planets that we have observed so far, that they have eccentric orbits and that they are found closer to their parent stars than expected.

A PULSAR PUZZLE

It is worth a brief aside to say that the first detected extrasolar planetary system was actually discovered by tiny fluctuations in the precisely periodic radio signals from a pulsar. A second case is now known. Since a pulsar is the stellar remnant left after a supernova explosion blows off 70% of its mass, an event of extreme violence, it is an even greater puzzle that planets exist in these cases than for the normal cases we have been discussing. The theoretical work done so far suggests that perhaps they formed out of the gas cloud blown off in the event. But this is not a settled issue.

PATTERNS IN PLANETARY CHARACTERISTICS

If the orbits of planets change and evolve with time in other star systems (contrary to our understanding of our own), then we can not use the characteristics of the orbits that we observe now to infer how the planets might have formed originally. Instead we need to look for something that doesn't change with time. Such a parameter may be the mass of the planet, and indeed there are some preliminary suggestions that the distribution of companion masses (analogous to the distribution of human weights or heights) may allow us to distinguish brown dwarfs from planets. It is not easy to derive the distribution of companion masses, because the ambiguity about the orbit inclination angle rears its ugly head once again. The analysis proceeds by assuming that the distribution of inclination angles must be random, and it can only be applied to a sample that has been selected and observed according to well-defined rules. The frequency of companions drops as you move towards smaller masses. For some reason that we don't understand there are lots of low-mass stellar companions in binaries, but hardly any brown-dwarf companions. In the middle of the range there is a minimum, the so-called brown-dwarf desert. Then, as you move further towards companions with masses as small as Jupiter, the frequency of companions starts to rise again. The shape of the distribution of companion masses seems to be telling us that we are looking at two different populations, things that form like planets on the small end, and things that form like stars on the high end. But this interpretation is very preliminary because the numbers of objects involved in the analysis are small.

It was fascinating to see that patterns were beginning to emerge in the characteristics of the population of newly-discovered "radial-velocity" planets, but until recently something crucial was missing. We live in a planetary system, but all the discoveries were of single planetary companions, one per star. What we really want to know is whether there are other systems of planets, and whether any of them look at all like our own. A giant step towards understanding the answer to this question was taken in 1999, with the announcement of orbital solutions for two additional planets in the upsilon Andromeda system. The two new planets are progressively more massive as one moves out from the parent star, and the orbits are progressively more eccentric. This configuration doesn't look at all like our solar system! Nevertheless, there is no doubt that the additional orbits are real, because they were discovered independently by two different teams using two independent data sets; the Marcy and Butler group on the one hand, and a team at the Harvard-Smithsonian Center for Astrophysics led by Robert Noyes on the other hand. Some of the other radial-velocity systems are also showing deviations that will require additional planets, so we can expect our understanding of planetary systems to improve as the orbits for more of them get solved in detail.

Although several of the planets discovered so far appear to have masses as small as Jupiter, all of them are in much smaller orbits with shorter periods. The detection of a real Jupiter, one with an orbital period of at least 10 years, is just at the edge of what we can now achieve. For planets with longer periods the amplitude of the orbital velocity is smaller, and we barely have the precision needed to detect an orbit with Jupiter's orbital velocity amplitude of only 12m/s. Indeed, all the orbits published so far have amplitudes larger than 50 m/s. In addition, the observations must be sustained over more than one cycle to be sure that the motion is periodic. Thus, it may be some time before we have convincing evidence for a solar system like our own, with a Jupiter patrolling the icy outer regions, warding off intruding asteroids and comets which might come cruising for a bruising into the inner solar system. (See Table 1.)

DIRECT DETECTION

At visible wavelengths Jupiter is a billion times fainter than the Sun. If Jupiter were all by itself, completely isolated from any star, we could detect it with existing technology out to a distance of more than 100 light years. Taking a picture of a planet like Jupiter in orbit around a star like the Sun is a completely different matter because of the overwhelming glare of the star. Such a detection is beyond the capability of the Hubble Space Telescope, even after it gets upgraded with the Advanced Coronographic Camera (which is designed to block the glare of a bright central object).

Moving from visible wavelengths into the infrared can change the situation a lot, because planets like Jupiter are hot enough to glow by their own thermal radiation, and at long wavelengths the contrast between the star and the planet can improve by as much as a factor of 10,000. Of course, it also helps if the companion is farther away from the glare of its parent star.

Although nobody has managed to get a convincing picture of an extrasolar planet yet, there is the wonderful example of the brown dwarf companion to Gliese 229, which itself is a nearby cool M dwarf star. This object was found by Ben Oppenheimer and his collaborators as part of a search of more than 200 nearby stars for substellar companions. Although the brown dwarf Gliese 229 B is very faint, it is well enough separated from the parent star (by 7 arc seconds) that it has been possible to obtain remarkably good spectra. At infrared wavelengths the spectrum shows strong absorption bands due to molecules like water and methane, very reminiscent of the bands seen in the spectrum of Jupiter. Evidence of methane-absorption bands, seen either directly in detailed spectra or indirectly in a comparison of an object's infrared to its red color bands, proves that the object is much too cool to be a star, with a temperature a bit below 1000 K.

PHOTOMETRIC TECHNIQUES

When a planet like the Earth transits in front of the Sun, it covers a tiny fraction of the solar surface. For a few hours a distant observer would see the light of the Sun drop by less than 1 part in 10,000. Changes in light this small are tough to measure, but not impossible, and there are two space missions, Kepler and Corot, that propose to look for such transits by carefully observing large samples of stars. The reason that large samples are needed is that transits can only be detected if the orbital plane of the transiting planet is almost exactly aligned with the observer. The chances of perfect alignment and of watching at the time of transit are together rather small.

With the discovery of giant planets in short-period orbits like the companion of 51 Peg, the prospects for observing transits improved dramatically. The dip in the light would be much deeper, something like 1%, and the chances for a transit would be much higher because of the small orbits. This motivated several teams to undertake searches for transits using ground-based telescopes. Although candidate transit events have now been shown at conferences, none have been yet been confirmed as planet transits; most have proven to be eclipsing binaries with grazing eclipses. Nevertheless, this technique looks very promising, and it offers the important advantage that the inclination would be known immediately for any spectroscopic orbit that might be derived for a transiting planet.

Another promising photometric technique is looking for microlensing. When a much smaller object crosses the line of sight to a distant star, Its gravitational lensing effect produces a short-term brightening. The duration of the event depends on the mass of the lensing object and on its speed across the line of sight. For an intervening star a typical duration is measured in days. For a planet the duration is much shorter. The trick is to catch a stellar lensing event just as it is beginning, and to monitor it continuously to see if there is a spike due to a planet orbiting the star. Networks of telescopes have been organized to carry out such monitoring, and it is only a matter of time before they will catch a microlensing event due to a planet.

SPACE ASTROMETRY

Traditional photographic astrometry using ground-based telescopes struggled to achieve an astrometric accuracy of a few thousandths of an arc second. Even the best modern ground-based techniques barely reach one milli-arc-second. In contrast to this, there are space missions now under intense study that expect to do almost 1000 times better! When these missions fly they will revolutionize the study of extrasolar planets. They will easily detect giant planets orbiting stars as far away as the star-forming regions in Orion and Taurus, and there is even some hope that they will be able to pick up Earth-like planets orbiting the nearest stars.

NULLING INTERFEROMETRY

One of NASA's long-range goals is not just to find Earth-like planets, but then to get their spectra to see if there is any evidence of absorption bands due to molecules indicating life. The first step is to suppress the glare of the parent star by a factor of about a million, so that the light of the planet can be isolated and detected. The present plan is to do this with a special array of telescopes connected together optically and electronically carefully tuned to null out the light of the central star using destructive interference of the light waves.

Then the next step is to measure the spectrum of the remaining light and look for evidence of life. The best region of the spectrum appears to be the infrared, where molecules such as water, methane, and ozone produce absorption bands. The ozone in the Earth's upper atmosphere comes ultimately from plant life, which uses photosynthesis to turn carbon dioxide and water into oxygen and food. The detection of bands in the spectrum of an extrasolar planet, if it revealed such molecules, would certainly provide a strong suggestion that life was involved there too. However, the argument is not foolproof, because there are other, inorganic processes that can liberate oxygen in a planetary atmosphere under just the right conditions, and the detection of ozone bands would need to be supported by evidence of other life-related molecules such as methane.

The notion of measuring the spectrum of an extrasolar Earth may sound mind-boggling, but in fact it doesn't appear to violate any laws of physics. The laws of economics may be another matter. It seems relatively easy to dream up marvelous ways to use our modern technology to look for planets and life elsewhere. Funding these ideas is the real challenge.

POSTSCRIPT TO LATHAM

By

WILLIAM R. ALSCHULER

The news about the discovery of extrasolar planets is so hot the pages that report it are smoking. In just the few months since this chapter was first set to print, eight new entries will need to be added to Table 1 (Masses and Orbital Data of Extrasolar Planets). These include a group of six planets discovered in October and November of 1999 by the team of Vogt, Marcy, Latham, Butler et al. One of these new planets orbits the star HD 209458, a solar-type star about 150 light years away. It orbits its star in about three and one half days. From the size and shape of its velocity curve it was found to have a circular orbit only four and a half million miles from its star, and a mass six-tenths that of Jupiter.

What makes this particular discovery extremely exciting is that it allowed a second and so far unique step to be taken, which provides new information about the planet. Based again on the shape of the velocity curve, it seemed likely that the planet's orbital plane is in the line of sight to Earth, and therefore the planet should transit—or cross in front of the disk of its star—once every orbit, just as Mercury and Venus on occasion transit across our Sun. It was estimated that the planet would reduce the star's light by about 1% as it passed in front of it. Latham furnished the orbital parameters and the transit prediction to Greg Henry on November 5th. On November 7th Henry used a telescope at Patagonia Mountain in Arizona, and at the predicted time the light from the star diminished in a steady fashion, just as expected, to a maximum dip of 1.7%, in good agreement with the estimate. Almost immediately after this was announced, another group independently confirmed that it had observed two other transits of the planet across star HD 209458 in September.

The rate of the brightness decrease, coupled with the measured orbital speed, allowed the teams to estimate that the planet, with a mass of .63 Jupiters, has a radius of 1.6 times Jupiter's radius. This means its density is .2 grams per cubic centimeter, confirming further that it is a gas giant like Jupiter. This swelling beyond the size of Jupiter was in agreement with the general prediction that any gas giant in a small orbit would be expanded beyond normal size by the intense heat of its star.

While you cannot say that we have seen this planet directly by its own light, we have seen its shadow. Thus it is a nonluminous object of defined size, and this serves to confirm that this candidate really is a planet, and by extension to offer strong support for the idea that all the other recent discoveries of planet candidates based on spectroscopy are, indeed, actual planets.

We can expect new planets to be found around other stars as the specroscopic surveys cover more and more of the hundreds of target stars on the survey lists. Furthermore, as time goes on perhaps some of the already surveyed stars will reveal large planets in larger orbits, because these have longer periods that can only be detected with longer runs of data.

As if the above were not enough, advances in all the other techniques described in Chapter Three seem to be arriving faster than expected. For example, there is a rumor that a group in Europe will shortly announce that it has successfully separated the spectrum of an extrasolar planet from the light of its parent star, and thus can make preliminary specific remarks about its composition. This result is said to be from ground-based telescopic observation. Also, a simplified design for a nulling interferometer has been demonstrated to work in a lab setup, and a working version is in design. With it there is every reason to expect that the light of a star can be blocked effectively and thus reveal the light of its planets as separate little dots. This is a truly exciting time in the search for other solar systems . . . and for indications of extrasolar life itself.

THE DRAKE EQUATION: A REAPPRAISAL

By

FRANK D. DRAKE

It has been thirty-five years since I first wrote the formula that has come to be known as the Drake Equation. The motivation was not to enlighten the world, but rather to organize rationally the program for the first scientific meeting ever, as far as I know, on the subject of extraterrestrial intelligent life. I was the lone organizer for that meeting, which would be attended by almost everyone in the world active in the subject—all twelve of them. Looking back over all those years, I think the equation has survived the test of time quite well, a rarity in science, and has become the basis of major searches for life now underway.

The survival of the equation is due, I think, to the fact it was constructed in the best tradition of science: The preferred explanation of a phenomenon is the simplest explanation. Don't get "clever" until the facts make you do so. Our knowledge then and now of the evolution of stars, planets, the molecules of life, and of systems of living things said that our star, its planets, and life on Earth, in all their complexity, are the result of completely normal processes that occur readily in this Universe. No freak events are required. Thus the basic premise behind the equation is that what happened here will happen with a large fraction of the stars as they are created, one after another, in the Milky Way Galaxy and other galaxies. People unfamiliar with the accepted pictures of cosmic and biological evolution might think the equation is highly speculative; in fact, it is just the opposite, since the phenomena it assumes to take place in the Universe are only those we are sure have taken place at least once.

There is actually an exception in the equation to that last statement, and one that causes the result to be very conservative and to bend over backward not to overestimate the abundance of detectable civilizations in the Universe. This is the inclusion of the factor L, the mean longevity of civilizations in a detectable state. We actually do not know that there is a limitation to this longevity; only the study of other civilizations will reveal the truth. However, the assumption of a limited longevity introduces into the equation our one area of almost total ignorance in such a way that it minimizes our estimates of the numbers of civilizations we might detect. In the end, then, the equation is carefully not speculative. Those who use it to contemplate life in the Universe, or to plan searches, are going to great lengths to be nonspeculative fuddy-duddies.

Thirty-five years ago the typical number of technological civilizations given by the equation for the Milky Way was roughly ten thousand years. This came from estimates based on observations and theory, in which all the factors in the equation but the last multiplied out to a value of about one, and we guessed that L was of the order of ten thousand. The observational evidence providing actual values for the factors in the equation has greatly improved over the years, but the end result has not changed significantly. There have been a multitude of laboratory experiments tracing the possible chemical pathways by which life might develop. We have seen in the interstellar clouds, in the comets, and in the meteorites the molecules of life or their chemical precursors, confirming that the chemistry of life is ubiquitous, and, quite separately, we have seen that the march toward life on Earth might have started even before our planet was formed. Similarly, in the fossil record we have seen evidence that there is more than one path to an intelligence species. Recent fossil evidence shows that there were a few relatively large-brained dinosaurs, which were well along the path to intelligent status; it is only through chance that we are the first on Earth.

In the same vein, our exploration of the planets has shown that there is a bewildering variety of planets and satellites just in our own system; for example, in the Jovian system we have Europa, with its surface of ice covering, probably, a complicated ocean, and right next to it the bone-dry Io, rich with active volcanos of sulphur. In recent times there has been a wealth of new information indicating that a large fraction of other stars has planetary systems. The underlying truth behind these discoveries, and others, such as that of the pulsars and quasars, is not surprising: In the Universe, anything that can happen will happen. And often. This is perhaps the Murphy's Law of the

Universe. The existence of life, and intelligent, technology-exploiting life, in large quantities, should not be a surprise.

Over all these years we have surmised that the most promising way to search was with radio telescopes though other methods are now in development. It is at wavelengths of a few centimeters that the Universe is darkest and quietest; we know this well, and so will the others. It is at such wavelengths that we can detect the faintest signals with the least expenditure of resources, and also where another civilization can communicate with us at least cost, if it so desires. Until recently, nevertheless, it was hard for us to search, because we didn't have the ability to listen to many frequency channels at once. Modern computer technology has changed all that, and now we can listen to millions of channels simultaneously.

The equation tells us that, with that capability, it is worth searching. There is a real chance that with realistic resources, and in an acceptable time, we will find one of those other civilizations. Widely, we are exploiting this opportunity through the several searches now planned or underway. We have entered the age of the greatest of all explorations, the search for intellect throughout the Universe.

MYSTERY OF
THE GREAT SILENCE

By

DAVID BRIN

I first heard the subject of extraterrestrial intelligence brought up at a scientific seminar in 1968, when a speaker suggested that pulsars—then newly discovered—might be beacons of an advanced civilization. He was only partly serious, but it was soon clear that most of those with tenure didn't like this kind of talk at all. Only a few years later, however, some of those who were angriest in 1968 applauded when Carl Sagan unveiled at Caltech a gold "message" plaque to be placed upon Pioneer 10, the first human artifact that would leave the solar system.

Soon scientists were discussing not whether extraterrestrial intelligences exist, but how to go about listening for signals from our nearest neighbors, adapting radio telescopes for the search and asking, "Is anyone out there?"

But the voices of the critics never really went away. For no sooner had it become legitimate to inquire, "Where are they?" than new questions were raised asking, "Why aren't they here already?"

But let's not get ahead of ourselves. To early xenologists it was dangerous enough talking about alien life forms without risking one's scientific reputation talking about interstellar travel. Thus, modern scientific xenology first dealt with the possibility of life springing up in isolation among the stars—yielding islands of sentience separated by vast distances and for all time.

Early students of this new science, no matter how daring, were faced with one major limitation: a near total lack of data. Still, certain scientific discoveries, combined with a useful philosophical tool, gave researchers the courage to make crude estimates.

First, it was found almost ridiculously easy to make amino acids and other precursors to living matter from abundant molecules such as methane, ammonia, and cyanogen. Harold Urey and Stanley Miller subjected a solution of these substances to electrical discharge and ultraviolet radiation and got an organic "soup" in short order. Furthermore, during the last two decades, radio astronomers have discovered great clouds of complex molecules drifting in space: ethylene, formaldehyde, and ethyl alcohol among them.

It's clear the raw materials for life are out there. But what about the right environments? For simplicity, we have to assume it's most likely for complex life to grow and evolve where we did, on planets orbiting stable stars. Rings of dust have been discovered circling nearby stars Vega and Beta Pictoris, and the host of newly discovered extrasolar planets leads many astronomers to believe stars like our Sun are naturally born with companions.

Finally, the philosophical tool mentioned earlier, which caps the legitimacy of xenology, is called the cosmological principle, or the "assumption of mediocrity."

Since Copernicus, astronomy has given us a series of lessons in humility, all leading to the conclusion that there is nothing special about where and when we are. First, the Earth was displaced from the center of the solar system, then the Sun became a nondescript traveler in orbit about the rim of the Galaxy. Finally, the Galaxy became merely one island universe among billions, and the Universe seems to have no "middle" at all.

The cosmological principle tells us we should avoid the temptation to think that there's anything unique about the Earth in space, time, or situation. Therefore, what has happened here might happen elsewhere, perhaps many times.

THE DRAKE EQUATION

The most popular way to guess at the possible distribution of technological species was invented by former Cornell and U.C. Santa Cruz Professor Frank Drake when he was at the Arecibo National Radio Observatory. It remains a widely accepted tool for xenological speculation.

Let N equal the current number of technological (radio broadcasting) civilizations in the Galaxy. Then

$$N = R. \, f_p \, n_e \, f_l \, f_i \, f_c \, L$$

There are reasons to believe that it is short about three factors. But we'll stay with this version for a while. During the 1960s, with plenty of up-and-down leeway in every parameter, Carl Sagan and others estimated that.

$$N = 0.01 \, L$$

This meant the average life span, L, of technological races determines the number present in the Galaxy at any time. If self-destruction is the common fate of "civilized" species, there might be no more than a handful in the Milky Way at a given moment. But if a reasonable fraction live long, the Galaxy might teem with intelligent life.

If the planets of a million stars held sophont races, then about one thousandth of a percent of eligible stars in the Galaxy would be orbited by thinking beings. The average distance separating these islands would be several hundred light-years—a gap easily crossed by radio waves.

This was the state of affairs in the early 1970s. The accepted model depicted isolated motes of intelligence separated by sterile tracts of space. Frank Drake and his associates began the search by looking at the nearest candidates. But they found only star noise coming from Epsilon Eridani and Tau Ceti.

Undaunted, they and others expanded the search. Telescopes turned and scanned. The Russians joined in enthusiastically. They too reported only negative results. (In the former Soviet Union, extraterrestrial intelligence was not only considered possible, but required by Leninist dogma.)

Astronomers suggested that no advanced species would waste energy broadcasting over the entire radio spectrum. To conserve power and attain a high signal-to-noise ratio, they would modulate over a very narrow frequency band. Yet even the second and third generations of eavesdropping devices, tuned to seek in narrow, so-called water-window or water-hole bands, have come up with nothing so far. Though better instruments have been built, and some radio xenologists are promising improved searches, others have begun glumly proposing that no one is "out there" after all, at least not in our vicinity.

Why this new pessimism? We've only been at the search for less than twenty years, using spare time and borrowed equipment. According to most calculations using the Drake Equation, the average distance

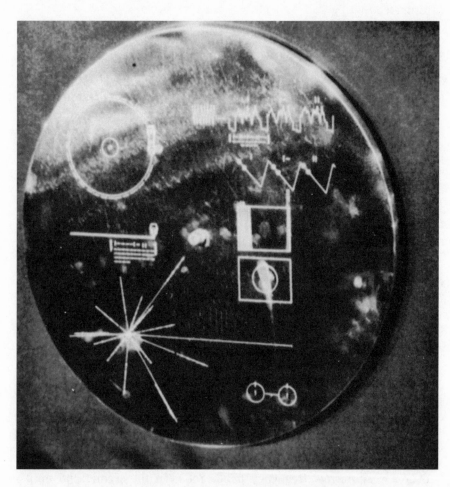

Figure 1. The Voyager record, attached to the spacecraft, contains coded information about us, our planet and our location in the Galaxy. *(Photo: Courtesy NASA.)*

between technological civilizations might be 600 light-years, or 200 parsecs. There are well over a million stars in a sphere that wide centered on the Sun. It would take a long time to search even the most likely of these, choosing only those radio bands we guess to be the best.

Two hundred parsecs makes "conversation" a little difficult. But a *Sesame Street* beacon would be as useful as ever, at that range. And just knowing extraterrestrials exist might profoundly boost poor Homo sap's sagging morale. Success, in the long run, seems assured to the persistent.

What has changed then? What has caused this spreading anxiety?

It's not the sort of thing one would expect to be a cause for pessimism. At first hearing, it sounds like very good news: starships are possible!

THE THIRD ERA OF XENOLOGY

Sometime in the mid-1970s, several prominent scientists challenged the conventional wisdom that intelligent life arises upon isolated islands, forever separated by the wide gulfs of interstellar space. Ron Bracewell, Robert Forward, and others demonstrated that it's possible, in theory, for spaceships to cross the emptiness between the stars. No "magic" is needed. It isn't necessary to repudiate Einstein. Whether by light sail or anti-matter rocket, humanity may be launching its own starships within a few centuries.

These starships will be nothing like the good old *Enterprise* of television. Limited to possibly a tenth the speed of light, they couldn't travel far by interstellar standards. But they might carry people, possibly several generations, in transit. The "slowboat" generation-ship of science fiction has been mathematically vindicated.

Why is this bad news? Because the possibility of starships presents us with a paradox that is difficult to overcome.

Consider: What would we do if we had starships? If history tells us anything, we would look around for nice real estate and start colonizing. In fact, we wouldn't even need to find planets; stable stars with asteroid belts would do. Professor Gerard O'Neil argues convincingly that cities in space may need little more than raw materials and solar power.

Once the new settlements had reached a high level of industry, they'd send out more colony ships of their own, to stellar systems even further out. Imagine a sphere of human settlement slowly expanding through space. Even limiting ship speed to a tenth of the speed of light, and allowing each colony plenty of time to industrialize, how long would it take for colonies to be planted three hundred light-years from Earth? Ten thousand years? Thirty thousand years?

Mankind has hardly changed in the last thirty thousand years. If we make a few social advances and avoid self-destruction, we should live long enough to fulfill the above scenario.

If *we* could do this, why shouldn't this sort of expansion occur with other sophont species? Isn't it likely many of those million high-tech races we spoke of earlier might also spread and colonize?

If many advanced life forms did this, the 200 light-year "average spacing" between races would be filled up in under 100,000 years!

In fact, all it might take is just one aggressive, colonizing species. Recent calculations by Eric Jones, of Los Alamos Laboratories, indicate a slowly expanding sphere of settled solar systems could fill the entire Galaxy within 60 million years. It's not unreasonable to imagine at least one out of a million civilized races living that long.

Finally, why haven't we met any wise old alien star robots? Frank Tipler, of Tulane University, calculates we should have by now. These robots, first prophesied by the great John Von Neumann, would go exploring like the Voyager and Viking space probes, but would also stop at each solar system to make copies of themselves to send onward. Tipler says just one such self-copying probe could become a horde, with one at every star in the Galaxy in under 3 million years. Such "Von Neumann machines" should have arrived long ago, and would have been waiting ages for Earth to evolve someone smart enough to talk to.

So we are faced with a new question—why do we see no signs that Earth has been colonized in the last 60 million years? And it's even more curious that we haven't seen signs of civilization near neighboring stars. Why have we picked up no radio signals when the stars should be humming with information and commerce?

Where is everybody? Does this really mean we're alone?

Debate over this issue has come as a shock to believers in SETI. Just when they seemed to have won acceptance, suddenly they had to contend with jokes that xenobiology was "the only scientific field without a subject matter."

These questions mark the traumatic awakening of xenology as an adult science. It marks the end of a short period of innocence. The dust has not yet settled, but one thing is clear: Some of our assumptions are wrong. The Universe might turn out to be considerably more complicated than the optimistic scientists of the late 1960s first thought.

THE GREAT SILENCE

We see no evidence for ancient alien cities in Earth's crust. Venus, Mars, and the asteroids appear to be untouched.

Most significantly, Earth, until less than a billion years ago, was populated for eons by only primitive prokaryotic bacteria, teeming in the oceans, with no life on land at all. A visiting starship need not have landed colonists. All they'd have to do is be careless with their garbage, or latrine, and the history of Earth would have been totally different; sophisticated alien parasites would have overwhelmed our primitive ancestors. Since this didn't happen, it seems unlikely aliens landed here during that time. (For a different view on the potential for damage by alien trash, see the articles by Clement; Benford.)

It certainly looks as though we've been alone for ages.

The quandary of the Great Silence has given the infant field of xenology its first traumatic struggle, between those seeking optimistic excuses for the apparent absence of sentient neighbors and those who enthusiastically accept the silence as evidence for humanity's isolation in an open frontier.

Eric Jones and Frank Tipler, in particular, think the apparent absence of ETIS (Extraterrestrial Intelligent Species) simply means this part of the Galaxy is uninhabited. Their "uniqueness hypothesis" implies that some or all of the key factors in the Drake Equation are really very small. For instance, some contend that intelligence such as ours may be an evolutionary fluke.

Then there is Michael Hart's contention that, though planets may be prevalent, habitable planets like Earth are rare. Alternatively, John Ball dredged up the science-fictional idea that Earth is a "zoo," and extraterrestrials are already here, observing us. (This implies we should add to the Drake Equation a factor to account for ET's *purposely* avoiding contact!)

Contact optimists, such as William Newman of Princeton and Carl Sagan of Cornell, have tried to make excuses for the extraterrestrials, suggesting truly advanced cultures would practice zero population growth. The rate of "galaxy-filling" calculated under their conservative assumptions is slow enough to suggest the nearest space-faring race might not have reached us yet.

Or our assumptions for f_l (the fraction of planets on which life originates) might be too high. Although the precursors of life—sugars, amino acids, nucleotides—seem likely to be common, it's possible the next steps might be much harder, requiring some rare catalyst to set off the process.

These and many other ideas have been presented to explain why aliens aren't here. (A complete catalog will be given later in this article.) All the hypotheses offered so far have problems, though. Some seem to contradict the best knowledge we have. Others, like the "zoo" theory, are untestable.

Let's consider one hypothesis xenological speculators have mostly passed up. It's a bit frightening. But maybe not as much as others we'll pick up later on.

THE FATE OF "NURSERY WORLDS"

In the Drake Equation the combined factor f^{ic}—the fraction of life-bearing planets on which intelligence and technology eventually evolve—is generally assigned a value of about one in one hundred. The xenologists who put forward the "one-percent" argument support it by citing the apparent fact that it took four billion years for Earth to give rise to merely one technological race. This is almost half the viable life span of the planet. Intelligent life would seem to be a rare and wonderful thing.

But is this assumption tenable? Let's consider the life cycle of a "nursery world," a planet with a stable biosphere in which the slow evolution to intelligence can take place.

Evolution appears to have proceeded gradually at first, then at an accelerating pace for 3 billion years. Except for the introduction of sexual reproduction, and later of angiosperms (flowering plants), there is no evidence even to hint the Earth was ever suddenly invaded by extraterrestrial flora and fauna. The Great Silence seems, at first glance, to have stretched through the entire Paleozoic.

If we assume Earth lay untampered with until at least the time of the Jurassic, we can guess that it takes about 3 billion years for life on a nursery world to evolve to a level of complexity that makes intelligence feasible.

But if humanity suddenly vanished? Would it take another 3 billion years for intelligence to arise on Earth again? If so, it's reasonable to accept the guess that only one or two technological species could erupt per habitable planet.

But *Homo sapiens* isn't the only species to have benefited from 3 billion years of evolution. Today's German cockroach may look like his distant ancestors, but he has accumulated many little tricks his cousins in the Triassic never heard of. The size of the genome of the raccoon and wolf (the number of genes in their chromosomes) is no smaller than that of man.

Consider what's happened since the Cretaceous-Tertiary Catastrophe, approximately sixty-five million years ago, that wiped out nearly every species of land animal massing more than forty kilos.

The creatures who went on to dominate the planet were small mammals: the early equivalent of mice, and tree shrews. We are among their descendants.

Now, despite the present arms race, man still lacks the ability to exterminate mice. The sudden demise of this star system's current technological race would not finish off the Earth as a nursery. If "mice" did it once they could probably do it again.

Perhaps suitable worlds must pass through long initial "fallow" periods before attaining a level of biological sophistication ripe for intelligence. Afterward, though, such planets might produce sapient species at fairly short intervals, depending on the time needed to recover from the damage done by the previous sentient race.

EXPANSION SHELLS

It is generally assumed that a space-faring species will expand into the Galaxy because of either raw curiosity or population pressure. For a race limited to slow-boat technology, colonization will take place only in a thin, growing shell surrounding an older, settled region within.

If population pressure is the primary motive for expansion, what of the long-occupied worlds in the interior, especially near the home planet? The words "population pressure" suggest the likely fate of these worlds.

Consider the settlement of Polynesia from roughly 1500 B.C. to about 800 A.D. (The island-hopping analogy is apt.) Eric Jones borrowed growth and emigration rates for his model of interstellar settlement from Polynesian history. The intrepid Polynesians testify to the likely viability of "star-hopping" colonization ventures.

Polynesia may, indeed, be representative of interstellar settlement, but not only in a pleasant sense. The Hollywood image of island life is paradisical, but Polynesian cultures were subject to regular cycles of overpopulation, controlled in war or ritual by culling adult male population. There are stories of islands whose men were wiped out completely.

Meanwhile, introduction of domestic animals disrupted island ecosystems. Many native species were wiped out.

The most severe example is Rapa Nui, also called Easter Island. Isolated thousands of miles from its nearest neighbors, it was as like an interstellar colony as any place in human history. Mankind may devoutly hope to do better when we finally do embark to the stars.

The colonists wrecked the virgin ecosystem of Rapa Nui. When no trees remained to make houses or boats, they had to abandon the sea and it resources, along with all possibility of escape. What remained was native rock—which they carved into hauntingly desolate images—and warfare.

The story of that place should be a lesson to make us all thoughtful.

Now, assume a settled sphere of expansion by an extraterrestrial intelligent species. What of the *inner* systems, within the sphere? The Polynesian example suggests a dismal image of increasing competition for dwindling resources with no escape valve for excess population, since all surrounding systems are in similar straits.

What happens to those inner worlds? In an old, settled system, all available asteroids would long have been turned into habitats. Safe inner orbits with unhindered access to solar power would be at a premium. Even the most efficient space structures will require frequent replenishment of gases such as oxygen, hydrogen, and nitrogen. Comets might supply part of this need, but terrestroid planets would be closer.

One might expect to see a profound cultural split between those living on planetary surfaces and those in space, as depicted by Larry Niven and Jerry Pournelle in their novel *Mote in God's Eye*. It would be simple to bombard cities with redirected asteroids. Factor L (average lifetime) clearly falls in such a case.

In any event, it would be the innocent higher animals who would suffer most in such a crossfire.

CYCLES OF RECOVERY AND EXPANSION

Recently scientists have uncovered thin layers of clay rich in exotic elements, including iridium (up to five times the normal abundance of some isotopes), at levels associated with the end of the Cretaceous period. Discoveries in locations from Italy to New Mexico seem to correlate with the great extinction. Some scientists conclude that a major meteorite impact on the Yucatan peninsula kicked up a great pall of dust, severely altering weather patterns (perhaps in conjunction with major volcanic activity that resulted in the huge lava fields in Asia called the Deccan Breaks), resulting in mass starvation.

The Cretaceous-Tertiary event wasn't the only one of its kind. At least four other mass extinctions are found in the sedimentary record, including one at the end of the Devonian and another at the Permian-Triassic boundary, approximately 225 million years ago. These events are less well understood and may have taken place over longer periods than the Cretaceous die-back, but we may compare the rough 10-to-500-million-year intervals seen with those suggested by Newman and Sagan for galaxy-filling by space-traveling species.

Here's one possibility to consider—might the ecological holocaust of the Cretaceous have been a local manifestation of the death spasm of a prior space-faring race, whose overpopulated sphere of settlement spoiled and self-destructed as the shell of colonization passed outward? It's farfetched of course, but also thought-provoking.

If this were so, all neighboring star systems might also have suffered ecological collapse at the same time. Earth might be the first nursery world to have recovered sufficiently, since the last wave of "civilization" passed this way, to develop a species with intelligence again.

Whether or not the end of the Cretaceous corresponded to the agony of dying star-farers, it may well be that colonizing cultures inevitably leave behind them wastelands empty of intelligence and living voices. If we humans initiate an era of interstellar travel of our own, we may find all around us the blasted remains of such an earlier epoch.

Would we then learn a lesson? Perhaps. But with the ever present opportunities for expansion, those humans who exercise self-restraint and environmental sensitivity toward their adopted worlds will not be able to force this tradition upon those who travel far away to establish newer colonies. A nucleus of selfishness may expand faster than a center of more rational colonization. While some settlers may preserve and protect local ecospheres, cognizant of their long-range potential, others may be rapacious.

Which type will we be? Clearly our environmental record here on Earth is a test. The list of extinct species, some of which might one day have become star-farers, is long and growing longer.

The Great Silence may be the sound of sands drifting up against monuments. It may be quiet testament to the fate of species that allow "population pressure" to be their motivation for the stars.

THE RETREAT OF THE CONTACT OPTIMISTS

In June of 1984, a new subunit of the International Astronomical Union gathered in Boston, devoted solely to discussing the question of extraterrestrial intelligence. At that meeting the trend of several years continued. The "Contact Optimists"—who have fought hardest to believe we have neighbors in space—continued to beat an organized retreat. They dug in behind fortress hypotheses offering excuses for the tardy, laggard extraterrestrials and explaining their strange failure to appear.

In so doing, the Contact forces have begun to sound downright gloomy.

Starships are impossible, some of them declare.

ETs kill themselves off before they get very far, others say.

Or *extraterrestrials are pinch-pennies, who would shrink back from the challenge of the stars.*

All this from scientists who once carried the science-fictional banner! Strangely, it is their opponents, the Uniqueness crowd, who now cluster in excited circles at these conferences, chattering about starships and galactic colonization.

Just who are the "conservatives" in an argument like this? We certainly do live in fascinating times.

With the possibility of star travel, and colonization, an average separation of a few hundred light-years starts looking trivial. Not only is the Drake equation no longer complete. We see that it doesn't even predict anything anymore!

When we introduce star travel, the Drake Equation suddenly needs three new factors:

V—the velocity at which an interstellar culture grows into space, pausing to settle likely solar systems and rebuild necessary industry, before again continuing its expansion.

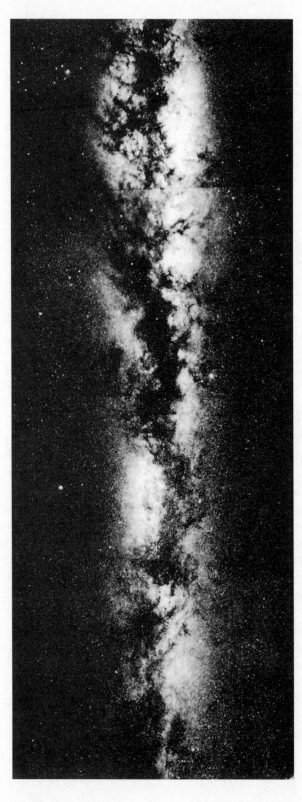

Figure 2. Photomosaic of the northern Milky Way. The constellations of Scorpius and Sagittarius are visible at the right. M 31 (the Andromeda Galaxy) is visible in the lower left. This is a close-up view of the left third of the frontispiece sky map. (*Photo: Courtesy the American Museum of Natural History.*)

L_z—the lifetime of a zone of colonization into which a species has expanded, after which the settled region becomes "fallow" once again.

A—an "approach/avoidance" factor, different for each culture, representing a "cross-section for discovery" by contemporary human civilization. (How likely is it we would even notice them? For example, a culture with a preference for settling on comets would never have visited Earth, and might exist undiscovered even now in our solar system.)

By including these factors in the appropriate formula one can try to predict C—the probability of contact between human beings and extraterrestrials. The seven factors of the old equation, plus the three new ones, give us a space within which to sort out our ideas, an organizational aid that was missing until now.

All ten probability terms are vital. Contact proponents admit that visits to Earth have been sparse, if they even have happened at all. They merely choose different explanations . . . or excuses . . . for the fact that we have observed no beings from other stars. It turns out the differences of opinion between Contact and Uniqueness forces divide quite simply according to which factor each uses to explain the absence of extraterrestrials.

Uniqueness advocates tend to concentrate on the left and middle of the Drake Equation. For instance, some used to claim that planets are rare, or that many Earth-like worlds get trapped into Venus-type runaway greenhouse effects, destroying any chance of developing life.

Other Uniqueness savants bitterly dispute this. Planets are plentiful, men such as Michael Hart say, but the odds of independently evolving life are small. Still others, such as Eric Jones of Los Alamos, claim life is probably common enough, but it is the step to *intelligence* that is a fluke here on Earth, unlikely to be repeated elsewhere.

Those on the Contact side disagree, of course. They believe technological societies should crop up all over the place. To account for the apparent absence, Frank Drake and Bernard Oliver hang on to a belief that star travel is impractical. Factor V does have its attackers, then, in the face of a tide of popular and inventive starship designs.

And hypotheses abound as to why extraterrestrials might choose to make themselves invisible . . . to avoid contacting us, or to abjure star travel even if it is possible, or to have neglected to settle our solar system in the more than 3 billion years that it's been prime real estate.

Any of those explanations might work for one or two races . . . maybe a dozen. But if ETIS are as diverse as men and women, the excuses run into trouble. Can the Contact people seriously contend that, out of millions of races, not one would behave as humans do in so many sf novels . . . setting forth in their space Conestogas to settle and alter their new homes?

(True . . . aliens "might think differently than we do." But if there are enough of them, ought not a *few* think like us?)

As always, the most entertaining Contact Optimist is the late Carl Sagan. Anxious to find an excuse for the missing aliens, and too smart to disdain starships, he came up with one of the most fascinating explanations. And in so doing he and his colleagues may have possibly done mankind a great service.

NUCLEAR WINTERS

In the Christmas 1983 issue of *Science*, there appeared an article entitled "Nuclear Winter: Global Consequences of Multiple Nuclear Explosions." It has come to be referred to as "TTAPS"—after the initials of its authors, R. P. Turco, O. B. Toon, T. P. Ackerman, J. B. Pollack, and C. Sagan. This historical document has shaken up thought concerning the potential consequences of modern major warfare.

If the models presented by the TTAPS authors are correct even within orders of magnitude, one can only conclude that the arms race between the great powers is a pointless waste of time and money. Even a "limited" nuclear war will devastate the Northern Hemisphere and leave it barren of civilization, nearly devoid of life.

It would not be due to fearsome blasts, nor even lingering radiation. Some fragment of America or Russia might survive those effects. Rather, it would be the dust kicked into the sky by as few as a hundred nuclear ground bursts, or soot from airburst-ignited fires, that would plunge the world into a frigid night from which very little might survive.

At least that's the contention of TTAPS. In the years following, there have been numerous follow-up studies, but no one has successfully disputed the article's orverall conclusions, that nuclear war could severely affect Earth's climate.

Very interesting—and perhaps vital for us all to think about—but what has all this to do with extraterrestrials?

Well, there is reason to believe the nuclear winter scenario had its birth in a struggle to find excuses for absent star-faring aliens!

Consider the position in which Contact proponents like Sagan found themselves. Unable to convince themselves starships are impossible, they had to come up with some universal mechanism to explain how both the number of extraterrestrial species and their rate of expansion could be small enough to explain the Great Silence.

Sagan's answer was to propose the following:

Assume that two types of species achieve technology—peaceful and aggressive. Peaceful races presumably lack the greedy drives that caused humans to seize every opportunity to conquer and spread, here on Earth. These quiet civilizations will expand to neighboring star systems slowly, if at all. So slowly, we can excuse their absence. They just haven't arrived here yet.

Aggressive types would push ever outward, filling the Galaxy as fast as Jones and Tipler contend. But those species must first pass through a dangerous phase—that period between developing nuclear weapons and viable star travel. Sagan says warlike species either cure themselves of their aggressive tendencies, or die.

In other words, the "optimists" are now suggesting the Galaxy is sparsely occupied by long-lived pacifists—who drive their starships only on Sunday, presumably—and by the planetary tombs of all the rest . . . species who couldn't learn to control themselves.

But for this rationale to work, there had to be an easily triggered mechanism for destroying civilizations. It must be more powerful than even bomb blasts or radiation . . . so compelling that one could envision it happening again and again, to every warlike race that failed to make the transition to a calmer mode of life.

Nuclear winter appears to offer Sagan's brand of Contact aficionado just such a mechanism.

A MENU OF EXPLANATIONS FOR THE GREAT SILENCE

Why do we seem to be alone?

Each of the explanations offered so far suggests a way to suppress one or more of the factors in an expanded Drake Equation in order to make the overall contact number fit observations of actual extraterrestrials . . . so far zero. Let's summarize a list of popular (and not so popular) explanations.

Starting from the left side of the Drake Equation, we begin with some favorite explanations of Uniqueness proponents.

Category One: Solitude

1. Habitable planets may be rarer than astronomers now believe. (Suppress factor n_e.)
2. Some unexpected "spark" may be needed to initiate life out of prebiotic compounds. (Suppress f_1.)
3. The final step to intelligence may require some "software miracle" that makes it far more improbable than currently expected. (Suppress f_i.)
4. Insatiable curiosity and manipulativeness, such as contemporary humans display, may be rare among intelligent species. (This effect would obviously suppress factor f_c.) As Author Poul Anderson put it: "The puzzle is why we're as bright as we are. Pithecanthropus was doing all right." He proposes that intraspecies selection, especially sexual, became fierce in proto-humans, leading to a strange animal that is uniquely clever and capable of fitting itself to live in vacuum or the bottom of the sea.

If any combination of ideas 1–4 are right, we may simply be the first tool users ever to come along. We are the "Elder Race."

Category Two: Graduation

5. Technological species may sooner or later discover advanced techniques that make radio and colonization irrelevant. (Still, it is hard to believe any race would abandon the electromagnetic spectrum—radio and light—completely.)
6. Space-faring sophonts might "graduate" to other realms or unimaginable endeavors, coming to look on planets and starships as mere toys. This would set a limit to the period of expansion, though not, perhaps, to exploration.

Either of these scenarios would lower our expected contact cross-section, A, with such a civilization. They might also tend to reduce V.

Category Three: Timidity

7. There might be reasons species develop an aversion to space-flight. For example, Carl Sagan suggested that the achievement

of immortality might make individuals reluctant to take even the slightest risk.

8. As discussed earlier, those species who don't destroy themselves may "cure" themselves of aggressiveness, and so become slow star-farers.

9. Intelligent species might develop a form of telepathy, through mind-computer links, which makes their lives far richer than existence as individuals. If this happened, they might grow reluctant to venture many light-days from the center of their civilization, in order to avoid, in effect, lobotomizing themselves.

Still, it's hard to imagine these notions applying in all cases, which is what we need from a convincing overall explanation for the Great Silence.

Category Four: Quarantine

10. Benevolent species may have a tradition of letting nursery worlds lie fallow for long periods, allowing new sentience to be nurtured there.

11. Observers might be awaiting mankind's social maturity, or may have quarantined us as dangerous. A galactic radio club might avoid too early contact, to let us develop our own unique culture, to contribute something new to the galactic melting pot.

12. No listing would be complete without including the far-fetched idea that aliens are already in covert contact with some on Earth. A charming Poul Anderson story depicts Earth's sole "member of the Federation" as an obscure tribe of southwest American Indians.

13. The *low rent* explanation suggests the Earth is simply too unattractive to be settled, or even visited by aliens. For example, Earth life forms rely almost totally on the left-handed isomers of complex organic proteins and amino acids. Other life forms could be right-handed.

14. Finally, it's possible Frank Tipler's imagined self-replicating robots, which should make star exploration cheap and easy for even the timid—might behave just a little differently than Tipler imagined. Perhaps there are hundreds of *friendly* probes, sitting

around the solar system, patiently waiting for us. Perhaps we must prove our ability actually to go out there in person before they will deign to say hello.

There is a problem with the quarantine scenarios, unfortunately. All appear to call for cultural uniformity in the Milky Way. . . . Some way for the pattern to be enforced for billions of years in a galaxy of constantly shifting neighborhoods and star formations. Such a rigid pattern would seem difficult in a relativistic Universe governed by the speed of light.

Category Five: Interstellar Wanderers

Perhaps waves of interstellar wayfarers *have* passed this way. Travel in vast slowboat starships might select for the sorts of beings who *like* living in space, who even come to abandon planet-dwelling as a lifestyle. This could lead to different behaviors.

15. Truly space-borne sophonts might greedily fragment terrestroid planets for building materials and volatiles, having a terrible effect on factor n_e, the number of planets that can support life.
16. Alternatively, they might have a tradition of cherishing nursery worlds, protecting them without any desire to use high-gravity real estate.

But we have looked over our asteroid belts in recent years, and they appear to have been untouched since the beginning of the solar system. No one seems to have disturbed them, yet these are the same small bodies such star-farers would covet—which our own grandchildren may be melting and reforming in a century or so.

Looking over our list so far, none of the explanations seems to explain the Great Silence in a convincing way. What's needed is a universal mechanism that acts impartially over long time scales, which would keep the numbers of extraterrestrial species small, or suppress their rates of expansion among the stars.

A few ideas have been proposed that seem to fit these criteria. The reader is warned that some may seem unsettling. If it's any consolation, I'll try to finish with an optimistic scenario . . . one that satisfies all the preceding criteria without being nasty.

Category Six: Dangerous Natural Forces

We've already mentioned the possibility Earth might have fallen into a "Venus Trap" . . . the runaway greenhouse effect that killed our sister world . . . or the perpetual frozen tundra of the "Martian Trap." Here are some other "natural" hazards. Any of them could have disastrous effects on the last four factors of the Drake Equation.

17. In its 230-million-year orbit round the Galaxy, our solar system regularly crosses regions of shocked gas clouds and hot young stars. These can be dangerous events. Spiral arms are where interstellar clouds compress to form new stars, and where supergiants end their quick lives in titanic explosions.

Perhaps advanced cultures eventually tire of playing galactic roulette and leave the spiral arms for good—setting up in the Milky Way's "halo" of older stars that drift in long, lazy orbits out of harm's way. That could explain why we don't see anybody flying around this part of the Galaxy: Those who *can* leave, do.

18. Were the dinosaurs really killed off by meteorite or comet impacts, which triggered major changes in the Earth's ecology? If so, were these and other collisions random? It has been suggested that a small dark, companion of the Sun, called Nemesis, or Shiva, orbits far beyond the comet belt, dipping in every 26 million years or so to scatter icy and rocky debris into the inner solar system. Alternatively, interactions with the galactic plane, or spiral arms, might trigger such events.

In any case, other solar systems might be in even worse shape than we are, so often smashed by cosmic debris that we're the first to climb up far enough to look around.

19. Our Milky Way may contain objects far more dangerous than mere shock fronts or falling rocks. Radio astronomy shows that many galaxies contain powerful, dangerous jets of relativistic particles, perhaps caused by huge black holes at the galaxies' cores. It's still unclear whether we share this galaxy with a compact version of such terrors, but already there is strong evidence for a black hole, of about 2.6 million solar masses, near the center of the Milky Way.

Category Seven: Dangerous "Unnatural" Forces

Nature can be malignant, as we have seen. But there are other dangers as well, dangers that might arise from life itself.

20. Migrational holocausts. This idea was discussed earlier. What happens to planets that are colonized by an expanding interstellar civilization? Unless the settlers leave large parts of their worlds fallow in wilderness preserves, or engage in "uplift" bioenginering of local higher animals, their mere presence is likely to do harm. A world probably cannot serve as a useful nursery of intelligence so long as it's occupied by a space-faring race. When the interstellar tenants finally vacate or die off, it may be a long time before a local species of tool users evolves.
So Earth might be the first nursery world to have recovered sufficiently—since the last wave of "civilization" passed this way.
21. Inevitable self-destruction is another cheery theme mentioned earlier, suggesting that many alien races found themselves where we now stand, on the teetering precipice between self-ruin and self-control; perhaps only a very few make it.
22. From physics and science fiction comes the dreadful notion of "deadly probes," which devastate life among the stars. A particularly paranoid advanced species might not want any potential competition to rise up elsewhere and so might send forth machines like Tipler's self-reproducing probes, but with a nasty edge. Whenever radio traffic indicates that new sentients (like us) have arisen, these robots would home in to destroy the infection before it spreads. This need only happen once for it to become the status quo, keeping the Galaxy silent and empty for billions of years.

Category Eight: A Grasp at Optimism

Is there any friendly explanation for the Great Silence? Isn't there any way the Universe could look the way it does and still let both sides in the debate get their dream—a galaxy with other minds to talk to, and yet still wide open for our great-grandchildren to have adventures in?
I have managed to come up with one.

23. The "Water Worlds" scenario. We've spoken of the Venus Trap and of a Mars Trap, which might yank Earth-like worlds toward conditions where life can't exist. This leaves us with the impression that Terra miraculously found itself straddling a narrow fence between two death sentences, and that might be true.

On the other hand, it might not. Recently, Professors Kasting and Pollack have published persuasive arguments that there is a deep valley, a cusp, between the Mars and Venus catastrophes. Within this valley there is another "trap," pulling toward it all planets within its reach. This is the pleasant trap of the Water World.

The existence of life on Earth has had powerful repercussions. It has taken most of the carbon out of the atmosphere, freed the oxygen bound in the rocks and regulated the planet's temperature so that it varies less than the heat output of the Sun itself. One result: the preservation of vast oceans.

If this turned out to be a common phenomenon, let's consider the possibility that the Earth is unusually *dry* for a water world. In other words, what if the vast majority of this kind of planet has far *less* dry land than ours?

Geneticists say that species diversity and rates of evolution depend on the size of the environment involved. It is unlikely that land creatures would develop to the complexity they have on Earth on a world with only island archipelagoes and tiny continents.

That doesn't necessarily mean *intelligence*, per se, is impossible on such planets. After all, dolphins and whales are pretty bright. But it does imply there'd be few places where "hands and fire" beings would develop the technology and basic outlook necessary to take to the stars.

There might be millions of intelligent species out there, ignorant and uncaring about starships, preoccupied with their own oceanic adventures. The result? Envision our descendants setting forth, as Jones and others anticipate. They find no other star-farers, and at first it seems they are all alone. At last, though, they discover other minds . . . minds that pose no threat, no danger.

Intelligent whales, or squid, or octopus . . . why should they refuse the roving humans' request to make use of local asteroids to build their cities and factories? If the strange-looking bipeds are willing to bring down exciting toys and machines, why not invite them to come take their vacations on the shores of the "useless" little islands, to splash and play and exchange philosophy lazily under the balmy sunshine?

Humans could be the voyageurs—the transporteers—carrying mail and slow philosophical discussion among the water sapients who will only be grateful for the service, of course, never jealous. Our great-to-the-nth grandchildren will have their adventures, and serve to tie the Galaxy together.

It sounds like a way to give both sides in our great debate what they want, without having to have a dangerous, malignant Universe, one that's out to get us.

I promised to end on a note of optimism, and I cannot do any better than that.

Now, if only it were true.

CHAPTER 4

Tuning In-Where To Look And Listen

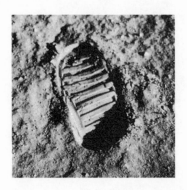

Assume that extraterrestrial civilizations do exist. Assume further that they communicate across interstellar distances. How do we find them? The Universe is vast: more than a hundred billion stars exist in our own galaxy alone, and there are a billion galaxies or more.

Michael J. Klein explains the strategies that radio astronomers use when searching for ETI. Thomas F. Van Horne shows how and why SETI will eventually move off our noisy, crowded Earth and establish observatories in space. Gregory Benford, internationally renowned both as a plasma physicist and a science-fiction author, suggests that we might search our own planet Earth for evidence that extraterrestrials— or their representatives—may have already been here.

WHERE AND WHAT CAN WE SEE?

By

MICHAEL J. KLEIN

LOOK TO THE STARS

L ooking up at the clear, dark sky, far from city lights, one can begin to appreciate how difficult it is to decide where to look for signals of intelligent extraterrestrial origin. Thousands of stars can be seen with the unaided eye, and thousands of millions can be photographed with large telescopes. Around which ones might there be planets capable of supporting life?

Astronomers estimate that our galaxy contains hundreds of millions of medium-sized stars like our Sun. These stars are sometimes called "good suns" because they are large enough and bright enough to supply the energy, heat, and light required to support life on a planet similar to Earth. They are also smaller than the huge, massive stars that have lifetimes of only a few hundred million years, a time that is probably too short for life to develop to an advanced stage. Good suns shine steadily for billions of years.

Our Milky Way Galaxy is a typical example of one class of galaxies that populate the Universe. The Milky Way is a spiral galaxy; stars numbering in the hundreds of billions form a highly flattened pinwheel that rotates around its center. The disk of stars is about 100,000 light-years in diameter but, except near the center, it is only about 2,000 light-years thick. The Sun is located in one of the spiral arms, about two-thirds of the radial distance from the center. From this vantage point most of the stars appear to lie in a sector of the galactic disk containing the galactic center, which happens to be in the direction of the constellation Sagittarius. In addition to the stars, dark lanes of light-absorbing interstellar dust are distributed along the galactic plane, which limits our view to a few thousand light-years. These clouds of gas and dust are known to be birthplaces of new stars and, on the basis of the latest evidence, new planetary systems.

Many SETI scientists believe that extra time and effort should be spent searching for signals along the plane of the Galaxy. They correctly argue that stars, including many good suns, are concentrated there. An alternative point of view contends that stars in the solar neighborhood are uniformly distributed out to a distance of a few thousand light-years. Within that sphere we find several million stars that appear to be evenly scattered across the sky. Putative signals from planets around these stars will tend to be stronger because they are closer to us. The numbers per unit area of sky favor the search along the galactic plane; the potential signal levels favor the solar neighborhood, which also includes a lot of good suns. The best bet is to try to accommodate both approaches.

The galactic center is so densely populated with stars that one might be tempted to concentrate a search in that single direction. However, the galactic center does not appear to be a very friendly place for life, at least not for life as we know it. Intense bursts of gamma rays, X rays, and energetic particles have been detected from the galactic center. A growing number of astronomers now think that a massive black hole, millions of times more massive than our Sun, may be responsible for the exotic radiation that is observed.

THE COMMUNICATION MEDIUM

Even if we knew the precise location of an ETI civilization, how can we know what method of communication they might choose to use? What form of energy will effectively carry information across the vast distances between the stars?

Nearly everyone agrees that photons are the answer. Photons are the massless packets of energy that characterize the particle nature of electromagnetic waves, which we recognize most easily as visible light. Other electromagnetic waves include gamma rays, X rays, ultraviolet and infrared light, and radio waves. The only difference among these various electromagnetic waves is their frequency, which is related to the energy of the photons. They all propagate through the vacuum of space, and most are easy to transmit and to receive. Even the simplest forms of matter, electrons for example, require at least a thousand million times more energy than photons to achieve speeds approaching the speed of light. Photon transmission is thus the speediest and most effective means of interstellar communication we know about. If we are correct in this analysis, for which frequencies (or energies) should we design and build our telescopes and detection equipment? Might there be *preferred* frequencies for interstellar communication?

Visible light is a candidate with certain advantages for interstellar communication. Our Sun, just like all the other stars, shines at all frequencies across the electromagentic spectrum. The peak of its brightness occurs in the visible part of the spectrum. Depending on its size and age, a star's brightness peak will be shifted a bit toward either the ultraviolet or the infrared, but the bulk of the energy from the class of good suns will be in visible light. It is possible that life evolving on planets orbiting these other stars would develop some form of "eyesight" that would match the frequencies of their stars' brightness peaks, just as we have. In other words, we all might have visual sensors at similar, but not identical, wavelengths. Might this characteristic be recognized as something common to all sentient beings and exploited to establish communication?

Instruments to search the sky at visible wavelengths are available, but to date little has been done to use the world's great telescopes expressly for SETI. This may be due to the fact that optical wavelengths do not appear to be the best choice from an instrumental point of view. The problem is competition! Anyone who designs (or pays for) a transmitter for interstellar communication would surely realize that a signal transmitted with a given power at almost any wavelength *other* than visible light would be more detectable at the receiving end than the optical signal, which could be lost in the glare from the star. For example, high-power microwave radar transmitters can literally outshine the Sun a billion times, and until recently most scientists considered this a telling advantage. However, new high-powered pulsed lasers of several types are able to outshine the Sun by factors of a thousand or more in both the visible and the infrared. As a result it seems worthwhile to look for such beacons, and optical and infrared searches are starting up. (See the chapter by Horowitz and Alschuler.)

Figure 1 shows the solar brightness curve compared with realistic signal powers that we could transmit at three frequencies (one microwave, one visible laser and one infrared laser frequency).

SEARCH STRATEGIES: WIDE VERSUS NARROW FIELDS OF VIEW

For the moment, let us assume that we can correctly guess the frequency of the signals we are seeking. A systematic search near every good sun in the Galaxy, star by star, could easily last several lifetimes. How can the search be accomplished in a reasonable time span of a few years? The answer depends on the kind of telescope selected for the task. As we gaze up at the sky, we can see a good fraction of a hemisphere at one time. When we use a telescope, our view of the sky is usually limited to a small patch of the sky. The telescope is billions of times more sensitive than the eye, but the field of view is highly limited. In general, the greater the sensitivity, the more restricted the field of view, and this holds for the entire electromagnetic spectrum, from the shortest gamma rays to the longest radio wavelengths.

Modern SETI projects require telescopes and signal processing equipment specifically designed to detect a signal, perhaps a very weak signal, in the presence of a flood of background noise. Of course the signal might *not* be weak. A highly advanced technological civilization might be inclined to transmit signals so intense that they would be obvious to anyone who happened to tune in. The fact that we have not yet discovered such signals perhaps suggest that the task will not be that easy, however.

Interstellar distances are so enormous that even the most powerful transmissions die away to a whisper as they propagate across the Galaxy. Earth's most powerful radio transmissions, which are routinely received by our spacecraft at the edge of the solar system, are fifty million times weaker when they finally reach the distance of the closest stars some four years later. These same transmissions would be a million billion times weaker if they were to be received at the center of the Galaxy. In SETI we are searching for signals; we are not transmitting. We do not know how far away the nearest transmitting civilization might be. To increase our chances for success, SETI instruments should be as sensitive as our technology (and budget) will allow.

GUESSING THE SIGNAL CHARACTERISTICS

Anyone who has ever been unexpectedly separated from a friend in an overcrowded amusement park has, in a small way, experienced the predicament of SETI scientists. Each person tries to guess what the other might do to solve the problem of finding each other in the crowd. The chances are much improved if the friends know each other very well. The size of the park also makes a difference. The challenge for SETI is to guess what "they" might do to make contact without benefit of knowing anything about them, without knowledge of where they might be located in the vastness of galactic space, and without information about the kind of signal they might choose to send.

Nevertheless, we are forced to make decisions if we wish to conduct an active search for evidence of extraterrestrial technology. Speculating among ourselves about what might or might be the best strategy costs little; building instruments and equipment to carry out a scientific experiment can be expensive. Following the example of space research projects, SETI scientists and engineers must consider a variety of potential approaches and finally make choices, often difficult choices, to develop an experiment that will have the best chance of success and yet be affordable to build and operate.

To date, the vast majority of search space that might contain ETI signals remains largely unexplored. The reason is that there is so much to explore! In this context, search space means something beyond the three-dimensional volume of the Galaxy. It is a multidimensional space that includes source location, signal frequency, power level, time of arrival, signal modulation, and polarization. ("Signal modulation" and "polarization" are technical terms that respectively describe how a signal changes with time to carry information and how it vibrates in a plane perpendicular to the direction the wave travels.)

Plausible limits for these "search space" parameters may be impossible to define. It is clearly not practical to look for all possible signals at all frequencies from all directions using instruments with the greatest sensitivity that our technology can provide. (However, it may be possible to construct a large, sensitive radio telescope that listens to a whole hemisphere of sky simultaneously, using phased-array radar techniques. See the chapter by Cullers and Alschuler.) Each reduction of search space not only decreases the search time and cost, but also decreases the chances for detection. Therefore, tradeoffs must be carefully made between sensitivity and signal character on the one hand, and spatial directions and frequency ranges covered by the search on the other. The objective is to select the most effective strategy within the constraints imposed by the limits on time, resources, and technology.

First we assume that the signals, if they exist, will be intentionally transmitted for detection by other technological civilizations. In other words, we assume that the signals are of a type that we are capable of detecting. If they do not wish to allow others to tune in, then it is unlikely that we will intercept their messages. We might look for "leakage" signals, an alien's version of our own commercial broadcasts or our military radar transmissions, which are expanding at the speed of light away from Earth within a growing sphere (now about one hundred thirty light-years in diameter). Leaked signals could be very hard to detect because they would probably be much weaker than beacons, and they might be unrecognizable to us. This is especially true if the senders are even slightly more technologically advanced than we are. Our eighteenth-century ancestors never could have detected twentieth-century television signals had they been sent to them with the most powerful transmitters of our day.

We assume that we are the technological infants who, for the near future anyway, will be searching by listening and looking. The transmitting societies must at least equal our technological level, for only in the last fifty years have we ourselves developed the capability of transmitting across interstellar space. If their technology happens to be far in our future, then we must rely on their desire to announce their presence to newcomers like us.

If a transmitting ET society wants its beacons to be detected, then what kind of signal would they choose? A logical approach would be to transmit signals that will stand out against the natural background emissions from the Galaxy and beyond. We look at the night sky and see the Moon, the stars, and our neighboring planets. But our astronomical instruments see much more. They pick up intense emissions from galaxies, quasars, huge interstellar clouds of gas and dust, black holes, and even the faint afterglow of the cosmic Big Bang that began it all. These sources of cosmic emissions are detected at all frequencies across the electromagenetic spectrum. However, the intensity is not the same at all frequencies.

As noted above, visible light would surely catch our attention if we could separate an artificial signal from the overwhelming glare of the starlight. This problem of contrast was until recently very difficult to overcome. Furthermore, signals at the highest frequencies, which include the gamma rays and ultraviolet as well as visible light and the near infrared, are absorbed and scattered by interstellar gas and dust clouds. This feature makes them less effective for interstellar communication over long distances than the far infrared wavelengths or the radio frequencies. Radio frequencies not only travel unhindered from the farthest parts of the Galaxy, they also happen to fall in the part of the spectrum where the background emissions from natural sources have minimum intensity.

The subject has been extensively studied and debated in the scientific literature and at professional meetings involving scientists from many disciplines. A systematic search of the radio frequency portion of the spectrum emerged as the initial strategy of choice for the detection of extraterrestrial signals, though other strategies are now emerging.

Even with a decision to begin the search with radio frequencies, the number of possible frequencies is still too large to cover economically. However, there are natural boundaries to the optimum radio frequencies for interstellar communications. There exists a natural "microwave window" that would be known to all technological civilizations in the Galaxy regardless of where they happen to reside. As the name implies, the window occurs at the so-called microwave frequencies, which coincidentally are used here on Earth for communications; we even use them for terrestrial culinary purposes. (See Figure 2.)

On a graph, with background noise plotted on the vertical scale and frequency plotted along the horizontal scale, the microwave window appears as a broad valley of low background emission lying between two steeply sloping "cliffs." The lower frequency wall is the result of intense emission from energetic electrons spiraling in the magnetic field of the Galaxy. This wall of radio noise rises steeply at frequencies below about 1,000 megahertz (MHz) or one gigahertz (GHz). The latter happen to be the frequencies we use for television, which work just fine here on Earth but would have to compete with the galactic emissions if we tried to transmit across interstellar distances.

The upper boundary of the window is caused by the so-called quantum noise that plagues all high-frequency amplifiers. This spurious noise grows stronger with increasing frequency, but the impact of this effect occurs well above the frequencies that are completely blocked in our atmosphere by oxygen. This means that the terrestrial microwave window, accessible from the ground, is not as wide as the free-space window that can only be utilized above Earth's atmosphere. Earth's atmosphere also contains water vapor, which further restricts the reception of high frequency microwaves. In the final analysis, the practical limits to listening for an ET signal in the terrestrial microwave window lie between 1 and 10 GHz. (Inside the window, the faint background noise is due to the universal blackbody radiation, the remnant of the Big Bang.)

THE WATER HOLE

The microwave window happens to include a special set of frequencies that has been identified as marking possible "signposts" for interstellar communication. Most of the background radio noise from the Galaxy is uniformly spread over wide ranges of frequency, rather like the static we hear from a radio tuned between transmitting stations. Several decades ago, however, excess radio noise peaks were observed by astronomers at a few discreet radio frequencies. The source of the noise was identified as spontaneous emission from atoms and molecules located in cool clouds of gas and dust distributed in the spiral arms of our Milky Way Galaxy. Each atom or molecule, upon excitation, randomly emits a short burst of energy at a very specific frequency. The random emissions from billions of atoms and molecules are detected as excess noise at a single frequency, which is different for each type of atom or molecule. Plotted on a graph, the excess emission appears as a spike rising above the background noise continuum. (Atoms in hot clouds showered by stellar ultraviolet emit in a similar way, but they exhibit bright emission lines at much shorter wavelengths; for example, in the visible or ultraviolet part of the spectrum.)

The process is a bit like crickets chirping in a large field. A single cricket might not be heard, but thousands of these randomly chirping insects can raise quite a din, and if they could all chirp identically at the same frequency, the sound would be even more noticeable.

To date several dozen molecules have been identified as sources of interstellar radio line emissions. Among the first radio lines detected were those due to neutral hydrogen atoms (at 1,420 million cycles per second or 1.42 GHz), the most abundant atom in the Universe, and the hydroxyl radical (OH⁻, with several lines near 1.65 GHz). These two species are widely observed by astronomers to map the spatial distribution and motion of matter in the Galaxy. The frequencies of these particular lines, coincidentally, happen to be close to each other in the quietest part of the microwave window.

Astronomers anywhere in the Galaxy would surely know about and study these line features just as we have. They might also notice that the two fragments are the constituents of the water molecule and that they are liberated when broken apart by intense ultraviolet radiation or by collisions with other molecules. If water is a uniquely critical component for life, might these facts about the radio lines of these molecu-

COMMUNICATION SIGNALS COMPETE WITH THE SUN

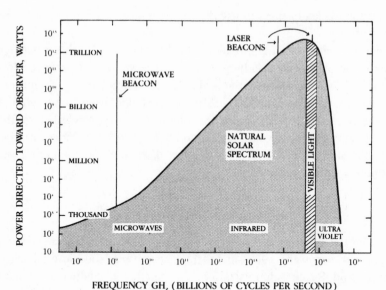

Figure 1. If a microwave, visible laser, or infrared laser beacon were directed at an observer from near a Sun-like star, it would appear as a spike against the natural spectrum as shown above. *(Diagram designed by M. Klein and W. R. Alschuler. Art by Elizabeth Wen.)*

THE MICROWAVE WINDOW
FROM EARTH'S SURFACE & FROM SPACE

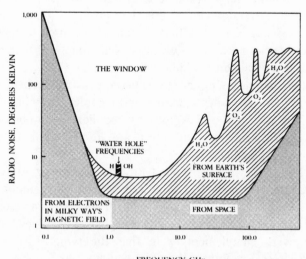

Figure 2. The dotted area represents the natural background of microwave noise in space. The hatched area represents noise contributed by Earth's atmosphere. The magic frequencies in the "water hole" are represented by the stripes. *(Diagram: Michael Klein, W. R. Alschuler. Art by Elizabeth Wen.)*

lar fragments lead others to use them as signposts for interstellar communication?

No agreement about the answer to this question has been reached among the SETI scientists here on Earth. The subject of preferred frequencies has been discussed and debated for years without resolution. A wide variety of special "magic" frequencies have been suggested, but none has captured the imagination of the majority. Nevertheless, the "water hole" frequencies discussed above tend to be included in most SETI plans. Perhaps the reasoning is based as much on romantic hope as upon scientific rationale.

THE NASA SETI PROJECT

The technical capability to search for radio signals of extraterrestrial origin matured in the 1980s under the leadership of the National Aeronautics and Space Administration. The agency developed a plan to conduct the most comprehensive search to date. The NASA SETI project was to be a ten-year effort using existing radio telescopes and specially designed receivers and digital signal processors to conduct a highly automated search of the "cosmic haystack" far more efficiently than ever before. Data from 20 million frequency channels flashed through the digital processor as custom-designed microprocessor "chips" and commercially available electronics processed the data at blinding speed. Several dozen of the most powerful general purpose supercomputers (e.g. Cray X-MP/18) would be required to match the speed of the special purpose hardware, which completed tens of billions of mathematical computations each second.

The automated receiving system simultaneously searched for signals in 20 million frequency channels and recorded anything unusual that stood out against the background noise. Follow-up observations were then made to determine which, if any, of the reported "events" were potential ETI signals.

The NASA Microwave Observing Project, which began (symbolically) on Columbus Day, 1992, followed two complementary search strategies: a high-sensitivity examination of nearby solar-type stars, designated the "targeted search," and a complete "sky survey." The two approaches were complementary in that the targeted search was designed to detect very faint signals that could be either pulsed of continuous, and the sky survey gave up a degree of sensitivity in order to survey the 99% of the sky that was not covered by the targeted search.

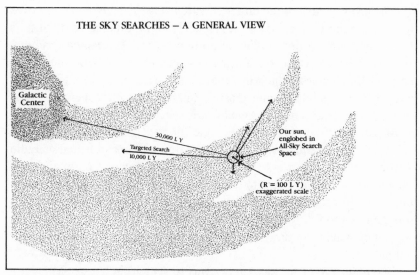

Figure 3-A. The Sun, in a spiral arm of the Milky Way, englobed in the all-sky search space. *(Diagram W. R. Alschuler. Art by Elizabeth Wen.)*

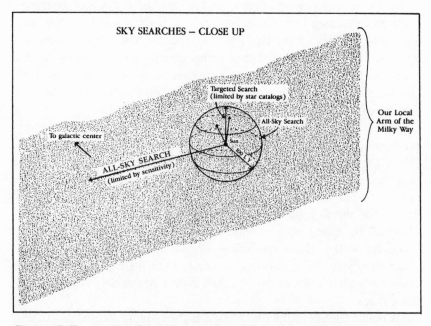

Figure 3-B. Close-up view of the SETI search space, and the limitations of each approach. The all-sky search is limited by the sensitivity of its receivers. The targeted search is limited to catalogued stars. *(Diagram designed by W. R. Alschuler. Art by Elizabeth Wen.)*

The primary task of the targeted search was to examine nearby stars that are similar to our Sun. Approximately eight hundred of these stars were identified within a radius of 80 light-years. Automated receiving systems designed to search for signals in the 1 to 3 GHz microwave band of frequencies (which includes the "water hole") were to be used with the world's largest and most sensitive radio telescopes. The 305-meter-diameter antenna at Arecibo was scheduled to produce the most sensitive search of stars in the one-third of the sky that can be observed at that equatorial site. Other large antennas located at radio astronomy observatories and at NASA's Deep Space Communication Complexes were planned to complete the targeted search at more northerly and southerly latitudes. The radio telescope at each site was programmed to follow each designated star for several minutes at each frequency, while the targeted search analyzer looked for complex signal patterns.

The objective of the sky survey was to search the entire sky over a primary frequency range from 1 to 10 GHz. The 34-meter-diameter antennas of NASA's Deep Space Communication complexes were to be used with support from other antennas of comparable size and sensitivity. The antennas were programmed to scan the sky in predetermined patterns calculated to complete the survey in six years. The entire sky survey would have been repeated about thirty times as the receiving systems were stepped through a series of adjacent frequency bands, each 300 MHz wide. As each scan progressed, power levels in each of the 20 million frequency channels were to be automatically analyzed for evidence of signals.

The spectrum analyzers for the targeted search and sky survey were similar but not identical. Multi-Channel Spectrum Analyzer (MCSA) systems were designed and prototype units were built for both searches. The targeted search MCSA produced multiple outputs with frequency bin widths that range up to a few tens of Hz. A modified MCSA for the sky survey produced a primary output bin width of about 20 Hz, along with a continuum channel (for comparison) about 1,000 Hz wide. These resolutions are between ten and a thousand times finer that the resolutions typically used for radio astronomical research (which looks at gas and dust clouds in our galaxy and external galaxies).

A major feature of the two MCSAs is their ability to process 20 million channels of data "on the fly." With 25 billion bytes of data screaming through the processors each second, attempts to record all the data

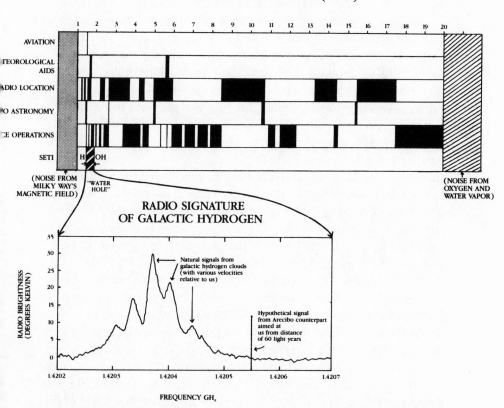

Figure 4. The frequency allotments to terrestrial and space activities, and the "water hole" frequencies are pictured at top. Below is an expanded view of typical natural radio noise observed from interstellar hydrogen. Superimposed there is a hypothetical ETI signal, respresented as a spike. *(Diagram designed by W. R. Alschuler. Art by Elizabeth Wen.)*

for subsequent processing is highly impractical. Consequently, the processors were programmed to differentiate potential ET signals from the confusing background of terrestrial signals and cosmic radio noise. The latter, which experience has shown to comprise more that 99.9 percent of the data, was discarded.

The SETI processors were designed for use for traditional radio astronomy purposes. Data with potential value for astronomical research was to have been saved during the course of the SETI observations. Plans were being developed to make the processors available for radio astronomers to use on a noninterference basis.

In 1993, as the first year of the ten-year observing program drew to a close, the U.S. Congress unexpectedly terminated the project. Observations were immediately stopped and the advanced signal processing sytems were shut down. Minimal funding was provided to preserve the signal processors for future use. The sky survey system was reconfigured for use at NASA's Deep Space Network for research in radio astronomy and the occasional search for signals from a malfunctioning spacecraft. The targeted search equipment was loaned to the SETI Institute, a non profit and privately funded research organization in Mountain View, CA. Many of the technical and science staff from the targeted search moved to the SETI Institute where they developed project Phoenix, a new SETI search that followed the principles of the NASA targeted search. (See the chapter by Cullers and Alschuler).

The NASA search for ETI never really got started. The few observing sessions that were accomplished in that first year were made with the prototype MCSA systems. The full capability of the search could not be realized without the operational processors that were under construction when the project was terminated. Targeted searches conducted with the giant Arecibo antenna would have been the most sensitive ever made and would therefore have been more likely to detect signals originating from the greatest distances. The range of frequencies searched and the variety of signal types that could be detected by the signal processors far exceeded the detection capabilities of previous systems. The "volume" of the multidimensional search space to be explored by the NASA systems was estimated to exceed the sum of all previous searches by at least tens of thousands and perhaps even tens of millions of times.

Fortunately, all was not lost when the project was terminated. Nearly two decades of scientific research and technology development produced by the NASA SETI program are being used and further devel-

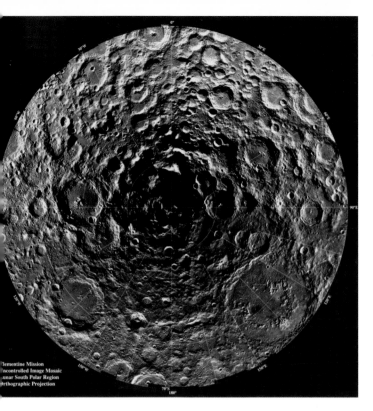

ve and below: False-color images representing radar data collected by the Clementine space-
t as it orbited the Moon in 1996. The areas shown are both centered on the lunar south pole. The
patch (bottom) is the area believed to harbor water ice. *(Photographs: Courtesy NASA/JPL.)*

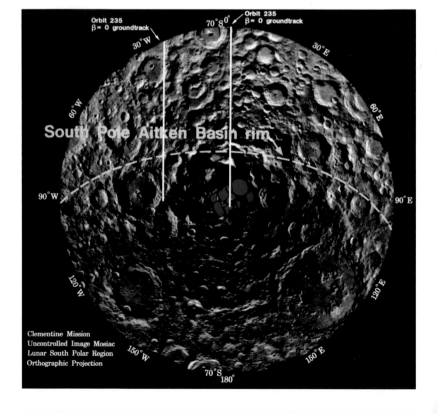

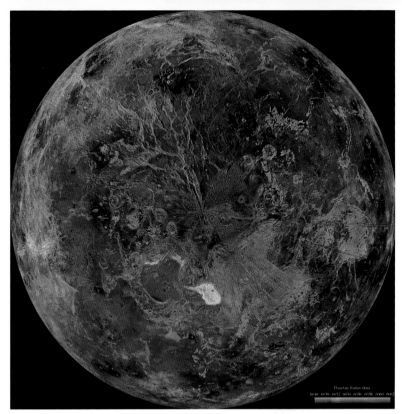

Above: Venus' surface was invisible to optical observations due to its solid cloud cover. The Magel
orbiter mission (1990-4) used high-precision radar that penetrated the clouds to determine the surf
relief for almost all of the planet. This false-color image codes red for the higher elevations, green for in
mediate, and blue and black for the lower altitudes. *(Photograph: Courtesy NASA/JPL and U.S. Geologi
Survey.)* Below: This is a false-color perspective image of Venus' surface, color coded to sh
rate of emission of energy, which is related to composition and surface roughness. *(Illustratio
Courtesy NASA/JPL and U.S. Geological Survey.)*

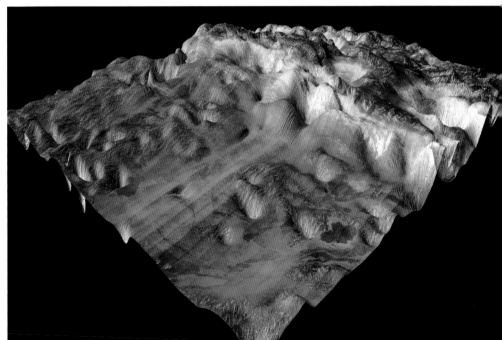

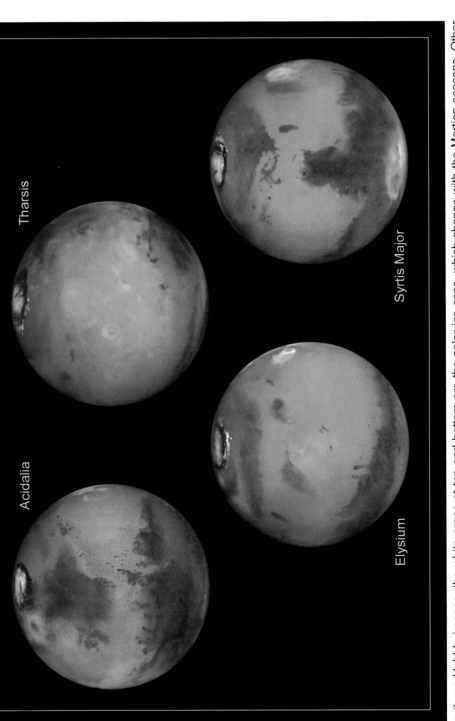

In these Hubble images, the white areas at top and bottom are the polar ice caps, which change with the Martian seasons. Other white areas are clouds in the thin Martian air. In the lower right image a curvilinear feature matches the appearance of the "canals" drawn by Schiaparelli and Lowell around 1900. (*Photographs: Courtesy Space Telescope Science Institute.*)

Tharsis

Acidalia

Elysium

Syrtis Major

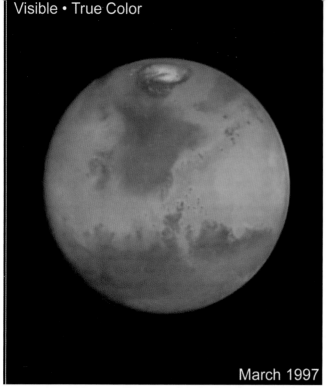

Visible • True Color

March 1997

Above and below: These two images are based on Hubble Space Telescope data. The top image is based on visible light and is colored to match the visual appearance. The polar cap is slightly pink due to the deposition of iron-rich dust on the ice. The bottom picture uses infrared camera data to portray the distribution of minerals, including water-bearing minerals. *(Photograph Courtesy Space Telescope Science Institute.)*

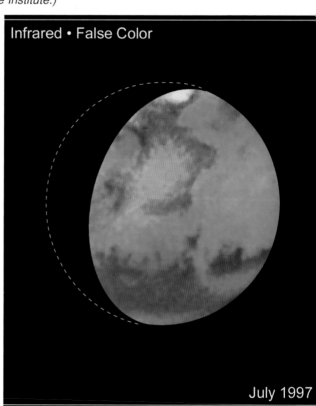

Infrared • False Color

July 1997

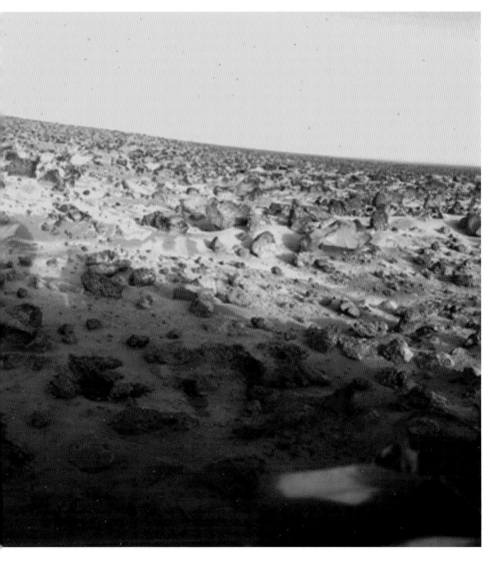

n 1979 Viking Lander 2 took this image of the surface from its site at Utopia Planitia. It clear-
y shows a white layer of thin, mostly-water ice on rocks and soil. This layer formed during a
easonal temperature drop that was cold enough to condense both water and carbon dioxide
ce onto dust particles, making them heavy enough to fall. The frost lasted about 100 days.
Photograph: Courtesy JPL.)

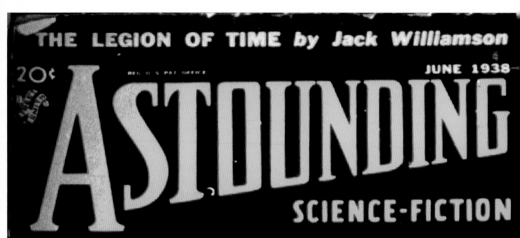

ASTOUNDING

SCIENCE-FICTION

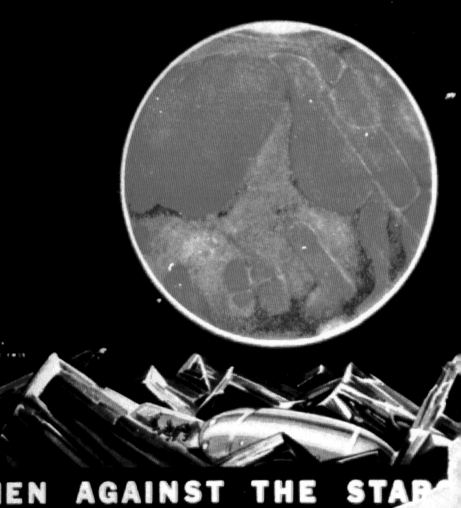

MEN AGAINST THE STAR

This portrait of Mars from a 1938 cover of a science fiction pulp magazine carefully portrays both planet's colors and the "canals" as drawn by visual observers of the then recent past, such as Lo and Schiaparelli. *(Courtesy William R. Alschuler.)*

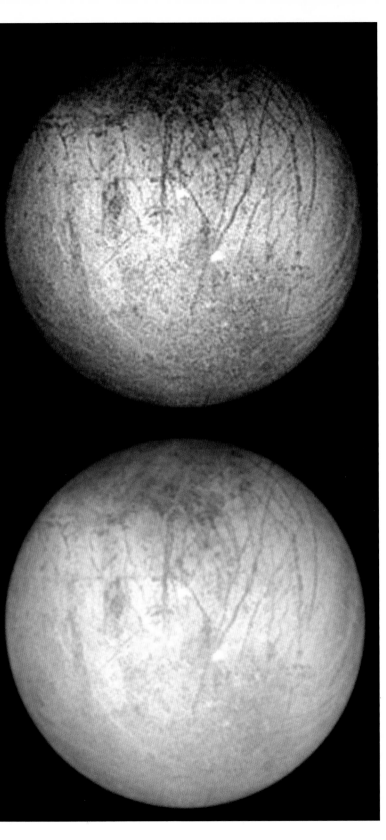

These images of Jupiter's moon Europa were produced by the Galileo spacecraft in 1997 and are composites of violet, green and infrared data. The left matches the visual colors and the right has exaggerated colors for improved contrast. The predominant white color is water ice, while the brown and yellow areas include minerals of so far unknown type. The dark lines are large fractures in the ice. (*Courtesy NASA/JPL.*)

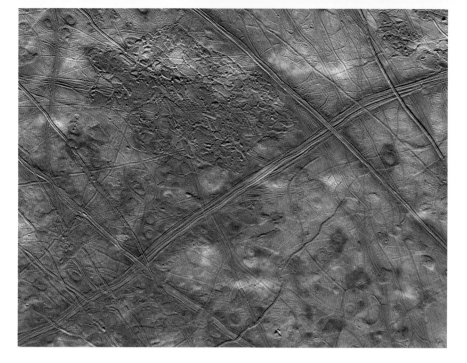

Above: This Galileo-probe image of Europa shows cracks, domes and ridges in the icy surface. The white areas are ice ejected from a relatively recent nearby impact crater. The area pictured is about 180 by 140 miles. *(Courtesy NASA/JPL.)* Below: The bull's-eye in this frame from the Galileo spacecraft is an impact feature on Europa's surface. It is about 85 miles in diameter, and the impactor is thought to have been about the size of a mountain. *(Courtesy NASA/JPL.)*

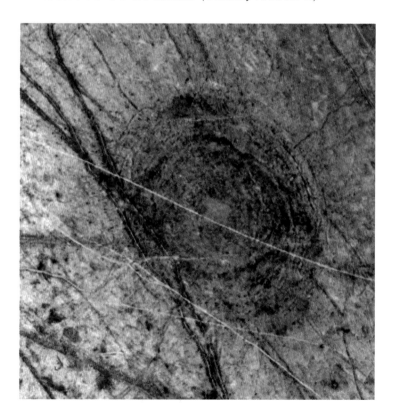

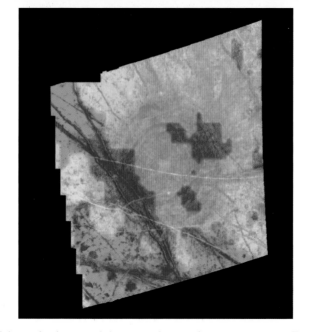

Above: This is a false-color image of the same impact-feature region on Europa shown on the previous page. The bull's-eye is mostly red indicating that it is water ice. The blue "veins" (cracks) crossing the terrain are rich in mineral salts like those found in Death Valley, California. *(Photograph: Courtesy JPL.)* Below: This is a false-color partial image that portrays the concentration of frozen sulfuric acid on Europa's surface. The acid results from the deposition of sulfur ions spewed out by the hyper-active volcanoes on the surface of the neighboring Jovian moon, Io. *(Photograph: Courtesy JPL.)*

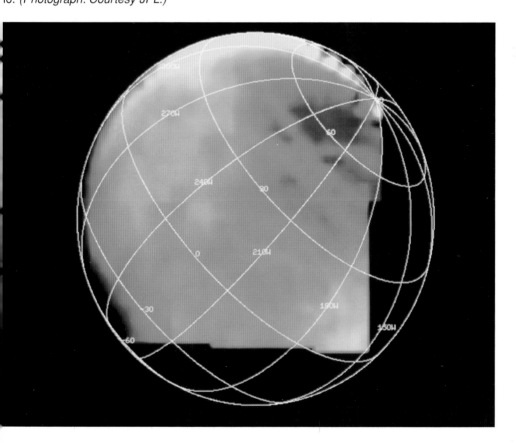

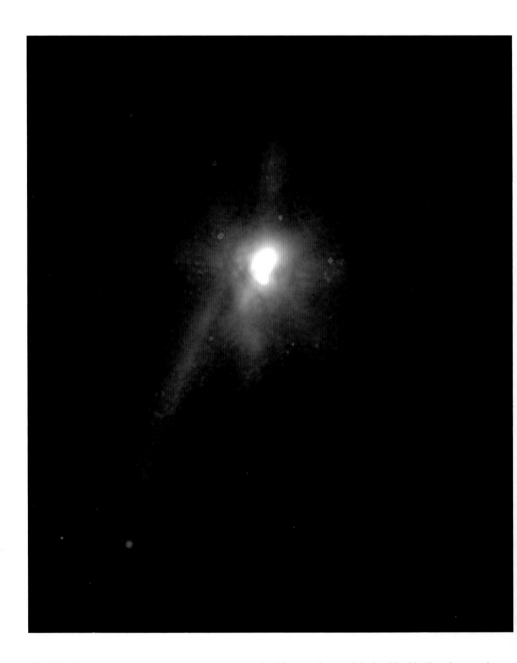

This Hubble telescope image shows a young double star (center) imbedded in the dust and gas cloud it formed in. Planets born in binary star systems may end up in orbits made unstable by the gravitational interaction of the stars. It appears that the luminous point at the end of the streamer of dust (lower left) is such a planet, ejected by its parent stars. It must be a large planet to be visible at all, but its disk is not resolved here. (Photograph: Courtesy Space Telescope Science Institute.)

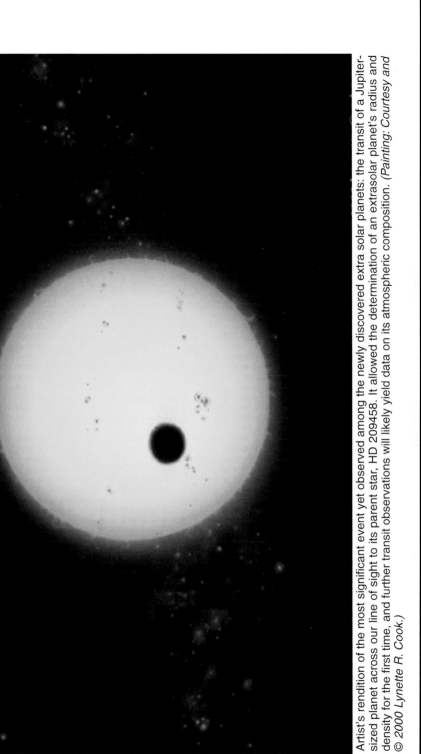

Artist's rendition of the most significant event yet observed among the newly discovered extra solar planets: the transit of a Jupiter-sized planet across our line of sight to its parent star, HD 209458. It allowed the determination of an extrasolar planet's radius and density for the first time, and further transit observations will likely yield data on its atmospheric composition. *(Painting: Courtesy and © 2000 Lynette R. Cook.)*

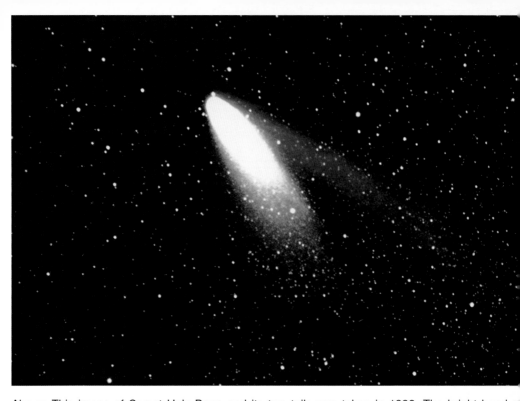

Above: This image of Comet Hale-Bopp and its two tails was taken in 1998. The bright head o
comet, the coma, is composed of dust and gas and masks the solid nucleus of rock, dust and ice.
bluish tail extending away from the comet is composed of singly ionized carbon monoxide particles
flouresce into visible wavelengths. The white tail is made of dust particles ejected from the comet a
nucleus is warmed by the sun. *(Photograph: Courtesy NASA/JPL.)* Below: This series of false-
images of the region around the nucleus of Hale-Bopp was taken by the Hubble Space Telescope
shows the changes in evolution of the nucleus as it moves to, and is warmed by, the sun. *(Photogra
Courtesy Space Telescope Science Institute)*

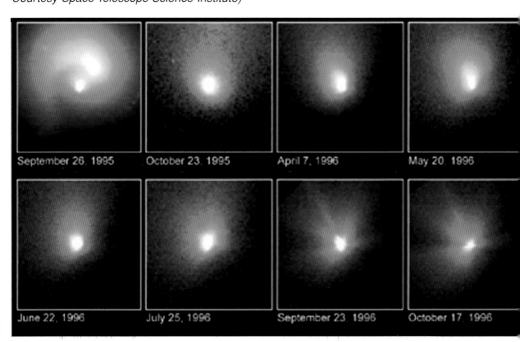

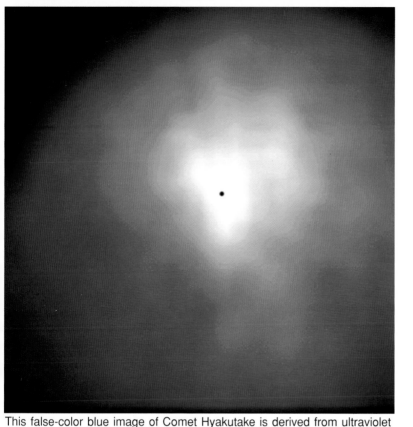

This false-color blue image of Comet Hyakutake is derived from ultraviolet observations showing details of the hydrogen gas evaporating off the nucleus, which is represented by the central black dot. Hydrogen is released when water ice evaporates and is cleaved by the high energy UV radiation from the Sun. *(Photograph: Courtesy Space Telescope Science Institute.)*

This false-color image of the nucleus of Halley's comet reveals that it has a pockmarked surface with an overall shape of a peanut, about 2 miles by 8 miles. The brilliant gas jets are confined to small areas on the sunny side of the object, whose slow rotation causes the jets to shut down as they pass into darkness, only to be replaced by others. This image is the result of combining and processing about 60 frames taken by the Giotto spacecraft in 1986. *(Photograph: Courtesy NASA/ JPL.)*

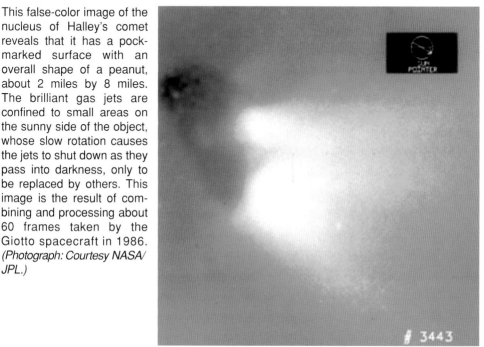

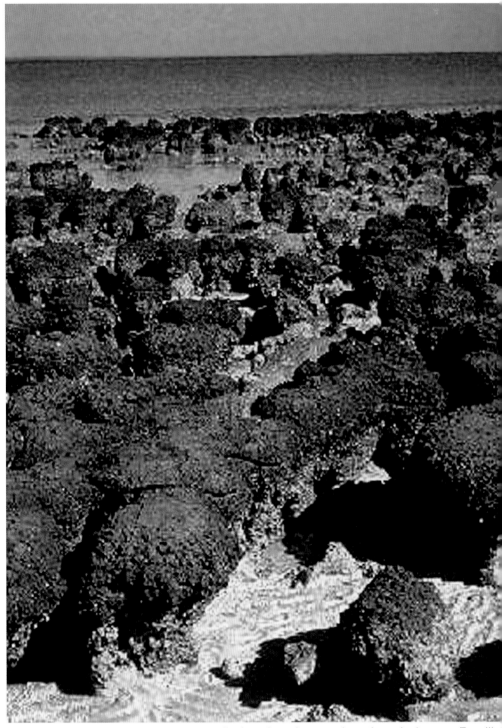

Above: Living stromatolites are generally found at the margins of tropical seas. Fossiliz
examples have been found going back to 3.5 billion years or more, and as such they represe
the oldest known examples of life on Earth in cellular form. *(Photograph: Courtesy Cyanos.*
www-cyanosite.bio.purdue.edu/index.html.)

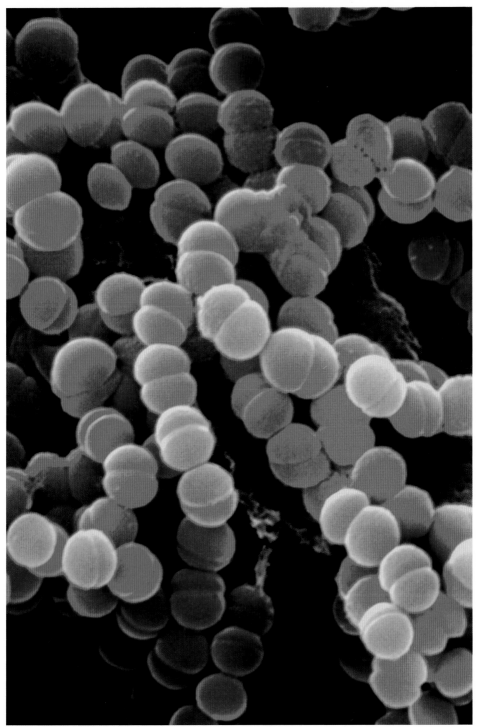

Above: An image of the bacteria streptococcus pyogenes. A similar form of this bacteria, streptococcus mitis, was found in the polyurethane foam insulation clipped from Surveyor 3 and brought back from the Moon by the late astronaut Pete Conrad. It is believed the bacteria in the insulation survived the voyage to the Moon and exposure on the lunar surface. *(Photograph: Courtesy Cells Alive!)*

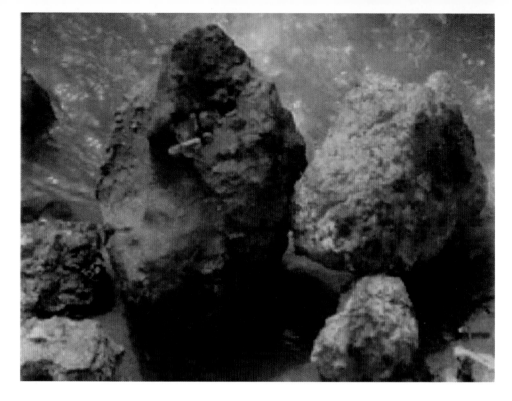

Above: These rocks are red because they are covered with an extremophile: the archaea single-celled organisms, sulfolobus solfataricus, that live in extreme conditions of high temperature and low oxygen. They are found in volcanic sites, both above ground and underwater at the mid-ocean vents. *(Photograph: Courtesy NASA.)* Below: The archaea, single celled organisms which may be of the oldest type on Earth, can survive extreme conditions as do these sulfolobus solfataricus, shown in the hot springs at Yellowstone National Park. *(Photograph: Courtesy and © 2000 Susan M. Barns.)*

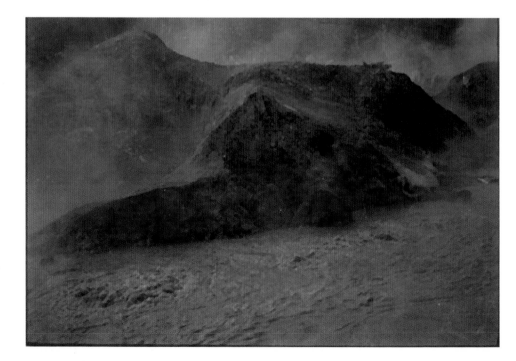

oped by the SETI researchers around the world. In the United States the research team at the SETI Institute, using private funding sources, completed the construction of the targeted search system and carried out significant SETI observations at the Parkes Radio Observatory in Australia and the Arecibo Observatory in Puerto Rico. A narrow band version of the sky survey continues to operate at Harvard University with support from the Planetary Society and a few private donors. New ideas to improve and expand our SETI search capabilities with new technologies continue to evolve. The NASA SETI project will surely be dwarfed by the technical capability of future projects but its contributions in the "early days," when mere speculation about ETI was replaced with well-planned scientific observations, will long be remembered.

RADIO FREQUENCY INTERFERENCE

Not all recent technological developments have been beneficial to the SETI effort. The microwave frequencies that are highly effective for interstellar communication are also effectively used here on Earth, and that is causing a problem for microwave SETI projects. Communications on the Earth's surface, communications with Earth-orbiting satellites, weather-radar, and radar to locate aircraft are but a few of the uses of the microwave spectrum that have become commonplace in our lives. Microwave ovens are in many of our homes. Every year the microwave spectrum becomes more and more crowded with a variety of signals (see Figure 4). The extremely sensitive receiving systems required for SETI are no longer able to filter out the cacophony of radio noise that permeates the sky. Some of these signals are so intense that they block out weak signals over a wide range of frequencies, not just their own. For astronomers and SETI searchers these are designated as Radio Frequency Interference (RFI).

It would be convenient if one were able to turn off these transmitters while SETI observations are in progress, but that approach works in only a few cases. The transmitters are licensed to operate at their assigned frequencies. It is not their fault that their transmissions interfere with SETI. So it is up to us to design our systems to avoid as much RFI as posssible. Special filtering techniques have been designed to address this problem but none is 100% effective. SETI researchers are faced with the problem of trying to hear a pin drop in a large ballroom filled with chattering guests, and more guests are arriving all the time!

SEARCHES FOR OTHER PLANETARY SYSTEMS

Since 1995 discoveries of planet-sized objects orbiting other stars in the solar "neighborhood" have been reported every year. These discoveries are based on the detection of infinitesimal changes in the wavelength of starlight caused by the gravitation pull of unseen companions orbiting a star. The discoveries to date are known as "indirect detections" because the existence of each planetary companion is inferred and not directly seen. The mass and the orbit of the unseen companion are calculated to explain the tiny changes in starlight observed. The technique works best on very large companions, that is, from planets at least as large as Jupiter to very small, very cool, starlike objects known as brown dwarfs. Detection of Earth-sized planets is very unlikely with ground-based telescopes.

Through its Origins Program, NASA is leading the way to develop and launch future space missions that will search for Earth-sized planets orbiting stars located in the "solar neighborhood" within approximately 50 light years of the Sun. The breakthrough technology that is required for the task is space-based interferometers. Optical Interferometers consist of one or more pairs of telescopes that are configured so that light from the telescopes is combined so precisely that the waves interfere with each other. The interfering waves add together to become brighter or cancel each other out, depending on the shape and brightness of the astronomical objects being observed. The detected output from the interferometer is processed in a computer to create an image that shows far more detail than either telescope could produce on its own. Interferometers can be built to operate at almost any wavelength from visible and infrared light to the longest radio waves.

NASA is developing large interferometers that will operate in space where the systems, free from the earth's turbulent atmosphere, will produce images of unprecedented resolution and clarity. One concept seriously being considered is the Terrestrial Planet Finder mission which would be a space interferometer operating in the infrared and specially designed to detect and image planetary systems. The system would survey a list of stars and produce images, so called "family portraits," of other solar systems as they are discovered. Even the nearest stars are so distant that we have no hope of imaging individual planets directly. However, the Terrestrial Planet Finder would be able to detect Earth-sized planets as points of light that can then be studied to determine whether the planet has an atmosphere and to search for chemical evidence of water and perhaps even the by-products of biological activity.

The potential to survey and catalog other planetary systems is a new capability that will surely emerge within the next two decades. The quest for discovering other planetary systems and the quest for detecting evidence of extraterrestrial intelligence seem to be converging in the latter part of the twentieth century. Wouldn't it be exciting if that convergence were to culminate early in the coming century with a detection of a signal from a planet imaged by the Terrestrial Planet Finder?

THE FUTURE OF SETI

by

THOMAS VAN HORNE

No matter what types of radio search systems may be used in the foreseeable future, one factor is likely to dominate. Radio Frequency Interference (RFI) is increasing around the world at an enormous rate, and any SETI project will either have to escape from it or learn to live with it. What with microwave data transmissions, cellular phones, local area broadband networks, police and military radars, aircraft transponders, and communications satellites, we are awash in a sea of intelligently generated signals. For SETI, this means we aren't just looking for a needle in a haystack. Much worse, we're looking for a slightly odd needle in a haystack full of them. Most current SETI listening programs are based on the techniques and instruments of radio astronomy. Yet even while the technology to receive and recognize ETI signals is rapidly advancing, the increasing volume of human-made noise is slowly crippling the world's great radio telescopes. Since about 1980, there has been growing concern that conventional Earth-based radio astronomy has only a few more decades of existence before transmitters of terrestrial origin obscure the entire radio sky just as city lights interfere with our ability to see the stars. Steps to preserve access to the sky and to restrict the extent of interference, at least at certain frequencies, are being taken by several groups concerned about astronomical research. But in the face of powerful commercial concerns, weak international enforcement powers, and military planners who think restricted frequencies are a good way to hide secret transmissions, there seems little chance that anything will stop the growth of RFI on and around Earth. To continue to operate at all, future SETI systems will either have to move beyond the range of human interference or else somehow learn to see through it. To avoid terrestrial RFI one could develop receiving facilities beyond geosynchronous orbit, clearly an expensive proposition. Nonetheless, in the early 80s, fueled by dreams of cheap access to space using the Shuttle, many space based schemes were considered. Such schemes offer a number of advantages to counter higher logistical costs. Freed from the strain of fighting Earth's gravity, orbiting SETI radio telescopes can be built with concentrating reflectors that are much larger than is possible on Earth. A large spherical reflector in orbit only has to be strong enough to hold its shape against the weak tidal stresses felt in orbit. It can be structurally very simple and can focus into a large number of free-flying feed horns and receiver systems to study a number of targets simultaneously with great sensitivity. A SETI facility beyond near-Earth orbit can protect itself from terrestrial RFI by means of a large screen held in position between the reflectors and the Earth. The schedule of observations and choice of targets for such a facility is potentially much more flexible than for a ground-based dish. Separated from the obscuring bulk of the Earth itself, the field of view of an orbiting antenna system includes the entire sky at all times, except for the area obscured by its protective RFI screen.

As the new millennium dawns, it still seems likely that space-based telescopes will eventually be shared by SETI researchers. The only question is when.

A variation on free-space antenna systems that also escapes the Earth's RFI environment is to use an enormous natural radio screen, the Moon. Near-Earth orbiting radio telescopes are still vulnerable to satellite RFI from sources in higher orbits than themselves, especially Earth's noisy ring of geosynchronous communications satellites. But because Earth's moon is tidally locked to our planet, the far side is protected from the entire area of terrestrial radio interference by a thousand miles of solid rock. There was, especially in the period following Apollo, considerable discussion of using the far side of the Moon as a haven for astronomy, associated with proposals that the U.S. and other nations establish a permanent manned presence on the Moon. If manned operations are being supported on the Moon for other purposes, it may well be that a high profile lunar program and the natural shielding might make radio astronomy from the far side attractive. It is possible to construct large-scale reflectors with a design similar to that of Arecibo, using some of the many impact craters on the lunar surface to form the support for a giant dish. The lower lunar gravity makes possible structures very large by terrestrial standards. There are also a number of disadvantages to far-side radio astronomy. Reflective dishes in lunar craters can't match free-flying dishes either for size or for flexibility of operations. Most important, it is unlikely that the entire far side of the Moon will be devoted solely to astronomy. If any other human activities, even exploration, are being carried on in that hemisphere, some form of communications link will be established. If communications satellites, as opposed to optical fibers, were used for those links, the shielded environment of the lunar far side would no longer be protected. Moves are afoot as I write this to protect the radio and optical environment of the lunar farside.

An alternative to escaping from the noise of human civilization is to learn to live with it. For years, radio observatories have used ingenious technical tricks to limit RFI problems. Digital signal-processing technology offers growing hope that advanced radio telescopes will eventually be able to subtract out signals, automatically identified as RFI. Growing satellite data bases and plans to tag aircraft, one of the most unpredictable interference sources, with automated position tracking, make this scenario daily more plausible.

The future of SETI is tied to what our technology can do. Over time, as our technology advances, new signal-processing techniques and new telescope designs will become available. Entirely new systems will revolutionize our search efforts.

SKA/ARGUS

One such innovative system concept is being prototyped in work currently underway at the Ohio State University (OSU) Electrosciences Laboratory. OSU SETI is testing a new signal processing system known as the radio camera as an astronomical instrument. A radio camera uses a phased array of antenna elements, receivers, and digital processors to create an image of the radio sources in its field of view. In a standard phased-array antenna system, like those used by large strategic defense radars, the signals from a number of small antennas are combined to synthesize an antenna beam like that of a single large antenna. The direction of that beam is determined by the way in which the signals are processed rather than by the physical orientation of the antennas themselves. Thus, a phased-array missile radar can point electronically to scan the sky much faster than a dish antenna could be mechanically moved to cover the same area.

To understand this a little better, consider how a well-known antenna works, say the standard parabolic telescope. Imagine that a wave front comes in from deep space, and that the axis of the parabola is aligned with the direction of travel of the wave.

This means that the wave causes the electric voltage of the capturing antenna to alternate between a maximum and minimum value as the wave continues to cross the antenna at the speed of light. At any instant of time, different parts of the wave front bounce off the parabola and are reflected through the focus of the antenna. This happens in just such a way that all the voltages of the wave add together at the focus and the signal's effect is maximized. Another way to look at this is to imagine waves on a lake. A focusing reflector bounces the waves into a spot where all the high ripples add together. It is rather as if one were to sweep up the water in the waves into one place. Now, with the increased power of computers, it is not necessary to focus the waves using reflection and geometry. Instead, one measures the wave front at each of many small antennas. The measurements are added in a computer with the correct time delays so that all the wave peaks add together as if received by a larger antenna of a certain shape pointing in a particular direction. Thus, we do digitally today what used to be accomplished with analog physical devices.

There is, however, a subtlety. An antenna small compared to a wavelength senses only a small part of the wave. It can be rotated in any direction without altering the measurement. This becomes obvious in the limit, since the antenna becomes a point for which all orientations are equivalent. Now, for antennas large compared to a wavelength, orientation matters. If the surface of the antenna lies on a wave front, the waves add together, raising and lowering the voltage across the whole antenna as time passes. On the other hand. if the antenna is rotated so that at a given instant of time it crosses wave maxima and minima, the high and low voltages tend to cancel each other out. The conducting antenna sees very little total signal.

This directional property of antennas is called gain. Because of their shape they favor certain directions. The larger they are, the more gain they have, or, to put it another way, the more of the wave they capture when properly aligned. Thus, in order for an array of antennas to see the sky, allowing their signals to be added digitally to synthesize the radio camera, each antenna must be small. Otherwise, all directions in the sky will not be equally visible.

A radio camera takes advantage of the fact that a digital phased array is not only able to synthesize a beam pointing in any direction but also can use the same set of data to synthesize every possible beam and look in all possible directions at once simply by changing the time delays of the addition of the "antennalet" signals. The OSU SETI project to develop an astronomical radio camera is named Argus. The goal of Project Argus is to create a radio telescope that is capable of imaging the entire sky simultaneously. Project Argus uses a phased array, consisting of small, essentially omni-directional, antennas laid out in an adjustable pattern. Each antenna is connected to its own receiver and digital-processing package. These send the digital data from each element to a central processing unit for storage and analysis. The final image is constructed by systematically processing the stored data until all possible independent views of the sky are synthesized.

Sensitivity will be determined by the total collecting area of the array, receiver noise, bandwidth being analyzed, and duration of the observation devoted to each sky direction. A thousand-element Argus would still have a small collecting area compared with a large dish like Arecibo. However, since it could see all the sky all the time, it would be able to capture large transient events such as pulses, not visible in any other SETI search. Also, because it would look at the entire sky rather than tiny pieces of it, Argus could use very large integration periods, the radio equivalent of long film exposures, to increase its sensitivity.

The limiting factor for Argus is data processing speed. This is proportional to the number of beams formed, the bandwidth of the incoming data, and the number of elements in the array. Obviously, one must decide what compromise to make given the processing power at any given time. However, whatever the prototype's capabilities today, they will be a hundred times greater in ten years. Argus, at least initially, would have to create a limited set of views of the sky using either snapshots to limit data or sequential examination of narrow frequency bands. However, as information processing technology advances and our ability to store digital data increases, this limitation will be greatly diminished.

The radio astronomy community needs truly vast collecting areas. Arecibo, the largest radio telescope in the world today, is limited to observations near the equator. There are several concepts currently planned to create antennas thirty times the size of Arecibo. Collectively, these are called the SKA (Square Kilometer Array). Some consider constructing the antenna out of vast numbers of elements, each looking in all directions. The difficulty is that, to create a square kilometer of collecting area, would require billions of antenna elements.

This makes the data processing very difficult. The most promising plan, a collaboration between Berkeley and the SETI Institute, proposes using satellite antennas, perhaps even those commercially manufactured for TV reception. These are cheap commercial devices and their individual collecting area is such that perhaps only a hundred thousand, as opposed to billions, would be necessary to form a square kilometer array. Each element would, like a satellite antenna, have directivity and, hence, gain. They could view a small patch of the sky, synthesizing all possible beams in that patch with high sensitivity and directionality. A prototype design is to become an actual radio telescope at Berkeley's Hatcreek Radio Observatory. It will be about a hundredth of a square kilometer, containing about a thousand dishes, and hence, is designated the 1HT or One Hectare Telescope. This collaborative venture, to be used half for SETI and half for conventional radio astronomy will be one of the largest radio telescopes in the northern hemisphere, useful in its own right, and, possibly, the prototype for the larger SKA. Because different beams can be synthesized simultaneously, the SETI and radio astronomy uses will not conflict.

Berkeley also uses data from Arecibo to run one of the most innovative experiments in computing today. This program, called SETI At Home allows Berkeley's analysis software to take advantage of idle cycles on computers of interested SETI enthusiasts, giving the equivalent of a thousand computing years each day of real time. In the first month of operations more than 700,000 people signed on and it is expected that by the time you read this there will be more than a million participants. Data from a 2 MHz band is digitized and sent for processing in packets to computers across the internet. The packets are processed by a screensaver, free from Berkeley, that searches for TV and radarlike signals. The packetized data is a sub-band of Berkeley's all-sky survey, SERENDIP. This survey, which examines 100 MHz of bandwidth, looks wherever the Arecibo telescope happens to be pointed, making a copy of the data as it streams in. Thus, it does not interfere with other radio astronomy. The sensitivity of SETI At Home is higher than the sky survey would have been because of the added internet computer processing, although it is not quite as high as the most sensitive targeted SETI surveys. It is difficult to quickly verify apparent detections since the data-taking process has no control over the telescope. Nevertheless, it is possible to look for signal types never considered in the real time searches. You too can participate. To find out how, come to the SETI Institute web site, **www.seti.org.**

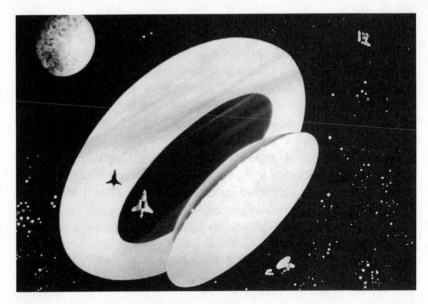

Figure 1. Orbiting radio telescope with RFI shield, as proposed by NASA. (*Art: Courtesy NASA.*)

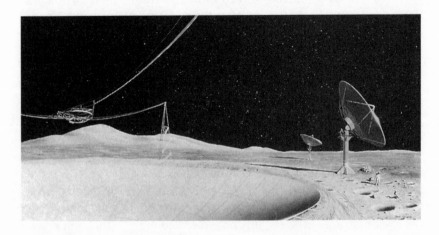

Figure 2. Using the body of the Moon as a shield from terrestrial interference, a crater dish on the lunar farside could be the best location for radio astronomy. (*Art: Courtesy NASA.*)

Though Berkeley'S SETI At Home is the first big experiment in distributed computing for SETI, it is not likely to be the last. The computing power of individual machines grows by a factor of ten every five years. Furthermore, the number of computers connected to the internet grows by a similar factor. If distributed computational power grows fast enough, and an Argus can be built from small antennas, the end result could be much like having thousands of large radio telescopes looking in every possible direction all the time. This can eliminate the entire question of where to look. Argus would look everywhere. An Argus SETI system would fill one entire slice of thecosmic haystack just by being turned on. OSU's Argus and similar radio camera systems may also be able to see around RFI entirely. Subtraction techniques could eliminate the strong sidelobes of signals that would otherwise make weak radio signals invisible. Radio sources near Earth, be they ground-based, airplanes, or satellites, move differently from sources at astronomical distances which are essentially fixed to the stars. In the ultimate radio astronomy system, we could form an image of every radio source that appears in the sky. So long as the radio receivers are able to handle the total amount of radio input from the sky without reaching saturation, such systems could only be significantly desensitized along the line of sight to strong interfering sources. The sky would have to get extremely crowded, even by today's standards, to disable an omnidirectional system.

Eventually, advanced multidirectional systems like Argus will be set up in space. The digital data they will store as they observe the Universe will be examined for intelligent signals just as it will be examined for information about the distribution of matter in distant galaxies. If we still have found no evidence of intelligence other than our own, we will have to make decisions. Will we begin broadcasting the messages we hoped to hear? Will we begin the development of the self-replicating intelligent probes that we failed to find (or that failed to find us)? Any discussion of the future of SETI must be speculative, because if the search is successful, everything about the field will change in ways we cannot hope to predict. But it may well be that before the systems being planned today are off the drawing board, we will have our answer.

ALIEN TECHNOLOGY

By

GREGORY BENFORD

Interstellar travel is a prodigiously expensive proposition. Sending a manned expedition to a nearby star would take about a thousand times the total energy now used annually in the United States. Though colonization of the planets seems a plausible long-term goal for us, an interstellar expedition would take about 100 million times more energy than establishing settlements on Mars.

Numbers like these lead many to assume that no alien technological society has *ever* carried out far-flung exploration of the Galaxy. Though surely any older race would have to expend vast reserves to send ships to our star, we should be careful in ruling out the prospect. We humans built the pyramids and climbed Mount Everest with no rational motive and at high cost. Of course, we have also abandoned great projects, like manned missions to our Moon. Similarly, for decades we have had the technical ability to build a truly spectacular building a mile high, but we don't. Judging the limits of the grandiosity of a species, even our own, is not easy.

Also, there are dangers in such assumptions, because they can stop us from considering how first contact might conceivably occur locally, near Earth. This idea animates the greatest of science-fiction films, *2001: A Space Odyssey.*

True, we have found no monoliths or other records of alien visits—at least, none we can seriously credit. But this may come from our lack of imagination, our inability to look in the right places. I think it is worth the time to seriously, dispassionately look into the possibility that intelligent beings may have visited Earth, or ventured into the solar system at some time in the distant past.

Thinking about this question in a systematic way is not easy. We are trained to believe that good, hard, no-nonsense thinking is the best way to attack problems. But here something different is needed—soft thinking, if you will. By this I mean the ability to speculate but remain within boundaries.

After all, any extraterrestrials who visited Earth possessed technology (and perhaps wisdom) far beyond our own. We should be properly humble about what such beings could do. This demands mental flexibility, to say the least.

It might well be that a race capable of journeying among the stars will possess a technology we would not even *recognize*, much less understand. Add to this the fact that these beings are truly alien, in all likelihood so completely strange that we could not even begin to count the ways they may be different—and the problem looks insoluble.

I don't believe things are quite so bad. We needn't guess every facet of a visitor's behavior; we only need to check if they have left anything behind as a calling card. Such an artifact must be recognizably artificial. If it was constructed by an alien intelligence it should stand out— indeed, was designed to do just that. Even here there are limits, though.

Let's look, for a moment, at one of the natural world's most fascinating coincidences. At total eclipse, when our moon moves between us and the Sun, a beautiful display occurs. The round moon perfectly overlaps the Sun's disk. Streamers of hot gas continually boil up from the Sun's surface, jets forming a bright halo around the Moon. This is a remarkable effect, quite dramatic. No other moon in the solar system provides such a floor show for its planet.

Is this accidental? The Moon has not always been in its present orbit, after all; tides drive it away from Earth at a rate of about two feet a year. A few hundred thousand years in the past (or the future) this exact overlapping of the Sun's and Moon's disks would not occur. No doubt eclipses would still be impressive, but much less so than now. It is striking that man's inquiring intelligence has evolved at just the right moment to appreciate this beautiful accident.

Or perhaps this additional coincidence—man's rise to civilization and the exact eclipse occurring at the same time—is no coincidence at all. Did some alien visitor accurately predict the evolution of intelligent apes and leave this massive signpost in our sky? The idea may seem absurd, but it is not impossible. This notion illustrates that the boundary between artifacts and natural coincidences is blurred.

Still, though we cannot anticipate the possible accomplishments of an alien technology, we can require that our knowledge of physical law and information not be violated.

Let's take a simple example. There is a cliche story plot that runs something like this: An alien interstellar expedition runs into trouble and must make an emergency landing on a lush, green, uninhabited planet. There is another disaster; maybe the native animals or bacteria kill most of the ship's crew. All but two of the aliens die. In the closing lines we learn that the virgin planet is third from its star, and the two aliens are named Adam and Eve.

This is nonsense for several reasons. The alien body chemistry would have to be exactly like the native life's—digesting the same sugars and amino acids, manufacturing blood cells based on hemoglobin, requiring precisely the same vitamins, and so on. This is most unlikely.

Even worse, how could we then explain the similarities we have with other primates? Did aliens bring them along, too? Fossil evidence shows a clear line of descent for mankind, all the way from 25 million years ago. Our ancestor proconsul certainly wasn't smart enough to build a spaceship, and even if he had been, why was he so peculiarly adapted to the ecology of Earth? Similarly, the integrated nature of all Earthly life, with its common chemical schemes and DNA-based reproduction, strongly suggests that no alien biology ever gained a foothold here. No, we are undeniably the sons and daughters of this Earth. We weren't dropped into our niche by accident. Leaving behind wildly un-Earth-like organisms as a signpost would be a tricky proposition, simply because they would have to compete with hardy natives (not to mention the problem of differing metabolism discussed above). Recent discoveries of plants using unusual chemistries in deep-sea volcanic vents prompted some speculation about how ancient these forms were, but they do seem to fit into local evolution. Unless even stranger forms lurk in some dark corner, we may dismiss the idea of bioartifacts as calling cards.

In the same way, we have to be careful about accepting any historical evidence of extraterrestrials. We need something more than vague legends about marvelous, miracle-working beings who live in the sky. Virtually all religions, past and present, require that the gods live underground and/or above the clouds. (After all, where else could they live—over the next hill? Then an unbeliever could refute an entire theology in an afternoon's walk.) Recently Soviet ethnologists conjectured that stories from the Bible are garbled versions of alien visits—even that Sodom and Gomorrah were destroyed by an atom bomb. There is simply no evidence for these ideas. Enough time has passed to erase radioactive elements or any other signature. Similarly, biblical accounts of spaceshiplike objects in the sky leave us with nothing to check.

A legend is only an aged yarn leading nowhere. We need something solid and unmistakable before such theories become anything more than armchair speculation.

At various times people have come forward with artifacts that they thought were evidence of alien visits. Some were well-meaning and others outright frauds. A Scotsman thought fused towers in Ireland and Scotland were works of high technology; it turned out they had been fired with peat, a process the Scotsman didn't know. Etruscan gems were mistakenly taken by some to be gifts from extraterrestrials because they seemed strange and sophisticated; they were finally proven to be man-made. Dr. Gurlt's Cube, a steel parallelapiped found imbedded in an ancient bed of coal, got quite a lot of press coverage but proved to be a hoax.

Lacking any historical evidence we can be reasonably sure of, we can turn our attention to the possibility that other beings left artifacts on or near Earth even before (or while) man evolved. In *2001: A Space Odyssey*, Arthur C. Clarke and Stanley Kubrick imagined such an artifact to be a monolith and endowed it with a decidedly theological purpose: the uplifting of man. This was a good dramatic device, but it is certainly not the only role an artifact could fulfill.

A second function of the monolith was set forth in the source for *2001*, an Arthur C. Clarke story, "The Sentinel." Here the idea was that the aliens left some guidepost or sentinel that would trigger a signal (a warning?) when man reached a certain technological level. This seems reasonable if our visitors wanted to know immediately when we developed. After all, they might want ample notice that we had discovered nuclear weapons or space travel, rather than learn a few centuries hence, when we come visiting them.

There is another role an artifact can play, beyond that of evolutionary guide or sentinel. Keep in mind that the distances between the stars are vast, our galaxy is many billions of years old, and intelligent races may not live very long in comparison. An alien expedition passing through our solar system long ago might never expect to return, or even to remain in this neighborhood of the Galaxy. They may, from experience with other races, know that civilizations do not survive for

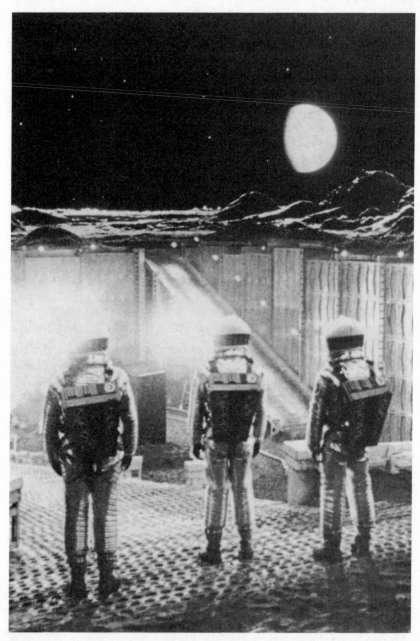

Figure 1. The most famous alien artifact in science fiction is the Monolith from Clarke and Kubrick's *2001: A Space Odyssey.* Here, it is discovered on the Earth's Moon. (*Photo: Copyright MGM 1968.*)

long on the cosmic time scale. Chances that Earth would evolve a culture worth knowing while our visitors' society was functioning were quite remote.

So perhaps they would leave some sign on Earth, as if to say, "Your intelligence is not alone." Even more, their artifact might serve as a legacy. In it they could store information, both scientific and cultural, which could extend the lifetime of a civilization. Perhaps it would serve as an epitaph for their own race, a kind of last defiant gesture against the forces of entropy that could bring down intelligent societies. On a small chip we can even now write an enormous wealth of knowledge; not much space would be required to leave a rich library inside some relatively indestructible vault.

Much cannot be conveyed by simple language alone, as every artist will tell you, and so objects might be left in a vault as well. Such a legacy would be of unimaginable benefit to mankind, a sort of colossal Pharoah's tomb containing new science and new culture. Discovery of this legacy would be the most important event in human history.

Monolith, sentinel, legacy– these are guesses, necessarily anthropomorphic ones, at the motivations of superior beings.

Then too, the agency that leaves the artifact may not be a living member of another race at all. The stars might be explored by computerized ships, not flesh and blood.

Sending living beings on voyages many light-years in length is expensive and inefficient, compared to computer-directed flights. NASA's experience indicates that unmanned probes cost a thousandth as much as manned ones. Even a vast, wealthy society would probably prefer to send unmanned ships for exploration and use members of their own species only on definite missions (say, colonization) to a known destination. John von Neumann, a great, innovative physicist, imagined that advanced computing machines could self-reproduce, using only raw materials. Set loose in the Galaxy, such machines could spread like rabbits in Australia. If so, we should see a night sky clogged with orbiting craft looking for asteroids to devour. We don't, so probably this means that intelligent space-farers don't unleash galaxy-gobbling devices, for sound, "ecological" reasons. After all, they may well value contact with others for cultural exchange, and see more in our solar system than a large asteroid belt to mine.

Even if we dismiss the argument that earlier alien societies would have filled the Galaxy, however, we should also remember the vast time scales that figure into interstellar exploration. Light takes many years to travel from one star to the next. Spaceships, even if they can travel at near light speed (a feat we are nowhere near mastering), would take very long indeed to visit the hundred billion stars of our galaxy. Man has been around in identifiable form only about two million years. Cro-Magnon man (ourselves) is about thirty-five thousand years old. Written records go back seven thousand years. These may seem like long times to us, who are granted only three score and ten. But life has been on Earth for billions of years and could have aroused the curiosity of a passing computerized spaceship long before man appeared.

If intelligence inevitably arises, once a stable ecology evolves on a planet, automated visitors might have been under instructions to leave some artifact. Where would they put it?

One obviously safe place is away from Earth entirely, in orbit about the Sun. A billion years ago it might have seemed equally likely that intelligence would evolve on Mars *or* Earth, so a signifier might be left in orbit between them. This probe, left behind by the main ship, would wait—drawing power from the Sun—until it detected signs of intelligent life on a nearby planet. From such a distance the only reliable evidence would be radio signals, the first indication of what we call modern technology.

If a radio signal ever came, the probe could simply repeat this signal, aiming its radio beam back at the source. A computer program could establish a common language, once firm contact occurred. This system has the advantage that the probe's radio signal, coming from a nearby orbit, would be much more powerful than a beam from the probe's home star, many light-years away. Also, the target planet (Earth) need not have very sensitive receivers.

Such a repeated playback would undoubtedly attract the attention of the natives—imagine the surprise of Marconi if he had found a mysterious echo to every transmission he made. For our purposes, the matter might be laid to rest right there: Marconi heard no echoes, therefore such a probe doesn't exist.

In 1935 Carl Stormer and Balthasar van der Pol, studying the atmospheric propagation of radio waves, detected echoes returning many seconds after the original signal. The time lag indicated reflection from an object many times as far away as the moon. These stood as riddles until the 1970s, when a British electronics engineer, Anthony Lawton, repeated the experiments. He showed that refraction of radio waves in the ionized regions of our upper atmosphere can give such delays, and concluded wryly that "long-delayed echoes would be a most cumbersome and unnecessarily confusing way of making contact. Surely the obvious thing a probe would be programmed to do would be to send its *own* signals and make itself as conspicuous as possible."

It seems unlikely that a probe orbiting around our Sun would simply stay there, giving no sign of its presence and waiting to be found. Picking out even a mile-sized object so far away is very difficult.

There are ways of narrowing down the search, though. In the early 1980s F. Valdes and R. A. Freitas, Jr., searched the lunar Lagrange points for artifacts. These are locations in space that allow remarkably stable orbits. An object left there would not be tugged by the weak but persistent influences of the distant planets. There are two Lagrange points near our moon where the combined influence of the Earth and Moon would allow an object to remain fixed for roughly a billion years. Valdes and Freitas looked for shiny objects reflecting sunlight and found nothing at these points, down to their observing limit of objects a few meters in size. (This was reported in *Icarus*, Vol. 55, p. 453.)

In the middle 1980s the late Michael Papagiannis of Boston University suggested using the infrared images of the night sky in another, similar pursuit. (Papagiannis never did not find enough funding from NASA to conduct his search.)

Without such a neat signature, there is little reason to visit just any small dab of light that orbits our Sun. One place we have visited at great cost, though, and will probably go on visiting, is our moon. Aliens might well have put the artifact there—whether monolith, sentinel, legacy, or some unimaginable variant. It would be difficult to ensure the stability of orbits around the Sun or Earth for millions of years (except at LaGrange points), but planting the artifact on the Moon would anchor it securely.

Covering the artifact with a few feet of lunar dust would bring another benefit: no more erosion by particles streaming out of the Sun (the solar wind) or interstellar space (cosmic rays). True, by the same stroke it becomes vulnerable to the occasional selenological activity on the Moon. Also, large incoming meteorites could still damage it. These are unavoidable dangers, but by leaving several widely spaced artifacts scattered over the Moon, the odds against all of them being destroyed by outsized meteorites can be made quite good.

There is another trouble with this theory—we have circled the Moon and landed on it, and no friendly radio message came out to greet us. Should we conclude that nothing is waiting for us there? Not necessarily.

For one thing, Kubrick and Clarke could be right. The tip-off that a monolith lies buried somewhere may be subtle, such as a local warping of the magnetic field. Or, as in "The Sentinel," the object may be a small pyramid sitting atop a mountain peak that literally must be stumbled across before humans recognize it for what it is. An artifact should try to attract attention, so it should be large and bright. But surface damage could have eroded these eye-catchers in a billion years, so we may need to look for rather subtle features. If these ideas are right, only a full-scale exploration of our moon would turn up anything interesting.

On the other hand, the radiation damage mentioned above may be quite important. Sensitive electronic components made today cannot withstand constant bombardment by high-energy particles; they must be shielded. If an alien artifact were to remain on the moon, operating for millions or even billions of years, blocking out the radiation must be a very serious issue. This means the object will be buried at least a few meters deep. Moon dust and gravel above it will stop particles, yes—and also radio transmissions.

To get around this, it would probably be best to have the artifact periodically protrude a radio antenna to the surface. There it would listen for transmissions from the Earth. The Sun is somewhat noisy in the radio wavelengths. To cut down on this noise, a sophisticated artifact would probably surface its antenna when the Sun is below the Moon's horizon.

What is a reasonable interval between appearances of the antenna? There is absolutely no way to tell. Over the long wearing course of eons, even a simple matter of extending an antenna can run afoul of accidents, so the period should not be too short. On the other hand, if the artifact were left in the first place to keep track of how rapidly humanity advanced, a frequency of once a century might be reasonable; this is roughly the life span of the beings that evolved on a planet, and may represent the minimum time needed to bring about a major technological advance. A sentinel that last emerged in 1890, before Marconi, would then be readying to look again in 1990.

All these factors depend strongly on precisely why the artifact was left. If it were a technological sentinel, to announce our graduation to the space-flight level, the Moon is a good site. Even better, place it on the Moon's other side, away from Earth. Then no freak radio contact with an Earthbound station would have occurred in our history.

If something is buried on the Moon's far side, and it does not surface frequently, contact with it may be postponed indefinitely. NASA plans call for very little activity on the far side in the foreseeable future—and difficulty of direct radio communication is one of the reasons. We may be in for a long wait for a call from a far-side sentinel. Nonetheless, it would be wise to keep an ear cocked for a stray signal that might be an aged but still functioning near-side sentinel, struggling to get through our ionosphere and be picked out of the commercially generated noise we ourselves are making. It would be ironic if we were blotting out word from the stars with a thick layer of cornflakes advertisements and *Star Trek* episodes.

But our visitors may be very wise beings indeed, and realize that all cultures need not develop very far technologically. What if Earth's natives never reached orbit or the Moon?

Lacking any data but out own case, we have no idea how probable it is that intelligence and technology are linked. Certainly if Earth were a planet of an older star, our crust would have fewer metals and heavy elements and we would have a hard time building spaceships. More to the point, do intelligent creatures necessarily desire technology? Our visitors must—otherwise they would never get here—but they might have encountered races that simply didn't think along technological lines.

We may have an example of such a race already on Earth: the dolphins. Our descendants may well remember our inability to recognize dolphin intelligence as our greatest folly, because we do habitually equate thinking with tool making. But an alien visiting Earth two million years ago might have found the dolphins the obvious evolutionary path for high intelligence. Dolphins are conspicuous in the oceans, making acoustic gossip picked up miles away, but who would take the time to scour the African forests for elusive tribes of tool-using primates? Or, realizing that dolphins and primates (which are the same age, evolutionarily) both had a good chance to form civilizations, aliens might have decided to leave a legacy that would be reached by both species.

After all, if you're leaving a legacy for a race you will very probably never meet again, does it matter whether they are fish or land-rover, tool-users or not? The dolphins might never discover fire, develop chemical fuels, or alloy metals—they certainly haven't yet. So they couldn't reach the Moon, even though they might have great use for the cultural record left by the visitors. Exploring the land would be difficult for dolphins, and flying in the air more so. The most obvious spot to leave a legacy for the dolphins would be the oceans.

The trouble with leaving any artifact beneath or near the wind, wave, and tide of the sea is obvious—corrosion. The aliens would need to be sure their legacy would be read and understood very soon—in which case, why not just teach it directly to the dolphins during their visit? (Which raises an interesting possibility: Perhaps the dolphins already have the legacy, transmit it by word of mouth to each generation, and don't consider us worthy of receiving it. *Touché*, fishermen!) In any case, an artifact left in the sea is surely gone by now; corrosion is swift. There remains the possibility that the legacy might be left on land, either for us for some future dolphin civilization.

Where would it be? Some place with little erosion, certainly, far from the oceans, away from areas of geological activity or places where large land animals could interfere with it. If the drifting of Earth's continents is typical of planets, and if our visitors knew the dynamics of plate tectonics, they could have selected sites with few earthquakes, volcanoes, or other severe changes.

The erosion rate is high near mountains and glaciers, so we can write off the great mountain ranges and many sites too near the North or South Poles. The great band of tectonic stress that loops over our planet like a baseball seam makes many other places, such as the California coast, unlikely. The Canadian sheet, a great area of very old, stable formations, would serve quite well if the glaciers had not so (relatively) lately steamrollered it. And so it goes for a large fraction of Earth.

Two sites do look promising: the interior desert of Australia and some southern portions of the Mongolian plateau. Australia offers the added bonus of being relatively cut off from Africa, where man apparently evolved. Our visitors might well have decided to leave any artifact as far from Africa as possible, reasoning that we would be further advanced by the time we found it.

Both these sites are relatively unexplored even today. Little grows there and few animals of any size are native. Many parts of Australia in particular are extremely hard to reach without mechanized transport or great endurance.

I am not a geologist, and the matter of guessing what sites have been most stable for very long times is a complicated one, best left to experts. The important point is that such sites may exist. Just this knowledge is not enough, though, because we return to the essential mystery of this whole discussion: Who (or what) are we dealing with? What sort of artifact would be left behind? How can we recognize it?

Obviously it should not seem natural. But after lying on Earth's surface for perhaps millions of years, it might not look very artificial by now. It must be covered by dust and gravel at least, if not rock formations of much greater weight. Without knowing specifically what its builders had in mind we cannot reasonably guess whether it could be designed to stay above-ground or not. It is impossible to say whether aliens who can fly between the stars (or send computerized ships instead) possess materials that can resist normal erosion, or have other special properties that give them away. Certainly if the artifact were large enough—say, the size of a mountain—and very regular in shape, we could spot it easily enough. Since we haven't, we should look for some more subtle beacon.

There are many attention-getting signs that do not depend on size—regular arrays, say, or differences in the quality of the light an object gives off (polarization or odd spectra). What kind of regularities? What sort of light? The possibilities are endless. For example, radar searches from orbit have already peered beneath the Sahara sands, finding "fossil" river valleys in the rock layers below. Radial rays cut in rock, pointing to a central origin, would be a simple sign of a legacy, safely buried under desert. Other methods will doubtless emerge as our surveys improve. The best we can do is look for the unexpected, and look very thoroughly.

Here we are in luck. We have detailed aerial photographic surveys of the our planet, made both from orbit and low-flying aircraft. Wide regions never before studied have been photographed through infrared and ultraviolet filters. The photographs are well systematized, so that information can be found from them conveniently and efficiently.

In the 1970s, after the first photos from Mars arrived via Mariner, it was pointed out that similar pictures of Earth with an optical resolution of one kilometer would have shown little evidence of man's civilization. Certainly we will need far greater resolution to see even one lone artifact standing in an arid desert. Thus, photos that display great detail will have to be painstakingly analyzed with a completely open mind.

A curious arrangement of a ridge line, a concentric pattern of rock formations, perhaps an abnormally high reflectivity in the ultraviolet or odd polarization—any of these could be either pure accident or, on the other hand, the first subtle clue.

Admittedly, there may be nothing in the Australian Outback or anywhere else. But a survey designed to discover such sites—or oddities on the Moon, in the asteroids, or at spots like the Lagrange points—could

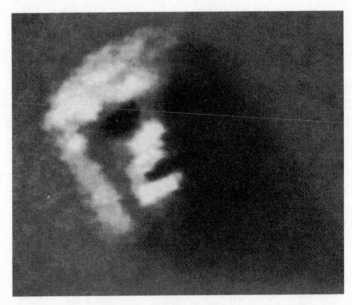

Figure 2a. A shot from Viking Orbiter (1979) showing the Mars feature which bears resemblance to the form of a human face.

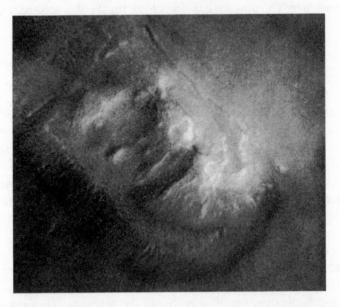

Figure 2b. The same feature imaged recently by Mars Orbiter. It shows that the feature is a naturally eroded rock formation, as expected by almost all Mars researchers. (*Photographs: Courtesy Jet Propulsion Laboratory/NASA.*)

yield interesting and significant insights into conventional astronomy or geology.

Healthy skepticism is important. For example, the "face on Mars" ferreted out from space probe photos of that surface is certainly a strange formation. It was deemed by NASA scientists almost immediately as a natural effect, but overenthusiasm by cranks for its possible ETI origin drove many scientists away from further work on it. The issue was settled by the recent high-resolution Mars Surveyor Orbiter images which prove that it is natural (see Figure 2). We risk being discredited if we give each possibility less than scrupulous study, which this one finally received.

Passive listening for radio calls requires that aliens send just when and how we choose to hear. The chances of this temporal coincidence may be quite small. Searching for artifacts can succeed if visitors passed by any time in the last several billion years.

This advantage should encourage us to undertake inexpensive searches. Computer analysis and image enhancement of Earth surface photos promise to make such studies possible as side projects to more mundane surveys, using few resources. The important point is that flexibility and an eye for oddities may yield enormous, incalculable rewards.

CHAPTER 5

SETI IN ACTION

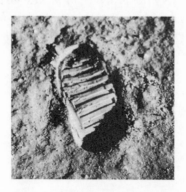

SETI is based on the fundamental fact that electromagnetic waves travel
at the speed of light, while spacecraft will necessarily be much slower.

The Universe is vast. The distance across our Milky Way Galaxy is
some 100,000 light-years. Other galaxies are millions, even billions of
light-years away. The fact that we can see the light of their stars in the
sky means that we could also receive their radio signals, if they were
sent with enough power. If they were sent at all. If there is anyone out
there to send signals.

In this chapter, Michael Papagiannis, first president of the I.A.U.
Commision 51 on Bioastronomy shows how radio searches of the sky
began, and who is doing them today. Paul Horowitz with astronomer
William Alschuler describes the evolution of his search philosophy and
the resulting increasingly challenging search programs carried out by
his group at Harvard.

In this chapter, SETI Institute scientist Kent Cullers and William
Alschuler explain how anyone with a personal computer can join the
search by joining SETI@Home. That project uses widely distributed
underutilized computer capacity (essentially, personal home computers)
to process data collected from large radio telescopes.

It is also possible for individuals—dedicated, inquisitive amateurs—
to participate in the search by collecting your own data on your own
telescope radio ("backyard radio SETI").

Amateur astronomers have made important contributions to the discovery of comets and asteroids. Ham-radio operators have helped to track artificial satellites and deep space probes. Pioneering research in the fields of electricity, meteorology, and heat flow was done by an amateur scientist named Benjamin Franklin. The race to find the first ETI signal is not entirely the province of professional astronomers with big telescopes. You can help, using equipment that is commercially available. Even if you don't make the first contact, you will have participated in the noble endeavor.

THE HUNT IS ON

By

MICHAEL D. PAPAGIANNIS

THE DAWN OF RADIO SEARCHES

Throughout history, schemes proposed or used to contact extraterrestrials have reflected the state of science of the times. With the Industrial Revolution of the nineteenth century, we begin to see more realistic ideas about how to contact other civilizations that were thought to inhabit other parts of our solar system, but none of them was implemented. The modern era of actual searches for extraterrestrial life and intelligence finally began in the twentieth century, following the development in the 1950s of the field of radio astronomy and the advent of the Space Age.

The first cosmic radio signals (radio noise from the center of our galaxy in the direction of Sagittarius) were detected by Karl Jansky in 1932, while he was studying radio interference from terrestrial sources at the Bell Telephone Laboratories in New Jersey. In 1938, Grote Reber built, in the backyard of his home in Wheaton, Illinois, the first intentional radio telescope. It had a dish thirty-one feet in diameter, which was used to produce the first radio map of the sky at a frequency of 160 MHz, near today's TV frequencies. Jansky showed that the galactic center, and a few discrete sources in the plane of the Milky Way, were strong sources of continuous radio static at several frequencies, and that the Sun was a weak radio source (except at times of solar flares).

During the Second World War, because of military needs (radar, etc.), there was great progress in radio equipment. A number of people observed the Galaxy's radio output at various frequencies and directions, always finding it to be of roughly uniform brightness independent of frequency. In 1951, Professor Edward Purcell of Harvard and his graduate student, H. Ewen, by looking along the Milky Way and observing a modest band of frequencies, managed to detect the first radio spectral line, a bright spike in the general static, emitted by atomic hydrogen centered at 1.42-GHz (at a wavelength of twenty-one centimeters), which had been predicted during the war by the Dutch astronomer Van de Hulst. Then in 1959, in their famous paper published in *Nature*, G. Cocconi and Philip Morrison recommended searching for radio signals from other stellar civilizations, and doing it near the hydrogen line frequency, which, they wrote, "Is a frequency that must be known to every observer in the Universe." They closed their paper with the statement, "The probability of success is difficult to estimate, but if we never search the chance of success is zero."

Only months later, in the spring of 1960, Frank Drake used the then-new 26 meter (85-foot) Tatel radio telescope of the newly established National Radio Astronomy Observatory (NRAO) in West Virginia to conduct the first radio search: looking for ETI signals near the hydrogen line frequency from two nearby Sun-like stars—Epsilon Eridani (10.2 light-years) and Tau Ceti (11.9 light-years). He observed them for about two hundred hours in a project he named Ozma (after the princess in *The Wizard of Oz*). Project Ozma marks the birth of modern SETI, i.e., of the new field of science that pursues "the search for extraterrestrial intelligence."

Looking back, we see that in just three decades of space exploration, we have landed men six times on the moon, and landed more than a dozen probes on Mars and on Venus; we have flown missions by the planets Mercury, Jupiter, Saturn, Uranus, and Neptune, and the Voyager and Pioneer space probes have already gone beyond all of the planets of our solar system. Soon they will become lost in the Galaxy, carrying sound recordings and golden plaques with the figures of a man and a woman, like greeting cards from the people of Earth to any extraterrestrial civilization that may find them.

The searches for life in our solar system have so far been negative, including the two Viking probes that landed on Mars in 1976 and tested its soil for biological activity and for the presence of organic compounds. Probes, possibly some manned ones, are being sent to Mars again during the next ten to twenty years to study our neighboring planet more carefully, because close-up photographs indicate that Mars may have had periods with liquid water on it.

A recent announcement by a NASA team that a meteorite found on

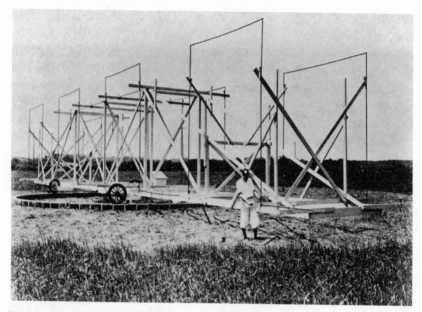

Figure 1. Karl Jansky and his rotatable radio antenna. With it he discovered that radio noise is emitted by celestial sources. (*Photo: Courtesy AT&T Archives.*)

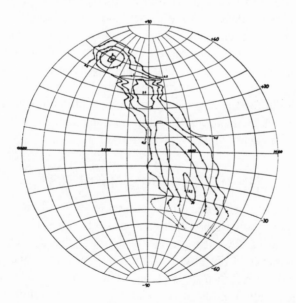

Figure 2. Grote Reber's contour map of celestial radio noise. The main contours coincide with the outline of the Milky Way and the galactic center. The concentrations at the upper left were eventually identified as a supernova remnant, and colliding galaxies. (*Source: The Milky Way.*)

the Antarctic ice cap, which everyone agrees is from Mars, harbors internal fossil and mineralogical evidence of microbial life was met with great scepticism by other scientific teams. The issue is not yet settled.

Probes are also being planned for Titan (the Cassini mission), the large moon of Saturn where prebiotic chemistry seems to be active. The Galileo mission, which recently visited the Galilean moons of Jupiter, found evidence that Europa, under its icy crust, may have a subterranean ocean of liquid water and hence the possibility of life. A follow-up probe to search for liquid water is now in design. Over all, however, the probability of finding life anywhere else in our solar system seems at present to be low, though higher now than before these discoveries.

The search for direct evidence of *primitive life* in other solar systems is still beyond our technical capabilities. With the rapid development of space astronomy, though, it seems likely that in the next ten to twenty years we will have large astronomical observatories in space and/or on the moon. These will be free from the problems caused by Earth's atmosphere and will allow us to make a more stringent search for planets around other stars than we have been able to carry out from the ground. Ultimately we hope to discover Earth-like planets, and to study them spectroscopically, searching for spectral lines of oxygen and ozone that would signal the presence of life. (Oxygen and ozone are highly reactive chemically, and therefore they cannot long exist in a planetary atmosphere without being continuously replenished through biological processes similar to photosynthesis.)

At present, however, the most likely way to detect the presence of life elsewhere in the Universe seems to be through radio signals sent to us by advanced civilizations. For this reason, SETI is now the area where we are focusing most of our search efforts.

THE DEVELOPMENT OF SETI

In the nearly forty years since the pioneering Project Ozma, scientists have carried out more than sixty search projects, most of them at radio frequencies, but a few also in the ultraviolet, the optical, and the infrared. Jill Tarter of the SETI Institute maintains an active file of all these projects. So far all projects together have accumulated approximately three hundred thousand search hours, and ten countries (United States, Soviet Union, Australia, Canada, France, Germany, Holland, England, Japan, and Argentina) have been active in this effort. Almost

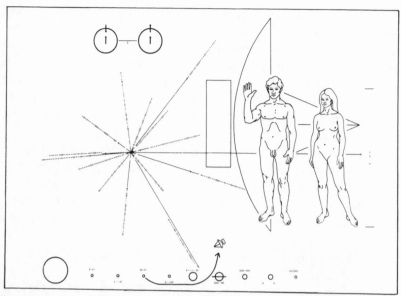

Figure 3. An image from the plaque being carried by the Pioneer spacecraft to the stars. It bears a schematic of the Pioneer's path out of the solar system, the hydrogen molecule, and the directions from Earth to various pulsars—along with codes for their frequencies. This information would give alien astronomers the date and place of origin of the spacecraft. (*Photo: Courtesy of The Astronomical Society of the Pacific; NASA.*)

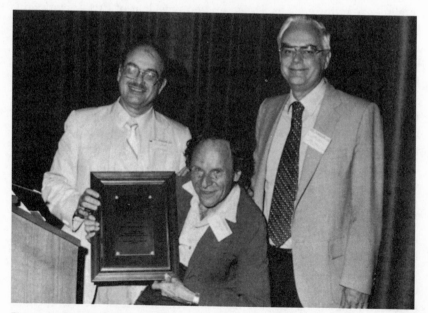

Figure 4. Pioneers of SETI. From left to right: Michael Papagiannis, Philip Morrison, and Frank Drake. (*Photo: Courtesy Michael Papagiannis.*)

all of these radio searches have been conducted at select "magic frequencies" as they are called—the characteristic spectral lines of common atoms, such as the hydrogen line at twenty-one centimeters, and
molecules and radicals, such as the four hydroxyl (OH) lines around
eighteen centimeters (about 1.665 GHz), in the hope that other stellar
civilizations will choose to broadcast at these universally known frequencies to make it easier for young civilizations, such as ours, to pick
up their messages.

Probably more than 90 percent of the search hours we have accumulated so far have been at the hydrogen line frequency, but unfortunately this strategy has not paid off. As a result we have reoriented our
efforts toward searches that will cover much wider ranges of frequencies. This was not possible in the early days of SETI, but technology has
advanced rapidly in these thirty years, and we can now search for signals simultaneously in many different frequencies using Multi-Channel
Spectrum Analyzers.

An important step in the development of SETI was the fact that the
International Astronomical Union (IAU), the world body in astronomy,
in 1982 espoused this new effort and established a special commission
for it, named IAU Commission 51—Bioastronomy. The term "bioastronomy" describes the new branch of astronomy that searches for life and
intelligence in the cosmos. I was the first president of IAU Commission
51, from 1982 to 1985. I was followed by Frank Drake (1985–1988),
now retired from the University of California, Santa Cruz, by G. Marx
(1988–1991), of Eotvos University in Hungary, and it is presently
headed by Stuart Bowyer at U.C. Berkeley. IAU Commission 51 grew
rapidly to a membership of three hundred astronomers from thirty-
three countries, established its own newsletter (*Bioastronomy News*),
and held its first IAU Symposium in 1984 in Boston, its second in 1987
in Hungary, and held its third in 1990 in France. Following the success
of our first IAU Symposium, the science magazine *Nature* asked me to
write a review article, which was published in 1985. The success of this
new IAU commission was a clear indication of the strong interest that
exists for this field within the scientific community, as well as among
the general public. Since then bioastronomy has been taken on by
NASA as the Astrobiology program (see the postscript).

Two other important contributions to the acceptability of SETI also
occurred in 1982. One was a letter in support of SETI that was prepared
by Carl Sagan, signed by seventy prominent scientists, including eight

Nobel laureates, and published in *Science*. The other was a recommendation from the committee on astronomy of the U.S. National Academy of Science for the expenditure of funds to advance SETI in the 1980s. The money was appropriated by Congress in the early 1990s but cut off in 1993. Some Federal money is going to sophisticated optical searches for oxy-water planets, but all the SETI projects are now funded outside of government.

The SETI projects conducted so far can be divided into three general groups: directed, shared or parasitic, and dedicated.

DIRECTED SEARCHES

These searches use a major observatory for a relatively sort period to carry out a specific SETI project. Typical examples are the following: P. Palmer and B. Zuckerman used the 91-meter (300-foot) antenna of the National Radio Astronomy Observatory (NRAO) in West Virginia to study the hydrogen line frequency looking toward 674 stars, in 5 hundred hours of observations. This project, which they named Ozma II, was conducted intermittently over a four-year period between 1972 and 1976.

J. Tarter, et al., from 1979 to 1981, used the Arecibo radio telescope in Puerto Rico (which, with a diameter of 305 meters, is the largest in the world) to observe 210 Sun-like stars in a 4-MHz band around the magic frequencies of hydrogen and hydroxyl. They also used a new technique and a CDC 7600 computer to obtain an excellent frequency resolution of 5.5 Hz.

Lord and O'Dea used the 14-meter (45-foot) diameter millimeter-wavelength radio telescope of the University of Massachusetts to look near the frequency of the 115 GHz line of the carbon monoxide molecule for strong beacons along the north portion of the rotational axis of our galaxy. This is a potentially magic location for beacons operated by supercivilizations, because from such a vantage position they would be able to have direct line-of-sight access to every part of the galactic disk, unobstructed by the dust and gas that lies in the plane of the galactic disk.

Another interesting search was undertaken in 1983 by Freitas and Valdez, who used the Hat Creek radio telescope in California to conduct a search at the 1.516 GHz line of tritium, which is the heaviest isotope of hydrogen (one proton and two neutrons). Since tritium is unstable and has a half-life of only 12.5 years, if found in the vicinity of normal stars it must be of artificial origin and hence most likely the by-product of huge nuclear fusion plants.

None of these searches had positive results.

Freitas and Valdez also used the seventy-five centimeter (thirty-inch) optical telescope of the Kitt Peak National Observatory (KPNO) to search for artifacts and probes possibly placed in our solar system by extrasolar civilizations. They looked for them at the magic locations of the L4 and L5 Lagrange points of the Earth-Moon and Earth-Sun systems. These are regions in space where objects tend to remain, even if perturbed by outside forces, and, therefore, the regions from which extraterrestrial stations could be observing Earth. Five of these special points were discovered by the French mathematician and astronomer Louis Lagrange (1736–1813). Three of them (the less stable) are along the line that connects the two major bodies, while each of the other two (L4 and L5), which are much more stable, form equilateral triangles with the two major bodies and travel with the smaller of the two, 60 degrees ahead of it and 60 degrees behind it, in its orbit around the larger one.

In 1978, W. Sullivan, et al., of the University of Washington, proposed that an alternative search strategy for ETI beacons would be to look in the direction of nearby stars for radio signals leaking unintentionally into space from advanced civilizations. As a test, Sullivan and Knowles used the Arecibo radio telescope to observe the radio leakage of Earth in the 150-500 MHz range, by observing reflections from the Moon. Strong television stations and powerful military radars were the most prominent sources seen. The space surveillance radar of the U.S. Navy in Archer City, Texas, for example, which operates at 217 MHz, emitting pulses in all directions with total power of 14 billion watts in a bandwidth of only 0.1 Hz, could be detected by a civilization with Arecibo-type telescope technology up to a distance of *20 light-years*. Knowles and Sullivan also did a limited eavesdropping search on a few nearby stars, using the Arecibo radio telescope and the Mark I VLBI (very long baseline interferometry) system, which, because of the large distances that separate its various radio telescopes, is able to achieve a high angular resolution and thus focus on a small region of the sky. Although this test run found no signals, it did show that eavesdropping is an alternative search process that is feasible and can also be pursued.

SHARED AND PARASITIC SEARCHES

Shared and parasitic searches either reanalyze archived data that had been obtained for other purposes for ETI signals, or they share in a parasitic or piggyback fashion the data being obtained by a radio telescope for an unrelated project, and process them for ETI signals as they are being obtained.

F. Israel of the Netherlands, working in 1981 first with DeRuiter and then with Jill Tarter, reanalyzed many of the 21 centimeter "noisy" sky maps that had been obtained with the Westerbork telescope array of Holland and had been stored by the Dutch astronomers. They were looking for strong radio sources in positions that coincided with known stars. In another project N. Cohen, et al., in 1980 reanalyzed their own surveys of globular clusters, looking for narrow-band signals at the frequencies of OH and H_2O masers (pure-frequency, high-intensity beams from dust clouds), at 18 and 1.35 centimeters respectively, that may get tapped by supercivilizations to produce strong signals in certain directions.

In 1980, S. Bowyer and D. Werthimer of the University of California, Berkeley, and their coworkers built an automated 100-channel spectrum analyzer to siphon off data obtained by a radio telescope for an unrelated project. This parasitic or piggyback SETI device was named SERENDIP and was used with the Hat Creek and Goldstone antennas. It was later upgraded to SERENDIP II, which has a 131,072-channel fast Fourier processor with a resolution of 0.49 Hz per channel. The system can operate unattended on a twenty-four-hour basis with practically any radio telescope. This project was extended into the 90s and is still in use (see the chapter by Cullere and Alschuler). In the mid-1980s I undertook a search for large artificial objects (such as space colonies or processing plants) in our solar system, and especially in the asteroid belt, which is an ideal source of raw materials (metals and water), to test the theory of galactic colonization; that is, the possibility that the entire Galaxy might have already been colonized by supercivilizations. I used the infrared astronomy satellite (IRAS) data bank of infrared sources in our solar system (mostly asteroids and a few comets). IRAS was developed by a group of scientists, of which I was a member, who assembled at the Infrared Processing and Analysis Center of Caltech to look for infrared objects in our solar system. My intent was to scrutinize about ten thousand images for infrared spectra that were too hot to be due merely to reflected sunlight, in the hope that artificial materials of energy-intensive industry would show up, much as our cities stand out as "heat islands." Unfortunately, due to insufficient funding I was not able to complete my search.

DEDICATED SEARCHES

Dedicated searches are performed by radio observatories that have SETI-dedicated facilities and conduct searches on a continuous basis. Three such projects, two of which are now in operation account for most of the observing hours accumulated thus far. The oldest of the Three was the Ohio SETI program, which was in operation from 1973 until 1996 under the direction of Dr. J. Kraus and Dr. R. Dixon. It used the meridian-transit radio telescope of the Ohio State University, which had a collecting area the equivalent of a parabolic dish 53 meters (175 feet) in diameter. The search was conducted at the hydrogen line frequency with the help of a fifty-channel filter bank with a resolution of 10 KHz (kiloherz) per channel. The Ohio SETI program was sustained with modest support from NASA and the tireless efforts of Kraus, Dixon, and many enthusiastic volunteers. A major false alarm in this project was the so-called "wow" signal recorded in 1977, which, in spite of repeated efforts, has not been found again. The project was terminated and the telescope torn down to make way for a real estate development.

Since March 1983 Professor Paul Horowitz of Harvard University and his collaborators have been operating the other SETI-dedicated facility using the 26-meter (84-foot) radio telescope of the Oak Ridge-Harvard-Smithsonian Observatory near Boston. This project is supported by the Planetary Society, a private organization which was headed by Professor Carl Sagan. Initally it had two 65,536-channel spectrum analyzers, with a frequency resolution of 0.03 Hz per channel. Horowitz and his colleagues then built a new-MCSA with 8.4 million channels and a frequency resolution of 0.05 Hz per channel, which provides a total bandwidth of 420 KHz, enough to account for practically all the Doppler effects due to the relative motions of Earth and the transmitting source. This second system was named Project META and started operating in September 1985. It covered all of the available sky at the hydrogen 21-centimeter line 5 times and also at twice the hydrogen frequency. This project has been succeeded by BETA, and Horowitz has recently begun optical and infrared searches. (See the chapter by Horowitz and Alschuler.)

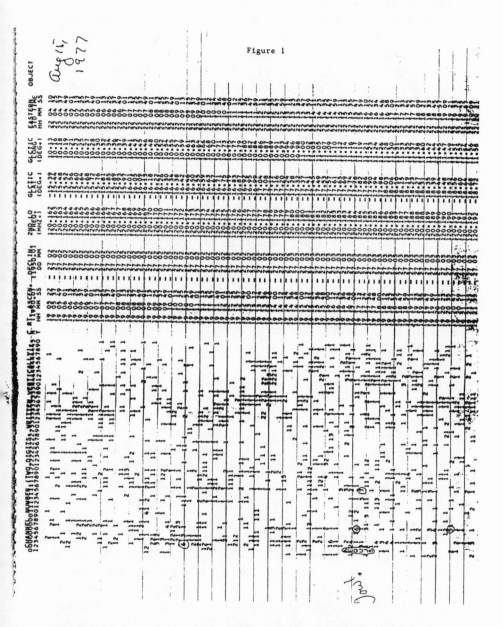

Figure 5. The "Wow!" signal. It was recorded on a computer prontout of radio noise intensity from 50 frequencey channels (digits and letters at left) at varying sky positions. (*Photo: Courtesy Robert Dixon; Ohio State University Radio Observatory.*)

A third dedicated facility, also supported by the Planetary Society, began to operate around 1991 near La Plata, Argentina. It is under the direction of Dr. Raul Colomb, and uses the La Plata thirty meter (ninety-one foot) radio telescope. Two of the members of the La Plata team worked with Horowitz to build the MCSA that was used initially in Argentina, essentially the same kind as the one used at Harvard. The exciting aspect of this new SETI-dedicated facility is that it is able to scan for the first time the southern skies that have been inaccessible to the other two SETI-dedicated facilities, both of which are in the United States.

THE NASA SETI PROJECT

The search for ETI radio signals is a multidimensional problem, which because of its complexity and size is often called the cosmic haystack. The dimensions of the "search space" include: coverage of the sky; frequency range; sensitivity; bandwidth; polarization; signal modulation; on-off periods, and more. Initially investigators, especially in the United States, had hoped that extraterrestrial civilizations would be transmitting at the hydrogen line to make contact easy. But extensive though not exhaustive searches by many observers at the hydrogen and a few other magic frequencies have produced no positive results.

With the rapid advance of technology, NASA embarked on the next generation of radio searches, namely to undertake systematic searches over wide frequency ranges in the microwave window (1-10 GHz) of Earth's atmosphere. This range is relatively free of cosmic radio noise and therefore is well suited for interstellar communications. Embedded deep in the microwave window is the "water hole" (1.4-17 GHz), which is especially noise-free, and therefore the most attractive range for interstellar radio communications. A point of great concern, however, is the rapidly growing use of this frequency range by our civilization for other purposes (such as satellite communications), which are bound to interfere with our future radio searches.

It is generally believed that SETI signals will be narrow-band to save power. Therefore, in order to have a good signal-to-noise ratio we need receivers with very narrow bandwidths, and since we want to explore a wide frequency range, we need a very large number of narrow-band channels. This function was fulfilled by special MCSAs that NASA developed, each with 8.25 million channels (slightly fewer than META), but with a much wider total bandwidth than the MCSA of

Horowitz. This new MCSA was constructed for NASA by a group at Stanford University headed by A. Peterson and I. Linscott. The highest frequency resolution was about 1 Hz per channel, giving a total bandwidth of about 8 MHz. It was able to analyze simultaneously the incoming 8 MHz frequency band into channels of 32, 1,024, and 73,728 Hz.

There were significant tradeoffs between the NASA SETI project and Horowitz's META project. The most important is the bandwidth of each channel, which in the META project was twenty times narrower and therefore secured a much better signal-to-noise ratio for very-narrowband signals. The NASA project, on the other hand, with channels that were twenty times wider, was able to cover a much wider frequency range, allowing for almost any conceivable relative motion between us and a source, which is actually its main objective.

Signals that exceeded a predetermined threshold chosen by the desired signal-to-noise ratio were flagged for further testing. Sophisticated signal detection algorithms were developed by NASA, and a considerable effort was made to achieve on-line processing of the data, a difficult task given the huge volume of incoming data with an 8-million-channel MCSA. Emphasis was also placed on the ability to detect pulsed signals and signals with a velocity-caused frequency drift (the velocity between us and the sender). The first 8-million-channel MCSA was ready in the early 1992, and went on line in October.

The prototype unit with 73,728 channels, together with several of the new signal-recognition algorithms, underwent tests with the 64-meter (208 foot) diameter Goldstone antenna in California. It was able to pick up the very weak (1-watt) signal beamed by the Pioneer 10 spacecraft toward Earth, from a distance of about thirty-five astronomical units (five billion kilometers)—the fringes of our solar system. It was also able to see clearly the frequency drifts imposed on this signal by the rotation of Earth and the relative motion of Earth and the spacecraft. Pioneer is now too faint but Voyager 2 is still being used as a test object, as it is in the process of passing through the boundary that separates the solar wind from interstellar space. After just a few months of searching this project was shut down in 1993.

The NASA SETI project was headed by Dr. John Billingham of NASA-Ames. His deputy was Dr. Bernard Oliver, and the project scientist was Dr. Jill Tarter; all are pioneers of SETI. The NASA SETI project had two components. The targeted search was the responsibility of NASA-Ames and, as mentioned elsewhere, emphasized high sensitivity to weak signals by concentrating only on a number of discrete sources. The sky survey was carried out by the NASA group at the Jet Propulsion Laboratory (JPL) headed by Dr. Michael Klein, and scanned the entire sky.

It is estimated that the NASA SETI project would have taken five to ten years, depending on how many of the 8-million-channel MCSAs became available. Thus, starting in 1992, it would have been completed around the year 2000, or the year 2001 as someone with a cosmic sense of humor once said. The targeted search, under Jill Tarter's direction, was taken over by the SETI Institute and is running strong. The all-sky search is not operating and Michael Klein is now running a forward-looking project to detect planets with oxygen around other stars.

PROGRAMS ABROAD

It is true that the United States has dominated the searches for extra-terrestrial intelligence and has piled up many more search hours than any other country in the world. It is also true, however, that several other countries have made significant contributions to this effort. Most prominent among them is the former Soviet Union, which was a leader in the early years of CETI (as they prefer to call it, using "Contact" instead of "Search" before ETI). In this effort, their leaders were I. Shklovskii, V. S. Troitskii, N. Kardashev, and V. I. Slysh. The effort has been compromised by the funding crisis in Russia.

Shklovskii wrote one of the earliest books on life in the Universe, published in the U.S.S.R in 1963. A version in English, significantly expanded by Carl Sagan, was published in the U.S. in 1966 with the title *Intelligent Life in the Universe*. Shklovskii died in 1985, but in the last ten years of his life he had become pessimistic about finding extra-terrestrial intelligence.

V. S. Troitskii was the leader in most of the searches that were conducted in the Soviet Union. In 1968 he carried out a search from his own Radiophysical Insitute in Gorki, targeted at ten nearby stars. In the 1970s he and Kardashev became the leaders of a major search that involved simultaneous observations from several stations around the Soviet Union, as well as from the ship *Academician Kurchatov* cruising near the equator. Measurements were made in the one-half to 10 GHz range, and the wide separation of the stations allowed them to estimate the direction of signals from the delays in their arrival at the different stations. It appears that they observed only terrestrial signals originating either in the ionosphere or in the magnetosphere of the Earth. In the early 1980s Troitskii was preparing a new search in Gorki that would have involved one hundred small (one-meter diameter) radio telescopes, operating at the hydrogen frequency, but he became seriously ill and the project was abandoned.

V. I. Slysh conducted a search at the hydroxyl frequency from 1970 to 1972 that was targeted at ten nearby stars using the Nancay radio telescope in France. More recently he conducted a sky survey of the 3-degree universal background radiation using a satellite radiometer at infrared wavelengths. The smoothness of the background ruled out the existence of Dyson Spheres, up to a distance of about three hundred light-years. Dyson Spheres are postulated megaconstruction projects, built by supercivilizations, which surround their star to utilize as much of its energy as possible, and thus their whole solar system would become a huge infrared (heat) source. A similar study was conducted in the late 1980s by Kardashev and Slysh using infrared data of the IRAS satellite to search again for Dyson Spheres (this became a rather strange preoccupation of the Soviet scientists). Their new sixty-five-meter (211 foot) millimeter-wave radio telescope in Samarkand is now approaching completion, and I was told that they plan to use it also for SETI.

Another interesting former Soviet project, called Mania, was conducted by Victorij Shvartsman, who used the 6-meter (19.5 foot) optical telescope of the Soviet Union in Zelenchuksksaya to search for optical pulses and for ultra-narrow spectral lines due to lasers. Shvartsman died in the fall of 1987, and the project was discontinued.

Several search projects have also been conducted in other countries. In 1977, for example, Wielebinski and Seiradakis used the 100-meter (325-foot) radio telescope in Bonn, Germany, combining a search for pulsars with a search for extraterrestrial signals. Starting in 1981 and continuing at intervals in the years that followed, Tarter and Biraud had been using the large radio telescope in Nancay, France, to observe three hundred stars at several of the magic frequencies. Paul Feldman and colleagues have repeatedly used the 48-meter (158 foot) Algonquin radio telescope in Ontario, Canada, to conduct radio searches, while in 1983 Sam Gulkis used the 63-meter (205 foot) Tinbinbilla antenna of the NASA Deep Space Network in Australia to conduct a search of the southern skies at 8 GHz. I have already mentioned the SETI-dedicated facility that was initiated in Argentina in 1991, and thus it must be quite evident that the search for extraterrestrial life and intelligence has finally become an international effort.

Characteristic of this development is also the fact that the "Flag of the Earth," which was designed by James W. Cadle and shows part of the yellow Sun, the blue disk of the Earth, and the small white disk of the Moon against the black background of outer space, is now flying on all observatories that are doing SETI work, to show that this is a joint effort of all mankind.

SOME CONCLUDING THOUGHTS

A simple comparison of the original Project Ozma to the Arecibo radio telescope with a powerful MCSA makes it obvious that we have made great technological progress in just three decades. A related question often asked is: why don't we postpone our searches until our technology becomes more advanced? I believe that the answer has two parts. The first is that we never know in advance the level of technology needed to succeed. It would have been a grave mistake, for example, to have asked the Wright brothers to wait for the discovery of the jet engine before trying to fly. They succeeded with far less, and on December 17, 1903, they opened the doors of the new field of aviation. I am sure that even if Drake could have known that 25 years later Horowitz would have an MCSA with 8 million channels for a search around the hydrogen line frequency, he still would have gone ahead with his Project Ozma, and rightfully so.

The second reason is that technology is like a ladder that we must climb one rung at a time, starting from the lowest ones. But as we climb higher, our horizons broaden and many new technological developments materialize—such as the jet engine in aviation and light-weight materials that withstand high temperatures in space programs, which also benefit many other fields.

After millennia of thinking and philosophizing about the plurality of worlds, we have finally entered the experimental era of SETI. We have already used space probes to search for primitive life in our solar system, and we are now searching with our radio, optical, and infrared telescopes for advanced civilizations in the Galaxy. It is a special privilege to live in the era that tries to answer experimentally profound, old questions about the prevalence of life, and especially of life with intelligence, in the Universe. With the many parallel special searches now in progress or planned for the near future, we can expect that in the next ten to twenty years we will learn much more about the presence of other advanced civilizations in our galaxy.

If we are to find them, this would certainly be the greatest discovery in the history of mankind. But even if after concerted efforts we were to conclude that we must be one of very few if not the *only* advanced civilization in our galaxy, this too would be an important result. Because knowing how rare our civilization is, among the hundreds of billions of stars of our galaxy, would hopefully make us realize how cosmically important it is to preserve it.

POSTSCRIPT TO PAPAGIANNIS

by

KENT CULLERS

Today, by whatever name, the SETI community has become a part of mainstream radio astronomy. Bioastronomy, exobiology, astrobiology, all have enough proponents that talks are given to define their differences. Generally, all of these refer to the study of astronomical signatures of life, from simple to complex. NASA has funded a $100 million program for astrobiology which studies everything except SETI. The IAU, International Astronomical Union, prefers the term bioastronomy since it focuses on how astronomers can find life, and this discipline includes SETI. In Europe, exobiology is all the rage, sometimes including SETI and sometimes not.

Whatever the venue, from Lake Balaton in Hungary, Santa Cruz, California, Italy on the beautiful island of Capri, or the big island of Hawaii, meetings discuss the detection of life beyond the solar system, and because SETI is privately funded today, it is always a part of the act. In any event, the search for life in the universe has become a science in its own right, and, at the millennium, relevant discoveries are coming fast.

As I write, I am sitting in a hotel room in Hawaii at the 1999 Bioastronomy Symposium which is held every 3 years by Commission 51, the Bioastronomy commission of the IAU. All the major scientific disciplines are here, represented by comet chemists, planetologists, spectrographers, anthropologists, signal processors and more. The level of excitement is very high. Today, we stand in an astonishing state of ignorance. We know how much we *don't* know. In just a decade, the early spectroscopic attempts to find planets have born fruit. Planets cannot yet be seen directly; twenty years of major NASA missions must yet succeed before that is even theoretically possible, but we can see the effects of planets on visible stars. As a planet orbits its primary star, it attracts this visible object just as the primary attracts the planet. Since the star is heavier, it moves much less than the planet. Nonetheless, the star's motion is visible, not directly as displacement, but as its derivative, velocity. Light from the star passing from telescope to spectroscope is directed through a gas with known lines in the visible spectrum. Comparison of the spectral lines of the star with those of the known, laboratory gas, allows an estimate of stellar velocity. The Doppler shifted stellar lines are compared with hundreds of lines in the laboratory gas, allowing random errors in the estimate to be averaged away. The high precision of the result allows the detection of planets in a way which does not depend on the distance of the star from us.

We know now that there are more planets outside the solar system than within it. The evidence for extrasolar planetary systems is tantalizing but very preliminary. Because large, nearby planets pull harder on stars than small distant ones, thus giving them higher velocities, most of the planets detected to date are Jupiter mass or larger, with orbits at least as close to their star as the Earth's. This does not mean, in any sense, that such a system is typical because the early results are so biased by the limits of air search technique. Even so, the systems discovered are so deviant from ours that most of our models for planet formation are being revised because of the new data. After all, we must be able to explain both our solar system and the new discoveries. The technique is new, so planets with long period orbits like our own Jupiter and Saturn have not yet been discovered in great numbers. So, we know there are planets, numerous planets orbiting single stars, but we have no idea yet what a typical solar system looks like.

As if this were not exciting enough, we have new hope for life in our solar system. Mars is again being actively explored because of speculation stirred by analysis of a meteorite, ALH84001, ejected from the Martian surface by a cosmic collision and collected in relatively uncontaminated condition from the ice of Antarctica. The meteorite contains carbon compounds and microstructures which may indicate that life existed on Mars billions of years ago. Most of the scientific community is not convinced that this proof is definitive, but everyone acknowledges its possibility, and is excited by the new opportunities in the early 2000's to test the reality of the conjecture. These tests have already begun with more accurate maps of Mars, will include a sample return, and even, possibly, a manned mission.

The new images of Mars have strengthened the conjectures of an early ocean, perhaps a hundred meters deep, covering half of the planet. If water is present, can life be far behind? Certainly, given what we know, the chemistry of life is possible given abundant water and the chemistry of an early Mars.

Speaking of water, Europa will be explored with detailed mapping early in the next decade. This Jovian satellite may have more liquid water than the Earth. An early conjecture, first put forth by Arthur C. Clarke in his 2001 science fiction series, has proven accurate. All of the evidence from recent surveys of Jupiter by the Galileo probe has shown an icy Europan surface with cracks typical of ice flows. Given the small solar energy flux at Europa, this evidence of a water-ice surface is unexpected, but tidal heating by Jupiter supplies enough energy to keep the satellite warm. If water is liquid, and it gets warmer as one approaches the planetary core, the life chemistry is possible, though it must grow in the dark.

However, we have found whole new domains of life in our own ocean depths and below the earth's surface. The life is exotic, by our standards, utilizing nonphotosynthetic chemistries. It is powered by geothermal energy, which originates from radioactivity on Earth, but likely would be tidally derived in Europa. Here at home, new estimates indicate that most of the biomass of Earth might be underground, in microbial reservoirs. Perhaps, life in the Milky Way Galaxy is mostly primitive, living safely below the surface of planets with internal energy reservoirs.

It may actually be the case that surface life is a hardy but minor branch of the living tree with roots deep within the planetary structure. Because we do not know the probability that life, once evolved, will become intelligent, NASA has developed missions to look for primitive, as well as intelligent life. This endeavor, expected to succeed in perhaps three decades, will image nearby planetary systems directly and analyze their spectra. Perhaps biological signatures like that of excess oxygen will indicate in an unambiguous way that life, at least primitive life, exists beyond our solar system. To do such imaging, multiple telescopes will be employed as interferometers so that planetary reflected light can be seen against the much brighter parent stars. With multiple telescopes, the bright, stellar image can be subtracted from that of the total solar system, so that only the planet's light remains.

This burgeoning of efforts to search for primitive life inside and outside the solar system does not exclude SETI. It may be, in the end, that looking for intelligent signals is the most direct and effective way to look for life. With a little help from our technological cousins, we could soon detect a signal of artificial origin, sent hundreds or thousands of years ago, from a distant star.

Bioastronomy, a new field brought into being by the IAU and others, is one of the most exciting of the interdisciplinary sciences. Filled with discoveries and hints of discovery, it promises a new bright era to correspond with the new millennium.

THE HARVARD SETI SEARCH

BY

PAUL HOROWITZ AND
WILLIAM R. ALSCHULER

G iven the overwhelming likelihood of extraterrestrial life, and the plausibility of intelligent life (by which we here mean life that has acquired the technology required to carry out interstellar communication), the central problem in experimental SETI is to predict the mode of communication that the sending civilization may be using to establish contact. During the past few decades there has been general agreement that, among the known possibilities, electromagnetic radiation is the method of choice (though one is certainly free to quarrel even with that choice), given its combination of speed, freedom from interference and absorption, and overall efficiency.

Even if we confine our attention to electromagnetic radiation, however, we are left with too many possibilities: the electromagnetic continuum offers hundreds of gigahertz of bandwidth in the regime called radio waves, topped by hundreds of terahertz of optical bandwidth, and so on up to the wavelengths we conventionally call X-rays and gamma rays. For good reasons the SETI establishment, if we can call it that, generally held the view, stable now for about thirty years, that microwave radiation is the optimum method for galactic communication. That conclusion rested upon the observation that at longer wavelengths one must contend with the radio noise pollution of the Galaxy (caused primarily by radiation from electrons spiraling in galactic magnetic fields), and that at shorter wavelengths one must contend with the effects of granularity of detection (or "shot noise") due to the particle nature of the radiation itself. Furthermore, communication through a planetary atmosphere like ours favors the long wavelength portion of this microwave interstellar band, approximately from 30 centimeters to 3 centimeters.

It is worth noting that this view—that centimeter-wave electromagnetic radiation is the galactic communication band of choice, particularly for establishing first contact (as opposed to routine communication, once contact has been made)—was never universally held, and there have been thoughtful proponents of infrared laser communication for years. For example, Schwartz and Townes, Kingsley, Betz, Ross and rather have all contributed to the idea. Our thinking in this area has evolved and Harvard-Smithsonian team searches, as well as searches at U.C. Berkeley and elsewhere are now expanding into the visible spectrum, due in part to lack of results in the microwave region and in part to advances in optical detectors, sources and computing power. Furthermore, if one permits the sending civilization to use existing natural radiation (rather than generating the signal from scratch), all bets are off: One could imagine constructing a giant venetian blind shutter, to cause the light seen from our star to wink on and off! In spite of alternative ideas, the advantages of centimeter-wave communication are enormous, hence their popularity: It is a remarkable fact that a pair of 300-meter diameter antennas communicating at a wavelength of 3 centimeters and at a range of one thousand light-years (within which there are roughly a million candidate stars similar to the Sun) would consume only about a dollar's worth of electricity per word transmitted. Given the maturity of microwave technology in 1960 (relative to infrared and optical), searches at centimeter wavelengths were the obvious first choice.

A thorough microwave ETI search protocol, then, would consist of a search of the entire sky (or at least the nearest 100 million stars), over the plausible microwave band, looking for radio signals that may be sent in the form of pulses, or carriers (a steady signal—the opposite of a pulse), or some combination ("pulsed carriers"). This is a tall order, and requires resources on a national scale, particularly if one insists on continuous (rather than consecutive) full-sky coverage.

History is littered with overly grand enterprises that tried to plan too much, too early. The same goes particularly for SETI, where we know too little (of the distribution of planetary systems, the prevalence of life, etc.). Furthermore, it isn't exactly easy to mount an effort on a multi-billion-dollar scale, particularly if one is interested in seeing it happen in one's lifetime. In fact, as described elsewhere, the U.S. Government's program was defunded by Congress; at the time of writing there is no nationally-funded SETI anywhere in the world.

With these considerations in mind, my group at Harvard began a series of modest searches for signals from extraterrestrial intelligence, based on the fundamental assumption that the sending civilization, being more advanced than we, would do their best to make it easy for us to detect their beacon signal. (They will be more advanced because: (1) less advanced civilizations do not have the technology to communicate at all—the slice of communicative history behind us is thin; and (2) Drake's equation requires long-lived technological civilizations, if there are to be significant numbers coexisting. Thus, most communicating civilizations will be more advanced; furthermore, the more advanced are by definition capable of more powerful transmissions, further favoring contact.)

And so we sought a guessable signal—one whose characteristics we can deduce without prior contact. In our first searches we applied the usual criteria: The method of communication should be efficient (hence microwaves), at a guessable frequency (something like the hydrogen line at 21 centimeters, as originally proposed by Cocconi and Morrison), with guessable modulation (we favor pure carriers, as we shall explain), and guessable allowance for the sender's velocity relative to us. These assumptions were tested and eventually modified.

"Modulation" is an interesting variable: will ET signals be sent as AM or FM, or some sort of sophisticated digital pulse scheme? The choice depends on what the signal is supposed to do.

Information theory teaches us that, in general, the best carrier of information is simultaneously the worst beacon. Thus the interstellar beacon engineer will probably separate the functions of establishing contact (i.e., the beacon) and conveying information (i.e., the communication channel). The beacon is what we seek initially, in the most difficult phase of establishing contact. For this purpose the most likely choices are either a pure carrier or a regular train of pulses. Good arguments can be made for each. We optimized our microwave searches for pure narrow-band carriers because: (1) they are easier to detect, using straightforward Fourier spectrum analysis techniques; (2) they stand out as clearly artificial, being a fraction of a hertz wide in a Universe where the narrowest natural spectral features are at least a kilohertz wide; (3) they are efficient beacons, permitting excellent received signal/noise ratios through coherent integration; and (4) they permit effective discrimination against terrestrial interference, owing to the particular time-varying Doppler shift signature that is impressed upon a true extraterrestrial signal by the effect of the Earth's rotation.

This matter of carrier bandwidth and Doppler shifts deserves further discussion and is true at all wavelengths. A pure (single-frequency) carrier is spread somewhat in frequency after passage through the turbulent charged plasma of the interstellar medium. For distances on the order of 1,000 light-years, the spreading is very slight, something like 0.1 Hz at the microwave frequencies we were interested in. We can optimize detection of carriers of that width by using a multichannel spectrometer whose channels have a matching bandwidth. We are now faced with a problem, however, because the Earth's rotation causes the received frequency to vary periodically up and down, or "chirp." This is both bad news and good news. The bad news is that we have to work hard and chirp our receiver to match the expected signal's chirp; the good news is that interfering terrestrial signals (from the intelligent life rumored to live on Earth) don't have the correct chirp signature, and are thus easily distinguished from the real thing (as well as being weakened enormously by the chirp operation).

Doppler shifts rear their ugly heads in yet another way. Interstellar velocities are quite large—tens to hundreds of kilometers per second, within our galaxy alone—and cause corresponding frequency shifts (which, unlike the "chirp" caused by the Earth's rotation, are unchanging with time) of a few megahertz, at microwave frequencies. We can handle this problem in several ways. One possibility is to build spectrometers of large enough bandwidth to cover all reasonable Doppler shifts; another is to assume the senders have transmitted their signals at a frequency precompensated for their motions relative to a guessable frame of reference. In the first case we need very large numbers of channels—several MHz total bandwidth, divided by channel widths of order 0.1Hz, or several tens of millions of channels; the second case requires many fewer channels; but with the required assumptions as to the intentions of the transmitting civilization, one is, of course, skating on very thin ice.

NARROW-BAND MICROWAVE SEARCHES

We carried out our first search along these lines in 1978 at the Arecibo Observatory's great 305-meter (1000-foot) dish antenna, the world's largest. In that search we looked at 185 Sun-like stars, seeking narrowband ET carriers with a channel width of 0.051Hz and total bandwidth of 1Khz, centered on the 21 centimeter wavelength of neutral hydrogen. This very narrow total bandwidth encompasses Doppler shifts corresponding to just 0.1 kilometer per second (km/s), which is much smaller than typical relative velocities of nearby stars (approximately 10 km/s); indeed, it is dwarfed also by planetary orbital velocities. (Earth's is 30 km/s.) In this first search we could not achieve greater bandwidth, given our off-line (no special hardware) spectral computation method. Our solution instead was simply to assume that the sender compensates his transmitted frequency so the signal arrives at the Sun at the true hydrogen frequency. This he does by making spectral observations of our Sun's visible light spectrum, from which he can deduce its velocity along the line of sight. The rest is easy. (Why aliens would consider our Sun a worthy target is another question.)

This search (*Science*, 201, 733, 1978) achieved the highest sensitivity ever; it could have detected a 5 kilowatt transmitter, connected to an Arecibo twin aimed at us, at the farthest star examined (eighty light-years away). Radioastronomy deals in weak signals, and this sensitivity corresponds to less than a micro-microwatt (10^{-12} watts) total power falling on Earth. No signals of extraterrestrial origin were found (bad news), but interference was completely rejected by the narrowband "chirped receiver" scheme (good news). We were unsatisfied with the restrictive assumptions that we were forced to adopt (precompensated transmitter frequencies), and we felt that the small amount of time available for SETI at busy radio telescopes was not enough. But we were pleased with the interference-free performance, and therefore planned a better search, the so-called Suitcase SETI.

Suitcase SETI (as it has been dubbed) was built at Stanford and NASA Ames Research Center, with support from the latter and the Planetary Society. It consisted of a dedicated spectrometer with 131,072 channels, chirped receiver, and on-line signal recognition and archiving of interesting signals; it achieved twice the bandwidth of the earlier search. We tested it at Arecibo, this time examining 250 favorable stars at another magic frequency, 2841 MHz, the second harmonic of the neutral hydrogen frequency (at the 21 centimeter line itself the radio sky is somewhat noisy, due to galactic hydrogen clouds; furthermore, transmissions at that frequency would interfere with radio astronomy. Both arguments provide plausible reasons to examine the harmonic frequency). We then installed it at the Oak Ridge-Harvard Smithsonian Observatory, where it operated continuously for over two years, beginning in March 1983.

At Harvard we covered 80 percent of the sky in a third search, an overlapping, nontargeted search called Sentinel. We used a 26-meter

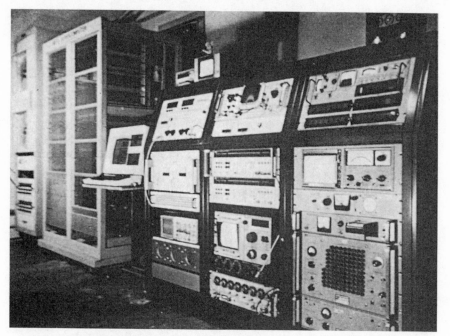

Figure 1. The META signal processors used to generate real-time radio spectra of incoming signals. (*Photo: Courtesy Paul Horowitz.*)

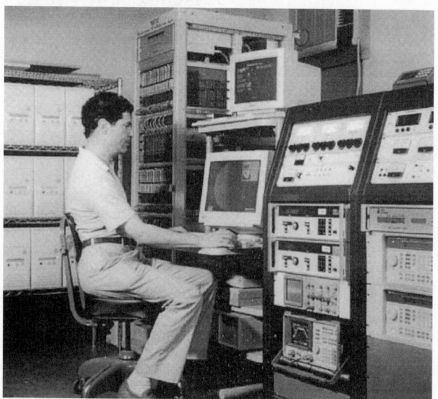

Figure 2. Paul Horowitz at the controls of the BETA signal processors. The tall rack holds the 250-million-channel spectrum analyzer that forms the heart of the search. To its left is the "backend" array of 21 Pentium processors; the double rack unit at right holds the radiofrequency and control electronics, with the operator's console tucked in the middle. BETA runs automatically under computer control, archiving data and sending email to its designers when exceptional candidate signals are encountered. (*Photo: Courtesy Paul Horowitz.*)

(84-foot) steerable dish antenna, with sensitive amplifiers feeding the modified Suitcase SETI spectrometer. We scanned the sky in "transit" mode—the antenna pointed at the meridian, examining a circular band of celestial latitude each day, after which the antenna was moved by one beam width north or south for the next day's SWEEP. At 21-centimeter wavelength, where beam diameter is one-half degree (and thus each point in the sky spent approximately two minutes in the stationary line-of-sight as the Earth rotated), it took about eight months to cover the whole northern sky. Although the system had 100 times less sensitivity than Arecibo, it had the advantage of full-time operation and full northern-sky coverage. It is of course impossible to quantify the tradeoff, knowing nothing about the distribution of possible beacons in the sky, or their signal strengths. There may be a very small number of very powerful signals up there, in which case the problem isn't sensitivity, it's persistence.

WIDER-BAND SEARCHES META

After two years' unsuccessful searching with Sentinel, we expanded the system to an 8.4-million-channel spectrometer, covering 400 KHz of total bandwidth (200 times as much as Sentinel) with comparable sensitivity. This system, called META (Megachannel ExtraTerrestrial Assay), lifted the constraint of assuming the sender has compensated for Doppler shifts relative to our Sun, as demanded by Sentinel and the earlier Arecibo search. Thus META could detect a generalized galactic beacon, not just the Sun-directed transmissions that the earlier searches required.

We built META I at Harvard, using twenty thousand integrated circuit chips and a half-million connections (all soldered by hand!). The architecture is a star-connected array of 144 processors, each using a 68000-type central processor, an arithmetic coprocessor, and memory. In operation, META cycled through frequencies corresponding to three guessable reference frames, namely the galactic barycenter (center of gravity), the cosmic blackbody rest frame (the frame in which the primordial remnant radiation looks the same in all directions), and the "local standard of rest" (the average motion of stars in our region of the Galaxy). As before, META's chirped receiver weakened local (i.e., worldwide) interference by a factor of about 100, and rendered it distinguishable from the expected celestial signature. META I ran reliably for nine years, during which it covered the northern sky five times, at

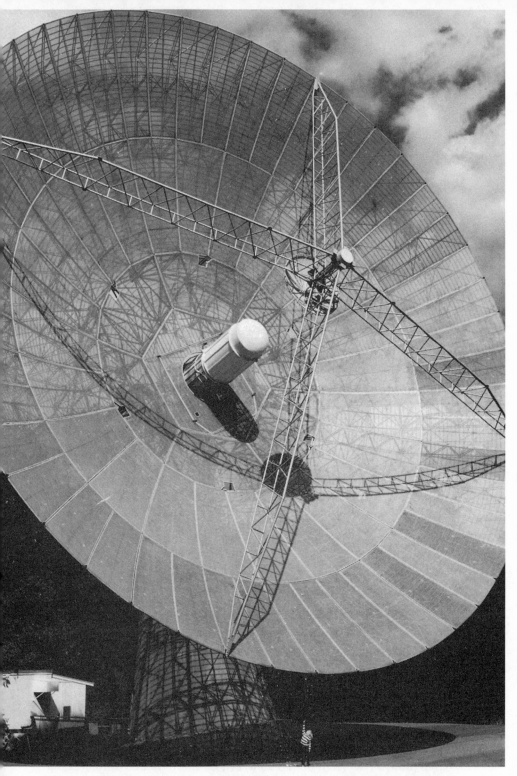

Figure 3. The 26-meter (84-foot) steerable radiotelescope at Harvard-Smithsonian's Oak Ridge Observatory in Harvard, Massachusetts. It is being used for dedicated searches for signals from extraterrestrial intelligence. That's Jacob Horowitz (the first author's son) at age 6, pointing to the fiberglass radome housing the Cassegrain feedhorns. (*Photo: Courtesy Paul Horowitz.*)

both 21 cm and its second harmonic. META II started to cover the southern skies in similar fashion in 1990. After excising obvious inter-ference signals, 37 candidate signals were found and their sky loca-tions revisited. None of them was ever redetected. (For technical details on META, see *Astrophysical Journal*, **415**, 218-235, 20 Sept. 1993. For a nontechnical summary see *The Planetary Report*, **13**, 5 (Sept/Oct 1993).)

BETA

Given the experience with META and the detection of nonrepeating sig-nals in other searches, we decided to make improvements to our exist-ing telescope and replace our electronics to increase our chances of detecting rare events and of rejecting Earth-based interference. We also wanted to cover the whole 1.4 to 1.7 GHz "water hole" of frequencies between the emission lines of hydrogen and the hydroxyl radical (H and OH), the constituents of water. For the latter consideration we designed "BETA" (Billion channel Extra Terrestrial Assay) to include 250 million channels covering the 320MHz-wide band. The bandwidth is covered in eight hops of 40MHz, each hop observing for 2 seconds.

To improve our certainty that a detected signal is celestial and not terrestrial, we designed a dual beam antenna feed, producing an abut-ting pair of beams ("east" and "west") in the sky. Any source that drifts first through the east feed and then the west feed at a rate consistent with the sky's apparent drift is of interest. (By this logic we would miss an alien ship's broadcast from near-Earth orbit, but that should be otherwise easy to detect!) We also added a third, low-gain horizon-sen-sitive antenna that detects terrestrial, but not celestial, signals. Any signal appearing simultaneously in that feed and the others is rejected. Only a signal obeying "east then west and never terrestrial" can be of true extraterrestrial origin. Following the theme of our earlier searches, that signal must also be of narrow spectral width, i.e., a narrow-band carrier. When such a signal is detected it triggers an automatic "leapfrog" movement of the antenna by about 5 degrees to the west, where it awaits an encore; this is repeated eight times in an effort to confirm or reject the candidate event.

To put it another way, each point in the sky is initially observed eight times in each of the two sky beams of 2 billion channels spanning the microwave waterhole. Strong candidates are reobserved with the same protocol an additional 8-fold, i.e., 64 more times. All interesting candidate signals, most of which are not sufficient to trigger leapfrogging, are archived for operator amusement.

BETA was turned on at Harvard/Oak Ridge Observatory in October, 1995. From that site we have observed all the sky from +60 degrees to -30 degrees declination at least twice. BETA has sifted a billion candidate signals and archived 3,500 that passed preliminary tests. No candidate has repeated (as of August 1999) or looks like an expected type of ETI signal.

TAKING STOCK

We have not done a final analysis of BETA data, but examination of the results of the META search allows some conclusions to be reached. Assuming that civilizations broadcast on the frequencies we searched near the hydrogen frequency at 1.4 GHz, we can say:

1) There are no civilizations with our energy resources (all devoted to signaling) broadcasting omni-directionally within 25 light years of Earth, and none anywhere in the Galaxy using an antenna like Arecibo (1000 feet in diameter) aimed at us.

2) A civilization using all the solar energy falling on its Earth-size surface for signaling would be detectable by META out to 2,500 light years if it transmitted omnidirectionally, and could be heard clear across the Galaxy if it used a 6-foot dish pointed in our direction.

Why haven't signals of extraterrestrial origin been detected, given some 50 searches so far? It is important to note that all of Earth's SETI activity to date has barely scratched the surface, in terms of sensitivity, spectrum coverage, and especially in observation time per candidate object—perhaps first contact comes only after a civilization has paid its dues, in persistence and sophistication.

OPTICAL AND INFRARED SEARCHES

However, another possibility is that we have been looking for the wrong kind of signal. Within a year of the its invention, interstellar signalling with lasers was suggested by Schwartz and Townes (*Nature*, 190, 205 [1961]), an idea that has since been elaborated upon by Betz, Kingsley, Rather, Ross, Werthimer, and others. But lasers were new devices, not very powerful in comparison with the mature microwave technology of that time; so most searches were done at microwave frequencies, where megawatt transmitters and large dishes were available, and where calculations showed that interstellar communication was clearly possible.

The situation is different now: Laser technology has enjoyed a Moore's Law doubling of capability every two years, and our lasers can now generate a megawatt of continuous output power, and a billion megawatts of pulsed power. "Earth 2000" technology increasingly employs photonics and fiber optics to replace the historical copper cables and long-haul repeater chains of microwave towers.

As laser technology has matured, the SETI community has begun to listen to the laser-SETI pioneers, with searches now begun at Berkeley, Columbus, and Harvard. This is not to say that first contact will not be via microwave beacon—rather, it has become clear that a powerful laser forms an altogether plausible beacon for initiating interstellar contact, and can efficiently target stars at distances up to a thousand light years (roughly the thickness of the galactic disk in our stellar neighborhood).

A LASER-TRANSMITTING STRATEGY

It is helpful to try devising a strategy of transmission and reception that forms, overall, an attractive scenario for interstellar contact. We don't intend to transmit; but with some idea of what they might be transmitting, we can mount a search.

Here is such a strategy: Imagine that intelligent civilizations are separated by several hundred light years (though this is probably optimistic). Each one is charged with the responsibility of illuminating all plausible stars within a hundred light years, in order to find young technological civilizations like our own. This they do by attaching a powerful pulsed laser (a petawatt, say) to a telescope like the Keck on Mauna Kea, Hawaii (it is 10 meters in diameter), and sending a nanosecond pulse to each candidate star. It would not be difficult to move from star to star, illuminating ten stars per second with a single pulse each. In 2 minutes the entire catalog (about 1200 stars) has been exhausted, so they just do it all over again . . . continuing without pause.

What do we, as one of the targeted stars, see? If we spend some time looking at each nearby star, we will be finally rewarded when we look at our advanced laser-firing star: Within 2 minutes we will see a laser pulse. Or will we? What about the dazzle of their star? Can a laser possibly outshine a *star?* (We assume, realistically, that we cannot distinguish the planet and its laser from the star; the light is mixed together.)

Here's the surprise: It turns out that such intense laser pulses would appear more than a thousand times brighter than the star itself! And, this statement is independent of distance, because both the laser light and the starlight grow fainter with distance by the same inverse-square law.

It turns out, happily, that such pulses are not significantly weakened or scattered by interstellar dust and gas over distances of a thousand light years. Not only do they outshine the parent star, they deliver a real wallop to the detector. For example, a Keck telescope on Earth would receive about 1500 photons (light quanta) from a single pulse as described above, if sent from a star 1000 light years distant. Within that radius there are roughly a million Sun-like stars, surely good candidates for life and intelligence. Finally, there are no known astrophysical sources of nanosecond flashes of light (and also very few terrestrial sources to cause interference).

OPTICAL SETI AT HARVARD-SMITHSONIAN

Our "laser SETI" experiment rides piggyback on an existing "radial velocity survey" of nearby solar-type stars, which has been running for a decade at the 61-inch optical telescope located at the same site as our radiotelescope. This survey is headed by David Latham and Robert Stefanik, and in fact it was responsible for the first unambiguous detection of an extrasolar sub-stellar companion, whose unglamorous name is "HD114762."

Our detector is attached to the side of the spectrograph doing that stellar survey, and it receives about $1/3$ of the starlight entering the telescope. That light is split into two by a beam-splitter, each of which illuminates a very fast photo-detector. The apparatus is designed to recognize simultaneous light flashes in the two detectors, the redundancy serving to eliminate false triggers from electronic hiccups that occur occasionally in such detectors. When a coincidence is detected, the electronics spring into action, keeping track of the intensity (roughly) and timing (rather precisely, to the nearest $1/2$ nanosecond) of the light flashes.

A typical observation of a candidate star lasts somewhere between 2 and 30 minutes, and typically we observe 30 different stars in a night. To date we have made some 5000 observations altogether, of some 2000 separate stars. "Events" are rare—at most a few in a night—and we have found no star that is the source of repeatable events. Based upon various tests we believe that this low background event rate is in fact dominated by detector and/or electronic artifacts, and we are working to isolate and eliminate it.

NEXT STEPS

We would like to eliminate false triggers completely. To accomplish this we are cooperating with Dave Wilkinson and his group at Princeton University, who are building an identical system for their on-campus 30-inch optical telescope. The two telescopes, located several hundred miles apart, will observe the same stars, at the same time. Any event that occurs simultaneously in both telescopes would clearly be a light flash of extraterrestrial origin. Even if not of intelligent origin, the mere detection of nanosecond flashes would be an important astrophysical discovery in its own right.

On a more ambitious note, we are exploring the practicality of conducting a whole-sky search for laser pulses. The idea is this: Our targeted search covers only one millionth of the sky (albeit the most interesting portion). By populating the focal plane of a telescope with a mosaic of fast detector pairs we can make a laser-SETI "camera," covering a few square degrees at once. We believe we can build such a camera, with 512 detectors, attached to a dedicated optical telescope, all on a modest budget.

Although we have described only our group's searches, it is imperative to note that both microwave and optical SETI projects are flowering at other sites as well, in particular the very powerful radio searches being conducted by the SETI Institute (Project Phoenix), by U.C. Berkeley (SERENDIP and SETI At Home), the southern hemisphere searches (Argentina: META II; Australia: Phoenix and others); there are also optical pulse searches by the pioneering U.C. Berkeley group led by Dan Werthimer, and also spectral "data mining" by the planet-hunters led by Geoff Marcy (looking for narrow laser spectral lines in their high-resolution spectra).

Geoff Marcy's group is going to look back at the collection of extremely high resolution spectra it is accumulating in its increasingly successful search for extrasolar planets. It is looking for and finding tiny Doppler shifts of lines in the stellar spectra due to the gravitational pull of unseen planets on the visible star, and the mutual orbits which result. Marcy's group realized they can also look for very narrow emission lines at laser wavelengths, which will show up at increased contrast on their spectra because of their superfine detail. It is a long shot because so many spectra have been taken over the years and examined in detail, and no such unnatural lines have been seen. Even at the more ordinary lower resolution of these older images a really powerful signal would have shown up.

Far more ambitious multibeam microwave phased arrays, as well as other advanced search technologies, are in the planning stage at the SETI Institute.

We conclude with the observation that SETI is an exploration, a search for plausible signals transmitted by an intelligent civilization with the intention of initiating contact with others. We do not know enough to know the prevalence of such civilizations, the likelihood that they are indeed seeking contact, or the method(s) they would favor for such contact. The best approach is probably a diversity of plausible approaches, each evolving as our technology improves and we gain experience. The recent interest in optical SETI should be seen as a reflection of this paradigm, not as a repudiation of radiofrequency methods. (In fact, if we had to choose just one method today, it would continue to be at microwave frequencies.)

Information on our searches can be found at:

http://mc.harvard.edu/hgroup.html.

In this work we have had the benefit of the following collaborators: Peter Backus, Dave Brainard, Joe Caruso, Kok Chen, Chip Coldwell, Raul Colomb, John Forster, Andrew Howard, Enrique Hurrell, Mal Jones, Sam Klein, David Leigh, Ivan Linscott, David Latham, Tap Lum, Guillermo Lemarchand, Brian Matthews, Juan Carlos Olalde, Cos Papaliolios, Allen Peterson, Skip Schwarz, Robert Stefanik, Anne Sung, Cal Teague, Mike Williams, Jonathan Wolff, and Joe Zajac. Primary support was provided by The Planetary Society, Steven Spielberg, NASA, and The Bosack-Kruger Foundation, with additional grants from the SETI Institute, the Shulsky Foundation, the Dudley Observatory, the Hofheinz Foundation, and NASA-Ames Research Center. Corporate gifts of equipment were received from Fluke, Hewlett-Packard, Intel and Micron.

We are indebted to the SETI Institute for sponsoring a set of workshops on next-generation SETI, at which we became educated about optical SETI.

INDIVIDUAL INVOLVEMENT

by

D. KENT CULLERS AND
WILLIAM R. ALSCHULER

F LASH BACKWARD. It is 5:00 a.m. Atlantic Standard Time, October 15, 1992. From the radar console where I sit writing this, the raucous jungle noises are nearly inaudible. Instead of these, the air conditioning hums, cooling klystrons and computers below the temperature of the tropical night.

If I were to take a ten-minute stroll, I could stand on a support platform five hundred feet above twenty acres of metal mesh, the largest radio antenna in the world. At this moment, whatever signals are falling on this giant antenna are unheeded. The control room is silent. Only the control operator and I are present. Normally, this room, with racks of receivers, amplifiers, and processing equipment is a beehive of activity. The Arecibo antenna performs radio astronomy experiments year round. People from all over the world requiring the extremely high sensitivity of this instrument propose research projects, and the telescope time is in great demand. Right now, however, something unusual, though not unprecedented, has occurred. An experiment has finished early. Part of the team scheduled to observe next, I am unable to sleep. The other team members are more sensible after a twenty-four-hour period of uninterrupted observing and data processing. They are sleeping so that when our new run starts in an hour, at least someone will be thinking straight. But now, I have just been given sole use of the telescope for the next hour. It is an awesome thought that I could do anything my heart desires. Unfortunately, I have no idea where to point the telescope to find an extraterrestrial signal. So, I begin checking the set-up we plan to use in an hour. Double- and triple-checking prevents mistakes. You have already read the arguments for the plausibility of extraterrestrial intelligence. These arguments are not proof. The scientific revolution has swept away countless attempts to deduce the nature of physical reality from first causes. Physics is an experimental science. Either communicating ETs exist or they don't. The debate on this subject will be settled by observation, not by logical deduction. Of course, those, like me, who are devoting their lives to a search for ET, believe that there is a good possibility of success given enough time and resources. Basically, this belief is why I am presently observing at Arecibo. The team gathered here is taking the first steps in learning how to carry out an automated search of the sky. I am the NASA SETI signal-detection team leader. My job is to tell the difference between a signal from ET and anything else that might look similar. Two phenomena concern me on this particular night. First, radio telescopes like optical telescopes, are susceptible to local interference. In the case of optical instruments, this may be light from nearby cities, which scatters into the field of view when the telescope is pointed at a star. Radio telescopes have much the same problem. Local radio transmitters, from taxicab radios to communications satellites, send stray signals into the Arecibo dish. Not only is the interference likely to be strong, but the signals have the systematic characteristics and patterns expected of intelligence. Consequently, they will pass the tests that should find a transmission from an extraterrestrial technology and discriminate against natural cosmic noise. How severe is this interference at our most important telescope site? At the moment, I am collecting the data to find out. The analysis will take months. Second, even if all interference from the local environment is successfully excised, noise can fool you once in a while. Noise is a random process. In searching the sky for five years over a wide band of frequencies, the total amount of data processed will be thousands of terabits (a terabit is 10^{12} bits). Each second, NASA instruments will process the information equivalent of several entire *Encyclopedia Britannicas*—several gigabits (10^9 bits per second). This information, almost entirely cosmic noise, will be, by analogy, random letter combinations. Sometimes, however, just by chance, a noise word will look like an intelligent signal. In principle, complete elimination of false alarms from random noise is impossible. However, I must know the expected false alarm rate·for my system. So far, on this observing run, the false alarm rate is that predicted from the theory. So what I'm doing is learning how to conduct a massive search of the sky, a look at many frequencies and many stars. It will begin in the middle 1990s and continue for about seven years. It will use the world's largest antennas. It will be a billion times larger than any search before. It will cost $100,000,000.

FLASH FORWARD. I sit now, revising my words in the summer of 1999. Part of this revision is a consequence of historical accident. The NASA search, after performing 0.1% of it's assigned task was halted by Congress in late 1993. Fifty million dollars of research money was deemed excessive. The government was not going to pay for SETI science.

Fortunately, private individuals in Silicon Valley had other ideas. They funded the continuation of the SETI search which, as we speak, has completed half of its planned mission. It will, by the year 2003, have surveyed the thousand nearest Sun-like stars, just as we planned, two decades ago, and more or less on schedule.

The second reason for this revision is technological. Computing has progressed faster than anyone expected. Computing capacity has grown by a factor of almost a hundred since 1992. The equipment first used to do the search, even though private enterprise doubled NASA's computing investment, is almost obsolete now. As we complete our search, I am designing new computer equipment with twenty times the capacity of previous systems. And I'm doing it at a quarter the cost and twice the reliability using commercial chips and CPU's.

Nonetheless, it is still proper to ask the question I posed in my earlier incarnation. The professionals have good support in the scientific community, access to large telescopes and the inside track to low cost computer hardware.

In the face of this, what can an individual do? Actually, individuals from the interested public can help a lot. The surprising fact is that skilled amateurs, using home-built equipment, can actually make technical contributions to the SETI effort. They can search at frequencies and for signal types that we will not. They can more easily test new ideas than we can in a large program. They can attain detection sensitivities comparable to those we have in the same search domain. It is even possible that an amateur proposal of exceptional merit can get time at a major observatory using state-of-the-art equipment. The rest of this chapter will tell you why this is possible and how you can start your own SETI program.

In the same way that computing advances have helped professionals, they have given a tremendous boost to amateur and semiprofessional efforts. This is primarily because the exponential improvements in hardware have put real processing power into the hands of many people. Essentially, programs performed by astronomers a little over ten years ago can be run now on your home computer. It's the old story. That old IBM you learned on that took up a room and cost a million dollars has been more than replaced by your thousand dollar desktop machine.

You can custom design your entire apparatus as outlined below, or, you can get data from the biggest radio telescope in the world and process it with a free screensaver. The program, called SETI At Home was put together by Dan Wertheimer and his colleagues in the astronomy department at U.C. Berkeley, and is supported by the SETI Institute and the Planetary Society. It is a great use of Internet time, and you can find out all about it by going to the SETI Institute website, www.seti.org. (See Fig. 1.)

The SETI At Home website is: **http://setiathome.ssl.berkeley.edu.**

There are two marvelous things about SETI At Home. The data you process is some of the best available anywhere in the world. The sensitivity of the search is world class. Best of all, the internet search looks for classes of ETI signals that the real- time searches do not. We know things today that we did not know in 1992. We have actually found more planets outside the solar system than inside. Most of the planets discovered are Jupiter-sized because the planet searches find massive planets best. If these Jupiters have moons, they will be rapidly orbiting their planets. This causes signals to shift frequency more than is expected from an Earth-like planet. Yet SETI at home searches a wider frequency-time domain for such signals. You may be the first to have your computer discover an ET signal.

If you do get notified of a possible discovery just remember that a signal may be terrestrial. Don't assume that all signals in your antenna are from space.

How big is a search?

If you are not an expert on radio, more particularly radio astronomy, but would like to plunge in, this section is for you. I will try to keep the math at a minimum, but many of the concepts are technical and require some thought. If you trust me utterly, dangerous at the best of times, you can skip to the end and accept the conclusions. For those of you still with me, here goes. I promise you that by the end we will have proved together that an individual with about three thousand dollars can search an uncharted region of the electromagnetic spectrum and a few stars more sensitively than has any ETI search conducted to date. In fact, it is within your means to look in a direction of your choosing and at a small band of frequencies more sensitively than will

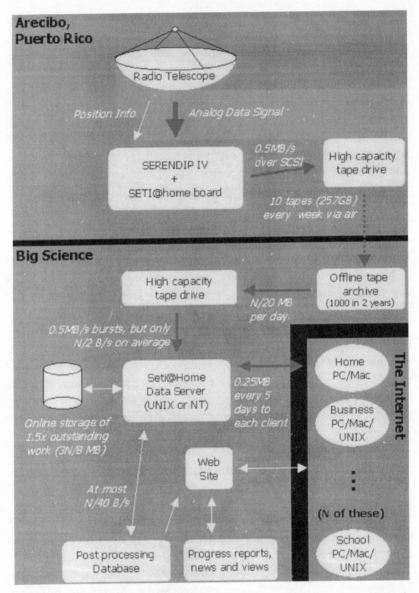

Figure 1. This diagram, which was taken directly from the SETI At Home website, shows the flow of information for the project, from telescope to home computer and back to the project center. You will see it when you visit the site, at

http://setiathome.ssl.berkeley.edu/setiathome_science.html

any search currently planned. This carries with it, however, a vitally important caveat. You must know where to look. To rephrase Lincoln, you can beat the professionals in some of the sky some of the time, but it's impossible in all of the sky all of the time. People like me in the SETI biz talk glibly of search space, nine-dimensional haystacks, and terabits to describe the size of their endeavors. Usually, after only an hour or two of argument, we can agree on what we mean. The fact that two people never use exactly the same numbers to describe the size of a particular ETI search shows how many hidden assumptions go into evaluating the effectiveness of methods for finding ETI.

Let us explain this by analogy with observing the sky visually. On a clear, dark night, how many stars can you see? In the visible Universe there are at least a million trillion stars. The unaided eye can see about two thousand of these in good conditions from any one place on Earth, at any one time. Primarily, this small number is due to the fact that most stars fall below the eye's detection threshold. A similar effect exists in radio astronomy, and its cause is easy to understand. For a signal to be detected, it must stand out against the background of receiver noise that is constantly present in any radio equipment. All objects in the Universe have a finite temperature, which is a measure of the energy in their particles' random motions. The important particles in your radio set are the electrons. Their average motion is the current which, when amplified, is the usable signal output. Finite temperature means that random electron motions will cause fluctuations in the receiver's output. If you connect a speaker to this output you hear noise called static. If you point your antenna to the sky you will, if it is sensitive enough, also hear cosmic static and other natural radio signals. If an incoming signal is much weaker than this thermal noise, it is not noticed against the background roar. If it is much stronger, it is obvious. Thus, we define the detection threshold for a signal, rather intuitively, as that level where the signal power is equal to the noise power. A signal becomes more detectable if we increase the signal power or if we cut the noise power. The important thing is their ratio, often called the SNR, signal-to-noise ratio. Obviously, we want to search as many stars as possible when looking for ETs. We cannot control the power of their transmitters. We can, however, decrease the noise in our receivers. One way is to cool the receiving equipment, thus decreasing the random electron motions. Another way is to divide the incoming data into small pieces, either in frequency or in time. The noise in each small piece of data is tiny compared to the noise in all the data taken together. If there is a signal in one piece, concentrated there, it will be more detectable in that segment alone than it would be against the noise in the entire data stream. The largest planned SETI endeavor, NASA's effort, carried on by the SETI Institute today, uses knowledge of signal processing to carve up the frequency and time dimensions in pieces likely to contain large signals but little noise. This search concentrates on continuously present or regularly recurring simple signals. Such searches are good at finding certain types of regularly pulsed radar signals as well as amplitude-modulated radio (AM) and TV transmissions with a narrow carrier wave component. Other transmission types, such as commercial FM stereo, are very poorly matched to NASA's search. Since the information in an FM signal is represented as frequency changes, the signal covers many channels in an irregular pattern determined by the transmission's content. If ETs only broadcast in FM stereo, NASA is unlikely to find the signal. The point is that even the largest planned computer processing systems on the largest available antennas, looking at the quietest frequencies for interstellar transmissions, cannot do it all. A lucky amateur could scoop the pros. In a later section, I will tell you about what the big searches are doing so you can see what they are missing. The one obvious advantage that professional astronomers have is antenna size or collecting area, and control over the telescope. Thus, professional searches can immediately discriminate against terrestrial interference, either by looking for signals with multiple antennas to prove their reality on the sky, or by moving single antennas on and off source to make a distant signal appear and disappear under observer control. Even SETI At Home is unable to make this discrimination, though its data comes from the world's largest radio telescope. An amateur, controlling his own antenna, can make such tests, though his antenna will be smaller. Overall, professionals can mount bigger searches. Professionals also have the advantage of vast information processing power. Bigger computers can look at more frequencies, wider bandwidths, for more signal types, in the same length of time (but amateurs may be able to slip in with unusual processing techniques just like SETI At Home; computer power is relatively cheap and getting cheaper). Most scientists feel that the probability of detecting ETI is proportional to the number of stars searched and to the frequency range covered. However, this is a rather general and approximate truth. For example, most astronomers feel that we should concentrate on stars like the Sun, stars that live long enough for life as we know it to evolve and that are relatively warm, maintaining a life-sustaining liquid element on nearby planets. Further, some frequencies, where natural noise is high or where local Earth-based signals obscure weak signals, are not likely to turn up ETI and professionals will ignore them. Nevertheless, assume that the probability of finding ETI is proportional to the number of stars and frequencies covered. The distance to which a signal is detectable, keeping everything like the receiver noise and incoming signal power constant, is proportional to the diameter of an antenna. The signal received by an antenna of constant size decreases with source distance, just like the force of gravity. If the distance is doubled between transmitter and receiver, the signal is decreased by a factor of four. This is the inverse square law at work. It applies because by the time the signal reaches the receiver from twice the distance, the same amount of transmitted power has spread over four times the area. The receiving antenna, still the same size, collects one quarter of the signal it had before. If a source's distance is doubled and the diameter of the antenna is doubled, the received signal strength remains constant. The signal per unit area is one quarter as great after the doubling, but there is four times as much antenna area to soak up the transmission. Thus, by doubling the distance and doubling the antenna size, the signal is just as detectable as before. Therefore, the detection range is proportional to the antenna diameter. It is a good approximation to assume that the number of stars within a given distance is proportional to the cube of that distance. In other words, in our region of space, the number of stars is proportional to the volume we can see. Obviously, on large scales this is not true. The Galaxy is shaped like a convex lens, not a sphere, so that in some directions volumes can be found that are almost empty of stars. For distances up to a thousand light-years, however, the assumption is good. Since the distance we can see out to is proportional to the antenna diameter, the number of stars is proportional to the antenna diameter, cubed. If we accept the assumption that the probability of finding ETI is proportional to the stars and frequencies searched, we get: $p=kfd^3$ where p is the probability of finding ETI, k is a constant known by no man (it is related to the result of the Drake Equation), f is the frequency range searched, and d is the antenna diameter. We are in the odd situation of knowing what is better, big antennas, lots of frequency coverage, without actually knowing what the probability of finding ETI really is. Nonetheless, we now know enough to see if an amateur can do anything useful in this age of professional ETI hunters. The antenna at Arecibo, Puerto Rico, is 300 meters across. A more typical amateur setup might use a satellite dish three meters across, one hundred times smaller. An individual can afford a PC to process his data. A professional can get a Cray-sized supercomputer, which runs about one thousand times faster. Frequency coverage is essentially proportional to the speed of data processing. So, if you substitute into the above equation you will see that the professional has a billion times (100^3 x 1000) the probability of the amateur of finding ETI.

This is true if you accept all the prior underlying assumptions. In the data-rich world of today, it is theoretically possible to test your favorite algorithm on data direct from professional radio telescopes, sent to you via the Internet. In this way, you might overcome the antenna disadvantage of amateur searches. However, SETI At Home does not allow this now. The screensaver implements a growing set of algorithms but also provides many safeguards against hoaxes and false alarms. So far, the developers are not willing to allow their data products to be manipulated by creative computer enthusiasts. Is it possible nonetheless for an amateur system to overcome the billion-to-one data and antenna disadvantage? I believe it is just possible, and I will explain why. Though professional searches cover much wider frequency ranges than amateur efforts, they do not cover all good frequencies. First of all, the NASA search and its private successors, Projects Phoenix and SERENDIP, don't cover all interesting frequencies and signal types. These projects cover frequencies for nearby Sun-like stars between 1 and 3 billion cycles per second (1-3 GHz) using Arecibo and other large antennas, and for the whole sky over limited frequency bands. They are sensitive to continuous signals like those of TV and to pulses like those of some radars. They do not see FM stereo, many types of military transmissions, or TV satellites, which also use frequency modulation. Many of our strongest Earth-based transmissions currently take place below a billion cycles per second (1 GHz). Stereo FM transmissions occur at about 100 million cycles per second. TV carriers occupy channels up to the highest UHF allocation at 800 million cycles per second. The professionals have ruled these out, at least for the time being, because most radio telescopes are not efficient at these frequencies and because the cosmic noise is slightly higher there than at the noise minimum. However, if you are an amateur in a radio-quiet location or you can arrange efficient interference filtering, you might want to search them. Good automated scanning receivers that cover them cost less than one thousand dollars. Remember that you are likely, unless you take precautions, to detect Earth-based signals instead of ETs.

So perhaps, you admit, there are some good frequencies left for prospecting. What about the obvious professional antenna advantage? All of the stars cannot be observed with the antenna at Arecibo, Puerto Rico. That antenna uses an unusual construction that makes it cheap to build, but which allows effective use only near the vertical. Thus, though a band of stars is visible as the Earth turns, only those near the celestial equator (which is almost overhead in Puerto Rico) can be seen. In all, only about one-third of the Sun-like stars can be viewed by Arecibo. The rest of the stars have been observed at other latitudes by telescopes ranging in size from thirty to sixty meters in diameter. We have fairly complete lists of Sun-like stars only to about one hundred light-years distance. Beyond this distance, stars like the Sun are too dim for us to be certain that they have been included in our databases. (The Sun would be about 7.5 magnitude, just too faint for the naked eye, at 100 light-years.) Project Phoenix is using the biggest available radio telescopes to look for a long time at the approximately one thousand nearby Sun-like stars that we know about. The rest of the sky, most of it, will be swept quickly by antennas having a diameter of about 30 meters. Projects BETA at Harvard and META in Argentina, supported by the Planetary Society used this strategy. This allows a complete, if less sensitive, look at the sky. The professional-antenna advantage over our amateur set-up using a three-meter dish is typically not one to a million, but something like one to ten thousand. Things are looking better. There is, however, another surprise. If he knows the frequency of ETI, an amateur can purchase software that does better signal processing than that planned by the professionals. This can increase amateur sensitivities for some particular star and frequency so that his antenna disadvantage is overcome completely. In some small part of the planned search, an amateur can do a professional job. Many amateurs, working cooperatively, may do even better. In fact, there is an organized amateur effort led by a professional radio engineer Paul Schuck Ph.D., Director of the SETI League. He has all the latest information on available amateur equipment from receivers to data processing. His web site is **www.setileague.org**. I am happy to report that his efforts were, in large part, inspired when he read the first version of this book. His organization even gave one of us (KC) an award based on this chapter. The world is a small place, and the Internet makes it smaller yet.

SENSITIVITY OF THE SEARCH

This is, by far, the most technical section in this chapter. It is my area of expertise, and by the end, some of you will undoubtedly say that I am lost in the details of my job. Unfortunately, the details are necessary for an understanding of why the NASA/Phoenix search has the strengths and weaknesses it does. If you, as an amateur, want to do it better, you must understand how to perform a sensitive search. Therefore, I will try to immerse you in the gripping details of signal processing without getting you lost.

TAMING FREQUENCY AND TIME

What frequency does middle C have? Is it the same for a piano, violin, and flute? If so, why do these instruments sound different? What frequency do you create when you whistle middle C? What frequency do you produce when you snap your fingers or turn on a light switch? What is the frequency of a gunshot? If you are certain of all the answers to the above questions, you probably understand the concept of frequency. Most people intuitively grasp what frequency is, since your ear is a frequency analyzer. To minimize the use of mathematics and to maximize the application of your intuitive understanding, I will use auditory examples in explaining what frequency really is. Of course, the concepts are equally valid when they are applied to fluctuations in radio receiver output rather than to those impinging on your eardrum as air pressure changes. Many people know that middle C corresponds to a frequency of 256 cycles per second. In other words, a middle C note causes air pressure fluctuations that have 256 maxima and minima per second. This correspondence is arbitrary and by tradition. Your ear, with a precision varying widely among individuals, can tell the difference between middle C and nearby notes. Some people even have what is called perfect pitch. Without any reference, they can tell you what note is being played on an instrument. If you, like me, are not one of the gifted few with perfect frequency discrimination, how can you determine the frequency of a note? Usually this is done either by comparison or by direct counting of the wave maxima. If you have ever tuned a musical instrument, you probably understand the comparison method. As you tune your instrument more closely to a standard pitch, you hear a beat, or difference in tone between the standard and the instrument being tuned. As the difference becomes small, it sounds like one note wavering in loudness at the frequency of the difference. You tune until the wavering stops. But what does stop mean? For me, it means a wavering of less than once in ten seconds. However, to be sure that I have tuned to this precision, I must wait for ten seconds to make sure the note of the two sources is not wavering too fast. If I were—more—willing to spend the time, I could wait a 100 seconds and get a more precise tuning. The point is that the precision with which a frequency is known depends on the time you have to measure it. Counting the number of maxima gives the same result. If you wait a second, you can, by counting, know that your note produces 256 crests in that time, not 255 or 257. Thus, you know the frequency to 1 cycle per second (CPS). If you wait 100 seconds, you can know the frequency to 1 cycle per 100 seconds or 0.01 cycles per second. Again, the precision of the measurement is greater as the time span of the measurement increases. This is a general principle of frequency measurement with applications in everything from radio to quantum mechanics. Whatever instrumentation you use, the product of the frequency error in CPS and the measurement time in seconds is always greater than or equal to one. There is another subtlety to the concept of frequency. Commonly, people say that a piano and a violin playing middle C produce the same tone. But everyone also knows that these two instruments have characteristic sounds that allow a musician and most other people to tell instantly what instrument is being played. The difference between the notes lies in the overtones of the sound. Both instruments produce sine waves at 256 cycles per second when playing middle C. However, they also produce weaker sine waves at multiples of this frequency, 512, 768, 1024 cycles per second, etc. It is the relative strengths of these overtones that give each musical instrument its characteristic sound. A pure frequency, like the one you whistle, is a single sine wave. It is possible, in fact, to create any wave shape, no matter how complicated, by adding sine and cosine waves together at appropriate frequencies and with appropriate strengths. Nowadays, makers of electronic music apply this principle with abandon. By adding together the right combinations of sine waves, they can synthesize the sound of any acoustical musical instrument ever made. They can also synthesize sounds that no physical acoustical music box could ever make. For those of us who like this sort of thing, this is much of the appeal of electronic music. So far we have unearthed two important principles of wave analysis. First, the frequency accuracy depends on the time interval over which it is measured. You cannot assign a frequency to snapping fingers or a gunshot because the sound is too short for accurate determination. Second, any wave shape can be synthesized as the sum of many simple sine waves with specific frequencies and amplitudes. This latter principle is very important in signal analysis because physical systems, whether in radio or music, tend to produce signals with large amounts of a restricted set of frequencies. A musical instrument, a TV station, or your local AM broadcast station all produce primarily one note. If one analyzes these signals to determine what frequencies and amplitudes are present, their strong primary notes stand out as obviously artificial in a natural world filled with random noises covering a wide range of frequencies with no outstanding components. Computers use a program called the FFT or Fast Fourier Transform to efficiently perform signal analysis in terms of sine waves. Fourier discovered the mathematical relation between arbitrarily shaped wave forms and sine waves in the early 1800s. Multiplying the output numbers from the transform by the appropriate sine or cosine wave and adding up all the results exactly reproduces the input data. In other words, the transform tells you how big each pure frequency is in a signal, compared with all the others. The computer always works with a finite time slice of the input. (We can't observe forever!) The output from that data, the amounts of sine and cosine waves present, is the frequency spectrum of the signal. Each number in the output applies to a particular frequency. The spacing of the frequencies in the analysis is consistent with the measurement principle for frequency. If the spectrum works on data that extends over one second, the spacing of the frequencies (the bin size) is one cycle per second. If the data extends over 100 seconds, the spacing of the frequencies is 1 cycle per 100 seconds or 0.01 cycles per second. We can imagine carving up a batch of data into time segments and running an FFT on each one. The data is then represented by the amount of sine wave amplitude for each frequency at a particular time. The sine wave amplitude is the amount of a particular frequency needed, during a particular time interval, to synthesize the data there. The output of the Fourier Transform can thus be viewed as an array of numbers with rows representing time and columns representing frequency. Each number is the sine wave amplitude in its own little frequency-time rectangle. The only restriction on the rectangular areas is that they satisfy the frequency precision rule. Fat or thin, the frequency interval multiplied by the length of time for the measurement must equal one.

This procedure would not accomplish much except that artificial signals of many classes look very different from the natural noise of the Universe when analyzed in this way. Noise in general is broad banded, with many frequencies present in about equal amplitude. If you tune your FM radio to a place on the dial where there is no station, you will find a roar like incoming surf or a waterfall. It sounds nothing like a whistle or a note on a violin. This is because no particular frequency dominates. In fact, all frequencies in the audible range for the human ear are present equally. Thus, in analogy with white light, in which all colors are equally present, the static in your FM receiver is called white noise. This noise is characteristic of most natural objects. Performing a frequency analysis is not effective on pure noise. A signal behaves quite differently, however. In the input, the signal, even if it is a pure sine wave, is spread out over time. But in the output, only one or at most a few frequencies contain all the signal amplitude. Thus, a few bins contain all the signal. The noise in these same boxes, however, is only a small fraction of the total in all the data analyzed, since this noise is distributed equally throughout the data stream. Thus, at frequencies where the signal is present, the SNR of the output is much larger than at the input to the Fourier Transform. Not all signals can be concentrated by a frequency analysis. FM signals, by their very nature, defy this type of processing. FM means frequency modulated. The output of an FM transmitter is a carrier whose frequency changes in proportion to the amplitude of the modulating signal. Thus, the transmission is spread over a wide band of frequencies. No frequency is occupied long enough to achieve much amplitude. Observing the band with an amateur scanner can be more sensitive than any professional narrow-band detector currently planned. On the other hand, AM radio and TV have a single sinusoidal component (the carrier wave) containing over half the power of the transmission. Though this unchanging continuous wave part of the transmission has no information content, it makes the construction of cheap receivers possible. If carriers are commonly used by technological civilizations, they are like no natural sources known. They can be made very pure, covering less than .001 cycles per second. A long Fourier Transform of 1,000 seconds produces frequency channels well matched to such transmissions. Any carrier is enormously large in its channel, and the noise is small.

There is a problem with looking for stable ET carriers in this way. First, it is not always possible to look at sources for 1,000 seconds. Second, frequencies as we observe them are not the same as the transmitted frequency. The ET, especially if transmitting from an Earth-like planet, is in relative motion with respect to our solar system. We can correct for the motions of the Earth relative to the center of our solar system, so this is no problem. However, we do not know the velocity of the ET source. As this velocity changes with the orbit of the ET world, the apparent frequency we see changes. This frequency shift is due to the Doppler effect. It is the same effect that causes a car horn to change pitch as a vehicle passes you or a whistle of a train to drop in pitch as it passes along its track. Thus, if each channel is too narrow, a signal will not remain there during the analysis and will drift over many frequencies instead of staying in just one.

The Project Phoenix search has compromised. For nearby Sun-like stars that are observed for a total of many minutes, the bandwidth of the frequency bin is about one cycle per second. This means that each second a new spectral analysis is made. Within one second, even a rapidly rotating or orbiting planet will not change velocity enough to move the received signal out of the 1 cycle per second bin. This does not apply, however, to moons that may orbit Jupiter-sized planets in earth-like orbits. In these cases, accelerations are much higher. SETI At Home is the only search which examines signals so as to detect these potential rapid drifters. Assume that the closest communicating civilization is a few hundred light-years away, sending a pretty strong signal. Since it is not one of our thousand nearest Sun-like stars, it is not in any catalogue. Thus, Project Phoenix will not do a high-sensitivity search in its direction using a large antenna and looking for a long time. It will be left, instead, for the attention of the all sky surveys. Such surveys use moderate-sized antennas, about ten times the diameter of a typical TV satellite dish at three meters. The hundredfold advantage in antenna area for the 30-meter dish means that a sky survey professional and an amateur looking at the same star would see a hundredfold difference in signal strength, in favor, naturally, of the professional.

INDIVIDUAL AMATEUR SEARCHES

Because they must cover the whole sky over a wide frequency range, the all-sky surveys moves the analysis band and direction rapidly, spending perhaps 1 second at each directional setting. If you were certain about your star and channel, you could actually equal or surpass their sensitivity for that frequency and direction by spending more time and processing power there. In particular, if you knew the frequency of the ET signal exactly, or even approximately, you could pour data from the output of a commercially available receiver such as an Icom ICR7000 into a digitizer attached to your PC. The approximately 3,000 cycles per second audio bandwidth could be sent through a computer program that synthesizes thousands of little filters. Each filter could be 0.01 cycles wide, one hundredth the width of a normal sky survey bin. The output signal to noise ratio in the correct channel would be just as good as that for the pros. The reason is that while they have a bigger antenna and one hundred times the signal, you have one hundredth the filter width and one hundredth the noise power. You can hear as well as any search is likely to do in our lifetime. The cost of this improvement is the narrower width of the FFT analysis channels and longer observation time. Your bandwidth is one hundred times smaller so each analysis takes one hundred times longer. Remember the accuracy rule. Thus, it will take you one hundred seconds. The reason each of your channels has the same energy that the pros have is that your analysis allows a hundred times as long for the signal to put energy into the channel. Thus, though the received signal energy per second is small because of your small antenna, it is compensated for by the longer time. You also probably own your antenna because you live in a rural area, which not only has no commercial TV but also no human interference—an advantage for the search! Of course, the problem with all this is knowing the exact frequency of the signal to camp out on. If the signal is drifting because of the motion-induced Doppler effect, your detection attempt will fail (unless you have a drift algorithm to match it) since the frequency will change while the analysis is being carried out. On the other hand, an extraterrestrial might intentionally stabilize his signal. He could either take out the Doppler shifts in the direction he is transmitting, just as we do for receiving, or he could transmit from a stable platform in deep space. With the computing power of today, a typical Pentium can test all the drift conjectures for an Earth-like planet or even for the moons of Jupiter.

BEAMED BEACONS

We know how strong a signal must be if we are to see it from Arecibo. The calculation is somewhat complicated, taking into account everything from antenna temperature to number of samples added. The net result is easy to state, however. The power of an ET transmitter broadcasting in all directions at once, just visible from Arecibo with today's most sensitive analyzers, is $P = 10R^2$ where R is the distance of the transmitter in light-years and P is in megawatts. The observation time is one hundred seconds. For a star twenty light-years away, (there are about twenty Sun-like stars that close), the required power is four billion watts. This is the total output of two large nuclear power plants; possible, but not trivial either. This, however, is the answer if the power is distributed by the sender uniformly over the whole sky. It goes out in all directions from the alien transmitter and just enough falls on the little portion of that enormous surface intercepted by the Arecibo antenna. There is just enough signal for detection. What if, instead, the alien civilization beamed directly at Earth, either because they had already received one of our own radio signals or because we orbit a Sun-like star. If they used an antenna like Arecibo, concentrating their energy a millionfold, the required transmitter power would be only four thousand watts. This is a power level many radio amateurs can produce with their rigs at home now, though in the U.S. it is illegal to use this much. There could be an intermediate case: a transmitter placed in the galactic plane, broadcasting an annular beam pattern that just irradiates the disk, might cut power requirements by factors of five to twenty-five times. Even a three-meter dish could receive a four-billion-watt signal from their Arecibo equivalent. Though such levels are not impossible, they may not be common. Obviously, if civilizations are to be seen at greater distances, the power levels must be even higher or observation times must be longer. The latter is where amateurs can shine. The important thing to remember is that most frequencies have not been searched even at the amateur level I am suggesting here. Most people using these frequencies are transmitting signals and looking for particular, rather strong, return signals. You can conduct, on most frequencies up to 2 billion cycles per second, a search thousands of times more sensitive than any done before, and you can do it with commercially available amateur equipment. If there is a stable, beamed signal out there in the solar neighborhood, you could be the first to find it. Before you get carried away and jump in your car for a trip to Radio Shack, remember that this only applies if you know the star and the frequency. An amateur effort is like the lottery. You could spend your lifetime playing and never win.

AMATEUR ANALYSIS OF THE PROFESSIONALS' DATA STREAM

There is a vital way that amateurs, even the public at large, can participate in SETI. As mentioned, NASA devised algorithms to analyze incoming data in real time (largely the work of the SETI Signal Detection Team). These detection methods filter out false alarms due to noise and terrestrial interference and recognize a simple signal. Experimentally, these techniques have been shown to be many millions of times faster for the low false alarm rates required than human searches are. Members of the NASA search, now Project Phoenix, are on the board of SETI At Home, and these same quality algorithms are applied to Arecibo data using the screensaver. It may soon be possible, however, to directly get data over the internet. Then it would be an operator's choice whether he or his computer did the analysis. A human search, for example, might look at the data on a video display as it comes in. Generally, any signal that is not a continuous carrier wave or a set of pulses will not be sensitively detected by typical computer algorithms. On the other hand, the human eye is very good at finding unspecified nonrandom patterns in noise. Just as a longshot then, some enterprising internet data provider might broadcast live on the web (SETI-TV) some of the SETI data. If you were looking and thought you saw a pattern, you could note the time and phone in a report to the SETI League at an 800 number. Judging by the reliability of UFO reports over the years, this idea has obvious problems, but amateurs with an original computer idea could tape this data for off-line (not real time) analysis. Anyone with a PC and the right equipment could try some tricks on selected data. SETI scientists have no plans to use human observers for initial data processing because although humans are creative in identifying patterns, the flip side of the coin is a high false alarm rate. Humans tend to find patterns, even when they are not there. Nonetheless, trained operators will sometimes look at data directly, even in the automated systems. In the end, we never believe data not accessible to our senses. There are two further caveats about this whole idea. Since a pulse or carrier wave is so simple to detect, it seems the likely choice for any ET beacon. Thus, any complex signal sent out is likely to be leakage, not a beacon, and thus weak to begin with. In addition, the modulation that carries the complex information will be weaker than the carrier, if there is one (which is likely to be seen first). So recognizing a picture seems unlikely. On the other hand, the suggestion about special reprocessing of the data may be feasible.

STEPS TO AN AMATEUR SETI OBSERVATORY

If, after the dose of cold water in the section on beaming, you still want to build a system, the parts are readily available. Check out the SETI League web site for up-to-date information. Although equipment today is much more stable and does more processing, the modular costs are about the same as in 1990 when we first gave them. A good receiver costs about $1,000. A good computer also costs about $1,000. The low noise amplifier, a mixer to shift frequencies into a convenient analysis band, if your receiver doesn't go high enough for you, and the digitizing card all cost $100 a piece. Satellite dishes with drives and computer control are $500. You might want to invest a little extra money in a broad-band feed, not the one tuned specifically for the TV satellite band. So for $3,000, you're off and running. This includes the cost of the filter bank synthesis program called a DFT. For a 3-meter dish and 100 seconds integration time, the sensitivity is better than 10^{-23} W/m^2. This yields a few false alarms per hour using a million channels, which today's computers can easily analyze.

DIRECTIONAL CONTROL

Pointing your antenna is easy. Anything that points a three-inch optical telescope is more than accurate enough for a radio telescope. (Mechanical strength is, however, another issue.) Radio waves are much longer than light waves. Even though your radio dish is tens of times bigger than a three-inch refractor, the waves it is focusing are millions of times larger than light waves. Therefore, the focus is much less precise for the radio telescope. You do, however, want good time signals and pointing coordinates, so that you and others can look again in a direction where you found a signal. Setting circles, or measured displacements from known celestial radio sources, will suffice (see Appendix A).

TRACKING THE SKY

Amateur searches for ETI signals can be carried out in various ways. Most TV dishes are permanently pointed toward a satellite. They can be used for SETI as stationary transit instruments that detect sky sources crossing the antenna beam as the Earth turns. This mechanical simplicity comes at a price. The satellite, which is interference for SETI purposes, is smack in the middle of the beam. This makes frequencies near its transmission frequency unobservable. Second, in the transit mode, each object will be in the beam for only a few minutes per day. Furthermore, if the dish is not repointed in declination (celestial altitude, with respect to the celestial poles), only one strip of the sky will be surveyed.

In order to attain more sensitivity, the radio dish should track the celestial source under study. To do this, a mechanical drive is needed. Pointing a radio antenna is easier than pointing an optical one because of the broader radio beam and because atmospheric effects are negligible for radio waves. However, as with optical tracking, the drive has to run one revolution per sidereal day, slightly shorter than the solar day. Accurate setting circles would also be useful. If these are not available, a PC with the right program can feed pointing data based on looking first at a celestial source with known coordinates. We can give no single recipe for adapting the dish to a drive. There are too many dish types on the market. It may be that one of the new types of table drives can be adapted to support a whole dish without disassembling its mount, thus preventing the invalidation of equipment warrantees, (see Appendix A). Perhaps further work on such drives can be coordinated through the ATM column of Sky and Telescope Magazine, or through the SETI League or another coordinating group.

SETTING UP AMATEUR GANGED SEARCHES: BIG COOPERATION

In spite of the simplicity and potential glory that might point you to individual searches, you should consider cooperative efforts. These can yield benefits in better sensitivity (signal to noise), time coverage, sky coverage, frequency coverage, and even spatial resolution, though the latter is probably less important and is more difficult.

TRACKING VERSUS TRANSIT

As mentioned, if a selected set of targets can be agreed upon, you and others can track and camp out on them. Many simultaneous detections of the same signal will allow each individual detector to use a lower threshold without increasing the overall false alarm probability. This increases total system sensitivity. If standard time marks are imposed and standard equipment and algorithms are used, then, in principle, tapes of signal intensity from many dishes can be combined to give greater signal strength. (Combining phase information would yield even greater gains. Unfortunately, this was beyond the state of the amateur art in 1992, but is on the edge of feasibility today. Check with the SETI League to stay on the cutting edge.) Even if signals are not phased together, the effective SNR improves in proportion to the square root of the total dish area observing simultaneously. If the dishes are all the same (say, three meters diameter), then the improvement goes as the square root of the number of participants; ten participants working simultaneously on one target will have an SNR about three times better than one observer. Given a nondrifting constant signal or one with long repetition period, daily reobservations can be added together to further improve the SNR. Further cooperation can search the same direction, parceling out various search frequencies to allow, for example, the tracking of drifting signals. Alternatively, round-the-clock observation is possible with an observation network spanning the globe. Observers over a range of latitudes can cover the whole sky in both hemispheres.

OTHER DATA

Could you find ET using a normal radio set? Probably not. After all, people have been tuning the bands for years. If signals from Out There were loud enough for normal electronics to find without directive antennas and computers, they would have been announced long since. If you don't want a construction project or a screensaver from SETI At Home, is there any other data you can analyze? Unfortunately not. This was particularly regrettable in 1990. At that time, if you were rich, a system such as SERENDIP complete with frequency shifting hardware, which surveys fifty thousand cycles per second bandwidth, could be built from completely commercial components. The total cost was a little less than thirty thousand dollars (exclusive of the antenna). Today, the $3,000 system suggested above is much more powerful. Nonetheless, now as then, I refuse to look at your low-probability events unless you take extraordinary care that you are not getting Earth-based interference.

One last thing. Amazingly enough, if you took a good commercial

```
1000000000000000000000000000000000000000001000011100
0000000010000010000001000001000000010001000000000000
0000000000000000000000000001000100001000000100000000
0000010000000000010001000001000000100000000010000100
0100000001110000000000000010000000000000010000000000
0000000000000000000000000000000000000000000000000000
0000100000100000010000010000110001000000000110000
0000000000000000000000001100001100001100000110
1101101101001100001100101100101100100100100100101001
0101001001000011000011000011000011000011000000001
0000000000011111010000000000000000000010000000000
0100000100000000000101101110010000000000000011111101
0000000000000000000000000010000000000000000000001000
1001110000000000010100000000000000010100100001100
1010111001010000000000000000101001000010000000000010
0100000000000000000100100000100000000000001111100000
0000000011111000000011101010000001010100000000000010
1010000000100000000001000101000000001010001001000
0000000000000100010010001000100110110011101101101010
0000100010000101010100010001000000000000000000010001
0001001001000100001000000100000000000011100000111111
0000011100000001111101000001010100000101000001010001
0000001000000000010000010000111000010000010000001000
0000000010000010001000100010000001000001100011000010
0000010001000100010000010000011000000011000001101
1000110110000011001111
```

Figure 2-A. An example of a digitally encoded message. It has the look of randomness.

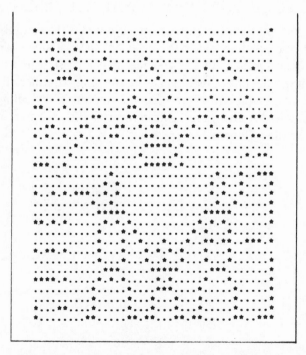

Figure 2-B. The decoded message of 2-A. Method used was to find repeating information, which first suggested arrangement of the data as a TV frame. Through further decoding, a picture emerged. *(Generated by Cipher A. Deavour.)*

receiver and listened for strange things on its output with a satellite antenna in standard scanning mode, you would be surveying most frequencies and positions in the sky at one thousand times the sensitivity anyone has ever used before. There could be a strong ET out there somewhere, just waiting for the right dish to point at the sky and listen to the right frequency. Maybe you will get lucky.

COORDINATION OF AMATEUR SETI WORK

The earlier version of this chapter inspired creation of the SETI League. Use this excellent resource. There are 2.4 million satellite dishes out there in the United States. If only 10 percent of those dish-owners decided to join in a ganged search, the combined effort would produce the equivalent of 25 Arecibos but the job of coordination is immense. The simplest thing to do now is to become a dues-paying member of the SETI League to become part of the act.

WRITE YOUR CONGRESSIONAL REPRESENTATIVE

For those of you who have given up on doing SETI yourself by this time, realizing just how daunting the search size is, please write your congressional representative if you feel that an ETI search is worthwhile. A few letters have real impact in Washington, especially if they are carefully thought out. There is, again, interest in including SETI in the broader NASA search for extraterrestrial life. A letter from you might make the difference.

CHAPTER 6

SEARCHING CLOSER TO HOME

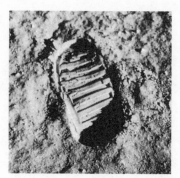

*T*he major part of this book is dedicated to the search for signals *from extraterrestrial intelligent life. This search is founded on the strong belief that intelligent life is likely to exist elsewhere. At the same time one could ask a prior question: if life is widespread in the univere, shouldn't we be able to find evidence of it in our home system? This seems increasingly possible as we discover more about the physical conditions of other bodies in our solar system, and also the amazing range of conditions under which life survives on Earth. If we could dis-cover life elsewhere—any other life, no matter how simple—it would have major implications for the search for intelligent life, greatly strengthening our resolve to carry on and dramatically impacting human philosophy, identity and religion. So it seems worthwhile to examine in greater detail the diversity of potential life-bearing environ-ments in the solar system . . . and on Earth.*

LOOKING FOR LIFE IN THE SOLAR SYSTEM

By

WILLIAM R. ALSCHULER

THE MOON

L et us begin our examination of life's possibilities with the Earth's closest companion, the Moon. We all "know" now that the Moon is a lifeless orb with no atmosphere and extremes of hot and cold. But when Galileo turned his telescope to the Moon 390 years ago and became the first to see the mountains, craters and dark plains in magnified detail, he assumed there was an atmosphere, running water and life. In fact he published speculations that there were intelligent beings walking the lunar surface. As telescopes improved these speculations were proved to be fantastical. Even with the greatest ground-based telescopes with the largest light-gathering power and greatest magnification, only the Sun's illumination angle ever changes on the Moon. There are no clouds, sparkling water, green vegetation or any moving objects to be seen. The temperature ranges from about 240°F in sunlight to about -220°F in the dark. Though there were rare reports, even in this century, of localized flashes of light seen with telescopes in some craters, these were never confirmed. The Moon's changelessness was well established by the middle of the 20th century, allowing Robert Heinlein to play off of this fact in his clever short story, "Nothing Ever Happens on the Moon."

When plans were being made to send astronauts to the Moon everyone assumed that there was no water; it was well established that in many places the lunar surface is dust. Unmanned Surveyor spacecraft were sent in advance of the Apollo program shots to gather basic data of general astronomical interest but also to sample potential landing sites to guide the goals and equipment designs for upcoming lunar geology missions. They were tripod-mounted probes with solar cells for power, a scoop to scratch the surface and instruments to measure other parameters. In addition, these landers laid to rest one major fear held by a minority of the scientific community: the astronauts would find their landing craft engulfed by a thick layer of dust when they attempted to set down. The Surveyors showed that this fear was groundless, that the dust layer was compacted and, though quite deep in some places, one would sink in a centimeter at most. The first astronauts almost died by landing on a boulder field rather than sinking into dust! In fact the dust did play another and largely unexpected role in the landings. It stuck to the spacesuits of the Apollo astronauts and was carried inside the landers, where it coated everything.

Nothing the astronauts observed or brought back changed our image of the Moon as a lifeless sphere, pitiless in its vacuum. The instruments left behind did however establish that there are a few things that change over time. The seismometers show sporadic shaking. Since the surface is free of any evidence of volcanic eruptions in the recent or medium-distant past, and there is no evidence of continental drift or plate tectonics (no continents or faults as we know them), these shakes cannot be of internal origin, and have been interpreted as meteor strikes. This is a reasonable assumption, but none of the astronauts actually saw a meteor impact for visual confirmation. None of the Apollo astronauts, nor their spacecraft or the instruments left behind, have been damaged by impacts either! The largest number of these impacts are from meteorites that are unrecordable by the seismometers. The astronauts also captured evidence of the solar particle wind of high-speed protons. These, along with the stream of micrometeors that come from the outer reaches of the solar system, constantly but slowly pulverize the surface rock into the thin dust we see now. The process is so slow that the astronauts' lunar footprints (one of which heads each chapter of this book) will probably be visible for millions of years.

Of course the face of the Moon itself is covered with evidence of change, but change long ago. All of the features, especially the craters and the lunar plains, were created by millions of impacts of fast moving large bodies from outer space. These fell mostly as the planets and moons were forming, 4.5 to 4.3 billion years ago. The great lunar planes are lava fields created when the crust cracked under giant impacts and the still warm rock of the interior flowed out. The large impacts continued at a steadily decreasing rate, but still occurred in more recent times, as shown by some of the giant craters, such as Copernicus and Tycho, estimated to be between 175 and 225 million years old. These have sharp-featured unfilled crater floors, splash-back central peaks, and large surrounding systems of light-toned splash marks, called rays, which have not yet been dulled by the micro bombardment to the color of surrounding soils.

Until perhaps fifteen years ago the lunar impact features were ascribed largely, if not solely, to the impact of rocky or metallic meteors. But with the growing knowledge of comets, and perhaps Sir Fred Hoyle's provocative thesis that their impacts bring us viral infections from beyond, interest developed in the influence of comet impacts on Earth in providing both water on a large scale and some of the building blocks of life. It gradually dawned on a number of people that comets would have hit the Moon in the same ancient era and perhaps there might be remnants of water there as a result. With this motivation, research was started with ground-based radar and instruments on Clementine, a probe that orbited and surveyed the mineralogical content of the Moon. These provided evidence in 1999 that there was indeed a small amount of water ice frozen on the surface, or perhaps under the floor of a crater at the lunar south pole. It might be in the form of a chunk of ice or it might be a sort of permafrost. In either case, it is assumed that it is the remnant of a comet strike from the era of bombardment, preserved in the darkness of the polar crater floor.

The estimate of volume led some commentators to suggest that it would be a fine source of water for astronauts when a lunar colony is established. However, if it really is the remains of a comet, it would be an extremely interesting sample of primordial material, perhaps left over from interstellar material from before the formation of the solar system. This water makes it even faintly possible that life existed on the Moon briefly, but only as an emigre, not native, having arrived via the comets. It would then be worthy of extreme care in handling, so as to allow analysis for life or the building blocks of life, without contamination from Earth.

This leads to a small but cautionary tale: At the time the first astronauts went to and returned from the Moon, there was some fear, in spite of the generally widespread knowledge that the Moon was hostile to life, that it might harbor unknown microbes that could be brought back and might devastate terrestrial life. As a result, a partial effort was made to take precautions against this possibility. This included the immediate placement of the astronauts after they landed into an isolation trailer on their aircraft carrier ferry, where they lived for more than a week after their return.

No exotic microbes were found and the practice was discontinued for later flights. However, microbes *were* found on the Moon. A later Apollo flight, commanded by Pete Conrad, landed at one of the Surveyor sites so that Conrad could walk over and snip off a piece of the lander, which he did, and bring it home for examination. It was found to harbor a species of common earthly infectious bacterium, cells of *streptococcus mitis*. It appears that in spite of the clean room precautions taken at the time the Surveyor probe was assembled, it became contaminated in handling and the bacteria survived both the launch and the trip to the Moon, as well as years in the high vacuum, solar wind and intense solar ultraviolet bombardment (or perhaps the particular part recovered was in shadow) while on the lunar surface. After extermination the bacteria were frozen, but can be revived by rewarming.

It is of course possible that the staph bacteria were a later contamination, created after the sample's return, but the scientists who found it think this is unlikely. If not, then we have a case of earthly bacteria surviving in what many consider impossible conditions, though these are the typical conditions of outer space near a star. And since they survived the solar radiation, it seems safe to assume they might survive an extended time in deep space between the stars, where as a rule there is no intense ultraviolet. It makes the whole idea that life could have arrived here from elsewhere a lot more believable.

MARS

Mars has long been seen as a place likely to harbor life. Galileo's telescope gave him a hint of the changes that occur regularly during each Martian year. Mars was observed to have a rotation period just a half-hour longer than Earth's. It's rotational axis is tilted sufficiently to create seasons, as is Earth's. The overall red color could be seen to be a blend that includes areas of green and brown that change with time, as well as white polar caps, which alternate in extent annually. With better telescopes the surface sometimes could be seen to be obscured by a haze that arises suddenly and was surmised to be from large dust storms, a supposition confirmed by the first Viking landers in the 1970s.

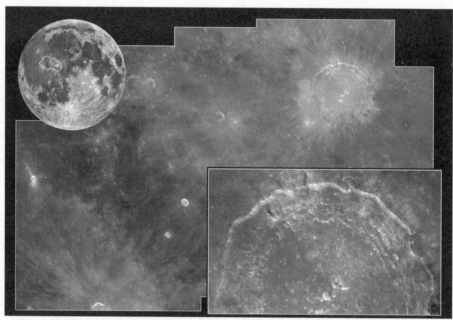

Above: The Moon's Copernicus Crater, as imaged by the Hubble Space Telescope (inset) and a ground-based photo taken from the Lick Observatory. *(Photograph: Courtesy Space Telescope Science Institute.)* Below: Copernicus again. This view of the 55-mile wide impact crater was taken by the Lunar Orbiter. *(Photograph: Courtesy NASA/JPL and U.S. Geological Survey.)*

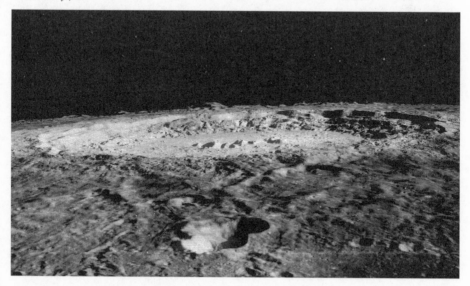

In the late 1800s Schiaparelli published visual observations of Mars in which he claimed to see curvilinear markings, like mixed up lines of latitude and longitude, which he called "canalli." An enthusiastic, serious and wealthy amateur astronomer in the U.S. who built his own observatory, Percival Lowell mistranslated the Italian as "canals" and proceeded on the assumption that Schiaparelli thought the features were artificial. Lowell spent years observing Mars intensively, taught himself to draw carefully what he saw, and produced beautiful and detailed drawings of the "canal" system. These were seen by many other observers, though photographs, which were increasingly employed in astronomy, did not show them (and they never have).

The colors of Mars seen by the Hubble look very similar to those recorded visually by Lowell, et. al. They also change seasonally and over longer terms, as recorded a century ago. The Hubble shows red regions turn to dark brown-green regions, and vice-versa. This probably has to do with dust deposition and other forms of weathering.

With the improvements in films and in spectrographs at the turn of the 20th century, astronomers were able to measure the temperature and composition of the Martian atmosphere. The results were rather discouraging to the notion of Martian life: at the equator in the day the temperature could rise as high as 60°F on occasion, but usually only rose to freezing. At night it often dropped down to 80°F below zero. This is more or less the temperature range of Antarctica during the middle of its winter. The Martian poles were more extreme. Analysis showed that the atmosphere contained free oxygen, carbon dioxide, nitrogen, argon and a trace of water vapor. All good, but the proportions were wrong: way too much carbon dioxide (95%) and too little oxygen (less than 1%) or water vapor. On top of that, the total atmospheric pressure was found to be very low (0.007 bars), 0.7% of sea level on Earth, and about equal to the pressure here at 100,000 feet. We would need a respirator to compress and separate the air enough for us to breathe. Because the air is so thin the shielding effect of Mars' atmosphere against ultraviolet radiation is much poorer than Earth's. It would constitute a significant hazard to unprotected humans and possibly a source of increased mutation for any Martian life. It is possible that the early air might have included free water vapor and could have been better shielded against UV than Mars is now. Water and carbon dioxide were found in the polar caps, though water ice dominated. The prospects of finding life were downgraded.

The Mariner (1971-2) and Viking (1976) landers and orbiters con-

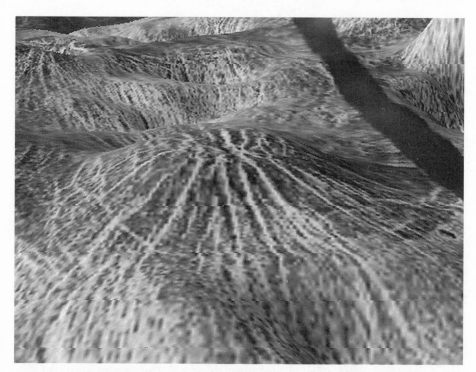

Our nearest neighbors in space, Venus (above) and Mars (below) are a study in contrasts. Venus's forboding surface is volcanically active and the pressure is severe enough to keep the physical profile of surface features extremely low. Mars, half the size of Earth, has a thin atmosphere and the remnants of water, as seen in this photo of water ice coating the rocks and soil. *(Venus Photograph: Courtesy NASA/JPL and U.S. Geological Survey. Mars Photogrpah: Courtesy NASA/JPL.)*

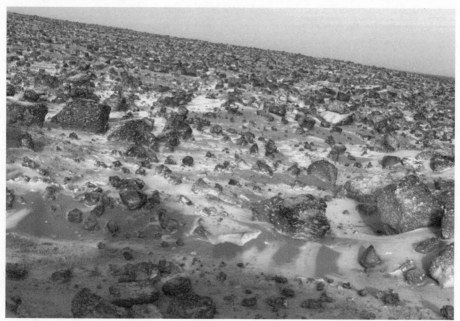

firmed the absence of canals but showed striking features not seen before. Giant volcanoes, the largest in the solar system, poke up to the top of the atmosphere and show that at one time Mars had a hot interior. There is no obvious set of continental plates, though the most recent orbiters show by their orbits that the northern hemisphere has a slightly smaller diameter than the southern, and this may mean that a simple system with two plates once existed. The latest orbiter surprised everyone by discovering areas of Mars with alternating stripes of north and south magnetism. These are found on Earth on either side of the midocean ridges and form a neat support for ocean floor spreading, continental drift and the quasiperiodic reversal of the geomagnetic field. Their fragmentary presence on Mars lends further support to the possibility that Mars once had plate tectonics.

A huge canyon dubbed Valles Marineris, deeper than the Grand Canyon and stretching a distance equal to two-thirds of the way across the United States, was also revealed. Viking and later unmanned probes clearly show stratigraphy in the canyon walls. The canyon path has a dendritic pattern that resembles fairly well water-cut canyons on Earth. Landslides are visible inside the canyon. Elsewhere in some flat areas are aligned teardrop shaped flat buttes that look like sandbars created in floods of water, tails pointed downstream. These features all resemble water-made landscapes here, but the similarity is not complete. Though majority opinion leans toward Mars having had a significant amount of free water in the form of an ocean, perhaps covering the depression in the north to a depth of 300 feet for up to 2 billion years, neither its presence nor its longevity is at all settled.

It should be noted that if an ocean did exist on Mars at one time, it would not have been affected by any tides. Mars does have two moons, Phobos and Diemos, but they are only 10 and 6 miles across respectively (they look like captured asteroids), much too small to create tides, the absence of which might have adversely affected the evolution of any early Martian life. It seems likely that the intertidal zone on Earth—the shores that are alternately underwater and revealed by the tides twice a day—were certainly significant habitats for the transition of life from sea to land, and perhaps also for the origin of cellular structures in the earliest one-celled organisms. Intertidal zones are where the earliest known life forms, stromatolite colonies of blue-green bacteria, are found.

Although the atmospheric composition of Mars is nasty, far from hospitable to current life on Earth, it is perhaps not too far from what is now thought to have been the atmosphere on Earth about 2.5 billion years ago, shortly after photosynthesizing bacteria began to pump oxygen into the air. The hunt for life on Mars, as of this writing, is far from over.

METEORITES FROM MARS

The impetus to send probes to search for life on Mars was given a further push by the announcement in 1996 that a team of university and NASA scientists, funded by NASA, had found evidence of life in a meteorite from Mars that was recovered from the Antarctic ice sheet. The big chill of collecting near the pole aside, finding meteorites in Antarctica is easier than just about anyplace else on Earth. There are almost no loose terrestrial rocks on the surface to confuse the situation; most are buried beneath the snow and ice. There is no concealing vegetation and little water erosion. And the dark meteorites stand out against the white surface. In some cases fields of meteorites that fell together in one shower have been found scattered over a small area. This fist-sized meteorite, numbered ALH84001, was examined in clean-room conditions and found to contain inclusions, minute cavities completely closed off from each other and the outside, which contained gas apparently untouched since its enclosure. When analyzed, the gas composition was an excellent match for the Martian atmosphere as measured by earthly spectroscopists and confirmed by the unmanned landers. The mineralogical composition was found to be consistent with that determined for the surface rock of Mars. Using radioactive dating, the age of the meteorite was determined to be 4.5 billion years, and it was found that the rock left Mars about 15 million years ago, presumably as a result of a major impact by a meteor from deep space, that it orbited the Sun for about 15 million years, finally reaching Earth and landing on Antarctica about 13 thousand years ago. All of these results were published at the time of NASA's announcement of the possible detection of fossil life signs in the meteorite, and were widely accepted. The evidence for its Martian origin was solid. Then controversy arose over the interpretation of the other part of the analysis.

The meteorite was drilled and sampled and portions were examined microscopically. In a number of locations, groups of tiny rods were discovered imbedded in the meteorite. They were all made of minerals, the usual case when life fossilizes slowly over time. They were dated to about 3 billion years ago. Their shape is similar to that of many earthly bacteria. However, their length is only about 1 micron (a thousandth of a millimeter) or less, about a factor of 10 smaller than the smallest, commonly known terrestrial examples. While there was no dispute over the presence of the rods and only minor contention that they represented earthly contamination, there was great unwillingness to accept them as fossil life on the grounds that they are too small to be bacterial. There is also a belief among some scientists that such structures can be deposited by purely geochemical processes and thus there is no need to invoke biological ones. The team also found carbonates, sulfides and oxides in the rock from Mars, all of which could have resulted from biochemical reactions. They also found traces of polycyclic aromatic hydrocarbons (PAHs) in the form of bulls-eye stains with non-uniform rings. Such compounds are often left as residues when bacteria fossilize.

The controversy continues. For each piece of evidence against the "life" interpretation, the original team has made a strong counter. And new evidence keeps coming in. For example, additional meteorites from Mars continue to be turned up all over Earth. Recent finds, dated as being 1.3 billion years old and 165 million years old, hold shapes that look even more like known bacteria and have lengths of 1 to 2 microns. Other researchers have recently discovered living nanobacteria in Australia's oil-bearing sediments that have lengths in the range 0.02 to 0.15 microns and contain DNA material, show growth, and have cell membranes. They are well below the size the critics have claimed as the minimum needed to contain the conventional structures of living cells. This work seems to support the original interpretation of the rods from the meteorite ALH54001, published in 1996.

The NASA research team has repeatedly asserted that these pieces of evidence support each other and that they thus have found traces of Martian life. The current majority believes that they have not. However, many think further sampling, perhaps in deeper layers of Mars, which may require humans to carry out the work, will eventually turn up fossil life of a simple sort, and perhaps even living microorganisms in the permafrost. *If* the theorized permafrost does exist. However, though Mars has long been the best candidate for finding life off Earth, there is now a second hot prospect . . . well lukewarm, anyway. It is Europa.

EUROPA

Europa is the second closest moon to Jupiter and one of the four bright moons discovered by Galileo in 1610. It is an off-white sphere covered

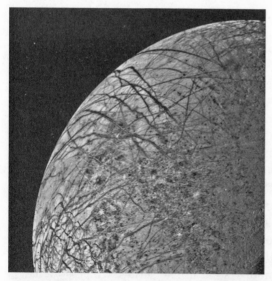

Left: Jupiter's frozen moon, Europa, as imaged by Voyager 2. Center: A close-up view of Europa, taken by the Galileo spacecraft, shows the frozen surface plates that have been broken and moved laterally. *(Photographs: Courtesy JPL.)* Bottom: A comparison of surfaces from Jupiter's moons. Left to right: Europa, Ganymede, and Callisto. *(Photographs: Courtesy NASA/JPL.)*

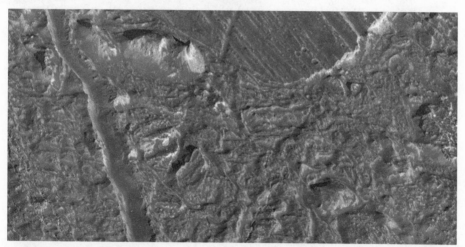

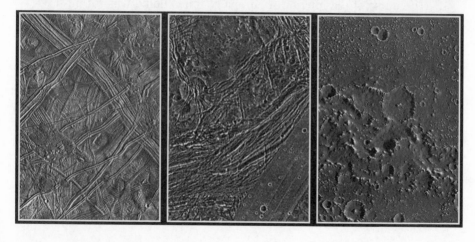

with a global network of irregular, venous, pale reddish-brown markings that intersect and split, and just a few impact craters. It looks
rather like the front surface of the human retina. The satellite's surface
is highly reflective and measurements soon showed that it is almost
entirely water ice. The relatively few impact craters implied that old
craters are constantly being wiped away by an active surface. The most
detailed Voyager images—and even better ones from the Galileo probe
now orbiting Jupiter—showed that the ice is riddled with seams, many
colored as described above. In general these look like pressure fractures
we see all over the north polar ice pack here on Earth, caused by the
motion of the water below. This resemblance was enough for many to
suggest that Europa was not solid ice to the core but might be covered
by a thick ice shell that encloses a liquid ocean, perhaps an ocean of
liquid water. While this was an obvious conclusion to draw because its
surface is water ice, Europa is a very cold place. It receives $^1/_{25}$ the
intensity of sunlight that illuminates Earth. The surface temperature is
only about -250°F. This is cold enough that molecules other than water
might be solid or liquid, depending (see the essay by Hal Clement).
However, the careful analysis of Galileo's flybys of Europa allowed its
gravitational field to be mapped in detail, which in turn permitted the
delineation of the interior structure of Europa with improved accuracy.
This seems to confirm that inside the ice there is liquid water, and
probably a solid rock mantle and an iron core. Europa is about the size
of our Moon, 1100 miles in diameter. Current estimates for Europa are:
an iron core 100 to 200 miles in radius, a rocky mantle about 800 miles
in radius, a liquid layer about 60 miles deep, and an ice crust perhaps
10 to 20 miles thick. The latter is a bit smaller than the thickness of the
Earth's rocky crust and much thicker than our north polar ice, which
on average is tens of feet thick and, at its greatest on the Antarctic cap,
about 3 miles deep.

Of course, if the interior of Europa contains liquid water it must be
above 32°F, which is much warmer than the surface. Since sunlight
cannot be keeping it this warm, another heat source must be doing the
job. It is possible that radioactivity in the rocky mantle plays a role, as
it does on Earth. However, the prime candidate for the responsible
energy source is internal friction, generated by the tidal force exerted
by Jupiter and abetted by the other 3 Galilean moons. The high gravity
of Jupiter varies rapidly with distance from it, with the result that the
nearest moons feel a greater tug on the side nearest Jupiter than on the
far side. This effect causes the moons to bulge on those two faces. (This

is a more extreme version of the same effect exerted by our Moon that creates tides on Earth.)

Assuming Europa's inner ocean is tidally heated to above freezing, what else can be said about its condition and the chances for life? As yet there is no hint as to how salty the water is. The fact that Earth's oceans are now salty may not be significant for the origin of life, since the salt is largely the result of washdown of minerals from the land by erosion. The early terrestrial oceans were fresh, and life originated while they were much less salty than they are now. The mineral content of any Europan ocean in general is unknown. But given the presence of a rocky core still being heated by tidal forces, and given the reasonably Earth-like mineralogy of other Jovian moons such as Callisto and Ganymede, whose surfaces are at least partly rocky, it is not unreasonable to speculate that at least a mild volcanism might exist in Europa's core that could transport an Earth-like array of minerals into its ocean.

The presence of internal heating would certainly drive currents in the Europan ocean, and the tidal forces referred to above will also likely play a role in generating currents. This is important because currents create gradients in mineral concentration and in temperature, and thus create varied potential habitats for life. The presence of a variety of ecological niches is almost certainly important as a source of selective pressure, a key to the evolution of life. In addition, volcanism could liberate both carbon dioxide and oxygen from the core. On Earth volcanism (as well as comets) was likely the main source of those gaseous atmospheric components, which are otherwise bound up in the rocks until biology does its work.

The amount of light under the ice shell must be quite low. The shell is thick compared to the thickest ice pack on Earth and will transmit little of the solar energy received at the surface, which is already diminished by a factor of twenty-five compared to Eart. In fact the conditions inside Europa may span the conditions at the extremes of the oceans on Earth. Near the surface, under the Europan ice, conditions should be similar to those under the ice packs on Earth. At the ice pack margins there are deep upwellings that bring a rich stream of minerals, in relatively oxygen-poor currents, up to the surface, and that is where the highest concentration of krill thrives. The krill are the micro- and tiny biota—plants, bacteria and animals—that form the bottom of the oceanic food chain on Earth. However their concentration is not as high under the center of the ice cap where the conditions and darkness are more similar to those likely on Europa.

At the ocean floor, if there are volcanoes on Europa, the conditions should be reasonably similar to those at the midocean ridges on Earth. There, in almost total darkness, we see lava emerging from the mantle below, water temperatures over 220°F though the water is kept from boiling by the extreme pressure. There is almost no dissolved oxygen, and there are high concentrations of many other elements. At these ridges we have found rich communities of tube worms, clams, crabs and other complex life. Even more important, we have also found single-celled organisms, bacteria and archaea, which feed off the minerals and have a metabolism that uses sulfur in place of oxygen and needs no light to survive. Many scientists believe the archaea, as their name implies, were the earliest form of life on Earth. Except for the lower pressure at the ocean bottom due to Europa's smaller gravitational force, and thus an increased tendency for boiling at the vents, the conditions are likely so similar that finding something on Europa similar to the archaea would not be a great surprise. Whether anything more complex exists is another matter. But it should be noted that on Earth the transition from single-celled life to complex life, which took place when the Earth was about 3.9 billion years old, was marked by a period of explosive variation. The fossils of the Burgess shale of British Columbia, the ediacara of Australia and certain newly found strata in China show a riot of species including a number of organisms thought not to fit in any existing phyla. (For an account of these discoveries and their implications see *Wonderful Life* by S.J. Gould and *Fossils of the Burgess Shale* by Briggs, Erwin and Collier.) The conditions on Europa have been as warm as they are now (or perhaps even warmer in the past if there are radioactive elements in the core to add to the tidal heating) for its lifetime, which is the same as Earth's, we believe. This suggests the possibility that there has been time enough for evolution and thus there might be complex life in Europa's ocean.

Given these considerations and the continuing stream of data from the Galileo probe that keeps improving our detailed coverage of the surface, it is not surprising that NASA is now planning follow-up missions to Europa. There is discussion of an orbiter to make detailed radar surveys, and of landers that might be able to drill through the ice crust and send down a microsubmarine on a reconnaissance cruise, and perhaps even return ocean samples to Earth.

From the reasonably high prospects for life on Europa, the possibilities get dramatically less favorable as we look around the balance of the solar system. The next candidate is Saturn's giant moon, Titan.

TITAN

Titan is the largest moon of Saturn. It is the second largest moon in the solar system with a diameter about 40% of Earth's, meaning that size-wise it is between Mercury and Mars. It is thus reasonable to think of Titan as another planet, one which happens to orbit a giant planet. It has been known since the 1940s that Titan has an atmosphere predom-inantly orange in color and quite deep, and since Stanley Miller's clas-sic experiments in the 1950s on the origin of life, it has been considered a possible site for the finding of primitive biology.

Until Voyager I's flyby in 1980, it was thought that methane was the prime constituent of Titan's atmosphere since the spectrum of nitrogen was not detected from Earth. Voyager I, however, found that the atmosphere is mostly molecular nitrogen, like Earth's, but the sec-ond-rank molecules are primarily methane, argon and hydrogen. Fur-ther down the list are hydrocarbons such as ethane, propane and ethylene, and then nitrogen-based cyanide, and carbon monoxide and carbon dioxide. The overall atmospheric pressure at the surface is 1.5 times that of sea-level Earth. The presence of molecular hydrogen in detectable quantities may seem odd since it is so light that it can easily escape the gravitational clutches of Titan even at Titan's low tempera-tures. Its presence must mean the hydrogen is continuously replen-ished. This is likely due to solar ultraviolet breaking up the methane and hydrocarbons high in the atmosphere where exposure to the Sun is significant. At lower levels there is shielding due both to the absorption of nitrogen and methane and also to the presence of a heavy "smog" of particles. The presence of the smog had been anticipated because polar-ization of Titan's light was significant and variable, and because the strength of the methane spectrum, which was discovered telescopically by Gerard Kuiper in the 1940s, varied a great deal with time. This sug-gested that the atmosphere was subject to occasional storms filled with particulates that polarized light and scattered it in all directions.

The Voyager data shows that the temperature at the surface is about 315°F, and that it decreases to about -375°F at an altitude of 30 miles, then it increases to -160°F at the top of the stratosphere. The tempera-ture rise is due to the upper atmospheric absorption of solar ultraviolet radiation. At the low end of these temperatures many of Titan's gases will condense and form part of the particulate smog. These condensates would be white or gray, thus leaving the question of what gives the atmosphere its orange color. At this time there is no complete answer.

The current best guess is that some of the hydrocarbons present are being turned into polymers, and that these chemical reactions may be taking place in reactions that occur on the surface of some of the organic condensates. Recent lab experiments have shown that in conditions similar to those in Titan's atmosphere dark polymers can form from hydrogen cyanide and acetylene, but no chemical with an exact match to Titan's spectrum and colors has yet been found.

The particulates in the smog are about 0.2 to 1 micron in diameter, as determined by Voyager. If the particles grow larger they become too big to float and will condense out in the cold conditions near the surface. Titan may have thin clouds of methane crystals at low altitudes. Ethane, present in small amounts, is the most abundant result of the ultraviolet destruction of methane. Ethane will condense at altitude and fall toward the surface. On its way it might form clouds or contribute to the general haze. However, when it reaches the surface it will be a liquid and calculations suggest it could fill a global ocean to a depth of about two-thirds of a mile. The ocean would contain dissolved nitrogen and methane as well as all the other atmospheric gases. The bottom might have a layer of carbon dioxide ice. If this "dry ice" can sublime, as it does on Earth, then its gas bubbles may keep the ocean boiling. Any surface that sticks up out of the putative ethane ocean will also be coated with this mixture of dry ice and hydrocarbon ices.

If you have the idea that icy conditions are not considered to be a barrier to the development of life you are correct. This is based in part on what we know of the next prospects: the comets.

COMETS

Though we have tracked the appearances of comets backward in time for (in some cases) more than two thousand years, our knowledge of their constituents and their physical conditions is largely due to work done in the 20th century. In 1882, telescope based spectroscopy showed that comets contain carbon, sodium and iron. R.S. Ball mentions in his 1886 book, *The Story of the Heavens*, the possibility that the increasingly curved tails of the comets are of successively higher-mass atoms and molecules. He names hydrogen, hydrocarbons and iron or chlorine in order. But it is not until the middle of the 20th century that a reasonably complete inventory of composition was compiled. From the spectra it was found that neutral molecules of hydrogen, formaldehyde, carbon monoxide, cyanogen, carbon dioxide, water, and many others, as well as light and medium metal elements, are present in the cloud immediately surrounding the comet's nucleus, called the coma. In addition, 1970s cometary UV spectra taken by rocket and satellite show there is an immense low density cloud of hydrogen surrounding the heads of comets, with diameters typically millions of miles: The tails usually exhibit a two-fold structure, a relatively straight blue-green tail that points nearly straight away from the Sun, and a yellow-white more fanned out tail that sweeps away from the blue tail and trails the motion of the comet. This double structure was vividly revealed in the tail of the wonderful Comet Hale-Bopp on its pass in 1998. Back in the 1950s, Fred Whipple characterized comets as being "dirty snowballs" that outgas and emit dust and dirt and this description seems apt, even in light of recent developments.

The blue tail is the gas ion tail, and the predominant color comes from ionized carbon monoxide. It and other ions are driven out by the pressure of the solar particle wind on the nucleus. When they emerge from the nucleus into the coma they interact at the front of the comet with the solar wind and its frozen magnetic field to produce a bow shock at the boundary. The ions, which are electrically charged, follow and trap the field lines. This fact shows up in the field-line-like structures of the ion tail. In fact these structures led to the inference of the existence of a solar wind in the 1950s. The dust tails are generated by neutral atoms that drag dust out of the nucleus as they evaporate. Since this gas is electrically neutral and the dust is nearly neutral, it is the pressure of sunlight that predominantly drives the dust away. When Halley's Comet made its last pass in 1986 several probes were sent through the tail, coma and very near the nucleus. The data from them showed that the coma gases were about 80% water, 10% carbon monoxide, $3^{1}/_{2}$% carbon dioxide and what is probably polymerized (i.e. long-chain) formaldehyde. The latter is very exciting because it is a clear hint that life-building organic chemistry has gone on in deep space, likely dating back to the cloud that formed the solar system or even before.

The nature of the dust was fairly speculative until those space probes passed close to the nucleus of Halley's Comet. They found the dust to be composed of three dominant types of particulates. The first, made of carbon, hydrogen, nitrogen and oxygen have been called "CHON" particulates. The second type is the silicates, similar to the rocks in the crust of the Earth, the Moon, Mars and the rocky meteorites. The third component is a mixture of the other two. In Hale-Bopp's pass observers also saw evidence of polycyclic aromatic hydrocarbons, that, as mentioned earlier, can be produced chemically or by life processes. These molecules were generated in the cold. An analysis of the water molecules in the ice deep inside Comet Hale-Bopp shows that ice has never been warmer than 25K (-400°F).

In any case the molecules are complex and thus compel us to believe that complicated molecules on the way to life, or life molecules themselves, are likely to arise in the cool, gassy and dusty conditions in deep space. Since comets sometimes impact planets, especially early in a solar system's history, these molecules may arrive on the backs of comets and provide a head start to life on a planetary surface.

Halley provided another intriguing surprise: its nucleus was revealed to be peanut-shaped, about 10 miles long by 5 miles in diameter, showed evidence of cratering and was also found to be an almost perfect black, one of the darkest surfaces in the solar system. This violated the long held idea based on the external appearance of brilliant white that the parent body of a comet must also be white. We now have to concede that at least the surface of the nucleus is more the dirt in the dirty ice than the ice. Just what is the nature of this dark layer? It is not settled but many think it is a hydrocarbon film, with an admixture of silicates. Something very like it may also explain the dark, nearly black colors of many of the most distant asteroids, as we'll see shortly. Based on the measured low density of Halley's nucleus, it may be that comets are made of porous ice rather than solid ice. If true, the porousness would be expected to act like a maze for light and contribute to the blackness of the surface, no matter the composition.

As the comet approaches to within three astronomical units (Earth distances from the Sun) the temperature in the comet rises and the ices begin to sublime. It is thought that throughout this process some of the particulates mixed in the gas condense on the surface to form the dark layer, which also insulates the interior. Then further sublimation is generated from local hot spots below the surface. The fact that there are localized jets of gas and dust was inferred from detailed observations of heads of comets. The images from the close pass at Halley showed such jets in detail.

The temperature of a cometary crust as it crosses the orbit of Earth should be about 85°F, and this was observed to be the case for Halley. Thus one could say that for most of each orbit the surface of a comet, like its interior, is in a really deep freeze, while for a small fraction, say 1% of each orbit, the surface becomes warm. It is likely that the organic chemicals found in comets, if produced there, have arisen slowly in the colder conditions, since those are so much more prevalent than the warm ones. In any case the findings of organics to date, coupled with the presence of water, are sufficiently tantalizing that NASA and ESA are considering various missions to comets to extract samples from their nuclei and return them to Earth for analysis. These missions would launch sometime after the year 2000.

ASTEROIDS AND METEORITES

The clues we have received about biochemistry from comets and the controversy over the Martian meteorite suggest the following question: What do we find when we examine ordinary meteorites that arrive from the outer solar system, presumably from the asteroid belt between Mars and Jupiter, or from much further out in the Kuiper Belt or the Oort Cloud? And how do we know where the meteorites come from anyway? Are some from the destruction of comets?

Meteorites have been more or less systematically collected since they were recognized to be extraterrestrial in origin in the 1800s, and appear in many natural history collections. There are more than 3,300 cataloged now and many are sold by dealers on the open market.

The origin of the majority of meteorites is actually thought to be well tied to the material in the asteroid belt for several reasons. When the overall colors of the various types of meteorites are examined in the lab and compared to those of the asteroids we have been able to observe, they fall into similar groupings by color, which correspond to compositional groups among the meteorites. Those groups are the iron-nickel or metallic meteorites, the stony meteorites, the carbonaceous chondrites, and some of mixed type. Another way of dividing them is into undifferentiated (chondritic) and differentiated meteorites. Other lines of evidence about origins include orbits that are similar to the Earth-crossing asteroids called the Apollos. These in turn can be worked backward to orbits in the Asteroid belt between Mars and Jupiter. Jupiter, the 800-pound gorilla of the outer solar system, is capable of throwing such bodies inward because of the resonant interaction of its orbit and gravity with theirs. There may be other asteroids with origins farther out, either beyond Neptune (the Kuiper Belt) or beyond Pluto by ten thousand times (the Oort Cloud).

In the late 1990s, the first observations were made of bodies from the Kuiper Belt, seen as they orbit. In just a few cases the largest telescopes have collected colors for them. The Kuiper objects are measured to be thirty to fifty miles across. The range of colors is from neutral gray to dull red. The latter is the expected color if carbon, hydrogen and other elements form into hydrocarbons, which process is promoted by the long-term bombardment of the cosmic rays that strike all objects in deep space. Since this range of colors is also found in the asteroid belt and in meteorites, it is reasonable to think that their history is at least partly common.

The elements most abundant in the Sun are present in the chondrites in about the same proportions. The stony meteors have about the same composition as the Earth's crust, and the metallic meteorites look similar in composition to the core of the Earth. Their origin seems to have been inside larger bodies, the size of moons or small planets. The evidence for this is both compositional and mineralogical. In the first case, the differentiated meteorites, especially the metallics, got that way by being subjected to temperatures high enough to melt the rock, during which gravity drew the metals and sulfur to the center of the bodies involved. This is a process just like smelting for purification. Many other meteorites (most of the chondrites) were not melted but were held at temperatures around 2600°F for many years, allowing elements to diffuse slowly and homogenize the composition of the silicate minerals. Again, this only seems possible if the chunk of meteorite was buried in a large body. Finally, small objects exposed to space develop a roster of certain unusual isotopes due to cosmic ray bombardment. Measurements show most meteorites were shielded from bombardment most likely by being inside something larger for most of their eons in orbit.

The meteorites with the closest connection to life are the carbonaceous chondrites. They carry a high load of hydrocarbons, as their name suggests. A number of them have been analyzed for hydrocarbons and two major classes have been found. Most recently polycyclical aromatic hydrocarbons, possible byproducts of life, have been found in the form of kerogen. Even more interesting, since the 1970s researchers have found amino acids in these meteorites. These include the twenty types of amino acids that form all terrestrial proteins. It was originally thought that these might be from terrestrial contamination, but an unusual fact prevents this conclusion. While the amino acids come in right- and left-handed varieties (they are said to be of opposite chirality), which are created equally in the laboratory, in living organisms the left-handed predominate. No one knows why this is. Yet in the meteorites equal amounts of left- and right-handed molecules are found. There is no known way to explain this by contamination and thus it seems well established that the meteoritic amino acids originated in space, before during or after they took their present form. One could also add that unless some process in space constantly renews them the meteorites they have been traveling in must have remained below about -225°F for most of their lives. Of course, given the low temperatures of objects of small size in orbits beyond Mars, this is not difficult to imagine!

These results seem to leave us with the possibility that the building blocks of cell metabolism originate in deep space, at relatively low surface temperatures, and then may shower down on planets as they form and are bombarded by the small but numerous leftovers of the cloud they are condensing from. It is still an open question whether these amino acids fry upon arrival, since the inner rocky planets had surface temperatures over the boiling point of water for millions of years. Perhaps it is only the later leftovers that count. When the Earth finally was cool enough to maintain an ocean, carbonaceous chondritic impacts might have been meaningful carriers of the building blocks of life. There are still question marks, however. For example, small meteors achieve high temperatures as they blaze through the atmosphere, likely enough to disintegrate the amino acids. On the other hand amino acids might survive the atmospheric passage in a large meteor, say a mile across, but the impact of this size object is in the class of catastrophic impactors. It would generate massive tidal waves, boil a significant part of the ocean and inject steam and dust into the atmosphere. If the object failed to break on impact the acids would be locked in. If it broke, they would have to survive the altered conditions produced on their arrival. Perhaps this is a paradox, perhaps not. More work on detailed models of such events needs to be done to better settle the question and to describe with more confidence their consequences for both ancient and present-day Earth.

VENUS

Venus represents a low-probability venue for life according to current theories, which are different from earlier notions. For centuries since Galileo saw its disk and discovered that from our vantage point it undergoes phases like the Moon, the opposite was true. It did not take long to establish that Venus's mass and diameter are almost identical to those of Earth. It was labeled as our "sister planet." Since it is only two-thirds as far from the Sun as Earth, it was assumed that Venus must be

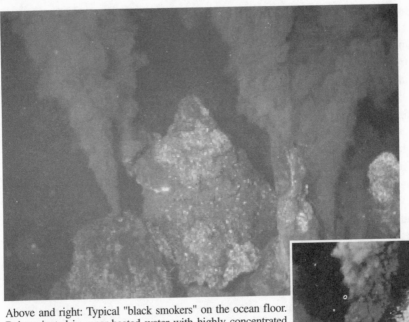

Above and right: Typical "black smokers" on the ocean floor. Being ejected is super-heated water with highly concentrated dissolved minerals. While a hostile place for humans, many strange creatures thrive in this extreme environment. *(Photographs: Courtesy U.S. Geological Survey.)* Below: Extremeophiles, in the form of streptococcus bacteria, were unintentionally sent to the Moon aboard Surveyor III (pictured), and when returned were alive and well.*(Photograph: Courtesy NASA/JPL.)*

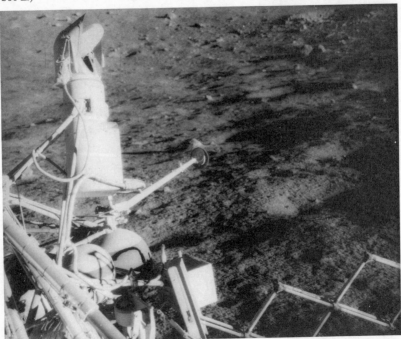

warmer, though majority opinion leaned toward the equivalent of an earthly tropical climate. With the advent of science fiction at the turn of the century, Venus became the site of many scenarios in which the terrain and climate were portrayed as hothouse jungles and swamps, reeking with decayed matter and populated with stinging beasts, carnivorous plants (perhaps inspired by the Venus Flytrap?), and intelligent versions of the Creature from the Black Lagoon. Sometimes Venus was seen as the site of rich mineral resources being mined by nasty Earth corporations that worked their slaves to death.

All this speculation was permitted because Venus presents a perpetually white, blank face to all outsiders. No creatures can be seen in the visible part of the spectrum—no atmospheric bands, no glimpses of the surface. This continued in the 1970s with the first Soviet Venus landers. The Venera series of spacecraft landed successfully in 1970, '72, '75, and '82. Venus's temperature and pressure were measured on the way down, and the findings were a surprise: up to 485°C (900°F) and a pressure 94 times that of Earth sea-level were found by the first probes and confirmed by the later ones. TV images from the 1975 and 1982 landers showed a remarkably dull landscape. The cameras, which died after two hours or less due to the extreme heat, showed slabs of rock and flat surfaced boulders on a relatively flat surface. There was little soil or sand visible, though some pebbles were seen. The color images of 1982 showed the rocks to be dark brown, black, and slightly orange, and the air to be a dull orange. A sample-collection experiment in two 1982 craft found the rock composition similar to an earthly basalt, and the images look like basalt, too. Nothing moved in the images and there was not a lot of evident erosion. No evidence of living things was visible.

Ultraviolet images of Venus's cloud tops were taken by the American Pioneer orbiters. Those taken by the orbiter in 1979 showed a cloud pattern generally like Earth's in its north-south split circulation. But Venus was seen to have just one circulation cell from equator to pole, whereas Earth has three of these Hadley cells. There were no images of hurricanes as on Earth, just a set of cloud bands that incline gently from the equator.

The information from the U.S. and Soviet probes about the atmospheric composition was quite frightening. In addition to the extremely high temperatures, the orange glow was found to be due to particulate clouds of sulfuric acid high in the atmosphere. The concentration of the stuff is not high but its optical effects are considerable. The atmosphere is 96% carbon dioxide, $3^1/_2$% molecular nitrogen, with traces of carbon monoxide, water vapor, sulfuric oxide, hydrochloric and hydrofluoric acid. The larger amount of carbon dioxide and molecular nitrogen on Venus compared to Earth results from the high temperature on Venus, which prevents them from being taken up by rocks as on Earth. In fact, the high temperature and pressure represent an extreme runaway greenhouse effect.

The abundance of water, carbon and nitrogen is low compared to the metals on all four terrestrial-type planets. Nonetheless, they play key roles in the atmospheres, and in at least one case, the life on those planets. If there was water on the early Venus, and there may have been, the high solar flux there would have raised the surface temperature and driven it into the atmosphere. The high ultraviolet flux at the top of the atmosphere (probably even higher then than now due to solar evolution) would have broken the water vapor molecules into hydrogen (H) and hydroxyl (OH). The high temperature at the cloud tops would rapidly have evaporated the hydrogen to space. The hydrogen loss would have removed any water and water vapor and dessicated the atmosphere to the point we see it today. At that point there would be nothing to dissolve and remineralize carbonates, and so as carbonates eroded out of the rocks the carbon dioxide it formed would remain in the atmosphere, increasing the greenhouse effect and thus the surface temperature. This would further bake out carbonates until the surface layer of rocks was exhausted of them. Finally Venus's current temperature, hot enough to melt lead, was achieved.

On Earth, all heat-driven processes received less solar input. Earth's inventory of water may have started at a larger value than Venus's. In any case, the early Sun may have been up to 20 percent fainter than today and at Earth's distance the chill might well have frozen the early oceans for up to two billion years. However the fossil evidence clearly indicates that the oceans have always been liquid. Therefore Earth must have had an internal source of energy and this almost certainly was the heat of radioactive decay in the mantle rock. This drove and still drives volcanism here, and volcanism releases large amounts of carbon dioxide. The high rate of carbon dioxide emission in ancient times would have driven the greenhouse effect to higher values than now, but with larger water oceans and lower UV intensity here than at Venus, the clouds of Earth would have moderated the solar input, negatively feeding back the greenhouse effect and also redissolving some of the newly liberated carbon compounds. And the high water vapor content of the air would not have so rapidly bled off hydrogen due to UV dissociation. So far, this seems to be a relatively stable system.

The polar icecap, which holds a record of the last several hundred thousand years, has been core drilled for samples. So far the results are ambiguous. They seem to say that a rise in carbon dioxide in the air *follows* rather than leads global warming at the end of an ice age. We don't yet know how to interpret that result. The fossil record shows that the Earth has gone through repeated ice and tropical ages, while never straying too far from the happy mean. Perhaps it can't run away with itself. Yet it is still disquieting to think that we are playing with fire (literally!) on such a gigantic scale. Any one of the extreme past departures in climate from the present one would create extreme discomfort and crises in agriculture for much of the world. It will happen someday if nature takes its course.

THE EXTREMEOPHILES OF EARTH

I have referred occasionally throughout this essay (and similar references are made in other essays) to the fact that Earth has produced quite an array of living organisms adapted to life in extreme ecological niches. That they exist is a relatively recent realization, and in fact some of the discoveries are the result of research supported by the space program. This is because extremeophiles are in niches that in their physical conditions at least approach some of those found elsewhere in the solar system. Further, the varieties of life in these extreme locations can be examined by prototypical instrumentation and algorithms, to test both the physical survival of the instruments and their ability to detect the presence of the life. (A failure of our technology to detect life when it is demonstrably there would be quite significant.)

The habitats of the extremeophiles of Earth can for the moment be divided into four environments, three of which are somewhat related to each other. These are: polar ice caps, hot springs and geysers, midocean ridges, and subsurface crustal rock. The polar caps include the ice itself and the water under the ice. Bacteria and certain lichens exist in the ice. The water under the edge of the north polar ice cap is rich in the microfauna called krill, which are the main dietary component for all sorts of larger creatures. Seals and walrus live on and under the ice. They eat fish that have evolved the equivalent of antifreeze, which allows them to survive in saltwater that is actually below the freezing temperature of freshwater. Fish and marine mammals eat invertebrates and krill. Polar bears hunt the fish and seals. Penguins and other birds live on the ice and hunt the fish.

Under the Antarctic cap, radar studies have revealed the presence of what may be a freshwater lake trapped 12,000 feet down. It is estimated that its last contact with the surface must have been at least 400,000 years ago. Since it is buried in ice, it is natural to ask why it is still liquid. The answer is likely that there is a volcanic hotspot below. This is regarded as a model for the possible under-ice ocean on Europa, and also as a precious legacy. So far no attempt has been made to sample it because a foolproof way to do so without risk of contamination has not been devised. Samples have been pulled from ice cores as close as several hundred feet above its surface and these have revealed bacteria of new types and previously unknown microorganisms.

Hot springs and geysers are spread over the Earth and in most places they are quite colorful. Though many people assume the colors are simple mineral deposits, in many cases they are actually colonies of living organisms: bacteria and archaea. One of the latter, *sulfolobus solfataricus*, produces a metabolic enzyme, alcohol dehydrogenase (ADH), in water that has a temperature of 190°F and in corrosive acid conditions not too much less acidic than the electrolyte in car batteries.

Other species of archaea are found in the midocean vents under even higher temperatures and much higher pressures. The vent communities are rich with clams, crustaceans and fish as well as single-celled organisms. Though the conditions are not too acidic, there is no light or dissolved oxygen. The water is full of minerals and at least some of the microbes live by metabolizing hydrogen and sulfur. Since early Earth conditions resembled the vent environment it may be that archaea of this sort represent the earliest life.

Another candidate for "earliest" is the metal digesting bacterium recently found $1^1/_2$ miles down some oil wells. If widely distributed, it is such a thick layer that it may be the largest single hunk of biomass on the planet (see the essay by Hal Clement). Perhaps a deep hole into cooler layers in the crust of Venus might reveal a similar population.

I would also like to draw your attention back to that amazing animal mentioned previously in the essay by Hal Clement, the tardigrade. It is not really a conventional extremeophile. It lives in a large number of places but under relatively benign, moist conditions. Yet if its environment dries up it goes into suspended animation and can revive a hundred years later without the kiss of the enchanted prince. Tardigrades have survived high pressure and vacuum, temperatures close to absolute zero and above boiling. They can survive exposure to intense nuclear radiation. Do these noted abilities of the tardigrade indicate that it has evolved through all these extreme conditions at one time or another? Where and when would it have found itself in such conditions? I propose these tiny monsters as worthy of study by anyone with curiosity and the energy to explore their local marshes.

CHAPTER 7

FIRST CONTACT—SEIZING THE MOMENT

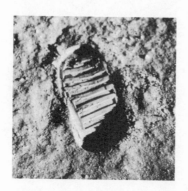

What happens after we make contact?

The world will change once we make unequivocal contact with another intelligent species. Our individual lives will change. Our societies will change. Perhaps not immediately, perhaps only imperceptibly at first. But the world will never be the same afterward. The change will be as enormous, and as permanent, as the results of the contacts between Europe and America that started 500 years ago. Michael Michaud takes us on a tour of some of the possibilities.

A UNIQUE MOMENT IN
HUMAN HISTORY

By

MICHAEL MICHAUD

Consciously and unconsciously, we are making contact with extraterrestrial civilizations more likely. The evolution of our technological civilization is making Earth electromagnetically noisier, with radio signals, television carrier waves, and radar pulses radiating outward into the Galaxy. Though we may not intend to call the attention of other civilizations to ourselves, we have been doing so for most of this century. We are making it more likely that other intelligences—if there are any—will find *us*.

At the same time, we have embarked on our own searches for life and intelligence beyond Earth, first with optical telescopes, then with planetary probes and radio observatories. So far, we have failed to find convincing evidence of another civilization. But, by extending the sensitivity and duration of our searches, we are making it more likely that we will find *them*.

Because we search for others, we tend to assume that they search for us. If we scour the skies with our instruments, send automated probes to other planets in this solar system, and imagine sending such probes to the planets of other stars, we assume that others are doing the same.

Yet this search for others may be an episodic cultural phenomenon in our own civilization, dependent on the values and perceptions of the time. The idea of a plurality of inhabited worlds has had its ups and downs throughout recorded human history; sometimes it was widely believed, and at other times it was widely rejected. This implies that other civilizations, if they ever start such a search, may not give it continuing attention over the millennia, particularly in the absence of a positive result. Thus the detection of another civilization, by us or by

them, may not be the result of a thoughtfully planned search conducted by astronomers sympathetic to it; it may come as a *surprise*. It
may be the unintended by-product of other activities, such as astronomy, planetary or interstellar exploration, or the gathering of military
intelligence. While there are strong arguments for radio as the preferred method of search, we should not exclude the possibility of other
scenarios, such as finding an artifact of another civilization in our own
solar system, or spotting the exhaust trail of an interstellar spacecraft.
Those too would be forms of detection.

Given the youth of our own technological civilization, probability
suggests that alien civilizations capable of detecting or communicating
with us would be older than ours and technologically superior. This
suggests that they are likely to find us before we find them.

THE CONSEQUENCES OF CONTACT

What happens if we do detect others, or meet them face to face?
Because of the probable technological superiority of the alien civilization, there is a presumption that the relationship will be an unequal
one, implying a submissive reaction on our part. But the consequences
of contact depend heavily on the circumstances of the detection, and
the state of our own civilization at the time.

At one extreme is the classic radio astronomy scenario, in which
our radio astronomers detect a faint signal that is the product of
another intelligence. After lengthy efforts, a message is deciphered, and
the wisdom of a superior civilization is revealed to us. The remoteness
of the aliens, perhaps hundreds or thousands of light-years away,
implies that they will be no threat to us, and that an exchange of
information may be the major outcome of contact.

At the other extreme is the direct contact scenario, in which an
alien spacecraft touches down on Earth, and we encounter extraterrestrials face to face. As envisioned in science fiction, the aliens could be
as benevolent as the cute alien botanist E.T., or as malevolent as the
marauding invaders depicted in the paranoia-charged atmosphere of
the early 1950s.

In our thinking about aliens, we reveal our emotional selves—our
predilections, our preferences. We are variously hopeful, naive, hostile,
intolerant; we display idealism, wishful thinking, insecurity, fear,
defeatism, even self-loathing. At one extreme, we think of aliens as
altruistic teachers who will show us the road to survival, wisdom, and

prosperity, or God-like figures who will raise humanity from its fallen condition. At the other, we see the aliens as implacable, grotesque conquerors whose miraculous but malevolently applied technology can only be overcome by simpler virtues.

These images are determined largely by our cultures, and by the circumstances of the time. Consider how American film and television portrayals of extraterrestrials changed from the weird and horrible invader of the 1950s *(The Thing, Invasion of the Body Snatchers)* to the benign aliens of the 1970s *(Close Encounters of the Third Kind)*, and then back to the repugnant aggressor of the 1980s television series *V* and *War of the Worlds*, and the 1990s movie *Independence Day* and TV's *X-Files*. We carry these images around in our heads, and they will influence the way we react to contact. (Of course, in other cultures people may carry other images.)

Our emotional and intellectual predispositions could be reinforced strongly by contact. Those humans who suffer deeply from guilt, who think that our species is uniquely evil, may fear retribution, a chastising of humanity; some may even welcome it. Those who despair at humanity's lack of wisdom, or who are frustrated by important unanswered questions, may see in the aliens a long-desired source of guidance and solutions, a living, law-giving deus ex machina. Those who perceive contact in the context of the more brutal episodes of human history may fear attack, invasion, or enslavement. We are likely to attribute motives to the aliens before we have real evidence.

Contact almost certainly would cause many more humans to attribute events on Earth to alien intervention (some already see this in the UFO phenomenon). There might be an upsurge in conspiracy theories, witch-hunting, and UFO sightings. But many of us would simply be excited by this new outside stimulus, with its suggestion of a break with conventionality and of new prospects for the future. Contact could be shared adventure for a species that badly needs one.

ANTHROPOCENTRISM GOOD-BYE

The most profound message from the aliens may never be spoken: We are not alone or unique. Contact would tell us that life and intelligence have evolved elsewhere in the Universe, and that they may be common by-products of cosmic evolution. Contact would tend to confirm the theory that life evolves chemically from inanimate matter, through universal processes, implying that there are other alien civilizations in addition to the one we had detected. We might see ourselves as just one example of biocosmic processes, one facet of the Universe becoming aware of itself. We would undergo a revolution in the way that we conceive our own position in the Universe; any remaining pretense of centrality or a special role, any belief that we are a chosen species would be dashed forever, completing the process begun by Copernicus four centuries ago.

The revelation that we are not the most technologically advanced intelligent species could lead to a humbling deflation of our sense of self-importance. We might reclassify ourselves to a lower level of ability and worth. This leveling of our pretensions, this anti-hubris, could be intensified if we were confronted with alien technology beyond our understanding. (Arthur C. Clarke has observed that any sufficiently advanced technology would be indistinguishable from magic.) We could feel even more deflated if the aliens, after contact, showed no interest in talking to us.

Contact also could be immensely broadening and deprovincializing. It would be a quantum jump in our awareness of things outside ourselves. It would change our criteria of what matters. We would have to think in larger frames of reference. Continuing communication with an ancient civilization would strengthen our sense of our own genetic and historical continuity, and could encourage us to take on longer-scale projects than we do now. Awareness of extraterrestrials would help to establish a new cosmic context for humankind; we would leave the era of Earth history and enter an era of cosmic history. By implying a cosmic future, contact might suggest a more hopeful view of the Universe and our fate, one less alienating than the cynical, materialistic, and limiting visions of the present.

Contact would remind us, as nothing else could, of our identity as a species. We would see the common nature of human beings defined by contrast with the aliens; the racial, religious, linguistic, and cultural differences among humans would seem minor by comparison. This could have a considerable unifying effect on humanity, easing tensions and encouraging cooperation within our species. But this new unity could be based as much on shared fear as on a sense of human brotherhood. If direct contact occurred, it could lead to a new racism, directed against the aliens.

Contact would give us the satisfaction of making others aware of our existence. If we detected extrasolar aliens, we would be strongly tempted to send a signal immediately to announce our presence, tell the aliens about ourselves, and begin spreading our own culture and values. But we have many causes for embarrassment about human civilization and behavior, and we might be tempted to disguise our problems and engage in posturing, inflating our stature and conveying an image of perfection. The aliens might not be above doing this themselves.

Contact also would be very reassuring to a species as doubtful about its future as we are. It would tell us that life and intelligence had survived and prospered elsewhere, even after acquiring powerful technologies. If the alien civilization were superior to ours, contact would suggest that intelligence is not an evolutionary dead end, and that the present state of human development is not final. More than any other event, contact could motivate us to transcend our present condition.

Contact would end the isolation of our species from other minds, giving us a new perspective on intelligence and on ourselves. At last we would encounter other beings who also worry about their survival, who feel the pain and joy of awareness, and who seek answers to many of the questions we ask about the purpose and destiny of intelligent life. We might enter a community of intelligence, gaining access to new knowledge and sensibilities, participating in a vast commerce of ideas among disparate minds. And we might join together with other civilizations in a mutual effort to assure the long-term survival of intelligence in the Universe.

THE KNOWLEDGE REVOLUTION

Contact could bring a knowledge revolution. Simply detecting aliens would bring us new knowledge about the evolution of life and intelligence, especially if we could identify the characteristics of their home star and planetary system. Even undecipherable signals could tell us much about their technology and their command of energy. Radio communication could allow exterrestrials to transmit vast quantities of information deliberately. Philip Morrison has suggested that aliens might send us a volume of information greater than that transmitted to medieval Europe from the ancient Greeks, stimulating a new and even greater Renaissance. By entering a communications net, we might receive maps of the Galaxy, and elaborate descriptions of the physical Universe and how it works. We might learn the histories of civilizations stretching far back into the galactic past, and become aware of alternative cultures, arts, social and economic systems, and forms of political organization. Deliberately or by implication, the aliens might tell us how they had survived. It is intriguing to consider how much we could contribute to the other side of the dialogue.

Alien knowledge, integrated with our own, could generate a dramatic forward leap in our sciences and our other academic disciplines. For the first time, we could compare our information and our perceptions with those of other minds in different environments, illuminating voids in our own knowledge and suggesting new generalizations. This almost certainly would lead to new syntheses, a boom in interdisciplinary studies as we perceived new linkages, and new branches of science. Dealing with this influx of new knowledge could force us into mind-stretching responses. Our curiosity would be stimulated by finding out how much we had not known. Contact also could reveal areas of shared knowledge, supporting our own conclusions; this might include religious concepts such as creation or a Supreme Being.

But we should beware of excessive optimism about this exchange of information; communication with an alien civilization may not be easy. No matter what we *wish* to believe, aliens, by definition, will be very different. While they may share some of our perceptions of physical reality and some of our evolutionary experiences, their evolutions would differ from ours in many ways, and we might share little in philosophy and culture. There could be serious problems of mutual unintelligibility, or misunderstandings caused by different ways of perceiving reality and by different cultural frames of reference. We might find that our own concepts of language, including mathematics, are narrow and idiosyncratic.

We also should not assume that the aliens will want to tell us everything. Transmitting the species data bank might not be the aliens' first priority. They might want to know first our capabilities and our intentions to assure themselves that their security would not be threatened. There might be things they would not want to tell us, such as how to achieve interstellar flight or how to create more powerful weapons.

Receiving knowledge much more advanced than our own, and the solutions to problems we have struggled with for years, could break the intellectual morale of some scientists and other scholars, and undermine support for some forms of research. Instead, we might simply wait for alien answers, and translate them into our terms. Humans concerned about their personal and institutional interests might resist the dissemination of some alien information, or seek to brand it as dangerous, immoral, or subversive.

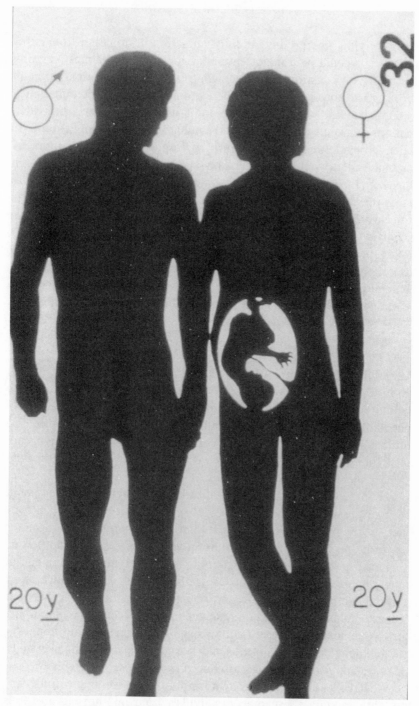

Figure 1. An image from the record sent along with the Voyager spacecraft, now on its way into interstellar space. *(Photo: Courtesy The Astronomical Society of the Pacific.)*

Receiving, interpreting, and disseminating information from extra-terrestrials could be a major enterprise for humanity, almost certainly requiring new institutions. Since control over this information could bring great power and status, there would be a strong temptation to monopolize the channel and to limit access by others. Individual nations or groups might attempt to conduct separate dialogues with the aliens to exploit contact for their own purposes. Political and govern-mental leaders would be concerned about the impact that contact could have on their populations, and might try to let through only those ideas they considered safe. National security policymakers might argue for classification of the contact and the information received. Some scholars, particularly those personally involved in the first contact, might be equally possessive about the information and the channel, especially if they distrusted governments and held a low opinion of the general population. Entrepreneurs might compete to get first access to alien ideas and to monopolize or patent those with commercial value.

THE FATAL IMPACT

The more intense forms of contact could have a fatal impact on our culture. Human history is littered with examples of cultural shock, of cultures that were destroyed or absorbed by other civilizations. An encounter with superior aliens could disorient our thinking, diminish our achievements, and shake our confidence. Even if the aliens meant well, their impact on us could amount to cultural imperialism; the missionary mentality may not be uniquely human. If the aliens were experienced in contacts with lesser civilizations and were concerned about the damage they might do, they might seek to reduce the shock of contact, or even avoid continuing it. But our own record in dealings between unequally powerful cultures gives us no reason for optimism.

In the cultural sense, contact could be the beginning of the end of humanity as we have known it. Contact's stimulus could produce a new cultural synthesis, leading to a new human civilization. Over time, our separate human culture might fade and vanish, becoming a quaint historical memory as it merged with a superior culture. Our anthropocentric religions might crumble, as superior aliens became our new gods, or as we adopted their religious concepts.

We have learned from our own history that a receiving culture cannot take in only those practices it likes from another culture; it is affected by the context of those practices, including the broader cul-

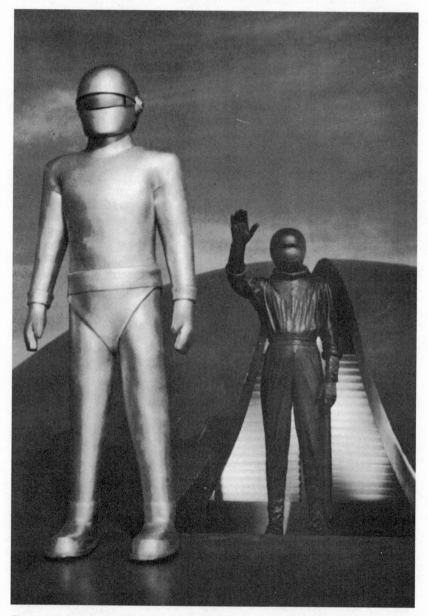

Figure 2. A friendly alien (Klaatu) and his all-powerful robot (Gort) are attacked by paranoid soldiers in *The Day The Earth Stood Still* in 1951. *(Copyright 20th Century-Fox, 1951.)*

ture. Alien ideas could influence our codes of behavior and styles of social interaction, our arts and our tastes. Humans might emulate alien ways, as we rush to fads and fashions now; this impulse could be stronger if we thought we were imitating superiors. There probably would be a reaction against this, a sort of nativist movement and counterreformation combined.

Alien technologies and new ideas about the possible forms and purposes of economic organization could spur economic change, perhaps suggesting new opportunities for innovation and growth, or less damaging prosperity. But they also might disrupt our economies, undermining the spirit of invention and independent initiative, forcing massive readjustment and unemployment, and threatening existing economic institutions. Fear of such possibilities could provoke a new Luddite movement against alien technologies.

Encountering an alien civilization also could force us to consider more universal bases for our laws, which would encompass alien concepts as well as our own. If direct contact were to occur, we would need to adjust our conception of the legal status of nonhuman life forms.

DANGERS

One of the things we tend to forget in our thinking about contact is how the aliens might react to *us*. Many scholars who have written on SETI have argued that there would be no danger in the remote contact scenario in revealing ourselves to aliens because: (1) more advanced beings would be peaceful and benign; and (2) interstellar travel is so difficult and expensive that we would be insulated by distance, making direct contact impossible. These assumptions need a closer look.

Extrasolar aliens may not share the ethical standards of fairness and regard for all species. They may show no more concern for alien intelligences than we show for whales and dolphins. They may think us unintelligent. They may have had violent histories, ascending the slippery slope from barbarism to civilization several times. Their experience with competition and conflict may have instilled in them a deep concern for security. They may have had bad experiences with earlier contacts, and might—at least at first—regard us as a potential threat. Contact might come as an unpleasant surprise to a species that had believed itself to be unique and superior; learning of another technologically advanced civilization might violate the integrity of their belief system and provoke a strong reaction. Even after the communications process started, misunderstandings could provoke a nasty response. And there is the danger that Freeman Dyson is right—that we may first encounter a species in which technology is out of control, a technological cancer spreading through the Galaxy.

Contact might bring the aliens here, at least to look us over. Studies such as the British Interplanetary Society's Project Daedalus indicate that interstellar flight might be possible (though by no means easy) even for a species only slightly in advance of our own. If we are already giving serious thought to interstellar travel, it may be commonplace for more advanced beings, who might enjoy longer life spans and access to more powerful means of propulsion. Contact with us might provoke even a non-star-faring species to interstellar travel, possibly bringing eventual direct contact. Even if attack or invasion are unlikely, the aliens might wish to confine us to our own solar system, and prevent us from achieving interstellar flight, as if they were isolating a virus. That could close off human expansion, and set a final limit to our growth.

Contact with extrasolar aliens, especially a star-faring species, could be the greatest possible stimulus to the human expansion into space. Finding that another species could travel across interstellar distances would suggest that we could too; it would draw us outward, first into our solar system and then to nearby stars. We might be motivated to spread human colonies away from Earth to broaden our options for survival, should contact imply possible eventual conflict with another species. Ultimately, the existence of an alien civilization would imply a limit to our expansion, at least in one direction.

Contact might draw us into some form of interstellar politics. We would have to think about how we should relate to other cultural and political entities, and ask what role *Homo sapiens* could play in a galactic society. We must hope that relations among civilization in our galaxy are not based on some sort of interstellar social Darwinism. As a newcomer, with limited capablities to affect anything beyond near-Earth space, we might have little influence at first. Galactic geopolitics might be meaningful only if contact was with aliens whose technologies were not much better than ours.

Contact, then, could be the most important event in the history of human civilization. Its effect on us could be both positive and negative, a gigantic stimulus and a demoralizing revelation; it could stir both hopes and fears on an unprecedented scale. It could involve us in a dialogue of centuries, bringing an incalculable richness of knowledge, physical instrumentalities, and cultural growth, and opening the door to a galactic society—or it could wreck our cultures and endanger our survival. Since we are in the process of making contact more likely, we need to prepare.

ORGANIZING FOR CONTACT

Despite the popularization of the idea of extraterrestrial intelligence, we are not ready for contact. We have not created the philosophical context or the institutional framework for a calm and rational relationship with aliens. That relationship will require a broad view of the importance of life in the Universe, and of its forms and its purposes. It will require us to accept the worth of beings sprung from different evolutions. It will require political and cultural sensitivity, and tolerance for differences. It will require a long perspective on the history of our own species, and a sure knowledge of our purposes. Successfully dealing with contact will require a significant degree of consensus among human beings, and a means for expressing it.

In 1972 humanity made its first deliberate attempt to communicate with extrasolar aliens when NASA attached plaques to the Pioneer 10 and 11 spacecraft that were launched that year to swing by Jupiter before heading out of the solar system. The plaques were intended to tell any alien civilization that found them about the nature of our species and our location in the Galaxy.

Given the unlikelihood that these probes will be found in the vastness of interstellar space, the act of sending this message is more symbolic than practical. However, thinking that any contact with an extrasolar species would only be the beginning of a much larger process, I published an article in 1972 that speculated about how we might manage our relationship with an alien civilization. I argued that we could learn much by studying relations among different civilizations on Earth, and by considering the lessons of diplomatic history. I concluded that we must be as ready as possible before interstellar negotiations begin. When a group of scientists led by Frank Drake sent a powerful radio message from the Arecibo observatory in Puerto Rico in 1974, I was one of those who raised the question of what right such a small group had to speak for the entire human species without broader consultations or prior agreement.

Further developing ideas about interstellar politics in published

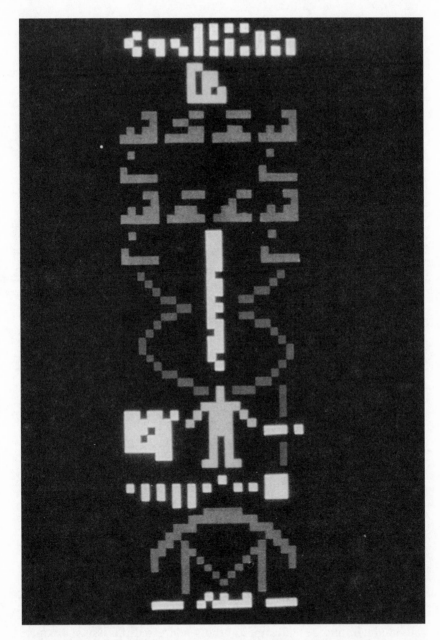

Figure 3. A coded message sent from the Arecibo radio telescope in Puerto Rico in 1974, in an experiment headed by Frank Drake. It had information about who we are and where we live.

articles over the next decade, I discovered that lawyers Andrew Haley and Ernst Fasan, among others, also had given thought to these issues. But there was no detectable interest in this subject in the world's foreign ministries, or in the United Nations.

In the absence of convincing evidence of extraterrestrial civilizations, we are unlikely to engage the sustained attention of most humans in such sweeping issues, so removed from ordinary life, or to create a permanent global institution for contact. But there may be ways to start modestly, by seeking agreement among the searchers on how we would handle the *detection* of an alien civilization.

In March 1985, Professor Allen Goodman of Georgetown University began circulating drafts of a paper titled "Diplomatic Implications of Discovering Extraterrestrial Intelligence," which included a proposed international "Code of Conduct" for SETI. That code contained four principles: (1) Anyone who discovers evidence of extraterrestrial intelligence will publicly report the contact; (2) any response will be formulated by a process of international consultation; (3) visiting extraterrestrials will be regarded as envoys entitled to diplomatic immunity, protection, and aid in the event of accident; (4) in the event that extraterrestrials appear to pose a threat to human health or peace, no nation shall act without first consulting the United Nations Security Council.

At the Congress of the International Astronautical Federation in Stockholm in October 1985, John Billingham, then chief of the extraterrestrial research division at the NASA Ames Research Center in California, proposed that a session at the next Astronautical Congress address the question of international agreements on four points: (1) The need to distribute the details of the discovery to all nations; (2) the establishment of a mechanism to distribute this knowledge; (3) how to determine if a response should be made and who should make the response; and (4) how to determine the content of the response. At the October 1986 Astronautical Congress in Innsbruck, Austria, Goodman presented a revised version of his paper, titled "Diplomacy and the Search for Extraterrestrial Intelligence." It included his proposed code of conduct for relations with extraterrestrial civilizations.

Goodman and several other authors addressed the issue in papers presented at the next Astronautical Congress, in Brighton, England, in October 1987. As co-chairman of the SETI session, I noticed that there was considerable overlap among the papers. I synthesized elements from the various proposals, boiling them down to one text. As the issues associated with handling a detection appeared to be quite different from the issues associated with sending a communication, I then produced separate drafts, one a proposed agreement on detection, and the other a proposed agreement on sending a response. I presented these drafts for discussion at a session of about twenty-five interested people at Brighton. We made good progress on the detection agreement, but discussions on the communication agreement quickly bogged down in broad moral and philosophical issues.

It was clear that it would be much more feasible to reach agreement on how to handle detection than on how to handle a reply. Volunteering to act as coordinator, I circulated drafts of an agreement on the detection of extraterrestrial intelligence to interested persons over the next year, making numerous minor revisions in the text as a result of their comments but preserving its basic principles, on which correspondents generally agreed. That draft agreement was endorsed by the International Academy of Astronautics in April 1989, and by the International Institute of Space Law shortly thereafter. It was submitted to the International Astronautical Federation, the International Astronomical Union, and the Committee on Space Research of the International Council of Scientific Unions for their endorsements. The agreement then was opened for signature by all of those engaged in the scientific search for extraterrestrial intelligence, in time for the planned start of NASA's expanded radio search in 1992.

The detection agreement is to be among the *searchers*, not among governments, as some institutions involved in the search, such as the Planetary Society, are not government-sponsored. Thus the agreement has no diplomatic status and is not an international agreement like the Outer Space Treaty. In fact, at the request of Czech legal scholar Vladimir Kopal, former head of the Outer Space Affairs Division of the United Nations, the agreement is now called a Declaration of Principles. The Declaration implicitly accepts an astronomical detection as the most likely scenario, but its principles could be applied to contact with another intelligent species on Earth, such as (possibly) intelligent dolphins.

The basic principles of the Declaration are those laid out by astronomer Peter Boyce in his 1987 Brighton paper: verify the evidence in cooperation with other observers, and then tell the world. The Declaration spells out procedures for handling the detection, including the recording of the evidence and the protection of the appropriate electromagnetic wavelengths. Many of the procedures were developed by astronomer Jill Tarter, former chief scientist of NASA's SETI program and now scientific director of the program at the SETI Institute. The Declaration also provides that no response to a signal or other evidence of extraterrestrial intelligence will be sent until appropriate international consultations have taken place, but leaves the mechanism of those consultations to another agreement, which could be developed from the second Brighton draft.

That draft addresses the profound questions of who should speak for Earth, and what should be said on behalf of our species. It states that communications with extraterrestrial intelligence will be undertaken on behalf of all mankind and provides that an international group will be formed to deal with the question of whether such a communication should be sent and, if it is, what its content should be. This proposed agreement is not essentially a matter of scientific research; it involves social and political questions of considerable magnitude. Refining it and gaining its acceptance by governments will be difficult. But that effort will force us to think big about our nature as a species, our shared interests, and our vision of the future.

Declaration of Principles
Concerning Activities Following the *Detection*
of Extraterrestrial Intelligence

We, the institutions and individuals participating in the search for extraterrestrial intelligence,

Recognizing that the search for extraterrestrial intelligence is an integral part of space exploration and is being undertaken for peaceful purposes and for the common interest of all mankind,

Inspired by the profound significance for mankind of detecting evidence of extraterrestrial intelligence, even though the probability of detection may be low,

Recalling the Treaty on Principles Governing the Activities of States in the Exploration and Use of Outer Space, Including the Moon and Other Celestial Bodies, which commits states as parties to that treaty "to inform the Secretary General of the United Nations as well as the public and the international scientific community, to the greatest extent feasible and practicable, of the nature, conduct, locations and results" of their space exploration activities (Article XI),

Recognizing that any initial detection may be incomplete or ambiguous and thus require careful examination as well as confirmation, and that it is essential to maintain the highest standards of scientific responsibility and credibility,

Agree to observe the following principles for disseminating information about the detection of extraterrestrial intelligence:

1. Any individual, public or private research institution, or governmental agency that believes it has detected a signal from or other evidence of extraterrestrial intelligence (the discoverer) should seek to verify that the most plausible explanation for the evidence is the existence of extraterrestrial intelligence rather than some other natural phenomenon or anthropogenic phenomenon before making any public announcement. If the evidence cannot be confirmed as indicating the existence of extraterrestrial intelligence, the discoverer may disseminate the information as appropriate to the discovery of any unknown phenomenon.

2. Prior to making a public announcement that evidence of extraterrestrial intelligence has been detected, the discoverer should promptly inform all other observers or research organizations that are parties to this declaration, so that those other parties may seek to confirm the discovery by independent observations at other sites and so that a network can be established to enable continuous monitoring of the signal or phenomenon. Parties to this declaration should not make any public announcement of this information until it is determined whether this information is or is not credible evidence of the existence of extraterrestrial intelligence. The discoverer should inform his/her or its relevant national authorities.

3. After concluding that the discovery appears to be credible evidence of extraterrestrial intelligence, and after informing other parties to this declaration, the discoverer should inform observers throughout the world through the Central Bureau for Astronomical Telegrams of the International Astronomical Union, and should inform the Secretary General of the United Nations in accordance with Article XI of the Treaty on Principles Governing the Activities of States in the Exploration and Use of Outer Space, including the Moon and Other Bodies. Because of their demonstrated interest in and expertise concerning the question of the existence of extraterrestrial intelligence, the discoverer should simultaneously inform the following international institutions of the discovery and should provide them with all pertinent data and recorded information concerning the evidence: the International Telecommunication Union, the Committee on Space Research, of the International Council of Scientific Unions, the International Astronau-

tical Federation, the International Academy of Astronautics, the International Institute of Space Law and Commission 51 of the International Astronomical Union.

4. A confirmed detection of extraterrestrial intelligence should be disseminated promptly, openly, and widely through scientific channels and public media, observing the procedures in this declaration. The discoverer should have the privilege of making the first public announcement.

5. All data necessary for confirmation of detection should he made available to the international scientific community through publications, meetings, conferences, and other appropriate means.

6. The discovery should be confirmed and monitored and any data bearing on the evidence of extraterrestrial intelligence should be recorded and stored permanently to the greatest extent feasible and practicable, in a form that will make it available for further analysis and interpretation. These recordings should be made available to the international institutions listed above and to members of the scientific community for further objective analysis and interpretation.

7. If the evidence of detection is in the form of electromagnetic signals, the parties to this declaration should seek international agreement to protect the appropriate frequencies by exercising the extraordinary procedures established within the World Administrative Radio Council of the International Telecommunication Union.

8. No response to a signal or other evidence of extraterrestrial intelligence should be sent until appropriate international consultations have taken place. The procedures for such consultations will be the subject of a separate agreement, declaration or arrangement.

9. The SETI Committee of the International Academy of Astronautics, in coordination with Commission 51 of the International Astronomical Union, will conduct a continuing review of procedures for the detection of extraterrestrial intelligence and the subsequent handling of the data. Should credible evidence of extraterrestrial intelligence by discovered, an international committee of scientists and other experts should be established to serve as a focal point for continuing analysis of all observational evidence collected in the aftermath of the discovery, and also to provide advice on the release of information to the public. This committee should be constituted from representatives of each of the international institutions listed above and such other members as the committee may deem necessary. To facilitate the convocation of such a committee at some

unknown time in the future, the SETI Committee of the International Academy of Astronautics should initiate and maintain a current list of willing representatives from each of the international institutions listed above, as well as other individuals with relevant skills, and should make that list continuously available through the Secretariat of the International Academy of Astronautics. The International Academy of Astronautics will act as the Depositary for this declaration and will annually provide a current list of parties to all the parties to this declaration.

Annex: Addresses of Institutions named in this declaration.

Annex
List of Institutions

Central Bureau for Astronomical Telegrams of the International Astronomical Union, Center for Astrophysics, 60 Garden Street, Cambridge, Massachusetts 02138, U.S.A.

Secretary-General of the United Nations, United National Headquarters, New York, New York 10017, U.S.A.

Director General, International Telecommunication Union, Place des Nations, CH-1211, Geneva-20, Switzerland

Secretary, Committee on Space Research, 51, Boulevard de Montmorency, 75015, Paris, France

Secretariat, International Astronautical Federation, 3-5 Rue Mario Nikis, 75015, Paris, France

Secretariat, International Academy of Astronautics, 3-5 Rue Mario Nikis, 75015, Paris, France

Secretariat, International Institute of Space Law, 3-5 Rue Mario Nikis, 75015, Paris, France

Secretariat, International Astronomical Union (IAU-UAI), 98 bis, Boulevard Arago, 75014, Paris, France

Proposed Protocol
for the Sending of Communications
to Extraterrestrial Intelligence

The signatories agree that communications with extraterrestrial intelligence will be guided by the following principles:

1. Communications with extraterrestrial intelligence will be under-

taken on behalf of all mankind, rather than specific nations, groups, or individuals.

2. Nations, organizations, and individuals will not unilaterally send communications to extraterrestrial intelligence until appropriate international consultations have taken place.

3. The signatories will not cooperate with attempts to communicate with extraterrestrial intelligence which do not conform to the principles in this protocol.

4. An international group including representation from all interested nations will be formed to deal with the question of whether such a communication should be sent and, if so, what its content should be.

5. If a decision is made to develop a communication to extraterrestrial intelligence on behalf of all mankind, the following principles will be observed:

a. Respect for the value of life and intelligence.

b. Respect for the value of diversity, including respect for different customs, habits, languages, creeds and religions, approaches to social organization, and styles of life.

c. Respect for the territory and property of others.

d. Recognition of the will to live.

e. Recognition of the need for living space.

f. Fair play, justice, mercy.

g. Reciprocity and quid pro quo.

h. Nonviolation of others.

i. Truthfulness and nondeception.

j. Peaceful and friendly welcome.

k. Cooperation.

l. Respect for knowledge, curiosity, and learning.

6. The drafters of a communication to extraterrestrial intelligence will consider detailed information about mankind to be a commodity of high value which will not be transmitted without due attention to human security and well-being, and to reciprocity.

7. In the event that extraterrestrials appear to pose a threat to human health, well-being, or peace, no nation shall act without consulting the Security Council of the United Nations.

CHAPTER 8

THE NEED TO KNOW

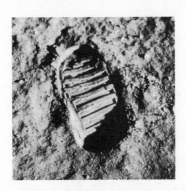

*The modern era of SETI began with the classic paper of Giuseppi Coc-
coni and Philip Morrison in 1959. Professor Morrison gives us the benefit of his thinking on the subject here, preceded by Arthur C. Clarke,
who has probably done more to make the public aware of SETI than any
writer of any generation.*

*The concluding words of Cocconi and Morrison's seminal paper are
as valid today as they were when first written, more than three decades
ago:*

> *"Few will deny the profound importance, practical and
> philosophical, which the detection of interstellar communica-
> tions would have. We therefore feel that a discriminating search
> for signals deserves a considerable effort. The probability of suc-
> cess is difficult to estimate, but if we never search the chance of
> success is zero."*

WHERE ARE THEY?

By

ARTHUR C. CLARKE

Early in December 1985, a group of distinguished astronomers gathered in Colombo, under the auspices of the International Astronomical Union, the Institute of Fundamental Studies, and the Arthur Clarke Centre, to discuss a subject which has long fascinated the general public, but which has only become scientifically respectable during the last two decades. I refer, of course, to the possibility of life on other worlds.

Now, this is a fairly new idea in Western thought, for the simple reason that from Aristotle onward it was assumed that Earth was the center of the Universe and that anything beyond it was some vague celestial realm inhabited only by supernatural beings.

The Sun was obviously a mass of fire, so no one except the gods could live *there*. And as for the Moon, it probably wasn't big enough for many occupants. . . .

The five planets visible to the naked eye—Mercury, Venus, Mars, Jupiter, Saturn—had been known to mankind since prehistoric times, and their curious movements had been a cause of much speculation. But no one, except a few eccentric philosophers, had any idea that they were all worlds in their own right—two of them enormously larger than the terrestrial globe.

It's an extraordinary fact that the East had guessed the true scale of the Universe, both in time and in space, centuries before the West. In Hindu philosophy there are eons and ages long enough to satisfy any modern cosmologist; yet until only a dozen generations ago much of Europe believed that the world was created around 4000 B.C. (I'm sorry to say that, owing to their misreading of the Bible, thousands of foolish people still believe such nonsense.)

The turning point in our understanding of the Universe may be conveniently dated at 1600, just before Galileo pointed his first telescope toward the stars. Shakespeare belongs to the century before the great intellectual revolution.

> *Doubt that the stars are fire,*
> *Doubt that the sun doth move . . .*

he wrote, circa 1600. He was wrong on both counts.

Of course, we know that the Sun *does* move—but not in the way that Shakespeare imagined. He thought it moved around the Earth, as common sense seems to indicate, and had no idea how distant—and how big—it really is.

And the stars aren't fire—although for reasons that were not understood until well into this century. They are much too hot! Fire is a *low-temperature* phenomenon in the thermal range of the Universe, much of which is simmering briskly at several million degrees, where no chemical compounds can possibly exist.

During the seventeenth century, the telescope revealed for anyone who had eyes to see that the Moon provided at least one other example of a world with mountains and plains, though not rivers and oceans. The moving points of light that were the planets now turned out to have appreciable discs—and one of them, Jupiter, had its own retinue of moons. Clearly, Earth was not unique; nor, perhaps, was the human race.

This was a shocking—even an heretical—thought, at least to those brought up in the Aristotelian school. Anyone who preached it too loudly, and especially near Rome, was likely to get into serious trouble with the Inquisition.

The classic example is, of course, Giordano Bruno (1548–1600), who was one of the first European advocates of the doctrine of an infinite Universe and the "Plurality of Worlds." Refusing to recant, he was burned at the stake in 1600. I wonder how many modern scientists would be prepared to emulate him in defense of their theories. . . .

And while we're on the subject of Renaissance astronomers, I'd like to remind you of one of the greatest ironies in the history of science.

In 1582 that remarkable man, Father Matteo Ricci, arrived in China with all the latest wisdom of the West. The Chinese regarded Occidentals as barbarians (and probably still do, though they're too polite to say so). But by tact, intelligence, and sheer goodness Father Ricci persuaded them that their superstitious concept of an enormous Universe enduring for vast eons was all nonsense: God put the Earth in the center of everything, and Adam and Eve in the Garden, only a few thousand years ago. As he proudly wrote: "The Fathers gave such clear and lucid explanation on all these matters which were so new to the Chinese, that many were unable to deny the truth of all that they said; and, for this reason, the information on this matter quickly spread among all the scholars of China."

Well! Poor Father Ricci! While he was persuading the Chinese to take a Great Leap Backward to Ptolemaic astronomy, Copernicus was destroying its very foundations in Europe. A few decades later Galileo (with an anxious glance over his shoulder at Bruno) would finish the job of demolition.

For the last 300 years, not very long in human history, all educated persons have known that our planet is not the only world in the Universe, and that its Sun is one of billions. The great voyages of the seventeenth and eighteenth centuries, during which European explorers "discovered" whole cultures that didn't even know they'd been lost, also prompted speculation about life on other planets. It seemed only reasonable that our enormous cosmos must be populated with other creatures, some of them perhaps far more advanced than we are. The alternative—that we are utterly alone in the Universe—seemed both depressing and wildly megalomaniac.

But how to prove it, one way or the other? We children of the Space Age can no longer remember how enormous even the solar system seemed, only a lifetime ago. Now the Voyager space probe is outward bound to the stars, about to pass the boundary of the sun's sphere of influence, having kept its appointment with Neptune, which, as recently as 1930, marked the frontier of the Empire of the Sun. That is an impressive achievement; even so, it will be tens of thousands of years before Voyager can cross the gulf to the nearest star.

Fortunately, we do not have to rely on *physical* contact to discover if there is intelligent life elsewhere in the Universe. We now assume, almost as a matter of fact, that any contact is likely to be by radio. Yet this in itself would have seemed incredible until well into this century. We take radio so much for granted that we forget how miraculous it is. Even the most farsighted prophet could not have predicted it—which is yet another example of what I call Comte's Fallacy.

Around 1840 the French philosopher Auguste Comte (1798–1857) was rash enough to make the following pronouncement about the limits of our knowledge concerning the heavenly bodies: "We see how we may determine their forms, their distances, their bulk, their motions, but we can never know anything of their chemical or mineralogical structure; and much less, that of organised beings living on their surface . . ."

Comte's monumental gaffe was in the same class as Father Ricci's. Within a few decades, the invention of the spectroscopes had utterly refuted his assertion that it was impossible to discover the chemical nature of heavenly bodies. By the end of the century, precisely *that* was the main occupation of most professional astronomers. Only the amateurs were still concerned with what Comte believed must always be the entire body of their science.

So it is very dangerous to set limits to knowledge or to engineering achievements. No one could have anticipated the spectroscopes; and no one could have imagined radio. They both exemplify Clarke's well-known Third Law: "Any sufficiently advanced technology is indistinguishable from magic."

There may be "magical" inventions or discoveries in the future which will settle the question of intelligent life in the Universe, but I do not think we really need them. Today's electronics can probably do the job, given a few more decades of determined application.

The giant radio telescopes which have been built for purely scientific purposes are quite capable—and this is a splendid example of serendipity—of detecting the sort of radio signals one would expect from an advanced civilization in our immediate galactic neighborhood. It would be ridiculously optimistic to expect immediate success, since we have had the capacity of making such a search for less that half a human lifetime.

Yet already this "failure" to find an artificial signal has produced a kind of backlash and has prompted some scientists to argue, "Perhaps we *are* alone in the Universe." Dr. Frank Tipler, the best-known exponent of this view, has given one of his papers that provocative title "There Are No Intelligent Extra-Terrestrials." Dr. Carl Sagan and his school argue (and I agree with them) that it is much too early to jump to such far-reaching conclusions.

Meanwhile the controversy rages; as has been well said, *either* answer will be awe-inspiring. The question can only be settled by evidence, not by any amount of logic, however plausible. I would like to see the whole debate given a decade or two of benign neglect, while the radio astronomers, like gold miners panning for dust, quietly sieve through the torrents of noise pouring down from the sky.

There is also another, and much more speculative, line of approach to this problem. Let me give an analogy to explain what I mean.

If a visiting traveler had surveyed our planet from space ten thousand years ago, he would have seen many signs of life—forests, grasslands, great herds of animals—but no trace of intelligence. Today, even a casual glance would reveal cities, roads, airfields, irrigation systems—and, at night, vast constellations of artificial light.

These "advertisements" of terrestrial civilization would have been beyond the imagination of our Stone Age ancestors. Can one set any limits to what might be achieved by a really advanced, long-lived society, with thousands of centuries of space-faring behind it? In particular, might it not have—literally—set its sign among the stars, as we have done upon the Earth? As long ago as 1929 the physicist J. D. Bernal, in one of the most daring works of scientific imagination ever penned, wrote: "It is unlikely that man will stop until he has roamed over and colonised most of the sidereal universe, or that even this will be the end. Man will not ultimately be content to be parasitic on the stars but will invade them and organise them for his own purpose . . . By intelligent organization the life of the universe could probably be prolonged many millions of millions of times. . . ."

Later writers have talked about "the greening of the Galaxy," and asked why the stellar sky is so untidy and badly organised. Where, indeed, are the Cosmic Engineers?

Perhaps, like ants crawling around the base of the Empire State Building, we simply haven't recognized what's going on all about us. During the last few decades, astronomers have been discovering some very strange phenomena in space, and have been straining scientific theories to the limits in attempts to find *natural* explanations.

Pulsars were the first example. In 1967, when Hewish and Bell discovered radio sources ticking away more accurately than any mechanical clock ever made by man, their first wild speculation was that they might be artificial. Indeed, no astronomer before 1920 could have explained how unaided Mother Nature could have contrived such a prodigy.

Well, we are now quite sure that pulsars are indeed natural (though amazing) objects—tiny dying stars acting like cosmic beacons as they spin madly on their axes. But there are other phenomena not so readily explained, and I should not be in the least surprised if the astronomers finally give up on them and admit: "We're sure that Nature can't be responsible. Somebody out there has forgotten to switch off the lights."

Or worse. The most chilling explanation I have heard of one titanic outpouring of cosmic energies is: an industrial accident. . . .

Nowadays, anyone who considers that alien supercivilizations may exist has to contend not with skepticism but with something much worse—credulity. Although the subject now affects me with uncontrollable fits of yawning, I would be failing in my duty if I did not say something about UFOs.

So here, as briefly as possible, are the conclusions I've come to after almost seventy years of study. (Sixty-nine to be exact, since I first read Charles Fort's *Lo!* in 1930. That monument of eccentric scholarship, published long before anyone had ever heard of flying saucers, listed apparent celestial visitations right back to the Middle Ages.)

1. There may be strange and surprising meteorological, electrical, or astronomical phenomena still unknown to science, which may account for the very few UFOs that are both genuine and unexplained.
2. There is no hard evidence that Earth has *ever* been visited from space.
3. If that *does* happen, there are at least three independent global radar networks that will know within a matter of minutes. And in the unlikely event that the U.S., Russia, and Chinese authorities instantly cooperate to suppress the news, they'll succeed for a maximum of forty-eight hours. How long do you imagine such a secret could be kept? Remember how quickly Watergate unravelled.

Having written thousands of words on the subject (and read millions) I refuse to go into further details. If anybody wants to argue, I'll merely quote one of my favorite book titles: "Shut up, he explained."

Finally, if *they* are out there—what do they look like? I suggest you go to the local zoo and take your choice. Nature tries everything at least once—and has lots of time and space for experimenting.

But I will tell you what they will *not* look like. We now understand the principles, if not the details, of human evolution. We specimens of *H. sapiens* are the product of thousands of successive throws of the genetic dice, any one of which might have turned out differently. If the terrestrial experiment started all over again at Time Zero, there might still be intelligence on this planet, but it wouldn't look like us. In the dance of the DNA spirals, the same partners would never meet again. As Loren Eisley wrote in *The Immense Journey* over thirty years ago: "Nowhere in all space or on a thousand worlds will there be men to share our loneliness. There may be wisdom; there may be power; somewhere across space great instruments . . . may stare vainly at our floating cloud wrack, their owners yearning as we yearn. Nevertheless, in the nature of life and in the principles of evolution we have had our answer. Of men elsewhere, and beyond, there will be none forever. . . ."

REFLECTIONS ON THE BIGGER PICTURE

By

PHILIP MORRISON

O ne of the most important occurrences over the thirty-plus years during which we have been thinking about SETI has been the event that did not happen: the discovery of some form of life on another planet. What has occurred that we did not foresee, but that supports our general view while complicating our detailed quantitative understanding, is the finding of complex polyatomic carbon compounds in a wide variety of cosmic contexts. From studies of the molecular species in the giant dense galactic clouds and from analysis of some asteroids and maybe satellites (in which we find indications of carbonaceous compounds), we have derived a renewed interest in carbonaceous meteorites themselves. This demonstrates a point on which biochemists were already very clear fifty years ago: The flexibility and peculiar subtlety of carbon compounds, as well as the high abundance of carbon, makes them preeminently the source of complex chemistry in the Universe.

When we seek the input of the physical sciences, we know that the practitioners are masters of a powerful deductive structure, with quantitative possibilities. Of course, they are beset by the necessary complexity of their models. They must try to pin down from some a priori model just what the first six or seven hundred million years of Earth history were like. They search for a necessary prelude for the biologists, something essential to the total picture of cosmic evolution. On the other hand, if the biologists were to explain why they needed certain conditions, perhaps it could be determined whether these conditions were at all plausible under some existing model. It is clear to me that strong interchange must go on in this domain. We have to learn a more interdisciplinary way of facing such problems.

A famous nineteenth-century interdisciplinary dispute illustrates this point. There was a lot of dispute, even full conflict, but no resolution at all; logic was clearly on one side, yet that side turned out to be wrong. I am talking about the famous problem of the time scale available for Darwinian evolution.

The absence of substantial observed changes in speciation in the natural world, as compared with the swift changes produced by domestic hybridization during the course of history, is a strong argument for the slowness of natural speciation. This argument was made even stronger by the fact that paleontology showed change clearly; therefore, you had to say that the time available in the geological record was very large. Darwin, while he was a man of extraordinary logical ability and in very simple ways a brilliant experimenter, often cutting right to the heart of the matter, was a bad mathematician. He could not calculate anything. He had a touching faith, however, in instrumental methods. His son writes that he discovered his father making measurements with an old paper ruler and writing these down to high accuracy. The son commented. "Well, you know that ruler is probably not right." So he got a better ruler; sure enough, his paper ruler was stretched and deficient. Darwin was depressed; the notion that a calibrated ruler, a thing you trust to measure with, might not be right was a breach of faith that he could hardly accept from his ruler-making colleagues! That was his style. He kept saying that his study of geological records suggested that there was a great deal of time indeed. He liked to put it that biology required almost infinite time. By this he meant a time quite long compared with all times that had been suggested so far.

Now comes Lord Kelvin, armed with the most powerful physics of the nineteenth century, who was able to show with computational hammer blows, one after another, that the time available for Darwin's evolution could not be one hundred million years, it could hardly be sixty million years, perhaps not even ten million years. For, if the Sun burns carbonaceous fuel or any similar chemical fuel, it can only last thousands of years—a palpably inadequate stretch of time. Even if it derives its energy from gravitation, we know its mass and we know its size, and we can show that it cannot last for more than a few tens of millions of years. Thus there was a direct conflict. Kelvin would come to the biologists and heckle them terribly by saying, "Tell me what time you want and I'll show if it can be; I can calculate everything." (He meant cooling and so on.) Of course, they couldn't name a time. They simply said, "Well, we know you're wrong. We feel it in our bones, in our fossils, but we can't prove it." So the evolutionists were regarded as people without any quantitative basis for their science, though they were, of course, onto something profound.

That was noticed by the distinguished geologist T. C. Chamberlain immediately after the discovery of radioactivity, about 1900. By 1905 or so, Ernest Rutherford himself gave a famous evening talk. It was a most distinguished and formal lecture to the Royal Society of London. As a young breaker of rules, a young discoverer, he noticed that in the front row sat Lord Kelvin himself, very elderly, but very stern, trying hard to stay awake and check on this young man who was going to talk about new forms of energy. (Kelvin didn't like radioactivity either, by the way.)

Rutherford tells us that he wondered how to avoid offending Lord Kelvin. Perhaps the famous man would get up and leave when Rutherford talked about the fact that nuclear energy can keep the Sun going for a good long time. Finally Rutherford thought of the right formulation. He said that he had been able to solve an old problem, whose magnitude and importance had been shown by Lord Kelvin when he pointed out that there was no known source of energy capable of keeping the Sun going. At last by experiment they had been able to find a new source, bringing out fully what Kelvin had shown all those years ago. Says Rutherford, Kelvin immediately went to sleep and the whole session was a huge success.

Let us look at a strategy: the strategy for catching food as a predator does. We are, after all, predators, both on berries and on bears; we belong to the hunting-foraging creatures. Suppose you were in the position of living on lobsters. That is a nice position to be in: It is achieved by some New Englanders and by all common octopi. Octopi are intelligent invertebrates—in some ways our analogs within the invertebrate kingdom.

Let us approach the octopus from the standpoint of a rational analysis of prey-seeking behavior. What is the situation? Lobsters are not as variable in behavior perhaps as some land animals, but still they are not all that uniform, either. It is quite likely that any particular desirable game, like lobsters, appears in fluctuating numbers within the field of action of any carnivore. There is little likelihood of a steady flow of lobsters, one dropping down every hour. Most hunters don't find it that easy. You've got to go out and scrabble around a little bit to get what you want.

When caribou are numerous, you should of course hunt caribou. When the Eskimo or the Indian hunter, skillful person that he is, finds that caribou are unhappily in short supply, he will simply redouble his efforts, for he is hungry, and back home the wife and kids are hungry. The whole situation is serious. The same tendency is found in every hunting-gathering mammalian predator activity.

On the other hand, an octopus has a much purer view. It behaves more like the theory of games predicts. When lobsters become few, an octopus does not seek in a frenzy to find those few lobsters or put up with eating mere crayfish. Heaven forbid! Instead the octopus goes to sleep—a most intelligent thing to do. Every once in a while it wakes up and looks out. "Any more lobsters around?" No. Back to sleep it goes again.

Such control over impatience, anxiety, and hunger is very hard for us to understand. Our thought is based on our design: namely, we have to generate one hundred watts of power all the time. There is a basal metabolism, roughly one hundred watts, that we expend. If we don't keep the machine fueled, we're in irreversible danger. But the octopus has no such base load demand. Cold-blooded, he is willing to relax to the ambient temperature of the warm sea environment in which he lives, provided only that every once in a while he can scrape up a fraction of a watt, turn the retina and its ganglia on, open an eye. That isn't too hard to do. Once you look at it coolly, you realize that human behavior goes completely against the sound principles by which an organism would adaptively go hunting. Whenever it is hard to hunt, don't continue to hunt with greater frenzy over longer hours, as we all do. On the contrary, take it easy. When conditions are not good, there is not much use in hunting. We humans can't adopt that principle, though, because for a couple hundred million years conditions were generally good enough so that somehow or other it was worth paying to keep our subtle electronics going—even during sleep—in order to have an opportunity to hunt well.

How different evolutionary structures can be! We need a special view of the lives of other creatures. If you now carry this logic over to some distant world, then it gives scope to the issues we are talking about.

The discussions of SETI show in detailed operational terms that we have already begun to make a clear plan. Certainly, a great deal of hope emerges. Indeed, we have remarkable new results based on spectroscopy: We have found other planets. We are setting up more appara-

tus dedicated to the purpose of finding planets, by spectroscopy, interferometry, by astrometry and with even more prceise techniques. I very
much hope that the entire scientific community will continue to support and applaud this effort, because it seems to be one of the most
important auxiliary searches that could be made. It is important even if
we never have a chance of getting radio signals. It can give us something else to look at than just the single Sun-planet system to which we
are so well adapted.

We can characterize attitudes toward SETI by involving the names
of two philosophers. First is the Aristotelian view, which seems quite
plain: Earth is the cosmic center; the heavens revolve around it, 1/R
reaches infinity here, and here is the right place! In this view, of course,
the whole outward-looking style is neither necessary nor desirable.
Astronomers can hardly accept that view; at least they have not
accepted it for several centuries now. They are not going to change,
and I am pretty sure that most of the other sciences will follow in turn.

The second point of view I like to attribute to Copernicus. Everyone
knows what that name implies, though I don't know if he actually said
it anywhere: namely, that this green-and-blue Earth is not all that different from the planets and the Sun and all those other things that circle and shine in the sky. They are themselves earthy or gaseous or
whatever, but they are physically real objects. Nowadays men have
walked upon one such object and shown that it is not different in kind
from the one we inhabit. Since we know Earth is also earthy, then it is
clear to us that these are only relative categories. Circular, shining, and
perpetual orbits was Aristotle's view; it was Copernicus who recognized
that Earth was no less circular, shining, and perpetual. We take a very
different view of the cosmos post-Copernicus. That has been the spirit
of SETI. The radical Copernicanism of the very first efforts is still
viable, though admittedly we have more judgment about where to look.

A curious situation has arisen under the power of intense modern
instrumental specialization. Our specialized tools and their data have
grown steadily. That is sharply reflected in the institutions of our universities, which are slow to change in the face of it. For example, many
universities still have a botany department and a zoology department,
but if you bring them any one of a number of microorganisms, they
can't say which department ought to study it! Perhaps it doesn't make
any difference. But our research structure is inherited from institutional

decisions in Scottish and German universities made 110 to 160 years ago. Sooner or later this will change. For all real large-scale engineering activities, such as NASA has carried out so successfully, we know that this is not the way to do it. Such activities require mission teams and a mix of specialties. The universities are going to have to learn, and some have begun. Examples of recently established interdisciplinary centers include the Whitehead Institute for biogenetics at MIT and the Bioastronomy Institute at Ames Field.

There is another narrowness of action, though not of intent, which characterizes university departments, and scientific publications and scientists in general: if it is too popular, it is somehow vulgar and wrong. You can't really speak to those people across the street. I live next to the chemists at MIT, but I never see them. I hardly know who they are, yet between physics and chemistry it is hard to know who should study what molecule. I myself am guilty. We form communities not based on the problems of science, but on quite other things. This is part of the general split between the intelligent informed member of the public and the scientist who speaks in narrow focus. But the great theoretical problems that I believe the world expects will somehow be solved by science, problems close to deep philosophical issues, are the very problems that find the least expertise, the least degree of organization, the least institutional support in the scientific institutions of America, or, indeed, the world.

Two of these, of course, are the great questions, "Are we alone?" and "How did life begin?" These questions are treated now in the elementary textbooks, because of the vigor of a few people over the last forty years, but they are hardly treated anywhere else. The further you go away from the freshman student, the less likely you are to find a colleague interested in it. This is beginning to change. Fifteen or twenty years ago, the radio astronomers, just to name a group of people I know quite well, were pretty hard to talk to about SETI in any way. It wasn't so much that they would disagree; that's fine—they still do. But they laughed, and that was not very pleasant. Well, now at least they are only smiling; that is a kind of gain.

One cure for this ill, though a difficult one, is the pursuit of a scientific discourse on a more philosophical, more consciously aesthetic, better-illustrated style, one willing to grapple with large problems, even though only small solutions can at present be offered for them. I think that science requires this mode too. I expect to see an enlarging of the disciplines to form at last an interdisciplinary pool, aware of larger philosophical issues. We need not try to solve them or to prescribe their limits, but we must recognize their human importance, their intellectual existence as an increasing element within scientific thought. If that were the only positive result from the SETI investigation, I think it would still be judged by history to have proved extremely worthwhile.

AMATEUR EQUIPMENT FOR SETI

By

D. KENT CULLERS AND
WILLIAM R. ALSCHULER

A s mentioned in the chapter on Individual Involvement, there are various requirements for radio equipment to do SETI. We can only summarize here and give suggestions for meeting them. Detailed treatment is beyond the scope of this book.

ANTENNAS

We have suggested that you use standard TV dish receivers, most of which are three meters in diameter (they can be purchased slightly smaller and also larger, up to four meters; the larger the better). For any type of SETI-observation technique you will need to point the antenna to various altitudes. The dish will feel varying forces and may be distorted as a result. If the dish distortion is too large, the focal sharpness will be ruined, which can lead to spillover and a wasted signal, as well as a shift of observed frequency. To check for this problem, you can run pieces of string from rim to rim across various diameters and chords, and check that they all touch where they cross, and stay touching at every pointing direction. If they don't, you need to reinforce the dish, which you should do with nonconducting materials. Also check to see that the feed does not sag out of the focal spot and that the dish shape is smooth. A non-pie-slice dish will likely be best in the latter respect.

ANTENNA MOUNTS

There are too many variations of mounts to catalog, but some common characteristics do exist. Most have a main vertical post (some are tripod

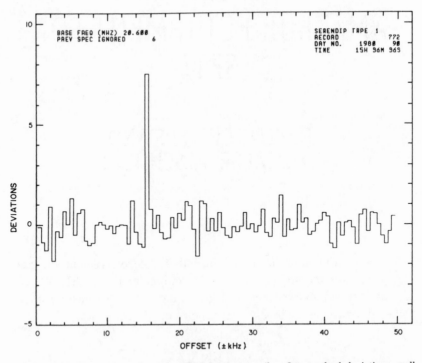

Figure 1. A radio spectrum found by FFT, showing a spike of 7 standard deviations—well above the detection level of 4.5 deviations. Terrestrial signals look like this, and so might ETI signals. *(Diagram supplied by Stuart Bowyer.)*

supported). The majority have a main tilted axis, the polar axis, which is set to point parallel to Earth's north-south axis. There is also often a stand-off yoke, which carries the dish at a slight tilt (often limited in range) to the polar axis. This tilt is to allow for your local parallax in viewing satellites; that is, the perspective shift you observe from being north (or south) of the Equator, looking up at an angle at satellites that are orbiting directly above the Equator. The majority also have a limited east-west axis adjustment, to allow pickup of the various satellites which are spaced out in orbit along the celestial equator. To use the dish to track celestial sources, you need to align the polar axis accurately to the pole, and make the yoke parallel to it. Thus you need to align the polar axis so that its plane is in the meridian (north-south) plane. You can start alignment using a compass, but will probably need to check at night using the stars, or have in hand a good map that shows deviation of magnetic from true north (or south). After that, you need to ensure freedom of rotation around the polar axis, for as much time as you wish to track potential ETI sources. Likely this would be for up to two hours, which would require rotation from fifteen degrees east to fifteen degrees west of the meridian. To automate this tracking, you will need to add a motor to the polar axis that tracks at the sidereal rate. You also need an axle to motorize, which may require you to modify the yoke or polar axis. To look at sources at any altitude above your horizon, you will need to have the freedom of pointing the dish from the pole to below the equator. This may require the unbolting of various actuator and lever arms. Before changing anything on a dish that is operating well as a TV receiver, be sure to inscribe marks on the mounting so that it can be easily returned to proper alignment for TV, between SETI sessions.

ANTENNA FEED

You need to check that your feed, which collects the radio energy at the antenna focus, will work well at the frequencies you have chosen for your SETI work. Alternate feeds can be purchased on the market.

THE RECEIVER

A major component of your system is the receiver. In years past, a receiver with the right frequency coverage would have been a major problem, since the only commercially available receivers monitored police, fire, and amateur FM, but were useless for general purpose VHF and UHF listening. Now you can buy, for just under $1,000, a general purpose scanner that covers the region from 25 MHz to 2.0 GHz, which includes the water hole frequencies around 1.5 GHz. Several models are available. Check with the SETI League or a local ham radio store. You should buy a Low Noise Amplifier (LNA) to connect between the antenna and your receiver. This combination will give you sensitivities comparable with those of professional radio tele-scopes. The noise power in a band of frequencies is proportional to the bandwidth and to a quantity called the system temperature. In many common electrical circuits system temperature is directly traceable to the system's physical temperature. If, for example, one measures the current in a resistor, one finds random fluctuations resulting from the thermal motions of individual electrons. These random motions are excited by thermal behavior of molecules inside the resistor. As the temperature of the resistor increases, the random motions get bigger and the random component of the current grows. Thus, the noise in any given frequency band increases proportionately. There is no intrinsic physical reason, however, that all circuits should behave like resistors. Though all of them yield outputs with random fluctuations, the constant of proportionality between these and the average output may be much smaller than those of simple resistive devices. Certain transistor devices, notably Gallium Arsenide Field Effect Transistors (GaAs FETs), tend to decouple the current carriers from thermal effects. Operating at room temperature (300K), amplifiers using these transistors have noise temperatures of about 100K, about a third of that in a room-temperature resistor. If you use as LNA a GaAs FET amplifier between your antenna and a broadband-scanning receiver, you can get effective noise temperature of 100K plus the antenna temperature (typically the latter is 50K; if you add shielding you can get to 10K or so). This is a system that an observatory operating in the early 1960s would have envied. So, first find an antenna. The better built the antenna, well-soldered connectors, smooth edges, etc., the lower the system noise temperature and the higher the antenna gain. Attach the antenna to the LNA with as short a cable as possible. Long runs of coax add to the system noise. After the transistor amplifier has increased the strength of the incoming signal hundreds of times, connection of the rest of the system is much easier. This is because the amplified signal and noise from the LNA dominates later stages in the system. The added noise of a slightly detuned receiver or too long piece of coax is insignificant compared to the amplified roar already coming into the system front end.

We suggest for a receiver the IC-R7000, a general-coverage scanner. This receiver is still valued, if you can find one, ten years after its original manufacture. There are, however, several equivalent models with simpler computer control. It is easy to use with a host of scanning modes. If you did nothing except scan frequencies throughout its range with your dish antenna pointed randomly at the sky, you would be exploring the unknown. Just listening to the receiver speaker, your search would, for most frequencies and directions in the sky, be thousands of times more sensitive than any performed to date. You can listen in a selection of modes: AM, FM (good for diagnosing interference, but not if you want to look for drifting signals), and SSB (Single Sideband) are all available. This last mode makes our radio and TV carriers come literally whistling up out of the noise as you tune by. You can set the scan rate of the device to be fast or slow over specified limits. For an extra sixty dollars, you can even install a speech card in the scan-

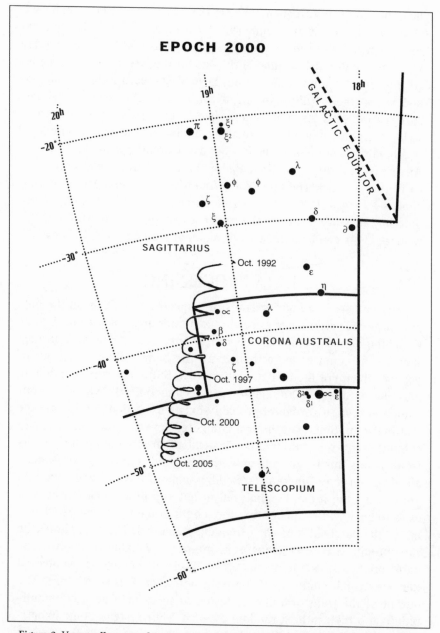

EPOCH 2000

Figure 2. Voyager II spacecraft positions. This chart shows approximate positions for Voyager II over the next several years. Note the "teapot" of Sagittarius; the proximity of the galactic center. The Milky Way has been omitted for clarity. Voyager's zigzag motion is the result of our changing viewpoint, as the Earth travels round and round the Sun. (*Diagram: W. R. Alschuler. Sky map after Phillip's Color Star Atlas.*)

ner. Then, on every frequency where there is a signal, the receiver will stop and announce the frequency. Put a tape in a recorder, and the receiver will turn it on only when signal is present. Then, once a day, you can monitor a short tape of the hits for the last twenty-four hours. All this can be done with nothing beyond standard radio technology and an operator willing to spend some time. The receiver, without speech card, sells for slightly less than $1,000. It is made by Icom, a well-known manufacturer of amateur radio gear, and can be purchased in a ham radio store or by mail order. For example, Henri Radio in Los Angeles, California, and Ham Radio Outlet in Sunnyvale, California, carry this product. The Low Noise Amplifier with connectors of your choice—I suggest BNC Type—can be purchased for about $100. When ordering, be sure to specify the frequency range of interest. As of this writing, LNAs can be purchased from, among others, the SETI League.

DATA PROCESSING

If you want to do a Fourier Transform spectrum analysis on the output from your scanner, you need a computer and a device to digitize the voltage so its value may be written into your memory. You must sample your data at more than twice the bandwidth coming out of your receiver. For the IC-R7000 in narrow, SSB mode, the sample rate must be at least 5,000 samples per second (5KHz). Whatever your computer, a digitizer board probably exists for it that can handle the required rate. Since you have a computer anyway, you may want to computer-control your scanner instead of programming it from its front panel. This is no problem with any good scanner today. Almost all of the receiver functions are addressable in ASCII. Once data is in your computer, it can be analyzed to tell you how much power is at each frequency. Remember that the length of data you analyze determines the bandwidth of each frequency channel. The data should be run through a Fourier Transform program, available in many standard mathematical tool kits. An excellent choice is Numerical Recipes, which comes in C, Fortran, and even Pascal versions. The output of the transform can be tested to see what sine wave amplitude is too high to be a random event in your system. Some experience will be required in order to set this threshold. Too low a threshold will keep you forever analyzing random noise and radio frequency interference. Too high a threshold will leave you in peace but may miss a weak signal.

Figure 3. Close-up of the Milky Way in the direction of the galactic center. Our galaxy's central bulge of stars lies above and below the dark lanes of dust that obscure the center. The tail of Scorpius, including the bright star Antares (imbedded in nebulosity) and a globular star cluster M4 (just above and right of Antares) lie above the center. *(Photo: Courtesy of American Museum of Natural History.)*

TESTING THE RIG

You can check your rig's sensitivity, tracking ability, pointing accuracy, and your software (filtering algorithms) by looking at various targets. These include: the TV satellites themselves, perhaps with a signal attenuator; the Moon, to pick up scattered signals of all types from Earth; bright pulsars; and the Pioneer and Voyager (and Galileo) spacecraft. You may wish to start by observing standard celestial radio sources and joining SARA, an organization for amateur radio astronomers. That way you can get your feet seriously wet before trying the more demanding tasks of SETI.

VOYAGER II AS A SETI TEST TARGET

Once you get set up to look for ETI signals, as discussed above, it will be a good idea to practice on some known sources with characteristics similar to those you are hoping to detect. A demanding test would be to listen for the signals from one of our distant space probes on its way to interstellar space. We suggest trying to listen to Voyager II, currently about 60 astronomical units from us and moving away from the Sun at about 3 A.U. per year. During Voyager's flyby the gravity of Neptune deflected it east and downward. Voyager II is now traveling systematically about 0.2 degrees eastward and about 2.0 degrees southward (below the plane of the ecliptic) per year. However, its apparent position against the background stars is also affected by Earth's orbital motion. This causes the spacecraft to undergo a back-and-forth, east-west cycle of about plus or minus 2 degrees at its current distance (much like the apparent motion of Neptune). This effect will diminish as Voyager's distance increases (see Figure 2). This means that, with a small radio telescope with an angular resolution of 10 degrees or so, you can expect to find Voyager II in your beam if you aim at: Right Ascension = 19 hours 30 minutes, and Declination = -45.0 degrees, for several years from now (2000). This position is just below the ecliptic, in the constellation Telescopium, near the star Iota Telescopii. This position is given for epoch 2000 star charts and will change slowly over the next several years, as described above. You may have to modify your receiver slightly to pick out Voyager's signal, which is at about 8 GHz, well above the water hole frequencies. It is only broadcasting about 20 watts, so the signal will be quite weak. Good hunting!

APPENDIX B.

STARS NEARER THAN 5 PARSECS

No	Name	RA	Decl	Proper motion	Parallax	Distance light years	Visual apparent: magnitude and spectral type
		(1950)					
1	Sun						$-$ 26.8 G2
2	α Centauri	14^h36^m2 − 60°38'		3".68	0".760	4.3	0.1 G2
3	Barnard's star	16 55.4 + 4 33		10.31	.552	5.9	9.5 M5
4	Wolf 359	10 54.1 + 7 19		4.71	.431	7.6	13.5 M8e
5	BD + 36°2147	11 00.6 + 36 18		4.78	.402	8.1	7.5 M2
6	Sirius	6 42.9 − 16 39		1.33	.377	8.6	− 1 5 A1
7	Luyten 726–8	1 36.4 − 18 13		3.36	.365	8.9	12.5 M6e
8	Ross 154	18 46.7 − 23 53		0.72	.345	9.4	10.6 M5e
9	Ross 248	23 39.4 + 43 55		1.58	.317	10.3	12.2 M6e
10	ε Eridani	3 30.6 − 9 38		0.98	.305	10.7	3.7 K2
11	Luyten 789–6	22 35.7 − 15 36		3.26	.302	10.8	12.2 M6
12	Ross 128	11 45.1 + 1 06		1.37	.301	10.8	11.1 M5
13	61 Cygni	21 04.7 + 38 30		5.22	.292	11.2	5.2 K5
14	ε Indi	21 59.6 − 57 00		4.69	.291	11.2	4.7 K5
15	Procyon	7 36.7 + 5 21		1.25	.287	11.4	0.3 F5
16	Σ 2398	18 42.2 + 59 33		2.28	.284	11.5	8.9 M4
17	BD + 43°44	0 15.5 + 43 44		2.89	.282	11.6	8.1 M1
18	CD − 36°15698	23 02.6 − 36 09		6.90	.279	11.7	7.4 M2
19	τ Ceti	1 41.7 − 16 12		1.92	.273	11.9	3.5 G8
20	BD + 5°1668	7 24.7 + 5 23		3.73	.266	12.2	9.8 M4
21	CD − 39°14192	21 14.3 - 39 04		3.46	.260	12.5	6.7 M1

No	Name	RA Decl	Proper	Parallax	Distance	Visual apparent:
		(1950)	motion		light years	magnitude and spectral type
22	Kapteyn's star	5 09.7 − 45 00	8.89	.256	12.7	8.8 M0
23	Krüger 60	22 26.3 + 57 27	0.86	.254	12.8	9.7 M4
24	Ross 614	6 26.8 − 2 46	0.99	.249	13.1	11.3 M5c
25	BD − 12°4523	16 27.5 − 12 32	1.18	.249	13.1	10.0 M5
26	van Maanen's star	0 46.5 + 5 09	2.95	.234	13.9	12.4 DG
27	Wolf 424	12 30.9 + 9 18	1.75	.229	14.2	12.6 M6e
28	G158−27	0 04.2 − 7 48	2.06	.226	14.4	13.8 m
29	CD − 37°15492	0 02.5 − 37 36	6.08	.225	14.5	8.6 M3
30	BD + 50°1725	10 08.3 + 49 42	1.45	.217	15.0	6.6 K7
31	CD − 46°11540	17 24.9 − 46 51	1.13	.216	15.1	9.4 M4
32	CD − 49°13515	21 30.2 − 49 13	.81	.214	15.2	8.7 M3
33	CD − 44°11909	17 33.5 − 44 17	1.16	.213	15.3	11.2 M5
34	Luyten 1159−16	1 57.4 + 12 51	2.08	.212	15.4	12.3 M8
35	BD + 15°2620	13 43.2 + 15 10	2.30	.208	15.7	8.5 M2
36	BD + 68°946	17 36.7 + 68 23	1.33	.207	15.7	9.1 M3.5
37	L145−141	11 43.0 − 64 33	2.68	.206	15.8	11.4
38	BD − 15°6290	22 50.6 − 14 31	1.16	.206	15.8	10.2 M5
39	40 Eridani	4 13.0 − 7 44	4.08	.205	15.9	4.4 K0
40	BD + 20°2465	10 16.9 + 20 07	0.49	.202	16.1	9.4 M4.5
41	Altair	19 48.3 + 8 44	0.66	.196	16.6	0.8 A7
42	70 Ophiuchi	18 02.9 + 2 31	1.13	.195	16.7	4.2 K1
43	AC + 79°3888	11 44.6 + 78 58	0.89	.194	16.8	11.0 M4
44	BD + 43°4305	22 44.7 + 44 05	0.83	.193	16.9	10.1 M5e
45	Stein 2051	4 26.8 + 58 53	2.37	.192	17.0	11.1 M5

(Source: Rowan Robinson, Michael. *The Cosmological Distance Ladder*, New York: 1985. W. H. Freeman & Co.)

GLOSSARY

BANDWIDTH: Any signal is broadcast over a certain more-or-less restricted range of frequencies, and any receiver is sensitive over a range of frequencies. These are called the transmitter and receiver bandwidths.

BIOASTRONOMY: The study of the signs of and conditions for evolution, and the possible structure of life on planets other than Earth.

BLACK HOLE: The core of a massive star that has gone supernova and whose collapse has continued past the neutron star stage to densities so extreme that space forms a "pocket" around it. Matter and energy are drawn into it and cannot escape.

CHIRP: A signal frequency is said to chirp (like a birdcall) if it shifts up and down cyclically. This can occur if either the source or observer is in orbit or rotates. Thus the Earth's daily rotation will cre-ate a fairly rapid chirp of any received ET signals.

DFT: A Digital Fourier Transform chip is a semiconductor-circuit chip specially designed to rapidly split a signal into its various frequency components using the mathematical technique called a digital fourier transform.

DOPPLER SHIFT: The observed frequency of any signal is affected by the relative motion of observer and signal source. The greater the velocity, the greater the effect. For velocities of approach, the frequency increases; for velocities of recession, it decreases.

ELECTROMAGNETIC SPECTRUM: The array of gamma and X rays, ultraviolet, visible light, infrared, and radio waves spread out in order of wavelength and energy. All are electromagnetic particle-waves (photons) that propagate through space.

KELVIN(S): A temperature scale invented by Lord Kelvin, in which absolute zero (−273 degrees C.) is the base. On this scale, the liquid range of water is 273°K to 373°K.

MAGIC FREQUENCIES: The most abundant atom in the Universe, hydrogen, and the most important water-related molecular fragment, OH, both have signature radio line frequencies, under interstellar conditions, near 1,500 MHz. They seem like natural choices to broadcast near, if you want to catch the attention of ETs similar to us. Thus these are "magic" frequencies, and the frequency band between them is the "water hole."

MULTICHANNEL SPECTROME-TER: A receiver-signal analyzer with the ability to collect signals in many different frequency ranges (usually narrow and side-by-side) simultaneously.

NEUTRON STARS: The leftover cores of massive stars that have gone supernova. They are extremely dense and often emit "lighthouse" beacons of radiation that we see as pulsars.

NUCLEAR WINTER: The rapid and prolonged cooling of Earth's climate, predicted as an unavoidable effect of even a limited nuclear conflict.

NURSERY WORLD: A planet ripe for life, undisturbed by external conditions.

PLANETESIMALS: Small agglomerations of rock in, or left over from, a forming planetary system, which may collect to form planets.

RADIO ASTRONOMY: The observation of celestial objects at radio wavelengths, using radio antennas and receivers.

RADIO LINE: Atoms and molecules have discrete internal-energy states unique to each type. A jump between states liberates (or absorbs) a photon of one frequency. For example, a cool cloud of hydrogen atoms emits many photons of 1420 MHz. If enough atoms emit similar photons they show up as a spike, or (radio) line, against the general background static.

STELLAR WIND: The moderately high-energy stream of subatomic particles emitted steadily by the Sun and, perhaps, most stars.

SUPERNOVA: The death of a massive star through violent explosion, the outburst of which rivals a galaxy in brightness. In the explosion, heavy elements are created and scattered into interstellar space.

XENOLOGY: The study of alien life-forms.

SUGGESTED READING

INTRODUCTION

GOLDSMITH, Donald. *The Quest for Extraterrestrial Life*. Mill Valley, Cal.: University Science Books, 1980.

SAGAN,C., Drake, F., Druyan, A., Ferris, T., Lomberg, and Sagan, L. S. "Murmurs of Earth: The Voyager Interstellar Record," Commemorative Edition CD-ROM Set, Warner New Media, 1992.

CHAPTER ONE

BATESON, Gregory. *Mind and Nature*. New York: Dutton, 1979.

COOKE, Donald A. *The Life and Death of Stars*. New York: Crown, 1985.

FERRIS, Timothy. *Coming of Age in the Milky Way*. New York: Morrow, 1988.

GARDNER, Howard. *Frames of Mind*. New York: Basic Books, 1983.

GRIFFEN, Donald. *The Question of* *Animal Awareness*. Los Altos, Cal.: Kauffmann, 1976.

MCDONOUGH, Thomas R. *The Search for Extraterrestrial Intelligence*. New York: Wiley, 1987.

PREISS, Byron and Frankoi, Andrew, eds. *The Universe*. New York: Bantam Books, 1987.

WALKER, Stephen. *Animal Thought*. London: Routledge and Kegan Paul, 1983.

CHAPTER TWO

SHKLOVSKII, I. S. and Sagan, Carl. *Intelligent Life in the Universe*. New York: Dell, 1968.

Time-Life editors. *Life Search*. Alexandria, Vir.: Time-Life Books, 1989.

CHAPTER THREE

BILLINGHAM, J., ed. *Life in the Universe*. Cambridge, Mass.: MIT Press, 1981.

DRAKE, F. and Sobel, D. *Is Any-*

one *Out There? The Scientific Search for Extraterrestrial Intelligence*. Delacorte Press, 1992.

MARX, G., ed. *Bioastronomy—The Next Steps*. Dordrecht, Neth.: Kluwer, 1988.

PAPAGIANNIS, M. D., ed. *Strategies for the Search for Life in the Universe*. Dordrecht, Neth.: Reidel, 1980.

CHAPTER FOUR

BRAMS, Steven J. *Superior Beings*. New York: Springer-Verlag, 1983.

BILLINGHAM, J. and Tarter, J. "SETI," in *Space Biology and Medicine*, Vol. 1, Ivanov, M., Kotelnikov, V., and Rummel, J., eds., American Institute of Aeronautics and Astronautics, Washington, D.C., 1993.

FINNEY, Ben and Jones, Eric. *Interstellar Migration and the Human Experience*. Berkeley, Cal.: University of California Press, 1985.

GOLDSMITH, D. and Owen, T. *The Search for Life in the Universe*. Reading, Mass.: Addison-Wesley, 1992.

MACVEY, John. *Interstellar Travel*. New York: Avon, 1977.

POYNTER, Margaret and Klein, Michael J. *Cosmic Quest: Searching for Intelligent Life Among the Stars*. New York: Antheneum Press, 1984.

SHOSTAK, S., ed., "Progress in the Search for Extraterrestrial Life," Astronomical Society of the Pacific (San Francisco), Conf. Series Vol. 74, 1995.

TREFIL, J. S. and Rood, R. T. *Are We Alone?* New York: Scribner, 1981.

CHAPTER FIVE

BALLARD, J. *Handbook for Star Trackers*. Cambridge, Mass.: Sky Publishing, 1989.

CULLERS, D. K., Linscott, I. R., and Oliver, B. M. "Signal Processing in SETI," Communications of the ACM (ACM/IEEE-CS Joint Issue), Vol. 28, No. 11 (November 1985).

DICK, Steven J. *Plurality of Worlds*. Cambridge: Cambridge University Press, 1982.

DRAKE, F. and Helou, G. "The Optimum Frequencies for Interstellar Communications as Influenced by Minimum Bandwidths." NAIC Report 76. (1978).

HOROWITZ, P. "Search for Ultra Narrowband Signals of Extraterrestrial Origin." *Science*, Vol. 201 (9178), 733-735.

OLIVER, B. "The Search for Extraterrestrial Intelligence." NASA SP-419, 63-73.

PAPAGIANNIS, M. D. *The Search for Extraterrestrial Life: Recent Developments*. Dordrecht, Neth.: Reidel, 1985.

PAPAGIANNIS, M. D. "Recent progress and future plans on the Search for Extraterrestrial Intelligence." *Nature*, Vol. 318 (1985).

SCHENKEL, Peter. *ETI: A Chal-*

lenge for Change. New York: Vantage, 1988.

SHOSTAK, S., ed. "Third Decennial US-USSR Conference on SETI," Astronomical Society of the Pacific (San Francisco), Conf. Series Vol. 47, 1993.

SULLIVAN, W. T., III. "Will the Next Supernova in Our Galaxy be Discovered with a Radio Telescope?" *Publications of the Astronomical Society of the Pacific,* Vol. 94 (1982), 901-904.

SWIFT, David. *SETI Pioneers: Scientists Talk About Their Search for Extraterrestrial Intelligence.* University of Arizona Press, 1990.

TAUB, Herbert and Schilling, Donald I. *Principles of Communications Systems.* New York: McGraw Hill, 1971.

WOOLEY, R., Epps, E. A., Penston, M. J. and Pocock, S. B. "Catalogue of Stars within Twenty-Five Parsecs of the Sun." *Royal Observatory Annual,* No. 5 (1970).

FASAN, Ernst. *Relations with Alien Intelligences.* Berlin: Berlin-Verlag, 1970.

GINDILIS, L. M., Dubinsky, B. A., and Rudnitskiy, G. M., "SETI Investigations in the U.S.S.R." Report Presented at the XXXIX Congress of the International Astronautical Federation, Bangalore, India, 1988.

HALEY, Andrew G. "Metalaw." *Space Law and Government. New York: Appleton-Century Crofts, 1963.*

MICHAUD, Michael A. G. "Extraterrestrial Politics." *Cosmic Search,* Vol. 1, No. 3 (Summer 1979), 11-14.

——"Interstellar Negotiation." *Foreign Service Journal,* Vol. 49, No. 12 (December 1972), 10-14, 29-30.

SULLIVAN, W. T., Brown, S., and Wetherill, C. "Eavesdropping: The Radio Signature of the Earth." *Science,* Vol. 199 (27 January 1978), 377-387.

CHAPTER SIX

BEATTY, J. Kelly and CHAIKIN, A. *The New Solar System,* 3rd ed. Sky Publishing Corp., Cambridge, 1990

CLOUD, P. *Oasis in Space,* New York: W.W. Norton, 1988

CHAPTER SEVEN

BILLINGS, Linda. "Is Anybody Listening?" *Final Frontier,* Vol. 1, No. 2 (June 1988).

CHAPTER EIGHT

CAMERON, A. G. W., ed. *Interstellar Communication.* New York: Benjamin, 1963.

COCCONI, G. and Morrison, P. "Searching for Interstellar Communications." *Nature,* Volume 184 (1959), 844.

COUSINS, Norman. "Why Man Explores." *NASA EP-125* (1976).

DRAKE, Frank, Wolfe, John, and

Seeger, Charles, eds.: *SETI Science Working Group Report.* NASA Technical Paper 2244, 1983.

FIELD, G., ed.: *Astronomy and Astrophysics for the 1990's. Volume I: Report of the Astronomy Survey Committee.* Washington: National Academy Press, 1982.

MORRISON, Philip, Billingham, John, and Wolfe, John, eds.: *The Search for Extraterrestrial Intelligence.* New York: Dover, 1979.

REEVES, H. *The Hour of Our Delight: Cosmic Evolution, Order, and Complexity.* Freeman, 1991.

SAGAN, Carl, ed.: *Communication with Extraterrestrial Intelligence.* Cambridge, Mass.: MIT Press, 1973.

SULLIVAN, W. *We Are Not Alone.* New York: Penguin Books, 1993.

RELEVANT ORGANIZATIONS

The Planetary Society
P.O. Box 91687
Pasadena, CA 91109
(The premier supporter of SETI research outside of the government.)

The Astronomical Society of the Pacific
1290 24th Avenue
San Francisco, CA 94112
(A leading association of professionals and amateurs with interest in SETI.)

Society of Amateur Radio Astronomers (SARA)
c/o Vincent Caracci
247 N. Linden Street
Massapequa, NY 11758
Membership is $20/yr for U.S., $21 for Canada, $28 for other foreign countries.
(The major amateur organization in radio astronomy.)

International Astronomical Union (IAU)—Commission 51 on Bioastronomy
c/o Stuart Bowyer, Acting President
Dept. of Astronomy
University of California at Berkeley
Berkeley, CA 94720
(The IAU is the largest international professional umbrella organization in astronomy.)

The National Aeronautics and Space Administration (NASA), Office of Public Information
NASA Headquarters
Code L
Washington, DC 20546
(You must know the material you want when you are calling, but there is no charge for U.S. citizens.)

The SETI Institute
2035 Landings Drive
Mountain View, CA 94043
Tel. (650) 961-6633
www.seti.org

CONTRIBUTORS

BYRON PREISS is editor of *The Planets*, *The Universe*, and *The Dinosaurs*. He is also co-editor, with William R. Alschuler, of *The Microverse*. He has collaborated on books and computer software with Arthur C. Clarke and Ray Bradbury. His project, *The Words of Gandhi*, won a 1985 Grammy Award, and his monograph, *The Art of Leo and Diane Dillon*, was a Hugo Award nominee.

BEN BOVA, besides being the author of more than seventy books of science and science fiction, has six times won the Hugo Award for best editor for his work at *Analog* and *Omni* magazines. He has also been a consultant to Woody Allen, Gene Roddenberry, and George Lucas on film and television projects.

WILLIAM R. ALSCHULER is the founder and principal of Future Museums, a museum-consulting firm providing program concept through final design for museums and exhibits with a science or technology content. Alschuler has a Ph.D. in astronomy from the University of California at Santa Cruz, and extensive university teaching experience in the sciences, holography and Lippmann photography, and energy conservation. He is currently a member of the science faculty at California Institute of the Arts. His first book for Byron Preiss Visual Publications, *The Microverse*, was published in the fall of 1989. He has authored one and co-edited three others since then.

HOWARD ZIMMERMAN is the editor in chief for Byron Preiss Visual Publications. He has edited or coedited nonfiction books on the search for extraterrestrial intelligence, dinosaur paleontology, astronomy and cosmology. More recently he edited a biography of Albert Einstein.

ISAAC ASIMOV's total of published books had passed four hundred volumes before he passed away in 1992. Although his Ph.D. was in chemistry, his popular nonfiction covered almost every imaginable subject, from quantum physics to the Bible. He won multiple Hugo and Nebula awards for science fiction. Among his novels are the Foundation series (winner of a special Hugo for Best Science Fiction Series of all time) and the Robot Series. He was also the father of the Three Laws of Robotics.

GREGORY BENFORD writes for the *Encyclopedia Britannica* in the areas of relativistic plasma physics and astrophysics. His highly regarded fiction work includes the novel *Timescape*, which won four separate awards. He was nominated most recently for a Nebula for *Great Sky River*. He is a member of the physics faculty at the University of California at Irvine.

DAVID BRIN's second novel, *Startide Rising*, won both the Hugo and Nebula awards. He was awarded another Hugo (his third altogether) for *The Uplift War*, set in the same universe. When he is not writing, he is a university teacher of physics.

ARTHUR C. CLARKE's achievements and honors are both scientific and literary in nature. Chief among them are his fellowship in the Royal Astronomical Society, the Hugo, Nebula, and John W. Campbell awards, the 1982 Marconi International Fellowship, a Fellowship of King's College, London, and an Oscar nomination (with Stanley Kubrick) for *2001: A Space Odyssey*. In 1979 the president of Sri Lanka nominated him chancellor of the University of Moratuwa, which is also the site of the Arthur C. Clarke Centre for Modern Technologies. His almost sixty books have sold thirty million copies in twenty languages, and he is credited as the inventor of the concept of the communications satellite.

HAL CLEMENT, a native of Massachusetts, holds degrees in astronomy and chemistry, and taught these and other sciences at the high school level for forty years until his retirement in 1987. He has been writing even longer, and is best known for producing so-called "hard" science fiction, in which the problems faced by the characters and the methods used in their solution both fit as closely as possible to currently understood science. His best-known novel is the science fiction classic *Mission of Gravity*. He is a retired air force reserve colonel, having flown thirty-five combat missions as pilot and copilot in Liberator bombers during World War II.

D. KENT CULLERS is the signal-detection team leader at the SETI Institute. He received his doctorate in physics from the University of California, Berkeley, in 1980, and joined NASA immediately thereafter. During the past ten years he has investigated ways to detect weak signals in a background of Gaussian noise and, in collaboration with the signal-detection teams, developed highly efficient algorithms and hardware for SETI. He is an Extraclass Amateur Radio Operator, and in a fundamental sense, SETI is an extension of his lifelong quest for distant signals. Dr. Cullers is married with two children. His hobbies include radio, playing the guitar, chess, and a great deal of science fiction reading.

FRANK DRAKE is retired from being professor of astronomy and astrophysics at the University of California, Santa Cruz. He received a Ph.D. in astronomy from Harvard University. He was affiliated for many years with the National Radio Astronomy Observatory and, later, Cornell University. At Cornell he was the director of the Arecibo Ionospheric Observatory and for ten years the director of the National Astronomy and Ionosphere Center, which operated the world's largest radio-reflector telescope at Arecibo, Puerto Rico. In 1960 he conducted the first modern search for extraterrestrial intelligent radio signals, Project Ozma, which was carried out at Green Bank, West Virginia. He was chairman of the U.S. National Committee for the International Astronomical Union, the chairman of the board on Physics and Astronomy of the National Research Council, the president of the Astronomical Society of the Pacific, and is still the president of the SETI Institute, a nonprofit corporation that carries out research related to extraterrestrial life with support from the planetary society and other private sources.

PAUL HOROWITZ received his Ph.D. in physics at Harvard University and is now professor of physics there. He has been senior research associate at NASA-Ames, and jointly developed SETI signal-processing software with that team. He is a world leader in electronics design, and his research interests span from cellular motility through pulsars to SETI.

MICHAEL J. KLEIN received his Ph.D. in radio astronomy at University of Michigan in 1968. His dissertation was based on extensive observations of the planets and their surfaces. He joined JPL in 1969 as a scientist in the Space

Sciences Division. He became supervisor of the Radio Astronomy Group in the Planetary Atmospheres Section in 1974. Dr. Klein has more than twenty years' experience in radio-astronomy research with special emphasis on the development of observational techniques and the application of microwave and submillimeter radio astronomical experiments in the study of solar system objects. He serves as program manager for for several deep space tracking and planetary detection programs, and is currently serving on the Arecibo Science Advisory Committee for the National Astronomy and Ionospheric Center (Cornell University).

DAVID LATHAM received his Ph.D. from Harvard University and is now a research astronomer at the Center for Astrophysics at Harvard/Smithsonian observatories. His special interests are brown dwarfs and extrasolar planets. He is on search teams that have made major discoveries in both areas including the first observation of an extrasolar planet in 1989, confirmed in 1996.

THOMAS R. MCDONOUGH is a lecturer in engineering at Cal Tech and an award-winning public speaker. He is also coordinator of the Search for Extraterrestrial Intelligence (SETI) program at the

Planetary Society, the 100,000-member international organization founded by Carl Sagan and colleagues. The *Los Angeles Times* named him "one of the rising stars to watch" in 1989. He is the author of the nonfiction books *The Search for Extraterrestrial Intelligence* and *Space: The Next 25 Years*, and of the science-fiction novel, *The Architects of Hyperspace*.

MICHAEL A. G. MICHAUD was director of the Office of Advanced Technology at the U.S. Department of State, where he was responsible for the foreign-policy aspects of space activities and other advanced technology issues and from which he recently retired. He is the author of one hundred published works, sixty-two of them on space or extraterrestrial intelligence. His publications include the 1986 book, *Reaching for the High Frontier*, a history and analysis of the modern American prospace movement. He is a member of the International Institute of Space Law, the Institute of Aeronautics and Astronautics, the American Astronautical Society, the Aviation/Space Writers Association, and several other space-related organizations. He holds a master's degree in political science from the University of California at Los Angeles.

PHILIP MORRISON took his Ph.D. in theoretical physics at Berkeley in 1940. For almost twenty years after the war he was on the physics faculty at Cornell. Since 1964 he has been at M.I.T., where he is now Institute Professor Emeritus. Among his accomplishments are serving on the Manhattan Project with J. Robert Oppenheimer and taking part in the Trinity test, the first atomic explosion. He believes that physicists owe their fellow citizens two services: better understanding of physics, and independent comment on modern war and how to avoid it through peaceful means. He has written several books and made films along both paths. Recently he and his wife, Phylis, wrote and appeared in a TV series on PBS called *The Ring of Truth*, which examined how science knows what it knows.

MICHAEL D. PAPAGIANNIS was born in Athens, graduated from the National Technical University of Athens, and received his Ph.D. in physics and astronomy from Harvard University. He was a full professor and chairman of astronomy, and the recipient of the Award for Excellence at Boston University. He was a member of the International Academy of Astronautics, the National Academy of Greece, a fellow of the AAS, a member and past chair-

man of the Space Science Panel of the NRC/NAS Associateship Program, and member of the Executive Committee of the Haystack Radio Observatory. He died in 1998.

DIANA REISS is a Senior Research Scientist at the Osborn Laboratories for Marine Sciences at The New York Aquarium of the Wildlife Conservation Society. Her research focuses on the cognitive and communicative abilities of bottlenose dolphins and comparative vocal learning and cognition. Using a combination of experimental and observational methods, much of her work has investigated the role of learning and the effects of social environmental factors on vocal development of dolphins. After completing her Ph.D., she established a marine mammal research facility at Marine World Africa USA and was Director of Marine Mammal Research from 1983 to 1991. Dr. Reiss has served as a member of the board of directors and as a scientific advisor for several organizations, including The Marine World Foundation, The Wild Dolphin Project, and the Marin Marine Mammal Rescue Center of California.

THOMAS F. VAN HORNE became a volunteer with the Ohio State University SETI project in 1987.

In 1988 he was appointed chief observer at the OSU Radio Observatory. He is in charge of the SETI project's data-analysis group and is coauthor with Robert Dixon of a paper describing the project's activities presented at the 1988 Toronto SETI conference. Van Horne is a professional computer programmer and long time science-fiction fan. He is on the team designing all-sky radio cameras.